THE PRESOCRATIC PHILOSOPHERS

Volume 1   Thales to Zeno

The Arguments of the Philosophers

EDITOR: TED HONDERICH
Reader in Philosophy, University College London

The group of books of which this is one will include an essentially analytic and critical account of each of the considerable number of the great and influential philosophers. Each book will provide an ordered exposition and an examination of the contentions and doctrines of the philosopher in question. The group of books taken together will comprise a contemporary assessment and history of the entire course of philosophical thought.

Already published in the series

Plato	J. C. B. Gosling
Meinong	Reinhardt Grossman
Santayana	Timothy L. S. Sprigge
Wittgenstein	R. J. Fogelin
Hume	B. Stroud
Descartes	Margaret Dauler Wilson
Berkeley	George Pitcher
Kant	Ralph Walker

THE PRESOCRATIC PHILOSOPHERS

Volume 1
Thales to Zeno

Jonathan Barnes

Fellow of Oriel College, Oxford

Routledge & Kegan Paul
London, Henley and Boston

First published in 1979
by Routledge & Kegan Paul Ltd
39 Store Street,
London WC1E 7DD,
Broadway House,
Newtown Road,
Henley-on-Thames,
Oxon RG9 1EN and
9 Park Street,
Boston, Mass. 02108, USA
Photoset in 11 on 12pt Garamond by
Kelly and Wright, Bradford-on-Avon, Wiltshire
and printed in Great Britain by
Lowe & Brydone Printers Ltd
Thetford, Norfolk
© Jonathan Barnes 1979
No part of this book may be reproduced in
any form without permission from the
publisher, except for the quotation of brief
passages in criticism

British Library Cataloguing in Publication Data

Barnes, Jonathan
 The Presocratic philosophers.
Vol. 1: Thales to Zeno.—(The arguments of the
  philosophers).
 1. Philosophy, Ancient
 I. Title II. Series
 182   B188   78-40273

ISBN 0 7100 8860 4

Contents

	Preface	ix
	Note on Citations	xiii

PROLOGUE

I	The Springs of Reason	3
	(a) *The art of thinking*	3
	(b) *Thales on magnets and water*	5
	(c) *Tradition and interpretation*	13

EDEN

II	Anaximander on Nature	19
	(a) *Pantological knowledge*	19
	(b) *The origin of species*	20
	(c) *The earth at rest*	23
	(d) *Τὸ ἄπειρον*	28

III	Science and Speculation	38
	(a) *Material monism*	38
	(b) *Anaximenes and air*	44
	(c) *Fairy tales or science?*	47
	(d) *The use of analogy*	52

IV	The Natural Philosophy of Heraclitus	57
	(a) *The great account*	57
	(b) *Nature's bonfire*	60
	(c) *All things are a flowing*	65
	(d) *A world of contradictions*	69
	(e) *Sage Heraclitus?*	75

V	The Divine Philosophy of Xenophanes	82
	(a) *A wandering minstrel*	82
	(b) *Summa theologiae*	84
	(c) *Theology and science*	94
VI	Pythagoras and the Soul	100
	(a) *Ipse dixit*	100
	(b) *The progress of the soul*	103
	(c) *Metempsychosis, mysticism and logic*	106
	(d) *Selves and bodies*	111
	(e) *Intimations of immortality*	114
VII	The Moral Law	121
	(a) *First steps in ethics*	121
	(b) *Eating people is wrong*	122
	(c) *Heraclitus and the laws of God*	127
VIII	The Principles of Human Knowledge	136
	(a) *The origins of scepticism*	136
	(b) *The foundations of empirical knowledge*	143

THE SERPENT

IX	Parmenides and the Objects of Inquiry	155
	(a) *Parmenides' journey*	155
	(b) *At the crossroads*	157
	(c) *The paths of ignorance*	165
	(d) *Gorgias on what is not*	173
	Appendix: *A formalization of Parmenides' argument*	174
X	Being and Becoming	176
	(a) *Parmenidean metaphysics*	176
	(b) *Melissus' metaphysics*	180
	(c) *On generation and destruction*	184
	(d) *Being and time*	190
	(e) *Eternity*	194
	(f) *The logic of becoming*	197
XI	Stability and Change	200
	(a) *The limits of the world*	200
	(b) *The Eleatic One*	204
	(c) *Homogeneity*	207
	(d) *Wholeness*	210
	(e) *Change and decay*	214
	(f) *The void*	217
	(g) *Corporeal being*	223
	(h) *The philosophy of Elea*	228

CONTENTS

XII	Zeno: Paradox and Plurality	231
	(a) *The Eleatic Palamedes*	231
	(b) *Large and small*	237
	(c) *Existence*	240
	(d) *Infinite division*	242
	(e) *The toils of infinity*	245
	(f) *The totality of things*	252
	(g) *One and many*	253
	(h) *The paradox of place*	256
	(i) *The millet seed*	258
XIII	Zeno: Paradox and Progression	261
	(a) *Sprightly running*	261
	(b) *Infinity again*	264
	(c) *Achilles and the tortoise*	273
	(d) *The arrow*	276
	(e) *Movement in a moment*	279
	(f) *The arrow blunted*	283
	(g) *The stadium*	285
	(h) *A most ingenious paradox?*	290
	(i) *Two last remarks*	294
XIV	The Ports of Knowledge Closed	296
	(a) *Parmenides on sense and reason*	296
	(b) *Melissus on perception*	298
	Appendix A Sources	303
	Appendix B Chronology	310
	Notes	312
	Bibliography	341
	Indexes (i) Passages	361
	(ii) Persons	367
	(iii) Topics	371
	Concordance	374

Preface

Anyone who has the temerity to write a book on the Presocratics requires a remarkably good excuse. The surviving fish from the Presocratic shoal, fortuitously angled from Time's vast ocean, have been gutted, anatomized, and painstakingly described by generations of scholars; and it might reasonably be supposed that further dissection would be a vain and unprofitable exercise.

The lucubrations of scholars have for the most part dwelt upon the philological and historical interpretation of Presocratic philosophy: the sources have been studied, weighed, and analysed; the fragments have been microscopically investigated, their every word turned and turned again in the brilliant light of classical scholarship; and the opinions and doctrines of those early thinkers have been labelled and put on permanent exhibition in the museum of intellectual history.

Yet if the linguistic expression and the historical context of the Presocratics have been exhaustively discussed, the rational content of their thought has been less thoroughly scrutinized. By and large, scholars have asked what the Presocratics said, and what external circumstances may have prompted their sayings; they have not asked whether the Presocratics spoke truly, or whether their sayings rested on sound arguments.

It is those latter questions with which my book is primarily concerned. My main thesis is that the Presocratics were the first masters of rational thought; and my main aim is the exposition and assessment of their various ratiocinations. The judicious reader will decide for himself the value of that essay and what success it may have achieved: it constitutes my sole excuse for offering this volume to his perusal.

My aim has imposed certain restrictions on the scope and nature of my treatment of early Greek philosophy; and it is proper for a Preface to acknowledge those limitations.

First, then, the book presents little in the way of philological scholarship. No writer on ancient philosophy can entirely forego scholarly suggestions; and any investigation of Presocratic thought will constantly make philological judgments and take sides in scholarly controversies. But classical scholars have raised great monuments to their art over the bones of the Presocratics. I rely largely on that work; indeed, I should not have had the audacity to write on the Presocratics at all had they not been richly provided with wise and learned philological commentary.

Second, I have little concern with history. It is a platitude that a thinker can be understood only against his historical background; but that, like all platitudes, is at best a half-truth, and I do not believe that a detailed knowledge of Greek history greatly enhances our comprehension of Greek philosophy. Philosophy lives a supracelestial life, beyond the confines of space and time; and if philosophers are, perforce, small spatio-temporal creatures, a minute attention to their small spatio-temporal concerns will more often obfuscate than illumine their philosophies. History, however, is intrinsically entertaining. A few external facts and figures may serve to relieve the reader from a purely abstract narrative: I hope that my occasional historical paragraphs may be of use to that end, and may do something to placate the historically minded reader.

Third, my treatment of early Greek philosophy is discriminatory. I shall, it is true, say something about most of the inmates of Diels-Kranz' *Fragmente der Vorsokratiker*; and Diels-Kranz' magisterial volumes are customarily taken to define the extension of early Greek thought. Yet such a definition is not wholly felicitous: it gives an artificial unity to a body of thought and doctrine that is, in reality, disparate in conception and various in purpose and intent; and it excludes those early thinkers—I have in mind the Hippocratic doctors, Euripides, and Thucydides—whose works had the good fortune to survive intact. I adhere to the convention that 'the Presocratics' are the men in the *Fragmente*; and the convention is, after all, not wholly without merit. But it follows that I cannot pretend to give a comprehensive account of early Greek philosophy.

Fourth, I shall have nothing to say about many of the interests of the Presocratics. We know a vast amount about Presocratic 'meteorology' and very little about Presocratic epistemology: I have little to do with the former subject, and much to say about the latter. The Presocratics did not work in departments and faculties as we do, and they saw nothing incongruous in treating ethics and astronomy in a single book. For the most part I have restricted myself to topics which would now be classified as philosophical. I shall not be greatly moved by the charge that my classification seems at times to be arbitrary; for in the last resort I have chosen to deal with those issues which happen to interest me and to fit my notion of what a philosopher might reasonably busy himself about.

My debt to the published literature on the Presocratics is incalculable; and it is only in part acknowledged in the Notes and the Bibliography. It would be invidious to pick out a short list of names from the long and learned catalogue of Presocratic scholars; but no one, I think, will object if I say that the writings of Gregory Vlastos have always proved a source of particular stimulation; and I wish also to confess an especial indebtedness to Professor Guthrie's invaluable *History of Greek Philosophy*.

My interest in the Presocratics was first aroused when, as an undergraduate, I attended a course of lectures given by Professor G. E. L. Owen. The views expressed in this book owe a lot to that masterly exposition; and I fear that Professor Owen, should he read my remarks, will find in them many a distorted ghost of his own former opinions. He has my apologies as well as my thanks.

The book was begun and ended at the Chalet des Mélèzes, a living reminder of a lost and better world. An early draft of the first part of the work formed a set of lectures which I gave at Oxford in 1973; but most of the labour was done in Amherst during the Fall of 1973, when I was a visiting professor in Classical Humanities at the University of Massachusetts. I am deeply grateful to the University for the honour of its invitation, and for ensuring that my time there was spent in a pleasant and fruitful fashion; and I must thank the Provost and Fellows of Oriel for granting me sabbatical leave for Michaelmas Term 1973. In Amherst I received valuable help from many hands; in particular, I thank Vere Chappell, John Guiniven, and Gary Matthews, whose criticism, keen, constant, but kindly, brought innumerable improvements to my rude thoughts.

Various parts of the book have been read in various places. An early version of Chapter IV, on Heraclitus, was delivered at Brooklyn College; pieces of Chapter VI, on Pythagoras, formed a paper read at Vassar College; some Eleatic thoughts were aired at the University of Minnesota, and others before the B Club at Cambridge; a part of Chapter XIII, on Zeno, was incorporated into a piece read at the University of Keele. On all those occasions I, at least, profited; and members of my different audiences may expect to see their pillaged suggestions in the following pages. In 1974 I gave a class on Zeno in Oxford, and the discussions there largely moulded my views on that enigmatic figure: I gained greatly from the acute comments of Nicholas Measor and David Sedley.

Work on the Presocratics has occupied me, on and off, for some three years. Throughout that time I have been aided and encouraged, sometimes inadvertently and often from importunate request, by very many pupils, colleagues, and friends; they will, I hope, accept this book as the tangible reward or punishment for their kindnesses. I am also deeply indebted to Mrs D. Cunninghame and Mrs E. Hinkes, who laboured long hours to produce an elegant typescript from a large and messy manuscript.

Finally, I must thank Ted Honderich, the editor of the series in which this book appears, and David Godwin, of Routledge & Kegan Paul: faced with a typescript far longer than they had anticipated, they reacted with self-control, sympathy, and helpful kindness. In particular, the division of the book into two volumes was their suggestion: the book was written as a unitary whole, and the two volumes should be considered as twin halves of a single work; but each volume has, I think, a certain unity of its own. (The division has occasioned one minor inelegance; for the Bibliography would not split as readily as the text. But that should not cause the reader any serious inconvenience.)

In studying the Presocratic philosophers I have constantly been impressed by the sagacity of Leibniz' judgment: 'these men of old had more worth than we suppose'. If any reader is encouraged by this book to join the Leibnizian party, I shall be well content.

J. B.
Chalet des Mélèzes

Note on Citations

Quotations of and allusions to ancient texts will often carry more than one reference; e.g. '1: Diogenes Laertius, I.24 = **11 A 1**'.

A bold arabic numeral accompanies the more important quotations, which are inset from the margin: that numeral documents the position of the text in this book. Thus the quotation labelled '**1**' is the first text of substance that I quote.

The source of every citation is specified: usually the author's name alone is supplied, and further information must be gleaned from Diels–Kranz; fuller details are given for more familiar authors (e.g., Plato and Aristotle), and also in cases where the citation is not printed in Diels–Kranz. Full citations follow the usual canons; and abbreviations of all book titles are explained in Appendix A. (But note here that 'fr.' abbreviates 'fragment'; that titles of the Greek commentaries on Aristotle are abbreviated by prefixing '*in*' to the abbreviated titles of Aristotle's works; that *SVF*, in citations of the Stoics, refers to H. von Arnim's *Stoicorum Veterum Fragmenta*; and that *FGrH*, in citations of certain historians, refers to F. Jacoby's *Fragmente der Griechischer Historiker*.) Thus 'Diogenes Laertius, I.24' refers to Chapter 24 of Book I of Diogenes' only work, the *Lives of the Philosophers*.

Almost all the texts I refer to are printed in the standard source book on early Greek philosophy, *Die Fragmente der Vorsokratiker* by Hermann Diels and Walther Kranz. References to Diels–Kranz, in bold type, cite chapter, section, and item (but the chapter number is omitted wherever it can be divined from the context of the citation). Thus '**11 A 1**' refers to the first item in section **A** of Chapter 11, 'Thales'. Chapters in Diels–Kranz are usually divided into two sections: section **A** contains *testimonia*; section **B** contains fragments. Sometimes, where no fragments survive, **B** is missing; sometimes a

NOTE ON CITATIONS

third section, C, contains 'imitations'. In the case of Chapter **58**, 'The Pythagorean School', a different principle of division is adopted. Readers should be warned that the **B** sections contain many texts whose status as genuine Presocratic fragments is disputed. (Citations bearing on Heraclitus, Empedocles, Melissus and Zeno sometimes carry an additional bold figure reference: those references are explained in the notes to the chapters in which they are used.)

Finally, where a numeral in plain type is suffixed to a bold type reference, it serves to indicate the line (or occasionally section) of the text in question. Thus '**31 B 115**.9' refers to line 9 of **31 B 115**.

All that is, I fear, somewhat cumbersome; and it makes for unsightliness. But I can discover no more elegant method of citation which is not annoyingly inconvenient.

PROLOGUE

I

The Springs of Reason

(a) *The art of thinking*

Logic is a Greek discovery. The laws of thought were first observed in ancient Greece; and they were first articulated and codified in Aristotle's *Analytics*. Modern logicians surpass Aristotle in the scope of their enquiries and in the technical virtuosity of their style; but for elegance of conception and rigour of thought he is their peer, and in all things their intellectual father.

Aristotle was conscious of his own prowess: commendably immodest, he trumpeted his achievement and solicited the gratitude of posterity. Yet God, as John Locke caustically observed, 'had not been so sparing to men as to make them barely two-legged creatures, and left it to Aristotle to make them rational'. If Aristotle's predecessors did not study the art of ratiocination, they were expert in its practice; if they were not logicians, they were thinkers of depth and power. Nor indeed was anyone better aware of this than Aristotle himself: Aristotelian man is essentially a reasoner; and Aristotle's writings describe and praise the attainments of those men who first discovered and charted the broad oceans over which the stately galleon of his own philosophy was to sail.

Pre-eminent among those voyagers were Plato and Socrates; but they too had at their disposal a serviceable set of navigational aids. The aids were prepared by a motley band of doctors and poets, scientists and charlatans, on whom their customary title imposes a spurious community. They are the Presocratic philosophers; and their works are the subject of this book. The term 'Presocratic' is stretched a little: some of the thinkers I shall discuss were Socrates' contemporaries rather than his seniors. And the term 'philosopher' is elastic by its very nature: my Presocratics are men of widely differing interests and professions. The storms of time have not been kind to them: their ships are wrecked, a few shattered planks alone surviving. But our meagre evidence shows something of the men: it reveals (to change the metaphor) that they sought out and drank from the springs of reason; and if that original and heady potation at times induced a trembling delirium in their brains, we still owe them an immeasurable debt for their precocious intoxication. Their tipsy gait taught us to walk more steadily; had they not drunk, we should only shamble.

The Presocratic philosophers had one common characteristic of supreme importance: they were rational. And it is their rationality which this book aspires to exhibit and to celebrate. But Presocratic rationality is often misunderstood, and sometimes mistakenly denied. Let me briefly elucidate my assertion that the Presocratics were rational men.

First, that assertion does not imply that the Greeks, as a race, were peculiarly devoted to reason or peculiarly devoid of superstition. Modern scholarship has abundantly illustrated how folly, unreason and the bonds of superstition were as oppressive in classical Greece as in any other age or land. The average Greek was doubtless as silly as the average Englishman; and the educated men of the sixth and fifth centuries BC were as barbarous and as bigoted as the educated men of today. The Presocratic philosophers were not typical of their fellows: they rose above the vulgar.

Again, it is a simple mistake to think that rationality is the hallmark or the prerogative of the natural sciences. The Presocratics were indeed the first empirical scientists; and in the history books it is the scientific endeavours of the early thinkers which hold pride of place. But reason is omnivorous; it does not pasture exclusively in scientific fields; and the Presocratics did not confine their reasoning powers to a monotonously scientific diet. It is the non-scientific aspects of Presocratic thought with which I am primarily concerned: I shall discuss their metaphysics, not their meteorology.

Third, it is not to be supposed that rational men must resolutely reject the supernatural. Scholars often, and rightly, contrast the naturalistic cosmogonies of the Milesian philosophers with such mythological stories as we find in Hesiod's *Theogony*. Yet the essence of the contrast is sometimes misrepresented: what is significant is not that theology yielded to science or gods to natural forces, but rather that unargued fables were replaced by argued theory, that dogma gave way to reason. Theology and the supernatural may be treated dogmatically or rationally: if the Presocratics reject the blank assertions of piety and poetry, that rejection by no means entails the repudiation of all things divine and superhuman.

Fourth, rational men are not obliged to dream up their ideas for themselves, aloof, autonomous and impervious to influence. classical scholars have, with limited success, investigated the origins and antecedents of Presocratic opinions. Many scholars having located, or conjectured, the source of an opinion, go on to infer that any argument offered for that opinion is mere rationalization: borrowed beliefs, they suppose, are necessarily unreasoned. The absurdity of that inference is patent: evidently, we may purchase opinions from other men and then advance them for our own. The Presocratics, like all rational men, bought many of their opinions off the peg.

Finally, what is rational is not always right; reasoned beliefs are often false; and reasoning—even good and admirable reasoning—is not invariably clear and cogent. Few Presocratic opinions are true; fewer still are well grounded. For all that, they are, in a mild but significant sense, rational: they are characteristically supported by argument, buttressed by reasons, established upon evidence.

Thus in saying that the Presocratics were rational men I mean no more than this: that the broad and bold theories which they advanced were presented not as *ex cathedra* pronouncements for the faithful to believe and the godless to ignore, but as the conclusions of arguments, as reasoned propositions for reasonable men to contemplate and debate. And in holding that the Presocratics were the fathers of rational thought I hold only that they were the first men self-consciously to subordinate assertion to argument and dogma to logic. Some readers may wonder if such a weak form of rationality is not too common a property to merit admiration: to them I commend the aphorism of Bishop Berkeley: All men have opinions, but few men think.

(b) *Thales on magnets and water*

The originator of natural philosophy, according to Aristotle, was Thales the Milesian (*Met* 983b20 = 11 A 12). Thales' name is connected with the solar eclipse of 585 BC; he and his native town of Miletus flourished at the beginning of the sixth century. The two theses on which Thales' reputation must rest are not, at first blush, remarkable for their sobriety: 'the magnet has a soul'; 'everything is water'. Yet the first judgment, I shall argue, betrays a keen philosophical eye; the second marks the beginnings of Western science; and both are supported by simple but rational considerations.

I start with the magnet:

> Aristotle and Hippias say that [Thales] gave inanimate things (*ta apsucha*) too a share in soul (*psuchê*), taking his evidence from the magnetic stone and from amber (**1**: Diogenes Laertius, I.24 = **A 1**; cf. Scholiast to Plato, **A 3**).

Aristotle's words have survived:

> It seems, from what they report, that Thales too supposed the *psuchê* to be a sort of motor, given that he said that the magnet has a *psuchê* because it moves iron (**2**: *An* 405a19–21 = **A 22**).

Aristotle does not name his reporter, but it is a plausible conjecture that he alludes to Hippias of Elis, the second authority named by Diogenes. Hippias, a fifth-century Sophist of some distinction, is sometimes hailed as the inventor of the history of ideas; but according to his own account he compiled not a history but a chrestomathy, a collection of wise or ingenious saws, culled from a variety of sources, and woven into 'a new and manifold argument' (**86 B 6**).[1] Thales' magnets and amber evidently caught Hippias' jackdaw eye; but where they lay during the century and a half from Thales to Hippias, we cannot tell.

The argument which Hippias preserved has a pleasing simplicity. Thales adduced two premisses:
(1) If anything has a motor, it has a *psuchê*;
(2) Magnets and pieces of amber have motors;
and he inferred that:
(3) Magnets and pieces of amber have a *psuchê*.
The sceptical will point out that only the conclusion (3) is unequivocally ascribed to Thales in our sources: premiss (1) is introduced by Aristotle with a cautionary 'it seems', and premiss (2) with the conjunction 'given that'. Perhaps the whole argument was constructed by Aristotle, or by Hippias, and falsely fathered upon Thales?

That melancholy supposition cannot, I think, be disproved; yet I do not find it plausible. Aristotle's 'given that (*eiper*)' most probably means 'since', and thus definitely attributes (2) to Thales; and in any case we can hardly fail to think that Thales rested his paradoxical view upon (2) or some equivalent premiss. And if we give (2) to Thales, it is clear that we may give him (1) to complete the deduction.

What is the sense, and what the cogency, of Thales' argument? The word *psuchê* is commonly translated by 'soul'; and in most contexts this translation is reasonable enough. Here, however, the standard translation masks the charm of the argument, and a heterodox rendering has some justification.

To have a *psuchê* is to be *empsuchos*. *Empsuchos* means 'animate' or 'living': *ta empsucha* and *ta apsucha* jointly exhaust the natural world, being the animate and the inanimate portions of creation. The *psuchê*, then, as Aristotle says, is simply 'that by which we are alive' (*An* 414a12): it is the source or principle of life in animate beings, that part or feature of them (whatever it may be) in virtue of which they are alive.[2] In short, an *empsuchon* is an animate thing; and its *psuchê* is its animator. Instead of 'soul', then, I propose the term 'animator' as a translation of *psuchê*; and I prefer the comic overtones of 'animator' to the theological undertones of 'soul'.

What are the criteria for life? According to Aristotle, 'things are said to be alive on several accounts, and if just one of these belongs to a thing we say that it is alive—viz. understanding, perception, change and rest in place, and again the change brought on by nourishment, and decay and growth' (*An* 413a22-5). More generally, 'the animate seems to differ from the inanimate by two things in particular, motion and perception' (*An* 403b25-7). Aristotle is not putting forward a philosophical thesis here: he is recording, and accepting, a commonplace. Anything that has powers of cognition, of which perception is the most common and the most evident example, is alive; and anything which has the power to alter itself or its environment, of which autonomous locomotion is the most evident example, is likewise alive. If the great marks of animation are the power to perceive and the capacity to locomote or to cause locomotion, then a *psuchê* or animator will be essentially a source of perception, or a perceptor, and a source of motion, or a motor.

Thales' argument now has a superficial plausibility. His first premiss is a platitude: motors—that is to say, self-starting motors—are, on Aristotle's own account, and in ordinary thought, animators or *psuchai*; and anything capable of autonomous locomotion is thereby shown to be animate. His second premiss is a matter of ordinary observation: magnets and pieces of amber are seen to possess the power to cause locomotion in other things and to move themselves. And the conclusion follows: magnets and pieces of amber are animate beings; they may not have the faculty of perception, but for all that they are alive.

Thales' successors ignored his argument. Later scientists felt the force of magnetic attraction, and offered crude mechanistic hypotheses to explain it; but they did not, so far as we know, stop to ponder Thales' curious conclusion.[3] Even Aristotle, who was aware of Thales' argument and who must have seen its power, says nothing directly against it; yet Aristotle hardly believed that magnets were alive.

Aristotle's psychology does, however, contain an implicit answer to Thales; and a short sketch of that answer may bring out the philosophical interest of the magnet.

The magnet, Aristotle would have said, does not initiate locomotion after the fashion of genuinely animate beings. Animate motion is necessarily caused by a 'desire', or *orexis*, on the part of the mover; it is, in a later jargon, preceded by a 'volition' or act of will. But magnets do not have desires or perform acts of will. Thus magnets may move, but they do not move in the manner of living things. To this, Thales has a retort: perhaps magnets do have primitive desires; perhaps their passion for knives and needles, and their indifference to silver churns, evinces a discrimination and a will? And if Aristotle adds that desire implies perception and judgment, Thales will simply say that the discriminatory capacities which magnets, like computers or potato-sorting machines, exhibit are primitive perceptions—and he will have some modern psychologists on his side.

Aristotle distinguishes between 'rational' and 'irrational' powers: if a has a rational power to Φ, then a can both Φ and refrain from Φing; if a's power to Φ is irrational, then a can Φ but cannot refrain from Φing. Animate movers have rational powers: they can withstand temptation, or be bloody-minded. But the magnet is weak-willed and intemperate; if a piece of iron is placed at a suitable distance from it, locomotion commences, and the magnet has no choice in the matter. Magnets are not free: that is why they are not alive.

I do not offer this as the correct rebuttal of Thales' argument; evidently the debate can continue. But enough has, I hope, been done to indicate that Thales' argument is not a naive aberration or a puerile sophism; it raises puzzles of a distinctively philosophical nature. Thales' magnet is the ancient equivalent of the clockwork animals of the seventeenth century and of our modern chess-playing computers: we know that mechanical toys are not alive; and we suspect that the most ingenious computer lacks something that every rabbit possesses. Yet if we attempt to justify those convictions or suspicions, we soon find ourselves lost in the thickets of the philosophy of mind. Vaugelas and Turing are justly celebrated for the challenge they made to lovers of the mind: Thales, I claim, deserves a small bow of recognition.

According to Hippias, Thales did not rest content with (3): he said, more generally, that inanimate things have *psuchai*. It is reasonable to associate this conclusion with the apophthegm 'everything is full of spirits' which, in various forms, is ascribed to Thales (Aristotle, *An*

411a7 = **A 22**; Aëtius, **A 23**; etc.: the same authorities present Thales with the view that the world as a whole has a soul, and Aristotle conjectures that this may have been the source of the apophthegm; but the opposite derivation is more probable). The purport of this generalization of (3) is uncertain: did Thales merely remark that (3) should prepare us for further surprises, that the world is not divided into animate and inanimate as easily as we might think? Should we rather press upon him the assertion that everything is animate, that the common distinction between animate and inanimate objects is illusory? And if we do press this upon him, are we to dismiss it as irresponsible enthusiasm? Or can we ascribe to him the philosophical reflexion that if the common criteria for distinguishing the living from the non-living yield results like (3), then those criteria must be vain creations of the human mind, marking no difference in external reality?

Such questions have no answers: even to pose them may be deemed a sign of speculative lunacy; and I turn hastily to Thales' second and more notorious contribution to rational thought:

> Thales . . . says that [the material principle] is water, and that is why he asserted that the earth rests on water (**3**: Aristotle, *Met* 983b20–2 = **A 12**).

Thus we have two aqueous asseverations:
(4) The material principle of everything is water.
(5) The earth rests on water.

I shall first consider (5).[4] Two chapters of Aristotle's *de Caelo* deal with the position and shape of the earth; and in his historical survey Aristotle adverts again to Thales:

> Some say that [the earth] rests on water. For this is the oldest theory that has been handed down to us, and they say that Thales of Miletus propounded it, supposing that it remains there because it can float, like wood or something else of that sort (**4**: 294a28–31 = **A 14**: again Hippias is probably Aristotle's source).

Here (5) is presented independently of (4) and with an argument of its own.

Some scholars discern a spark of genius in the argument: Thales' quick spirit tackled the grand and remote question of the earth's support by a homely analogy with floating logs; as Newton sat beneath his apple-tree and invented gravity, so Thales sat on a river-bank dreaming of astronomy. Yet Thales' spark is dim: had he amused himself by throwing stones into his river, he might have inferred that whatever the earth floats upon it is not water. The analogy will not do.[5] In any case, Thales' answer recalls Locke's Indian philosopher, who held that the earth rests on the back of an elephant, the elephant on a tortoise, and the tortoise on 'something, he knew not what'. Aristotle puts the point briskly: 'as if the same argument did not apply to the earth and to the water supporting the earth' (*Cael* 294a32–3 = A 14). And that, I think, disposes of Thales' claim to genius here.

For all that, Thales' argument has an extrinsic importance. First, its analogy provides the first example of a marked characteristic of Presocratic thought: from Thales onward, analogical illustration and argument are frequent; the analogies are often drawn from humble and unscientific areas, and they are sometimes spun out with some ingenuity. I shall discuss this at more length in a later context (below, pp. 52–6).

Second, Thales offered the first non-mythological answer to a standing problem in Greek science. Aristotle explains the problem with unusual lucidity: 'It would take, I suppose, a somewhat dull mind not to wonder how in the world it can be that a small piece of earth, if released in mid-space (*meteôristhen*), moves and will not stay where it is (and the bigger it is, the faster it moves), while if you were to put the whole earth in mid-space and release it, it would not move; in fact, heavy as it is, it is stable. And yet if you took a moving piece of earth and took the ground from under it before it fell, it would move on and downwards as long as nothing obstructed it. Hence puzzling about this naturally became a philosophical problem for everyone' (*Cael* 294a12–20). Two apparently obvious truths generate the puzzle: first, the earth is clearly at rest; second, the earth is clearly in mid-space. The conjunction of the two is paradoxical, given the observed behaviour of portions of earth.

Thales answered the paradox by denying that the earth is in mid-space; his successors, noticing the infelicity of his proposal, attempted other solutions. Their attempts are sophisticated and of some interest; and they too will be discussed at some length (below, pp. 23–8).

Thales' other watery thesis, (4), poses intricate problems of interpretation. Scholars agree that he cannot have stated (4) as it stands; for it uses the terminology of a later age. Yet (4) encourages the ascription to Thales of some such sentiment as:

(6) Everything is from water (*panta ex hudatos estin*).

It is easy to imagine that Aristotle rendered (6) by (4); and parallels to (6) can be found in the earliest remnants of Presocratic thought.

Was Aristotle's interpretation of (6) correct, and was Thales a

'material monist'? If Aristotle is wrong, what can Thales mean by (6)? I shall return to these questions later. Here, leaving the sense of (6) partly indeterminate, I ask why Thales assented to such a strange hypothesis, and why he should have subscribed to:
(7) There is some single stuff from which everything is,
which is immediately entailed by (6).

Our texts provide no answer to these questions; but it is not hard to excogitate one. (7) offers what is, in a very obvious sense, the simplest hypothesis that will account for the constitution of the world: unity is simpler than plurality; a postulated unity is more fundamental than a plurality. Science always strives for economy and simplicity in explanation; and in adopting (7) Thales was only proving himself an embryonic scientist; he saw that (7) was eminently simple and because of its simplicity he adopted it as a hypothesis.

Given that Thales subscribed to (7), why did he pick on water as his basic stuff, and plump for (6)? Aristotle and Theophrastus supply a set of arguments, which amount to the claim that water is essential in various ways to the existence of living creatures (*Met* 983b22–7 = **A 12**; Simplicius, **A 13**; cf. Aëtius, I.3.1). Now Aristotle's remarks are explicitly conjectural; and Theophrastus joins Thales with Hippo of Rhegium, a fifth-century thinker of little note who later adopted (4) as his own (cf. Hippolytus, **38 A 3**; Alexander, **A 6**; Philoponus, **A 10**): most scholars suppose that the arguments were propounded in a work of Hippo's and projected back onto Thales by the Peripatetics. They may be right: other arguments can be invented (it is usually observed that water, alone of the common constituents of the world, is regularly found in gaseous, solid and liquid states); or we may prefer to suppose that Thales adopted water as a whimsy.[6] But Hippo's reasons are not recondite; nor are they wholly unintelligible reasons, given Thales' psychological views: living creatures are far more prevalent than we ordinarily think; water is evidently necessary for their existence; water is not readily generated from any other stuff; hence water must be a basic constituent of the world. And since, by (7), there is at most one basic constituent of the world, thesis (6) comes tottering in as a conclusion. It does not take a giant intellect to knock holes in that reasoning; but at least there is a piece of reasoning, and not a mere prejudice, to attack.

The two theories which I have just examined show that Thales was no mean thinker. He offers reasoned views on abstract and philosophical subjects, and he merits his traditional place of honour at the head of Western science and philosophy: he was 'the Originator of this sort of Philosophy' (Aristotle, *Met* 983b20 = **A 12**; cf. *Cael* 294a29 = **A 14**). *Vixerunt alii ante Agamemnona*:

Theophrastus cautiously supposed that Thales had predecessors whom his own genius eclipsed and hid from the eyes of history (Simplicius, **B 1**). Certainly, Thales was not the first man to think about cosmogony; but what little we know of his predecessors does not contain much that is rational or philosophical in spirit. There is myth, and there is genealogical theogony. Apart from that, a few tantalizingly abstract phrases from the seventh-century Spartan poet Alcman peep coquettishly through the veil of time, exciting the imagination without satisfying the desire.[7] And there is the bizarre figure of Pherecydes of Syros: Aristotle called him a 'mixed' theologian (*Met* 1091b8 = **7 A 7**), whose work was only partly mythological; and his cosmogony, of which we have substantial fragments, seems in some respects to mediate between Hesiodic myth and Ionian science. But Pherecydes was almost certainly a generation younger than Thales; and in any case his fragments contain nothing of philosophical interest: he is at best a 'literary curiosity'.[8]

In his cosmic speculation, then, Thales had a few uninteresting predecessors. In psychology no one, so far as we know, had preceded him.

It would, of course, be a mistake to infer that Thales was a lonely revolutionary, indulging in abstract ratiocinations remote from the practical concerns of the world. On the contrary, tradition represents him as one of the Seven Sages: early stories depict him as an engineering consultant to the Lydian army (Herodotus, I.170 = **A 6**) and as a national statesman urging Pan-Ionian federation against the Persians (Herodotus, I.75 = **A 4**); and the early record was embellished by a host of later and less trustworthy raconteurs. Most famously, Thales is said to have predicted an eclipse of the sun, which interrupted a battle between the Lydians and the Persians. The story is told by Herodotus (I.74 = **A 5**), but it was known earlier to Xenophanes (**21 B 19**) and to Heraclitus (**22 B 38**). What lies behind the story is uncertain: Thales' prediction cannot have been based on any abstract astronomical theory, and it will not have pretended to any degree of accuracy; probably he had picked up some lore from the East.[9] However that may be, he surely showed some interest in matters astronomical; and Eudemus of Rhodes, who was set to write the Peripatetic history of the exact sciences, duly made him the first astronomer (fr. 144W = Diogenes Laertius, I.23 = **A 1**). Thales also stood at the head of Eudemus' history of geometry, where he was credited with the proof of several abstract theorems.[10] It is no part of my brief to list or assess those ascriptions; and the heated controversy they have aroused will deter all but the most reckless from advancing an amateur opinion. One report, however, will usefully serve to introduce the subject of my next section.

(c) *Tradition and interpretation*

Thales is said to have discovered the theorem which appears as I.26 in Euclid's *Elements*: Triangles *ABC, abc* are identical if $AB = ab$, angle A = angle a, and angle B = angle b.

> Eudemus in his *History of Geometry* ascribes this theorem to Thales; for he says that it was necessary for him to apply it in the method by which they say he proved the distance of ships at sea (5: Proclus, A 20).[11]

Evidently Eudemus did not find a statement, let alone a proof, of Euclid I.26 in any work of Thales; rather, he found ascribed to Thales a method of calculating the distance of ships from the land; he judged that the method required the application of I.26; he assumed that Thales did apply I.26; and he inferred that Thales had discovered, or even that he had proved, I.26. The weakness of Eudemus' inference is plain enough; and if Thales' geometrical reputation rests wholly on such Peripatetic speculations, we shall be wary of thinking him a geometer at all: birds are not aeronautical engineers.

Eudemus was working in the dark. Aristotle, who relied on the reports of Hippias, had come across no writings of Thales' own (or at any rate none bearing on the subjects which interested him); and it is improbable that Eudemus was any more fortunate than Aristotle.[12] Indeed, there was considerable uncertainty in antiquity over Thales' writings, and a strong tradition supposed that he had written nothing at all (Diogenes Laertius, I.23 = A 1).

Such reflections are dispiriting enough in themselves; generalized, they induce a grisly scepticism about our acquaintance with Presocratic thought as a whole. No piece of Presocratic philosophy has survived in its entirety;[13] in most cases we have only a few *disjecta membra*; and those fragments—sentences, mangled phrases, or single words—are as often as not known to us only from the quotations of late sources, who cite them to display their learning or to make a polemical point. We rely, then, on the 'doxography'—on reports, by later authors, of the opinions and arguments of their remote predecessors. For Thales we have no fragments at all; for many later thinkers we are little better off; and even where we possess a page or two of the original, the doxography remains important, both as a source of doctrine not presented in the fragments, and as a means of setting those jewels in a suitable foil.

Then how reliable is the doxography? It is a vast and variegated thing: it stretches in time from the fifth century BC to the fourteenth century AD, and most of the surviving authors of antiquity contribute to it. This tumultuous and many-channelled stream welled in the Lyceum, whence most of its waters derive. The chief source, it seems, was Theophrastus' large study *On the Opinions of the Physicists*; but only a few fragments of that work survive,[14] and we must usually drink from the lower reaches of the stream where the waters are stale and muddy. Moreover, the stream is contaminated. First, many of the later doxographers were not scholars but silly hacks who, by accident or design, regularly mutilated or distorted the Theophrastan material; and in any case they had at their disposal not Theophrastus' original work but some poor epitome and refashioning of it. Second, Theophrastus himself was not a historical purist: imitating his master, Aristotle, whose treatises are regularly prefaced by schematic doxographies, he presents earlier theories in terms of his own philosophy and earlier theorists as lisping Peripatetics.[15] In short, the doxography flows from tainted sources through tainting channels: if it happens to preserve a little pure water, that is a lucky chance.

The doxography is unreliable. Our knowledge of the Presocratics must rest upon their *ipsissima verba*. Few *verba* survive. Hence our knowledge of the Presocratics is exiguous.

I believe that our knowledge of early Greek thought is indeed exiguous: despite the labours of scholarship and imagination, we possess little firm evidence; and it was all so unimaginably different, and so very long ago. Yet we need not plunge to the very depths of sceptical despair: ignorant of most, we know a little. First, Thales is not a typical figure: for most of the major figures in Presocratic thought we do still possess a modest collection of genuine fragments; and it is often plausible to believe that these fragments preserve the most important and most interesting of their philosophical doctrines. Obscurities and uncertainties abound; the fragments hide as much as they reveal; and the doxography is almost always indispensable. For all that (as readers of this book will discover) the fragments form an archipelago of islets in the dark ocean of our ignorance.

Second, the doxography is not utterly despicable. Acute philological scholarship has established the complicated interrelationships of our surviving sources;[16] and we can often reconstruct with some probability the views, if not the words, of Theophrastus himself: science can filter out the impurities which the doxographical stream picked up in the course of its long passage. Nor am I convinced that the Peripatetics were poor, let alone dishonest, historians. They wrote, as we all do, in their own jargon and for their own ends; and they were sometimes slapdash and sometimes inconsistent. But inconsistency is always detectable, and often corrigible; and there is little evidence of widespread carelessness. Thales, indeed, supplies us with a fine example of Peripatetic scholarship: Aristotle himself makes it plain that he is working from second-hand reports, and not from original documents; he indicates, more than once, that his opinions are speculative; and he states with candour that the line of reasoning he ascribes to Thales is conjectural. Moreover, the Aristotelian terminology of his reconstruction will mislead only the most myopic scholar: the Peripatetics do not pretend, and we do not believe, that Thales himself used the phrase 'material principle'; rather, they pretend to express Thales' old thesis in their new terminology.

'But surely,' some will complain, 'such rephrasing of an argument is in itself an unhistorical anachronism; and it is quite enough to condemn an interpretation.' If that complaint is correct, then all attempts to understand the Presocratics are doomed to failure; for understanding requires rephrasing or translation. But the complaint is foolish. Consider, as an elementary example, the connexion between my sentences numbered (1)–(3) above, and Thales' ancient words. It is my contention that sentences (1)–(3) express exactly the same argument that Thales once expressed. The differences between my argument and that of Thales are formal, not substantial; in particular, they reside in three notational devices which I use and Thales did not. First, (1)–(3) set the argument out in deductive form, whereas Thales presented it informally. That device is at worst a harmless pedantry; at best it adds clarity to the articulation of the argument. Second, my argument is mildly formalized: its component propositions are numbered (later arguments will wear the slightly more daring finery of logical symbols). This device, again, is purely clarificatory. Third, (1)–(3) are written in English, not Greek: that device is by far the most dangerous of the three: yet few, I suspect, will insist on keeping the Presocratics concealed in their original tongue.

The Peripatetic approach to the Presocratics is not, in theory, any more reprehensible than the approach adopted in (1)–(3) and common to most modern interpreters of ancient thought. If we are to do more than parrot the fragmentary utterances of the past, we must translate them into a modern idiom. The attempt at translation may, of course, cause disfigurement; but that is a weakness in the translator—translation itself is both intrinsically harmless and philosophically indispensable.

Yet if I defend the doxography against the wilder charges levelled at it, I do not wish to encourage sanguinity. We know remarkably little about the Presocratics. Their texts are frequently obscure in content; and they are usually pigmy in extent. A historian of philosophy who has studied the seventeenth century has difficulties enough; but he possesses a vast mass of moderately intelligible material, and we need not despair of constructing a detailed and well-rounded account of the thought of that period. With the Presocratics nothing like that is true. There are bright patches of detail, and a few dim suggestions of a more general pattern of development; more than that we can never expect. And I cannot refrain from adding the essentially frivolous comment that such a state of affairs is not wholly depressing: in a sea of ignorance the pursuit of truth is more exacting; and darkness adds excitement to the chase.

Enough of such generalities. Later chapters will have occasion to discuss particular instances of doxographical malpractice, and to raise more detailed problems of anachronism in interpretation. The aim of the preceding paragraphs has been to advocate a moderately cheerful scepticism. Our evidence for Presocratic thought is slight and fragmentary; but it is not wholly unreliable. We possess some titbits of knowledge: whether or not they constitute a nourishing and a savoury philosophical meal, the reader's palate must decide; he has, in the theses of Thales, a sort of *hors d'oeuvre*: I hope that his appetite is whetted for the dishes that follow.

EDEN

II

Anaximander on Nature

(a) *Pantological knowledge*

Anaximander was a younger contemporary and a fellow-citizen of Thales; we need not accept the conventional statement that they were teacher and pupil, in order to believe that the younger man knew and was stimulated by his senior's excogitations. Anaximander became 'the first Greek whom we know to have produced a written account *Concerning Nature*' (Themistius, **12 A** 7).[1]

Of that work barely a dozen words have survived; but the doxography enables us to judge its scope and pretensions. It was vast: there was a cosmogony, or account of the original formation of the universe; a history of the earth and the heavenly bodies; an account of the development of living organisms; descriptions of natural phenomena of every sort, and infant studies of astronomy, meteorology and biology; and a geography illustrated by a celebrated *mappa mundi*. Nature, *phusis*, embraces every object of experience and every subject of rational inquiry except the productions of human contrivance; and the Presocratic systems of thought were generally spoken of as accounts *Concerning Nature (Peri Phuseôs)*. An account concerning nature would begin with cosmogony, and proceed to a description of the celestial universe. It would investigate the development of the earth, of terrestrial life, and of the human animal; it would describe the clouds, the rains, and the winds, the rocky structure of the land, and the salt sea. It would rise from the inorganic to the organic, treating of topics botanical and zoological; it would look at the typology of species and the anatomy of individuals. It would turn to the mind, and study the psychology of sensation and action; and it would ask about the extent and the nature of human knowledge, and about the proper place of man in the natural world. An account *Peri Phuseôs* would, in brief, encompass all science and all philosophy.

Thales, we may imagine, first indicated that vast field of intellectual endeavour. Anaximander was the first to map it out; and his chart, with a few additions and modifications, determined the range and aspirations of almost all subsequent thought. Anaximenes, Xenophanes, and even Heraclitus; Empedocles and Anaxagoras and the Atomists: all worked and wrote in the grand tradition of Anaximander: other men are specialists, their specialism was omniscience.[2]

Even through the thick fog of time which separates us from Anaximander, we can perceive the flashings of 'an intellect of truly amazing grasp and audacity'. The range of his mind was matched by a powerful reasoning capacity and an ingenious imagination. His astronomical system illustrates his intellectual virtuosity: the earth is at the still centre of the turning cosmos; about it lie concentric wheel-rims, one for the stars, one for the moon, one for the sun; the wheel-rims are hollow and filled with fire; and heavenly bodies are holes in these rims, through which shines the enclosed fire (Aëtius, **A 21–2**). Applications of this theory accounted for the various celestial happenings, and it was worked out with a dedicated mixture of mathematics, insight and fantasy.[3]

In this chapter I shall discuss first, Anaximander's 'Darwinism'; second, his account of the stability of the earth; and third, that small fragment of his work which contains the earliest extant words of Western Philosophy. My treatment will not exhibit Anaximander as a systematic thinker; but it will, I hope, show the characteristic virtues and vices of his temperament.

(b) *The origin of species*

And again, [Anaximander] says that in the beginning men were born from creatures of a different sort, because the other animals quickly manage to feed themselves, but man alone requires a long period of nursing; hence had he been like that in the beginning too, he would never have survived (6: pseudo-Plutarch, **A 10**).

Other reports, which do not agree in detail, make men's first parents fish or fish-like creatures who retained their human offspring in their bellies until they were able to fend for themselves (Hippolytus, **A 11**; Plutarch, Censorinus, **A 30**). A further notice indicates that Anaximander's speculations were not confined to his own species:

Anaximander says that the first animals were born in the moisture, surrounded by prickly barks; and that as they reached maturity they moved out on to the drier parts where their bark split and they survived in a different form (*metabiônai*) for a brief while (**7**: Aëtius, **A 30**).[4]

Thus a theory of human phylogeny was embedded in a broader account of the origins of animal life.

The theory that life began in the wet parts of the earth was accepted by many of Anaximander's successors.[5] It is tempting to connect it with another hypothesis:

At first, they say, the whole area around the earth was moist, and as it was dried by the sun the part which vaporized made the winds and the turnings of the sun and the moon, while what was left is the sea; that is why they think that the sea is becoming smaller as it dries out, and that in the end it will at some time all be dry (**8**: Aristotle, *Meteor* 353b6–11 = **A 27**).

Theophrastus ascribes the hypothesis to Anaximander (Alexander, **A 27**). The doxography gives no further details, but a remarkable set of observations ascribed to Xenophanes of Colophon, whose life span overlapped with that of Anaximander, gives grounds for conjecture:

Xenophanes thinks that a mixing of the earth with the sea is occurring, and that in time it is being dissolved by the moist. He says he has the following proofs: shells are found in the middle of the land and in the mountains, and he says that in Syracuse in the stone quarries there have been found impressions of fish and of seals [?], and on Paros an impression of laurel in the depth of the rock, and in Malta prints of all sea creatures. And he says that this happened some time ago when everything was covered in mud, and that the impression dried in the mud (**9**: Hippolytus, **21 A 33**).[6]

Xenophanes' theory was different from Anaximander's in at least one respect; for he held that the earth was gradually getting wetter, not that it was drying out. But in other ways he may have been imitating his Milesian predecessor. Perhaps Anaximander elaborated a cyclical theory of hydration and dehydration; and perhaps he relied on the sort of fossilized evidence that Xenophanes used—for if he had not heard of the findings in Malta and in Syracuse, Paros at least was near home. And scholars plausibly guess that Anaximander observed and was impressed by the gradual silting of the harbour at Miletus and the general recession of the sea along the Ionian coast.

All that suggests an expansive theory of the origins of life: 'The earth is gradually drying out from an originally water-logged condition. The first living creatures, then, will have been of a fishy variety, to whom a watery environment was congenial. Only later, as the earth dried, will land animals have developed from those aquatic aboriginals. And man, in particular, must have had a peculiar sort of ancestor, given the weak and dependent nature of the human infant.'

On the strength of this theory Anaximander has been hailed as the first Darwinian; and there are grounds for praise: the animal species were not, in Anaximander's view, immutably fixed at their creation; and their development was determined by the nature of their environment. Here we have, in embryo, evolution and the survival of the fittest. Both those 'Darwinian' aspects of Anaximander's theory are found, a century later, in Empedocles. Much of Empedocles' zoogony is strange and disputed (see 31 B 57-62; Aëtius, A 72); but he surely held both that the earliest living creatures were very different from those with which we are familiar, and also that many of those early creatures were, for various reasons, incapable of surviving and perpetuating themselves. The Aristotelian doctrine of the immutability of species later gained a stranglehold on men's minds; and it is only just that we should honour Anaximander and Empedocles for their insight.

Nevertheless, praise should not be lavished with fulsome disregard for accuracy; and the grand theory presented to Anaximander is neither as cohesive nor as evolutionary as I have made it seem. First, our sources do not connect Anaximander's hypothesis of a drying earth with his zoogonical theories; and since, according to Aëtius, the first animals were amphibian and lived at a time when the earth already had dry parts, the physical hypothesis may well have been entirely divorced from the zoogonical theories. Anaximander is perhaps more likely to have been moved to his watery zoogony by the sort of considerations which led Thales to adopt water as a 'first principle' (above, p. 11).

Second, there is no trace of evolution, in the sense of gradual change, in Anaximander's theory. Aëtius implies no more than that the first generation of each species emerged from prickly barks or shells. There is no suggestion that this mode of reproduction occurred more than once; or that the first generation had been preceded by a line of prickly ancestors; or that, once hatched, the first cats and cows, hyenas and horses, differed in any respect from their present descendants. Nor is the speculative origin of mankind evolutionary: it seems probable that the 'fish-like' parents of the first men were similar to the prickly cradles of the other animals, the only difference being that the human barks did not split until their contents were at a relatively advanced stage of development. Censorinus (**A 30**) says that the first men did not emerge 'until puberty'; if his report is accurate, Anaximander's motive is transparent: he wants to ensure that the first generation of men will survive long enough to reproduce and care for a second generation. Anaximander did not envisage a long and gradual alteration in the form and behaviour of animal species in response to their changing environment. He did not ask how the species we know came to have the characteristics we observe in them. His question was simply: How did living creatures first come into being and propagate? And his answer was a genial fantasy.

(c) *The earth at rest*

In the orthodox opinion, the early Ionian astronomers are divided by a deep gulf. On the one side stands the majority, whose accounts, though pretentious in design, are in execution crude and sketchy, offering imprecise and piecemeal observations on individual problems with no attempt at synthesis or quantification. On the other side stands the lone figure of Anaximander, 'the earliest known type of a mathematical physicist, at any rate outside Babylonia', whose theories rest on a proper scientific methodology 'critical and speculative rather than empirical'.[7] Both sides of this contrast are overdrawn: Anaximander was not quite the purist his admirers imagine, and his colleagues were not as different from him as they have been made to appear. Nevertheless, his astronomy remains an astonishing achievement, and nowhere more so than in his account of the earth's position in the universe.

Anaximander punctured Thales' water-bed: he realized that any solution to the puzzle of the earth's stability needed something stronger than an analogy and deeper than a cushion of water (see above, pp. 9–10). His own answer, which Aristotle expounds and discusses at some length (*Cael* 295b10–296a23 = **A 26**) meets these requirements, and enables him to reconcile the apparently conflicting facts that the earth is at rest and that the earth is in mid-space.

Aristotle's report runs thus:

There are some who say that it [sc. the earth] stays where it is (*menein*) because of the similarity (*dia tên homoiotêta*); e.g., among the ancients, Anaximander. For what sits in the middle and is similarly related to the extremes has no more reason (*mallon outhen . . . prosêkei*) to go upwards than downwards or sideways;

but it is impossible for it to make a movement in opposite directions at the same time: so of necessity it stays where it is (**10**: *Cael* 295b10–16 = **A 26**).

Aristotle is echoed in the doxography:

[Anaximander says that] the earth is in mid-air (*meteôron*), overpowered by nothing, and staying where it is on account of his similar distance from everything (**11**: Hippolytus, **A 11**).[8]

Both Aristotle and Hippolytus speak, in slightly different fashions, of 'similarity': their vague references can be filled out in more than one way, and we have no means of knowing which filling is authentic. The interpretation I offer is speculative; but it fits the words of our reports, and it consists with Anaximander's general cosmology. A *cosmic spoke* is a straight line drawn from the centre of the earth to the boundary of the finite cosmos. A spoke s_1 is *similar* to a spoke s_2 if every point, p_1, n units from the earth along s_1 is qualitatively indistinguishable from the corresponding point, p_2, n units from the earth along s_2. Hippolytus' text suggests that *all* cosmic spokes are similar; Aristotle implies the weaker supposition that for every cosmic spoke there is a similar spoke opposite to it. (Two spokes are 'opposite' if they form an angle of 180° in all planes at the centre of the earth.) In fact, Anaximander needs no more than:

(1) For any cosmic spoke s_i, there is a distinct spoke s_j such that s_j is similar to s_i,

and I shall use (1) as though it were Anaximandrian.

The inference turns, according to Aristotle, on the proposition that the earth does not move because it 'has no more reason' to go in one direction than in another. Implicit in this is the second of the 'two great principles' on which, according to Leibniz, all reasoning is founded: it is 'the Principle of Sufficient Reason, in virtue of which we believe that no fact can be real or existent, and no statement true, unless it has a sufficient reason why it should be thus and not otherwise' (*Monadology*, §32).[9] The Principle can be applied, and Anaximander's argument articulated, in more than one way; I shall present the argument as a *reductio*.

Let us suppose that the earth is moving, i.e., that it is travelling along some cosmic spoke, say s_1; thus:

(2) The earth is moving along s_1.

Anaximander assumes that the motion described in (2) must have some explanation. He is, I suggest, implicitly relying on some such principle as:

(3) If a is F, then for some ϕ, a is F because a is ϕ.

From (2) and (3) he may validly infer:
(4) For some ϕ, the earth moves along s_1 because s_1 is ϕ.
Suppose that the explanatory feature of s_1 is G, then we have:
(5) The earth moves along s_1 because s_1 is G,
and hence, trivially:
(6) s_1 is G.
Then, by (1) and (6):
(7) Some s_j distinct from s_1 is G.
Suppose, then:
(8) s_2 is G.
At this point, Anaximander needs a further principle, that explanations are 'universalizable'. An appropriate formula here is:
(9) If a is F because a is G, then if anything is G it is F.
Between them, (3) and (9) amount to something like a Principle of Sufficient Reason: (3) asserts that happenings need *some* explanation; (9) indicates how that explanation must be a *sufficient* condition for what it explains.
Now from (5), (8) and (9) there follows:
(10) The earth is moving along s_2.
Since nothing can move in two directions at once, (2) and (10) are incompatible. Hence, by *reductio ad absurdum*, (2) is false: the earth must stay where it is.

Anaximander's argument is clean and ingenious; and it reveals an awareness of certain central features of our notion of explanation. 'Even if we knew nothing else concerning its author, this alone would guarantee him a place among the creators of a rational science of the natural world.'[10] But the argument is hardly convincing. I ignore certain *a priori* objections to premiss (1): the premiss is a scientific hypothesis—a Popperian conjecture—and not an inductive generalization; and if hypothesis is preferable to induction, the status of (1) is a tribute, not an objection, to Anaximander. Moreover, (1) is no isolated hypothesis: it is part of an elaborate description of the heavens (see above, p. 20), which is designed both to save the phenomena and to guarantee cosmic 'similarity'. Nor will it do to object that Anaximander rules out, *sans* argument, any transcendental differences between cosmic spokes. Anaximander is doing astronomy; and astronomy exists as a science only if the gods do not capriciously intervene in the workings of the world. That there is no transcendental, divine, or capricious intervention in natural processes is a presupposition fundamental to the very enterprise of science.

Nonetheless, premiss (1) will not stand. Despite its ingenuity, Anaximander's astronomy does not work: it ensures the 'similarity' required by (1)—though not the stronger 'similarities' implicit in

Aristotle and Hippolytus—but it does not 'save the phenomena'. As an astronomical hypothesis it is falsifiable; and it was immediately seen to be false. Anaximander's argument is scientifically untenable.

Philosophically, there are those who reject the Principle of Sufficient Reason: some attack (3), others attack (9). Opponents of (9) ask why certain features should not simply have an effect on some occasions and not on others: freak weather conditions caused today's typhoon, even though the very same conditions had no devastating effect yesterday. Opponents of (3) may simply point to the occurrence of chance events. More subtle antagonists will ride Buridan's ass: equidistant between two bottles of hay their steed would, were the Principle right, starve to death. In fact, the donkey eats: either there is no explanation for its taking this bottle rather than that, in which case (3) is false; or else the donkey's attraction to this bottle is explained by a feature which that bottle also possesses, in which case (9) is false. This *reductio ad asininum* was anticipated by Aristotle: he compares Anaximander's arguments with 'the argument that a hair which is subject to strong but uniform tension will not break, and that a man who is hungry and thirsty to an extreme but equal degree will abstain alike from food and drink' (*Cael* 295b30–3).

I shall touch on these issues again in later chapters. Here it is enough to remark that the objections to (3) and to (9) are not conclusive against Anaximander; for (3) and (9)—like the prohibition on divine intervention—are, in a certain sense, presuppositions of any scientific astronomy: if either (3) or (9) lapses, then the goal of astronomy itself is unattainable, and we cannot find universal laws explanatory of the celestial phenomena. Any wise man, therefore, will strive to maintain (3) and (9), even if he cannot show them to be true *a priori*; for to abandon them is to abandon the highest ideal of science.

Anaximander's successors are often alleged to have betrayed his memory, retreating to primitive, Thaletan, thoughts and quitting the speculative heights to which he had ascended. Thus Xenophanes said that the earth 'reaches downward to infinity' (**21 B 28**; cf. Aristotle, *Cael* 294a21–8 = **A 47**); and Anaximenes had the earth 'riding' on the air (Aëtius, **13 A 20**; cf. **B 2a**). Anaximenes was followed by Anaxagoras and Democritus (Aristotle, *Cael* 294b13–23 = **13 A 20**) and by Diogenes of Apollonia (Scholiast on Basil, **64 A 16a**); and his theory became an orthodoxy, alluded to in poetry and prose, and guyed in comedy ([Hippocrates], Euripides, Aristophanes, **64 C 2**). Empedocles alone offered something similar to Anaximander; but his theory is only half intelligible, and that half is wrong.[11] Anaximander's argument is once ascribed to Parmenides and

Democritus (Aëtius, **28 A 44**); and another source has it that 'Empedocles and Parmenides and almost all the old sages' adopted it (Anatolius, **28 A 44**). But neither of these accounts is trustworthy; and in all probability Anaximander's argument was not taken up again until Plato laid hands on it.[12]

Nevertheless, I do not think that Anaximander's successors were primitive revivalists: he saw what Thales had missed, that the earth may rest in mid-air, *meteôros*, without solid support; and his successors did not relinquish that insight. It is true that in Xenophanes' singular case the earth is *meteôros* only in a Pickwickian sense; but it still differs from Thales' earth in needing no support: an infinitely extended column of earth need and can have nothing holding it up.[13] Of the Anaximeneans, one is expressly said to have held that the earth is *meteôros* (Hippolytus, **59 A 42**); and it is a reasonable conjecture that the others did too. Like Anaximander, they rejected a support for the earth, and sought to reconcile stability and suspension in mid-air; seeing the faults of Anaximander's reconciliation, they offered an account which turned on the observed physical characteristics of the stuff filling celestial space, and not on the conjectural mathematical features of space itself. The earth is physically suspended in air; it is not mathematically suspended by abstract reason.

Of the many pieces of evidence the Anaximeneans adduced for their theory (*Cael* 294b22), only one has survived, and that is not particularly impressive (*Cael* 294b13–21 = **13 A 20**). Nor does the Anaximenean theory provide much philosophical pabulum: compared to Anaximander's argument, it is boring. For all that, Anaximander's successors were not his inferiors; charmed by the elegance of his suggestion, they were sadly conscious of its failure to save the phenomena, and the views they advanced in its stead were intellectually dull but scientifically progressive.

A modern reader will feel a certain impatience with all this misplaced ingenuity. Why, he will ask, did the Presocratics not abandon the hypothesis of a stable earth and so dissolve their whole problem? The answer is that they were too scientific to do so: Anaximander followed Thales in accepting a stable earth; and he was in turn followed by most of the later Presocratics.[14] A few Pythagoreans dared to displace the earth from the centre of the cosmos and let it run around a central fire; but their view was deemed bizarre, and remained unfashionable (see below, vol. 2, p. 81). For once, common sense held the day: when we stand on the earth we have none of the sensations associated with motion; we do not feel the blast of the wind or see the clouds rushing past in regular procession; and the pit of our stomach assures us that all is at rest. As the great Ptolemy observed, 'it is perfectly plain from the phenomena themselves' that the earth is still (*Syntaxis* I.7).

Daily observation confirms the stability of the earth, just as nocturnal observation proves the mobility of the stars. In any case, a moving earth would not solve the Presocratic problem, but merely displace it. The question Thales raised in connexion with the earth would arise again in connexion with the new cosmic centre: *why*, whatever it is, does it remain still in mid-space?

Progress will be made here not by astronomy but by philosophy: the Presocratics needed a closer understanding of the concept of motion before they could improve their scientific hypotheses. Zeno's work laid the foundations for such an understanding (below, pp. 290–4); but even after Zeno there is little evidence of any reflexion on what we mean when we ascribe motion or rest to heavenly bodies. The only text I know of refers to an obscure and probably fourth-century Pythagorean:

> Hicetas of Syracuse, as Theophrastus says, believes that the sky, sun, moon, stars, and in a word all the celestial bodies, are at rest, and that except for the earth nothing at all in the universe moves; and when the earth twists and turns about the axis at great speed, all the effects are just the same as they would be if the earth were at rest and the heavens moved (**12**: Cicero, **50 A 1**).

Hicetas' theory is almost certainly geocentric; his earth revolves on its axis and not about the sun or central fire; and his astronomy is crude and readily refuted. Nonetheless, Hicetas shows some flickering sophistication in his handling of celestial motion; and the Zenonian moral is beginning to be learned.

(d) Tò ἄπειρον

The first fragment of Greek philosophy is short, dark, and attractive. Besotted scholars see in it the first strivings toward abstract and metaphysical thought: the fragment, they maintain, breaks new ground in the science of theoretical cosmogony; it introduces the potent notion of infinity into Greek speculation; and it allows us to ascribe to Anaximander a sophisticated and superbly rational theory of the primordial principle of the universe.[15]

In this section I shall first set out the famous fragment, together with its doxographical context; then construct an optimistic account of Anaximander's reasonings; and finally criticize that account, reluctantly sprinkling a little cold water on Anaximander's warm reputation. There are very many problems raised by the fragment which I shall not take up.

We owe the fragment to Simplicius, whose text reads as follows (the interpolated numerals are, of course, my own addition):

> Of those who say that [the principle] is one and in motion and unlimited, Anaximander, son of Praxiades, a Milesian who became successor and pupil to Thales, said that [i] the unlimited (*apeiron*) is both principle (*archê*) and element (*stoicheion*) of the things that exist, [ii] being the first to introduce this name of the principle. He says that [iii] it is neither water nor any other of the so-called elements, but some other unlimited nature, from which all the heavens and the worlds in them come about; [iv] and the things from which is the coming into being for the things that exist are also those into which their destruction comes about, in accordance with what must be. [v] For they give justice (*dikê*) and reparation to one another for their offence (*adikia*) in accordance with the ordinance of time—[vi] speaking of them thus in rather poetical terms. And [vii] it is clear that, having observed the change of the four elements into one another, he did not think fit to make any one of these an underlying stuff, but something else apart from these (**13: A 9 + B 1**).

The first principle or element of things, the original and originating mass of the universe, was *apeiros*, unlimited. What limits did it lack? Common sense suggests the boundaries of space and time; and scholarship adds the determination by fixed qualities. Thus we might imagine Anaximander's universal starting-point to be spatially infinite, sempiternal, and qualitatively indeterminate: in the beginning, before the cosmogonic moment, there was a mass of qualityless stuff, unlimited in extent and infinitely old. Why conjecture such a strange start for the familiar world? The doxography suggests a mesh of four arguments.

Argument (A) is extracted from sentence [vii] of text **13**. The argument turns on the phenomenon of 'elemental change', and runs as follows:
(1) Each so-called 'elemental' stuff can change into one or more of the other 'elemental' stuffs.
(2) If a stuff S_1 can change into another stuff, S_2, then neither S_1 nor S_2 underlies all change.
(3) If S is the stuff of all things, then S underlies all change.
Hence:
(4) The stuff of all things is not one of the 'elemental' stuffs.
The changes we observe daily are underlain by the 'elements': we

observe modifications of earth, air, fire and water. Hence only those elements are candidates for the post of all things; and their candidacy is defeated by argument (A). The *Urstoff*, we can only conclude, is indeterminate. What underlies even elemental change can have no qualities of its own; it must be Aristotelian 'prime matter', a 'something we know not what' (cf. *Met* 1069b19 = **59 A 61**).

Argument (B) is found anonymously in Aristotle: Aëtius (**A 14**) ascribes it to Anaximander.[16] Aristotle is listing reasons why philosophers have been persuaded of the existence of something actually unlimited:

> Again, because only in this way will generation and destruction not fail—if that from which what comes into being is abstracted is unlimited (**14**: *Phys* 203b18–20 = **A 15**).

Thus:
(5) New things are perpetually being generated.
(6) All generation is the alteration of some pre-existent stuff.
Hence:
(7) There has always existed an infinitely large stock of stuff.

Argument (C) forges a link between (A) and (B); it too comes from Aristotle:

> There are some who make the unlimited body [a stuff distinct from the four 'elements'], and not air or water, in order that the others should not be destroyed by their unlimitedness; for they stand in opposition to one another—e.g., air is cold, water moist, fire hot—and if one of them were unlimited the others would already have been destroyed; but in fact, they say, it [sc. the unlimited body] is something else, from which these [are generated] (**15**: *Phys* 204b22–9 = **A 16**).

Simplicius (**A 17**) refers the argument to Anaximander; it can be expanded as follows:
(8) The *Urstoff* of everything is spatially infinite.
(9) Each of the four elements is opposed to, i.e. tends to destroy, the other three.
(10) If a is spatially infinite, and a tends to destroy b, then for some n a will destroy b within n units of time.
(11) For any n, the *Urstoff* has existed for more than n units of time.
(12) No element has been destroyed.
Hence:
(13) The *Urstoff* is distinct from each of the four elements.

Argument (C) thus uses the conclusion of (B) to confirm the

conclusion of (A): it infers qualitative indeterminacy from spatio-temporal infinity.

Finally, *argument* (D) shows that any unlimited body must be a principle. Again, the text is the *Physics*:

> It is reasonable that they all make [the unlimited body] a principle. For [viii] it can neither exist to no purpose, nor can it have any other power except as a principle; for everything either is a principle or is from a principle, and the unlimited has no principle—for then it would have a limit. [ix] Again, it is both ungenerable and indestructible, being a sort of principle. For what has come into being necessarily has an end, and there is an end of every destruction. [x] For this reason, as we say, there is no principle of this but this seems to be a principle of the other things and to encompass everything and to govern everything (as those say who do not propose any other causes apart from the unlimited, such as mind or love); and this is the divine; for it is immortal and deathless, as Anaximander and most of the *phusiologoi* say (**16**: 203b4–15 = **A 15**).

Part [x], it is argued, is certainly Anaximandrian; but [viii]–[x] forms an organic whole: hence [viii]–[x] as a whole is Anaximandrian, and we have before us 'a second virtual citation from Anaximander's book, comparable in importance to the famous sentence preserved by Simplicius'.[17] In particular, we can assign to Anaximander the following argument:

(14) Everything is either a principle or derived from a principle.
(15) If a is unlimited, a has no limit.
(16) If a has no limit, a is not derived from a principle.
Hence:
(17) If a is unlimited, a is a principle.

Aristotle here uses 'unlimited' to refer to spatial infinity; we should get a slightly better argument if we took 'unlimited' to refer to sempiternity: any derivative body is temporally posterior to its source; hence no temporally infinite body can be derivative.

A small nest of intertwined reasonings supports Anaximander's unlimited principle, and at the same time elucidates its nature. There is an unargued hypothesis that the processes of generation will never give out: generation requires an infinite source; infinity and the generative function alike require an indeterminate source; and any infinite mass can only be a principle of things. The nest is not tidy but it seems cohesive and strong. Was it built by Anaximander? Or are the materials used in its construction late and synthetic? I take the arguments in turn.

An examination of argument (A) demands a nearer look at the passage of Simplicius. Simplicius is quoting Theophrastus, who is quoting Anaximander.

Argument (A) comes from sentence [vii]; and though [vi] shows that Simplicius is certainly reporting some of Anaximander's own words, [vii] is beyond the boundary of his quotation. (Indeed, it has been cogently argued that [vii] is Simplicius' own comment on the paragraph [i]–[vi] which he has excerpted from Theophrastus.)[18] Thus argument (A) is Anaximandrian only if Simplicius' comment on [i]–[vi] is correct. I am not sure how Simplicius reached his opinion: perhaps he supposed that 'the things that exist' in [iv] must include the elements; and inferred that [iv]–[v] recognize elemental change. He then ascribed to Anaximander the Peripatetic deduction of a non-elemental stuff. To assess his ascription we must analyse [i]–[vi].

Sentence [v] is fairly clearly the 'somewhat poetic' utterance referred to in [vi], and it (or at least most of it) is therefore securely Anaximandrian.[19] What of the earlier sentences? Sentence [ii] has roused passionate debate: did Theophrastus mean to assign the term 'principle' or the term 'unlimited' to Anaximander? It has, I think, been shown that Theophrastus assigned both terms to Anaximander, 'the unlimited' in [ii], and 'principle' in another passage (see Simplicius, *in Phys* 150. 18).[20] In that case, sentence [i] may well be a close paraphrase of something in Anaximander's text. Sentence [iii] is more puzzling: its final clause, containing the curious phrase 'the worlds in [the heavens]', seems archaic to some scholars; but the reference to the 'so-called elements' cannot be Anaximander's. We infer from [iii] that Anaximander said something to the effect that 'the principle is not water, nor earth, nor anything of that familiar sort'. But Diogenes Laertius has a subtly different account:

> Anaximander said that the unlimited is principle and element, not distinguishing it as air or water or anything else (**17**: II.1 = **A 1**: cf. Aëtius, **A 14**).

Did Anaximander positively deny that 'the unlimited' was water or the like? Or did he rather refrain from asserting that it was water or the like? The question is not merely trifling; for the view that Anaximander's principle was qualitatively indeterminate loses in plausibility if he did not positively distinguish it from the elements. Yet I do not see that we can answer the question; indeed, we cannot tell whether Simplicius or Diogenes better represents Theophrastus' judgment.

The doxography conflates sentences [iii] and [iv] (see Cicero, **A 13**;

Aëtius, **A 14**); and some modern scholars concur. But [iii] and [iv] seem to state theses which are perfectly distinct: [iii] deals with the generation of the heavens from 'the unlimited', in a word, with cosmogony; [iv] deals with the generation and destruction of 'the things that exist', with the production of the furniture of the world from its component stuffs or 'opposites' (cf. pseudo-Plutarch, **A 10**).[21] Sentence [iii] deals with the creation of the cosmos; sentence [iv] with the changes that take place within the cosmos.[22]

Sentence [v] connects to [iv] by the particle 'for' (*gar*): what connexion is thereby signalled? The sentiment expressed abstractly in [iv] is ancient and popular:

> Dust to dust and ashes to ashes,
> Into the tomb the Great Queen dashes.

Thus we might suppose that [iv] is, if not a quotation, at least a close paraphrase of Anaximander. And we might ascribe the *gar* to him, thus: 'Natural objects eventually are resolved into the elements from which they sprang (plants rot and form earth and moisture); for no one element perpetually gains at the expense of another—local gains are followed, in time, by compensating losses.' If we connect [iv] and [v] in this way, our interpretation does, I think, support Simplicius' inference in [vii]; at least, it ascribes elemental change to Anaximander. For on this interpretation the generation of natural objects must, characteristically at least, involve an elemental change: only if, say, the production of rain from cloud is construed as an elemental change of air into water will it constitute an 'offence' or encroachment. When clouds yield rain, water gains upon air: to preserve the cosmic balance of stuffs, the rain must at some time turn back into cloud.

The reconstruction is intelligible; but it is not obligatory. Some scholars ascribe [iv] to Theophrastus, and give the connecting particle *gar* to him rather than to Anaximander. The sense of [i]–[vi] is then this: 'Anaximander made "the unlimited" a material principle, i.e. something from which everything comes and into which it is destroyed again (= [i], [ii]). For (a) he *says* that everything comes *from* "the unlimited" (= [iii]); and (b) he accepts the *general* principle that things are destroyed into what they came from (= [iv]), as his own words (= [v]) show'.[23]

This second account of [i]–[vi] is, I think, the more plausible; for it explains the Theophrastan passage as a whole, whereas the ascription of [iv] to Anaximander leaves the connexion between [i]–[iii] and [iv]–[v] inexplicable. As an interpretation of Anaximander it is highly speculative; for [v] does not evidently suggest [iv] as an interpretative gloss. Moreover, it will hardly support Simplicius' inference in [vii]. For all that, it is likely to represent the original sense of Theophrastus' argument.

I return to sentence [vii] and argument (*A*). On any account of [i]–[vi], [vii] is at best an ingenious conjecture, applying a Peripatetic thesis about elemental change to a deeply hidden implication of Anaximander's argument. This is the most favourable construction to be put on [vii]: the most probable construction is that [vii] is a baseless invention. And there is an independent reason for doubting the authenticity of (*A*): premiss (2) is hardly likely to have been embraced by Anaximander. At all events, it was implicitly rejected by his follower Anaximenes, who took air to be the basic stuff of the world and yet was quite happy to let air change into other stuffs.

Perhaps, then, it is argument (*C*) that gives Anaximander's reason for picking 'the unlimited' as his first principle. Premiss (11) is certainly authentic: 'the unlimited' was 'eternal and ageless' or 'immortal and deathless' (Hippolytus, **A 11**; Aristotle, *Phys* 203b14 = **A 15**; cf. **B2**).[24] Premisses (9) and (12) refer anachronistically to 'the elements'; but the anachronism is trifling, and (9) and (12) together make a plausible reading of sentence [v] of the fragment. Premiss (10) has a Peripatetic ring to it; yet it might, I think, have been advanced, perhaps in a somewhat crude or metaphorical formulation, by Anaximander.

If we are prepared to ascribe (*C*) to Anaximander does that make 'the unlimited' a qualitatively indeterminate 'prime matter'? It is perfectly plain that a mass of 'prime matter' could not constitute a cosmogonical principle. The *Urstoff* was self-subsistent; and any self-subsistent stuff has definite qualities: a piece of stuff, however airy and abstract, cannot be neither Φ nor non-Φ for every value of Φ. Aristotle, it need hardly be said, was well aware of this (cf., e.g., *GC* 329a10).

But if the 'unlimited' was not entirely characterless, what was its character? In several passages Aristotle talks of *phusiologoi* who took as their principle a stuff 'between' (*metaxu*) the other elements; and he probably had Anaximander in mind. According to some scholars, Theophrastus thought that Anaximander's principle was a 'mixture' (*migma*) of all stuffs. These passages are all controversial,[25] but one thing is fairly clear: if the Peripatetics did actually ascribe a *metaxu* or a *migma* theory to Anaximander, they were whistling in the dark. Anaximander's text gave them no light; and I guess that they did not know what Anaximander thought, for the excellent reason that Anaximander himself did not know what to think.

Argument (*C*) assumes, in (8), the spatial infinity of the universe.

That proposition is the conclusion of argument (*B*). The argument is invalid, as Aristotle points out: 'In order that coming to be should not fail, it is not necessary that there should be a sensible body which is actually unlimited. The passing away of one thing may be the coming to be of another, the whole being limited' (*Phys* 208a7–10). This objection is overcome by adding a further premiss to (*B*), viz:
(18) The material supplied by the destruction of existing things cannot be used in the generation of new things.
But it is implausible to ascribe (18) to Anaximander. Sentence [iv] of the fragment, whether or not it is Anaximandrian, is not, strictly speaking, incompatible with (18): [iv] does not imply that the dust produced by destroying a thing is equal in mass to the dust consumed in its generation; and it is not grossly implausible to imagine that the processes of generation and destruction involve a certain wastage of stuff. Sentence [v], however, suggests fairly strongly that Anaximander had some sort of equal balancing in mind; and the probability is that he would have rejected (18).

Argument (*B*) can be repaired without the help of (18); instead of (18) we may add:
(19) The mass of existing things is perpetually increasing.
An adherent of (19) believes that the cosmos is expanding; and there is no direct evidence that any Presocratic held such a belief. But there is a sentence from Anaxagoras which apparently commits him to an expanding universe; and in some respects at least Anaxagoras was a scientific traditionalist.[26] If Anaxagoras embraced (19), perhaps he took it from Anaximander.

It is pertinent to quote here a fragment of Anaximander's pupil, Anaximenes:

> Air is close to the incorporeal; and since we come into being by an effluxion of this, it is necessary for it to be both unlimited and rich, because it never gives out (**18: 13 B 3**).[27]

Anaximenes thus advanced argument (*B*); and he was thereby committed to either (18) or (19). I incline to favour (19), and to take that as some slight evidence for Anaximander's acceptance of (19). Certainly, Anaximenes' adoption of (*B*) makes its ascription to Anaximander more plausible.[28]

What, finally, of argument (*D*)? The end of [x] is Anaximandrian; and many scholars tie the whole of [x] to him. I shall return to this passage later on; here it is enough to say that Aristotle's text in no way implies this wholesale ascription. Moreover, [ix] is, I think, a version of an argument advanced by Melissus (see below, pp. 194–7); and in that case there is no historical unity underlying the logical unity of [viii]–[ix]. Aristotle himself makes this plain enough; for he refers to 'all' the *physiologoi* at the beginning of the passage, and to 'most' of them at the end. We have no reason to ascribe [viii] to Anaximander; [viii]–[ix] is an Aristotelian concoction, prepared from several different Presocratic recipes.

With arguments (*A*) and (*D*) removed, Anaximander's thought about the material principle of things becomes less complicated; yet it remains rational: the principle must be *apeiros*, or spatially infinite, in order to support perpetual generation; and, being *apeiros*, it must be distinct from any of the ordinary cosmic stuffs. Arguments (*B*) and (*C*) together yield a reasoned structure of thought.

It must be admitted, however, that the grounds for ascribing even (*B*) and (*C*) to Anaximander are uncertain; and that uncertainty can easily be aggravated. A powerful chorus of scholars proposes a new etymology for *apeiros*: it is formed not from alpha privative and the root of *peras* ('limit'), but from alpha privative and the stem of *peraô* ('traverse'); and the etymological meaning of the word is thus 'intraversable'.[29] Whether or not this is correct, it is in any case clear that Anaximander could have used *apeiros* of the unimaginably huge: in Homer the sea is *apeirôn*, immense, not infinite. I am inclined to believe that *apeiros* does indeed mean 'unlimited', but that spatio-temporal infinity is not the only criterion of unlimitedness: a mass of stuff may reasonably be called 'unlimited' because of its untraversable vastness, or because its boundaries are indeterminate ('like a fog-bank or the warmth of a fire'), or even because of its qualitative indeterminacy.[30]

Thus the word *apeiros* does not, in itself, show that Anaximander's *Urstoff* was literally infinite. And if it was not, then argument (*B*) loses its point. Some scholars find the source of Anaximander's conception of his *Urstoff* in Hesiod's description of the horrid chasm between earth and Tartarus (*Theogony* 736–43); that chasm is vast, not infinite. Hence *to apeiron* is not 'the Infinite' but 'the Vast'; and its origin is to be found not in cosmogonical ratiocination but in poetical inspiration. In that case, argument (*B*) is probably a rationalization fitted to Anaximander's semi-poetical utterances by a later and more prosaic age.

We might, I suppose, allow that *to apeiron* is only 'the Vast', and that Hesiod inspired Anaximander. For all that, may not arguments (*B*) and (*C*) have been in Anaximander's mind? 'Why must the original mass have been so huge?'—'To support its innumerable offspring.' 'What can its character have been?'—'Vague and obscure, but certainly distinct from the stuffs familiar to us.'

We find ourselves in a desert of ignorance and uncertainty; so, I suspect, did the Peripatetic historians. It is possible that Anaximander set his views down with luminous clarity, and that the monster time devoured his book before the Peripatetics could read its pages; but I doubt it, and I suspect that our uncertainty about Anaximander's meaning reflects an uncertainty and lack of clarity in Anaximander's own mind.

Indeed, I guess that Anaximander's interest in cosmogony has been vastly overestimated, and his achievement consistently mispraised. The partial and fortuitous survival of an obscure utterance has given him an undeserved reputation for metaphysics. That sentence, hinting darkly at a huge primordial *tohu-bohu*, was perhaps supported by a sketchy paragraph of argument; and it was undeniably an impressive exordium to Anaximander's book *Concerning Nature*. But in the context of Anaximander's thought as a whole it had little importance: what mattered was the detailed science that followed: the astronomy, the biology, the geography. Anaximander set natural philosophy on the course it was to follow for many centuries: it is no diminution of his genius to say that his contribution to metaphysical philosophy was of less moment.

III

Science and Speculation

(a) *Material monism*

Anaximenes, the third of the Milesians, is by general consent a poor man's Anaximander: his theories were those of his master. An innovator in detail, he was an imitator in all essentials. And the two main innovations he can be credited with prove him to have lacked the vigour and temerity of Anaximander: he allowed the earth to rest in archaic luxury on a cushion of air; and he smirched the metaphysical purity of Anaximander's unlimited principle by turning it into a mass of gross, material air.

I dissent from that orthodox assessment. First, Anaximenes' two acknowledged innovations are both, I think, improvements on Anaximander's theories. Anaximenes, who evidently studied astronomy with some assiduity,[1] perceived the scientific untenability of Anaximander's argument for the earth's stability, even if he did not question the philosophical adequacy of his version of the Principle of Sufficient Reason. And his own airborne earth is, as I have already argued (above, p. 27), no mere regression to the childish position of Thales. Again, Anaximenes, who wrote in 'simple and economical' language (Diogenes Laertius, II.3 = **13 A 1**), will have seen that Anaximander's 'rather poetical' style disguised a somewhat vague and perfunctory thought as far as the first principles of cosmogony go; and his own theory has the modest merit of replacing Anaximander's indeterminate principle and uncertain cosmogonical operations with a plain, intelligible stuff and a pair of familiar and comprehensible processes.

Second, our evidence, such as it is, suggests that Anaximenes was the more thorough, the more systematic, the more rigorous, and the more scientifically inclined of the two men. Ancient opinion favours this assessment: Theophrastus devoted a monograph to Anaximenes' theories (Diogenes Laertius, V.42); and in the fifth century Anaximenes was taken as the paradigm Milesian.[2]

> Anaximenes said that the principle is unlimited air (**19**: Hippolytus, **A** 7).

Anaximenes, like Thales and Anaximander, was presented in the Peripatetic tradition as a 'material monist', as a thinker who accepted as the fundamental axiom of cosmology:
(1) There is some single stuff which is the material principle of everything.
It is time to keep a promise made on an earlier page and to look more closely at the claims and credentials of 'material monism': was it, as Aristotle thought, the prime Milesian doctrine?

As it stands, (1) is Aristotelian in its mode of expression: 'principle' or *archê* (in non-philosophical Greek, 'beginning' and sometimes 'rule') was indeed used in a philosophical context by Anaximander (see above, p. 32); but it probably did not assume its Aristotelian sense of 'explanatory principle' until much later. 'Matter' or *hulê* (non-philosophically, 'wood') was in all probability an Aristotelian invention. But, as I have already remarked, these linguistic points are of no great significance: Aristotle sometimes uses as a synonym for *hulê* the phrase 'to *ex hou*' ('the thing from which': e.g., *Phys* 195a19); and he often expresses the proposition that X is *hulê* of Y by a sentence of the form 'Y is from X'. Such non-technical expressions were of course available to the Milesians; and it may be conjectured with confidence that the men whom Aristotle takes for monists uttered sentences of the form:
(2) Everything is from X.

Finding sentences of the form (2) ascribed to the Milesians, Aristotle interpreted them by way of (1). His interpretation cannot be accepted without ado: (2) may, but need not, express material monism; for 'Y is from X' may express more than one relation between X and Y. Aristotle was fully aware of the fact: in *Metaphysics* Δ 24 he catalogues several of the ways in which 'being from something (*to ek tinos*) is said' (1023a26; cf. 1092a22–35). Five of these ways can be stated and illustrated as follows: if Y is from X, then either
(i) X is the stuff of which Y is made (as a statue is made *from* bronze); or
(ii) X is the source from which Y comes (as plants grow up *from* the soil); or

(iii) *X* is the agent which generated *Y* (as a child comes *from* his parents); or

(iv) *X* is the event which causes *Y* (as a battle may arise *from* an insult); or

(v) *X* is replaced by *Y* (as day comes '*from*' night, or a tan '*from*' pallor).

Modern commentators add a sixth way: *Y* is from *X* if

(vi) *X* is the stuff from which *Y* was made (as paper is made *from* rags).

(vi) is distinguished from (i) as originative from constitutive stuff.

In ordinary English the distinction is sometimes expressed by a contrast between 'from' and 'of'. Thus the paper I write on was made from rags; but I will not say that it is made of rags (for I am not writing on rags). The wine I drink was made from grapes; but I will not say that it is made of grapes (for I am not drinking grapes). Again, the pane I gaze through is made of glass; but I will not say that it was made from glass (for no glazier processed glass so as to turn it into windowstuff). The diamond I cut the pane with is made of carbon; but it was not made from carbon (for no alchemist transmuted carbon into diamond for me).

The question, then, is this: Are we to interpret Milesian utterances of (2) by way of (i), as Aristotle would have it? or rather by way of (ii) or (iii) or (iv) or (v) or (vi)? A scholar who rejects Aristotle's interpretation will suppose that Thales and his successors were engaged in cosmogonical speculation and not in constituent analysis, that they were concerned to discover the original stuff from which the world was put together, and not to divine the underlying materials of its present furnishings. Aristotle believed in an eternal cosmos, rejected cosmogony, and was an exponent of constituent analysis; naturally he read his own interests, and interpretation (i), into the Milesians; and the doxography naturally followed Aristotle. But what is natural may also be wrong; and the Peripatetic version of Milesian monism may be an anachronistic invention, not an historical truth.[3]

That view is supported by two general considerations: first, (1) is wildly implausible in itself, and would hardly have presented itself spontaneously to the Milesian mind; second, (i) was, so to speak, philosophically unnecessary in the days of innocence before Parmenides, and would not have been embraced by the Milesians as an unhappy but inevitable presupposition of cosmology.

The first consideration I find unconvincing: does interpretation (vi) really give a more 'plausible' thesis than (1)? Is it much more plausible to suppose that everything started from some one stuff than to suppose that everything is ultimately composed of some one stuff?

Both views have the same point of appeal: simplicity. And both face the same difficulty: the amazing diversity of things in the world around us.

The second consideration requires further exposition. Aristotle says that the monists, because they posit a single material principle, 'think that nothing either comes into being or perishes' (*Met* 893b12 = **A 12**); 'they say that so-called simple coming into being is alteration' (*GC* 314a8): change is nothing but an alteration in the properties of some piece of the basic stuff. Now that view of change would only have been resorted to, it is asserted, after Parmenides and his Eleatic followers had argued for the impossibility of generation and destruction. Hence material monism presupposes the cogitations of Elea and cannot have been advanced in Miletus.

The philosophical content of this argument will exercise us later. Here it may be said, first, that the Aristotelian inference is by no means obvious. It assumes a strict, Aristotelian analysis of generation; and even with that analysis it is only valid on the further assumption that bits of the basic stuff cannot themselves be generated. Aristotle is eliciting a thesis to which, in his view, the Milesians were committed: although he asserts that they 'say' that generation is alteration, he means only that 'it is necessary for them to say' it (*GC* 314a10), that they are committed to it. He does not mean that they expressly asserted it; still less that they stated it from an uncannily prescient desire to pre-empt Parmenidean objections.

Nor, secondly, is there any reason to believe that only Parmenidean worries could provide a motive for monism: a straightforward yearning for simplicity will lead in the same direction and provide explanation enough of any *nisus* towards monism.

Are there, on the other hand, any general considerations that support the Aristotelian interpretation? One line of argument suggests that if the Milesians intended (vi) then they also intended (i); for the distinction between (vi) and (i) seems, in some cases at least, to be illusory. If my table was made *from* wood, then it is made *of* wood. If a cake was made *from* flour, milk and eggs, then it is made *of* flour, milk and eggs. And in general, if Y was made from X, then it is made of X. Aristotle's mode of argument at *Metaphysics* 983b6–27, where he introduces material monism, seems to show both that he accepted the inference himself, and that he ascribed it to the Milesians. Two fragments of Xenophanes, separately transmitted, read as follows:

Everything which comes into being and grows is earth and water (**20: 21 B 29**).

For we all come to be from earth and water (**21**: **B 33**).

It is plausible to conjoin these lines: **B 33** supports **B 29**, and Xenophanes makes an explicit inference from originative to constitutive stuff—from (vi) to (i).

Now if Y was made from X by a ϕ process, then it is easy to infer that Y consists of X ϕly processed, and hence that Y consists of X. But the validity of the inference depends on the nature of the ϕ process: if ϕing involves abstracting, say, the inference is evidently invalid: Bovril is extract of beef, not beef; salt is produced from brine, but is not brine. Aristotle made the point; and he also observed, implicitly, that it is easy to confound valid and invalid versions of the inference (*Top* 127a17). Can we, then, suppose that the Milesians tacitly inferred from 'The cosmos was made from X' to 'The cosmos is made of X'? The plausibility of the supposition depends, in part at least, on the nature of the cosmogonical process: if the cosmos was constructed like a cake from its ingredients, the supposition has something to be said for it; if the cosmos was extracted like gold from ore, the supposition is implausible. Clearly, the Milesians must be approached individually; and we must ask of each cosmogony whether it suggests an Aristotelian reading.

Thales said:
(3) Everything is made from water.
According to Hippolytus, Thales held that:

> Everything is composed from it [sc. water] as it thickens and again thins out (**22**: *Ref Haer* I.2; cf. Galen, **11 B 3**)

Now if Y comes from X by 'thickening' or 'thinning', by condensation or rarefaction, then surely Y is made of X. If ice is condensed water, if it is made from water by a process of condensation, then it is made of water; and in general, if everything is made from water by condensation or rarefaction, then everything is made of water. Thus Hippolytus' report speaks for an Aristotelian interpretation of (3). It has been urged that the Aristotelian interpretation does not fit Thales' account of the earth's stability (**A 12** : above, p. 9); but I see no force in that. Hippolytus' report is, however, weak evidence: it may only be a doxographical conjecture. Prudence leads to a confession of ignorance; we know too little about Thales to judge the sense in which he intended (3).

The case of Anaximander is more complex. His principal claim is:
(4) Everything is from the unlimited.
The cosmogonical process is referred to as a 'separating out' (*ekkrinesthai* : Aristotle, *Phys* 187a20 = **12 A 16**) or a 'separating

off' (*apokrinesthai* : Simplicius, **A 9**; pseudo-Plutarch, **A 10**). Pseudo-Plutarch contains the fullest account of Anaximander's cosmogony:

> And he says that something generative of hot and cold was separated off from the eternal thing at the generation of this universe; and a sort of sphere of flame from this formed around the air about the earth, like a bark round a tree; and when this was broken off and shut off in certain circles, the sun and the moon and the stars were formed (**23: A 10**)

Thus first the 'unlimited' principle ('the eternal thing') gives rise to 'something generative'; then this generative stuff or process produces 'the hot' and 'the cold', i.e. the basic materials of the cosmos which are characterizable by means of those 'opposites'; and finally the furniture of the heavens is formed from the basic materials.

The cosmos was thus made from—and probably is made of—the basic materials. But what is the relation between the 'unlimited' principle and the materials? Was 'the unlimited' simply a generating agent, and should (4) be understood in terms of (iii)? But then from what were the basic materials made? Was 'the unlimited' rather the 'reservoir or stock from which all Becoming draws its nourishment',[4] and is (4) to be understood in terms of (ii)? But that suggestion is incoherent unless we assume that (4) is also to be read in terms of (vi), so that the 'unlimited' principle is a mass of *Urstoff* from which (by some entirely unknown operation) the basic materials are produced. The doxography was evidently perplexed: Simplicius, having said that the 'unlimited' is an Aristotelian substrate, adds that Anaximander 'does not produce generation by an alteration in the element, but by a separating off of the opposites' (**A 9**), so that the 'unlimited' is not a substrate after all. The Peripatetics did not know what to make of Anaximander's cosmogony. It is possible that they failed to understand his text, or that they did not possess it in its entirety; but, again, I am more inclined to suppose that their perplexity reflects a vague or incoherent account by Anaximander himself.

With Anaximenes a little light shines through. His principle reads:
(5) Everything is from air,
and the doxography has preserved an account of his cosmogony:

> Anaximenes, son of Eurystratus, a Milesian who became a companion of Anaximander, himself says that the single underlying nature is indeed unlimited, like Anaximander; but he does not make it indeterminate, like him, but determined, calling

it air. And he says that it differs from one thing to another in rareness and density—rarefied, it becomes fire, condensed, wind, then cloud, still more condensed, water, then earth, then stones—and everything else comes from these things (**24**: Simplicius, 13 A 5).

The parallel accounts in pseudo-Plutarch (**A 6**) and Hippolytus (**A 7**) show that Simplicius is faithful to Theophrastus here.

Anaximenes' principle is air, present in unlimited quantity; and his cosmogony is achieved by the twin operations of rarefaction and condensation, which in effect amount to the single operation of change in density. Rarefied, air becomes fire; condensed, cloud, water, earth, and so on; and thus are engendered all the stuffs of the familiar world. Anaximenes introduced rarefaction (*manôsis*) and condensation (*puknôsis*) into cosmogony, though those particular terms may not have been his own (cf. **B 1**); and the operations became an orthodox feature of Presocratic science.[5] Certainly, the processes have a cosmogonical significance: the earth we stand upon and the clouds we gaze at were originally formed by the condensation of a vast mass of air. But they also serve to provide a quasi-chemical analysis of the constituents of the present world order. For, as I have argued, the inference from 'Y was produced from X by a Φ process' to 'Y is made of X' is eminently plausible and natural when the Φ process is one of condensation or rarefaction; and there is, I think, no cause to doubt that Anaximenes was a material monist in the standard Aristotelian sense.

The Milesians were cosmogonists, concerned to name the originative stuff and state of the world. Yet Anaximenes at least also gave an analysis, in Aristotelian vein, of the present stuff of the world; and he was thus a material monist. With Thales and Anaximander we must rule *non liquet*; and we may hazard it that nothing was clear either in the writings or in the minds of those men. Aristotle boldly offers them a coherent view; but though the Aristotelian interpretation gives them something which they might have said had they said anything clearly, we may prefer to leave their accounts in the dimness which they themselves designed.

(b) *Anaximenes and air*

The doxography reports the first principle and the initial processes of Anaximenes' cosmogony: some sort of motion produces variations in the density of the *Ur*-mass of air, and the basic stuffs of the universe are generated. We also have a quantity of information about Anaximenes' astronomy and meteorology, from which it is clear that the cosmogonical operations also account for many of the phenomena of the present world.

Between these two sets of reports there is a gap. Simplicius' summary notice that 'everything else comes from these things' (**24**) is unrevealing. Is he reporting an '*etc.*' in Anaximenes' text, or is he rather abbreviating a wealth of Anaximenean detail? If the latter, did Anaximenes suppose that change in density sufficed to produce all the stuffs that there are, or were supplementary operations called upon? No generative operations other than rarefaction and condensation are ascribed to Anaximenes in our sources; and it is most reasonable to believe that all stuffs were somehow to be generated by the agency of those operations alone.

So far, I have spoken only of the generation of stuffs; and it is a notable feature of Ionian speculation as a whole that its primary concern is with the different materials found in the world. The twin operations of condensation and rarefaction may have seemed sufficient to explain the generation, and the composition, of stuffs such as vapour and rock, wood and flesh; but they are plainly impotent to generate substances, or informed parcels of stuff, such as clouds and pebbles, trees and men. The stuff wood may be compressed air; but trees, even on the crudest analysis, are wood shaped in such and such a way. Flesh and bone may be generable by condensation; but if we want to account for the presence of organic bodies on the earth we need more than lumps of suitable stuffs. In Aristotelian jargon, the Ionian theories touch on the material constitution of things but say nothing about their form. Anaximenes may have thought that he could explain the formal aspect of at least some substances (cf. pseudo-Plutarch, **A 6**: sun, moon, stars); but he appears to have given the question little thought. It was not until the middle of the fifth century that form became a philosophical issue, and then it was tangled in the thickets of Pythagoreanism.

The Pythagoreans associate form with number; and here it might seem that Anaximenes in a sense anticipated them. His cosmogony takes relative density as the one essential feature of stuffs, in terms of which their remaining properties are to be explicated: any stuff is simply air at such and such a density. Now to us density is a quantitative notion, amenable to measurement: thus Anaximenes' physics is fundamentally quantitative, and it adumbrates that principle which comprises 'the very essence of science': 'that quality can be reduced to quantity'.[6] Quantitative sciences allow a mathematical development: seventeenth-century physics advanced precisely because it sloughed off qualities and paraded in its quantitative underskin; and the frailty of modern psychology or economics is due to the false or fantastical quantifications they rely upon.

Was Anaximenes really a precocious quantifier, a Presocratic Boyle? Alas, I suspect he was not. Greek scientists were in general averse to, or incapable of, the application of mathematics to physical processes and phenomena; and there is no evidence that Anaximenes' theory encouraged them to attempt any such application. Nor is there any evidence that Anaximenes himself had any such application in mind: he had no scale and no instrument for measuring density, and for him density was a quantitative notion only in the weakest sense. The scientific appearance of his cosmogonical operations is due to chance, not to insight.

How did Anaximenes attempt to justify or commend his grand theory? We might ask him four questions: (a) why suppose that some single stuff originated and underlies the variety of appearances? (b) why suppose that *Urstoff* to be air? (c) why require an unlimited quantity of air? (d) why generate from air by means of condensation and rarefaction?

To question (a) the only plausible answer is, once more, the compelling attraction of simplicity: the fewer the primitives, the better the system. A single stuff and a single operation (or pair of complementary operations) constitute, from a systematic point of view, the best possible hypothesis. Question (c) is answered in **B 3**, which I have already commented upon (above, p. 35). Fragment **B 2**, which I discuss in a later context (below, p. 55), is sometimes seen as an answer to (b). That leaves (d).

Hippolytus reports that 'the most important factors in generation are opposites—hot and cold' (**A 7**). The two factors recur in a passage of Plutarch:

> As old Anaximenes thought, we should not leave the hot and the cold in the class of substances, but treat them as common properties of matter which supervene on changes. For he says that the compressed and condensed part of matter is cold, and that the thin and loose (that is the very word he uses) is hot; and that hence it is not unreasonably said that a man releases both hot and cold things from his mouth—for his breath is cooled when pressed and condensed by his lips, while if the mouth is relaxed the exhaled breath becomes hot by rareness (**25: B 1**).

Only the single word 'loose (*chalaron*)' is a direct quotation from Anaximenes;[7] but Plutarch plainly regards the whole argument in which that word is embedded as Anaximenean, and I am prepared to follow him.[8]

It seems, then, that Anaximenes' cosmogonical speculation began from the familiar paradox that we blow on our hands to warm them and on our porridge to cool it. Observation showed that the hand-warmer huffs with open mouth, while the porridge-cooler whistles through pursed lips; and a further simple observation indicates that the hot air is thinner than the cold: it is palpably less firm against the hand. At this point theory takes over from observation: first, Anaximenes supposes that the thinness of the hot air and the thickness of the cold air are causally connected to their temperature; and he advances the general hypothesis that what temperature a mass of stuff has is determined by its density. Thus changes in temperature are explicable in terms of rarefaction and condensation. Second, Anaximenes generalized his hypothesis further, and suggested that all the properties of a mass of stuff are determined by its density: just as rarefaction can account for the heat of fire, so it can account for its colour and its characteristic motions; just as condensation can account for the coldness of a cloud, so it can account for its opacity and woolly structure. Finally, the theory was applied to a variety of disparate phenomena—astronomical and meteorological—and to that extent confirmed or corroborated.

We need not embrace Anaximenes' conclusions in order to admire his principles and his methodology: observations of a puzzle situation lead him to form explanatory theories of successively greater generality. And the final theory has many of the hallmarks of science: it is highly general; it is devastatingly simple; it explains the original puzzle; and it applies to, and can therefore be tested against, a mass of superficially unconnected phenomena.

(c) *Fairy tales or science?*

Then is Anaximenes a Greek Galileo? And were the early Milesian cosmologists the world's first natural scientists? The question has aroused passion and dispute. At one extreme, there are scholars who think that 'a new thing came into the world with the early Ionian teachers—the thing we call science—and . . . they first pointed the way which Europe has followed ever since'.[9] At the other extreme, it is maintained that the Milesians are properly regarded not as the precursors of science but as the successors of the ancient poet-seers, lay dogmatists concerned to propound a secular *Weltanschauung* and unconcerned to defend it by the tiresomely rational methods of the scientist.[10] Those who prefer a middle path imagine that the Milesians strove towards scientific status but did not quite attain it: 'the *phusiologoi*, despite their eagerness to use the senses for all they were worth, failed not only to use but even to understand the experimental method of modern science'.[11]

The controversy has been muddled by two facts: first, the identity of the disputed terrain is shifting and uncertain; second, the disputants unconsciously bring quite different philosophical presuppositions to their arguments. It is worth indicating at the start some of the things to which all parties assent.

First, none of the Milesian theories is true: the Milesians do not compose a Greek Royal Society; and their Transactions would not make any contribution to the sum of scientific knowledge. They and their successors made and recorded various true observations; but the assembly of those observations into true or well-confirmed theory was a long process which the Milesians scarcely began.

Second, none of the Milesians aspired to the sort of precision we require in a scientific theory: their views are incurably vague; and underlying this vagueness is a complete innocence of the delights of measurement and quantification.[12] Thus Anaximenes, as I have remarked, made no attempt to state what degree of compression turned air into cloud or water, or to formulate an equation correlating density and temperature. As a result, his theories are peculiarly resistant to testing: it is simply not clear in what way they are to be 'applied' to the phenomena, nor, hence, what observations will confirm and what refute them. It might be added that Anaximenes' descriptions of his original puzzle and of his observations are negligent and unrigorous: his theory cannot explain the puzzle, since the puzzle is misdescribed. (The outstanding exception to this generalization about Milesian theorizing is provided by Anaximander's astronomy: that was decked out with precise mathematical hypotheses about the arrangements of the heavenly wheels.)

Third, it will be agreed that the Milesians had certain intellectual aims which are, in a broad sense, characteristic of science: they wanted to describe the phenomenal world; they wanted to explain what the phenomena were and how they were produced; and they aimed at giving an explanation which did not appeal to chance or to stray divinities.

Fourth, the Milesians had some grasp—implicit in their approach if not explicit in their writings—of certain methods of explanation which are also, in a broad sense, characteristic of science: they advanced highly general hypotheses which could (they thought) be applied to and explain the phenomena; they gave reasons for their opinions, however bizarre those opinions might seem; they drew inferences and they suggested analogies or 'models'.

If these points are agreed upon, wherein lies the dispute over the scientific standing of the early Greek thinkers? It is sometimes thought to lie in the question of whether the Milesians adhered to 'the experimental method': crudely put, the Milesians did not indulge in experiments and hence were not scientists.

It is true that, as far as our knowledge extends, the Milesians did not experiment; indeed Greek science as a whole can produce only a handful of experiments, and those are all of a fairly unsophisticated sort.[13] The reasons for this are not hard to guess. Yet I am inclined to think that experimentation is not an essential tool of science, and indeed that in some sciences it is of little or no account. An experiment, after all, is merely the artificial generation of observable phenomena. Experimental observation has certain advantages over observation *au naturel*: the experimenter can isolate the phenomena which interest him, and he can exercise some control over their production. Nevertheless, it is the observable products, and not the manner of their production, which are scientifically significant. In many of the biological sciences (in anatomy, say, or taxonomic botany) experiment has little or no place; in the human sciences (sociology or economics) experiment is not often acceptable; in certain of the physical sciences (astronomy is the prime example) experiment is rarely possible; and in some special sciences (for example, palaeontology) there is no room for experiment at all. The Milesians had a copious abundance of data to explain: 'pioneers, with so many fresh phenomena waiting to be observed, they felt no urge to manufacture more. Having abundance, they saw no need for superabundance.'[14] And in any case, the sciences they showed most interest in are not experimental in any serious sense. Certainly, the devising of a few tests would have enlivened and improved Presocratic science; but the lack of an 'experimental method' does not bar the Presocratics from the halls of science.[15]

Perhaps, then, the Milesians failed because they ignored 'the inductive method': they failed, that is, to live up to Baconian canons of scientific procedure. 'The inductive method' may be interpreted in a procedural or in a logical fashion: it may enjoin either that the garnering of data should precede the formation of theory, or that any formed theory should be supported by a mass of data. Both interpretations have this in common, that they require the scientist to be an ardent collector of particular facts.

The inductive method has fallen on hard times; and few, I imagine, would maintain that an inductive procedure is either essential or even particularly useful to science. Indeed, it is a popular view that the blind collation of data is inimical to the scientific spirit, if not a positively incoherent pursuit. Yet it is reasonable to think

SCIENCE AND SPECULATION

that data are not wholly irrelevant to science: a theory which is supported by a vast number of disparate facts is, I suppose, still preferable to a theory which has no support; and whatever our attitude to Bacon, we are unlikely to conclude that the collection of observational data is simply irrelevant to the scientific enterprise.

How do the Milesians fare if they are measured against these standards? We do not know if they attempted to follow an inductive procedure. I have supposed that Anaximenes' theorizing began from his observations of the effects of breath; but that is merely a guess. He might, for all our sources can tell us, have elaborated his theory first and only later come across the porridge puzzle. In any case, Anaximenes' procedure was hardly inductive even if my guess is right: one observation does not make an induction. Then did Anaximenes support his formed theory by amassing a collection of phenomena to which it might be applied? Here the answer is clearly affirmative. The doxography does not allow us to say how large was the *corpus* of Anaximenes' observations, or whether they were the result of personal inspection, or exactly how the observations were supposed to be related to the general theory; and we may well imagine, as I have already said, that neither the observations nor their subsumption under the theory were carried out in a particularly rigorous fashion. Nonetheless, it is beyond reasonable dispute that Anaximenes had a mass of empirical evidence which, he believed, indirectly corroborated his general theory. And that, I submit, is enough to make him as inductively minded as any scientist need be. In general, it seems fair to conclude that 'the alliance between careful observation and bold speculation is not only natural but essential in early Greek thought, the very condition for the creation of science and philosophy in the Greek sense'.[16]

Finally, a third method, the 'critical method', has been judged the especial mark of scientific endeavour. An adherent of the critical method will be most concerned to refute theories, whether his own or others'; he will elicit the particular implications of a general theory and prove them against the facts of observation; he will occupy himself in devising strenuous and varied tests, and he will not rest until he can invent no more hurdles for a theory to stride.

I am not certain that the 'critical method' constitutes a methodology; and I am certain that the 'critical method' is not specifically scientific. Criticism is a feature of rational procedure in every branch of intellectual study; philosophers and historians are not excluded from a form of thought which physicists and geologists may indulge in. Nonetheless, it is obvious enough that a sharp critical acumen and a determination to probe and test hypotheses are intellectual virtues of a high order; and it is apposite to inquire whether the Milesians possessed them.

The common view, I think, is that they did. The history of Presocratic thought is customarily seen in an Hegelian light: thesis and antithesis alternate in dialectical interplay, each new theory springing from the head of its predecessor. Criticism and refutation thus supply the very structure of Presocratic thought, and the 'critical method' is the key to an understanding of the first development of science.

It is, of course, indisputable that the Presocratics knew and were influenced by the views of their predecessors; and the influence was often negative. I have already purveyed the commonplace conjecture that Anaximenes' innovations were devised in response to the inadequacies of Anaximander's theories; and many similar cases will be noted as this book proceeds. Moreover, we have direct evidence of such awareness. Thus Xenophanes referred to Thales (**21 B 19**) and criticized Pythagoras (**B 7**); Heraclitus abused Pythagoras and Xenophanes (**22 B 40**); Hippo and Zeno may have animadverted on Empedocles (Aristotle, *An* 405b2 = **31 A 4**; Suda, **29 A 2**); Diogenes of Apollonia wrote *Against the Natural Scientists* (Simplicius, **64 A 4**); and Democritus attacked Anaxagoras (**68 B 5**) and Protagoras (**68 B 156**). Such references can easily be multiplied; and the Hippocratic treatises offer examples of the substance behind them.

Yet it is one thing to know and to reject one's predecessor's views, another to adopt the critical approach to science and philosophy; criticism, after all, is more than the mere contradicting of an opponent. And it is a remarkable fact that the art of critical or destructive argument scarcely appears in Greek thought before Socrates. The earliest examples I know come in the *Dissoi Logoi*, a treatise on which I shall say more later (in vol. 2, pp. 215–20). Section 6 of the work discusses the question of whether virtue and wisdom can be taught; the author advances some arguments for a negative answer, points to their weakness, and concludes thus: 'That is my argument—you have beginning and end and middle; and I do not assert that it can be taught—but those proofs do not satisfy me' (**90 A 1**, §6.13; cf. §2.23; §3.15; §5.9). That passage makes, clearly and for the first time, the crucial distinction between rejecting an argument for a conclusion and rejecting the conclusion itself. The art of criticism cannot thrive unless that distinction is grasped.

The critical innocence of the Presocratics appears in two forms. First, there is no Presocratic instance of a philosopher criticizing an *argument*; we might expect the successors and opponents of Parmenides to have investigated the structure of his reasonings and explained where it was weak or defective. Yet no example of such investigation survives: neither Empedocles nor Anaxagoras tells us where and why he thinks Parmenides errs, even though both thought that Parmenides did err. Nor does any philosopher before Aristotle tell us what is wrong with Zeno's paradoxes.

Second, and more surprisingly, we have hardly any instances of philosophers criticizing a *theory*. We may well assume that the successors of Thales thought his water thesis mistaken; yet no text tells us why they thought so, or what counter-examples they offered or imagined. Still less do we find self-criticism. Anaximenes' theory suggests to us any number of critical tests; yet there is no evidence that Anaximenes applied any of them. He may have thought, vaguely enough, that compressed earth becomes harder until it turns to stone; yet he does not seem to have attempted the easy task of compressing air—in a leather wine-skin, say—to see if it turned to cloud or water; and there is no evidence that he ever investigated the implications of his thesis that density and temperature were directly proportional.

Our evidence for the Milesians is slight and fragmentary. It is possible that their writings contained critical inquiries which later authors did not think fit to preserve; it is possible too, that the Milesians regarded criticism as a necessary propaedeutic to construction, but scorned to sully their finished publications with such preliminary observations. At all events, we can scarcely avoid the assumption that the Milesians and their successors sometimes rejected earlier theories, and did so on rational grounds. Yet the evidence lends great plausibility to the thought that the Milesians were more interested in construction than in destruction, and that their energies were too absorbed in the creative task of system building to dwell long on the less sublime business of criticism and refutation.

What do these reflections suggest? It is, I believe, perverse to deny that the Milesians were scientists—and great scientists at that. Their scientific shortcomings were not methodological: they approached their problems in an admirable fashion; and their failures were due not to lack of understanding but to lack of developed techniques of observation and theory construction. Their methodological failing was general and not specifically scientific: intoxicated by the delights of construction, they did not care to submit their buildings to the rough winds of criticism.

(d) *The use of analogy*

A striking feature of Presocratic thought is its use of analogy.[17] In

Thales' account of the floating of the earth we have come upon the first simple example of this pattern of thought. The most celebrated and elaborate analogies are found in the fragments of Empedocles: one long passage (**31 B 84**) compares the structure of the eye to the structure of a lantern, in order to explain how it is that our eyes 'flash'; a longer and notoriously difficult fragment (**B 100**) accounts for respiration by a detailed comparison with a *clepsydra* or pipette. But examples can be found in every early Greek thinker; and since the scanty doxography on Anaximenes presents us with several interesting analogies, I shall discuss this widespread 'thought pattern' by reference to him.

Historians of ancient thought sometimes treat analogy as an antiquated device; and sometimes they imply that all analogies are logically on a par. Neither of these notions is correct. First, analogy, in one form or another, is a constant—perhaps a psychologically indispensable—accompaniment of scientific thought: the vogue word 'model' is a modern synonym for 'analogy'. Second, an analogy may be invoked for a variety of purposes, only one of which is properly denominated 'argument from analogy'.

Here are seven passages in which Anaximenean analogies appear:

The soul, being our air, controls us, and breath and air encompass the whole world (**26: B 2**).

The stars move . . . around the earth, just as a turban winds round our head (**27**: Hippolytus, **A 7**).

And some say that the universe whirls like a mill-stone (**28**: Aëtius, **A 12**).

Anaximenes says that the stars are fixed in the crystalline in the manner of nails . . . (**29**: Aëtius, **A 14**).[18]

Anaximenes says that the sun is flat like a leaf (**30**: Aëtius, **A 15**; cf. **B 2a**).

Anaximenes says the same [about thunder] as him [sc. Anaximander], adding the phenomenon we observe on the sea, which gleams when cut by oars (**31**: Aëtius, **A 17**; cf. **12 A 23**; Aristophanes, *Clouds* 404–7).

Just as in old buildings certain parts collapse though not struck, when they have more weight than strength; so in the earth as a whole it comes about that certain parts are loosened by age, and, being loosened, fall and cause the parts above them to tremble. They do this first when they break away (for nothing of any size breaks away without moving what it adheres to). Then, when they have collapsed, they meet something solid and spring back again, like a ball which, when it falls, bounces back and is as often driven back as it is sent up from the ground on a new flight (**32**: Seneca, *nat quaest* 6.10 = Diels-Kranz, I.488.30–5; cf. **A 21**)

These seven examples fall into two, or perhaps three, groups.

First, analogy is often used merely as a rhetorical trope, to add colour and vivacity to a flat description. This is pretty clearly the case in **28**: the phrase 'like a mill-stone' adds nothing new to the verb 'whirls'. Example **27** is obscure; but I assume that it is a joke, designed more to enliven than to illuminate Anaximenes' account of the stars. It is likely that **30** also belongs to this class.

Second, an analogy may be more than entertaining but less than explanatory: we observe that an F is G, but find the observation somehow puzzling; analogy with more familiar cases of things which are G may serve to remove our puzzlement. Example **29** is of this sort: the small stars are evidently fixed somehow to the vault of the sky, yet we may wonder how they can stay up there. The observation of nail-heads fixed in an overhead beam shows that the fixture of the stars need not be paradoxical. Again, in **32** the superficially surprising phenomenon of the earth's quaking without being struck is made intellectually palatable by the observation that old buildings will sometimes tumble without being struck. It may be that **31** is a further example of this type; and **30** too may belong here: the sun can float on air, just as leaves can (cf. **A 20**; above, p. 28).

Analogies of this second type are susceptible to a strong and a weak interpretation. Taken strongly, **29** is supposed to show *how* the stars remain in the sky: they are the upper surface of a long spike which is sunk into the sky and thus holds them in place. So construed, the analogy does indeed aim to be explanatory. Taken weakly, **29** is intended to show only that the stars *can* remain in the sky, and not to offer a suggestion about *how* they are fixed. So construed the analogy has no explanatory pretensions, and Anaximenes might as well have added 'or like flies, or pieces of paper glued to the ceiling'.

The difference between the strong and the weak interpretations is not clear-cut: removal of puzzlement slides insensibly into explanation; and it is usually hard to tell what interpretation an author intends (unless he explicitly offers two or more analogies). For all that, the distinction is important. Some students of computer science attempt to simulate human behaviour and to show how it can be that certain sensory inputs into human organisms elicit certain cognitive or motor responses. Computer simulation may be an enlightening discipline; but it does not claim to show how human organisms work: that a computer can produce the same results from the same materials as I can, does not show that I and the computer work in the same way. Other students of computer science speak of artificial intelligence; they aim not to simulate but to reproduce—and hence to explain—human performances. There are thus two distinct ways in which computers may serve as an analogy or 'model' of the human mind; the second way, evidently, makes far stronger claims than the first.

Finally, analogies may be called upon in argument. Observing first that a is F and also G, and secondly that b is F, we infer that b, too, is G. Example **26** is commonly taken in this sense, and is treated as Anaximenes' reason for thinking that air, rather than any other stuff, is the material principle of everything. It is then to be paraphrased as follows: 'We men contain an airy soul; and that air keeps us together, i.e., keeps us alive; the universe as a whole contains air: hence it is air that keeps the universe together, i.e., supplies its underlying stuff.' Air sustains men; so air is probably the *Urstoff* of the universe.

That interpretation of **26** is, I suppose, possible; but it is not demanded by the text (which contains no inferential particle),[19] nor is it a happy interpretation (for the argument it ascribes to Anaximenes is scandalously jejune). Argument by analogy is in effect induction from a single case, and as such it is essentially lacking in probative force; moreover, in the case of **26**, the terms of the analogy are not identical, and the interpretation is obliged to introduce the phrase 'keep together' in order to produce a show of identity. It is preferable to think that **26** contains no argument at all, and *a fortiori* no analogical argument; rather, it presents one of the considerations which may have determined Anaximenes to fix on air as his basic material: if Thales preferred water because water is essential to life, Anaximenes preferred air for the self-same reason. Example **26** does indeed give an answer, or part of an answer, to question (b) of p. 46; for it helps to explain why Anaximenes picked on air as his *Urstoff*. But the answer is not based on analogical argument; and neither in **26** nor elsewhere do we find an argument from analogy in Anaximenes.

Indeed, I do not think there is a single argument from analogy in any of the Presocratics. And that is a happy conclusion: analogies may be scientifically important; they may serve, psychologically, to illuminate a dry exposition or to dispel a puzzlement; and they may be useful, methodologically, in suggesting a synthesis or provoking a generalization. But they have no inferential status: argument 'from analogy' is one of the numerous species of bad argument.

IV

The Natural Philosophy of Heraclitus

(a) *The great account*

When, in his lectures on the history of philosophy, Hegel came to Heraclitus, he was moved to an extravagant effusion: 'Here we see land! There is no proposition of Heraclitus which I have not adopted in my logic.' A prominent opponent of Hegelianism is no less effusive: Heraclitus' fragments, far from adumbrating teutonic dialectics, reveal 'a thinker of unsurpassed power and originality', a Greek Wittgenstein.[1] The truth is that Heraclitus attracts exegetes as an empty jampot wasps; and each new wasp discerns traces of his own favourite flavour.

The existence of such diverse interpretations of Heraclitus' philosophy will sow the seeds of despair in the mind of any honest scholar; and that luxuriant plant receives nourishment from a consideration of the history and nature of Heraclitus' text. We do possess over a hundred fragments from Heraclitus' pen; but many of them have reached us through the labours of two early Christian fathers: Clement of Alexandria saw Heraclitus as a pagan prophet of the Last Judgment; and Hippolytus of Rome made him, for polemical purposes, the spiritual father of Noetus' Monarchian heresy. Moreover, Heraclitus had earned the dubious benefits of popularity even before his Christian renascence; for Cleanthes the Stoic had attempted to give a stamp of authority to the teachings of his master Zeno by deriving them from the ancient doctrines of Heraclitus (Diogenes Laertius, IX. 16 = **22 A 1**).[2]

We see Heraclitus reflected in the distorting glasses of patristic piety and Stoic special pleading. And in their pristine state his doctrines were not easy reading: according to an old fable, 'Euripides gave Socrates a copy of Heraclitus' book and asked him what he thought of it; Socrates replied: "What I understand is good; and I think that what I don't understand is good too—but it would take a Delian diver to get to the bottom of it" ' (Diogenes Laertius, II.22 = **A 4**).[3] Theophrastus tartly observed that 'from impulsiveness, some of what he wrote was half-completed, and the rest inconsistent' (Diogenes Laertius, IX.6 = **A 1**). Heraclitus the Obscure, the Riddler, the oracular prophet, stands dark and majestic in the early history of philosophy. He set out to imitate 'the king whose is the oracle at Delphi', who, in Heraclitus' own words, 'neither states nor conceals, but gives signs' (**B 93** = **14 M**;[4] cf. Lucian, **C 5**).[5]

Interpretation may thus appear a Herculean task. Yet the filth of the Heraclitean stables has perhaps been exaggerated. First, the textual tradition is not irremediably contaminated: Stoic and Christian accretions are readily recognized and readily removed; and we have enough of Heraclitus' own words to reconstruct his thought without continual reliance on the doxography. Moreover, the obscurity of Heraclitus' writings is customarily misrepresented. He is, like all the Presocratics, given to a vexatious vagueness; he frequently propounds paradoxes; and he has a mild penchant for puns. But puns are harmless and paradox is not always obscure. The fragmentary state of Heraclitus' surviving words often makes his sense opaque; but I do not find his style particularly 'oracular'; he does not present his thoughts in 'riddles' (though he once quotes an old chestnut); and if he sometimes produces similes and analogies, it is gratuitous to suppose that his every remark must be construed unliterally, as the surface sign of an underlying profundity. At all events, I shall proceed on the assumption that Heraclitus usually means what he says. I do not share Nietzsche's view that 'probably no man has ever written as clearly and as lucidly' as Heraclitus; but it will, I hope, emerge that what he says is not always bible black.

We have, moreover, a clear starting point. Fragment **B 1** = **1 M** is twice said to come from the beginning of Heraclitus' book,[6] and we have no good reason to doubt the testimony (Aristotle, *Rhet* 1407b16 = **A 4**; Sextus, **A 16**). The fragment reads:

> And of this account (*logos*) which is the case always men prove to be uncomprehending, both before they hear it and once they have heard it. For although everything comes about in accordance with this account (*logos*), they are like inexperienced men when they experience both the words and the deeds of the sort which I recount by dividing up each thing in accordance with its nature (*phusis*) and saying how it is; but other men do not notice what

they do when they are awake, just as they are oblivious of things when asleep (33).

Aristotle pointed out the syntactical ambiguity of Heraclitus' first sentence, an ambiguity which I imagine to have been deliberate and which is preserved in the translation by the clumsy placing of 'always'; and scholars since Aristotle have devoted much labour and ingenuity to the explication of the fragment. I shall only touch on one exegetical point before stating what I take to be the chief contentions of the passage.

Most scholars have found in '*logos*' a technical term, and they have striven to discover a metaphysical sense for it.[7] These strivings are vain: a *logos* or 'account' is what a man *legei* or says. We may suppose that our fragment was preceded, in antique fashion, by a title-sentence of the form: 'Heraclitus of Ephesus says (*legei*) thus: ....'.[8] The noun *logos* picks up, in an ordinary and metaphysically unexciting way, the verb *legei*; it is wasted labour to seek Heraclitus' secret in the sense of *logos*.

It does not, of course, follow from this that Heraclitus had no 'metaphysical' theory to propound, no 'Logos-doctrine', as the commentators have it. On the contrary, 33 makes it clear that his 'account' must include or embody something like a general 'law of nature': 'everything happens' in accordance with the account. Thus Heraclitus' first claim is that he can offer a general account of the world, and that he can do this by explaining what is the *phusis* or essential nature of each thing. Second, he maintains that most men are woefully ignorant of this account: they are 'like the deaf' (B 34 = 2 M); they live in a dream world (B 89 = 24 M) 'as if they had a private understanding' of how things are (B 2 = 23 M).[9] Third, he says that most men do not even know what they are doing or how to act.

Of these three claims this chapter will investigate the first: later chapters will deal with Heraclitus' second claim and the epistemology which underlies it, and with his third claim and the rudimentary ethical theory it suggests. There is, I think, something to be said for the view that this ethical theory was the summit of Heraclitus' thought; but modern discussions inevitably and reasonably spend many more words on the metaphysical foothills.

'Everything happens' in accordance with Heraclitus' account: the account is 'common to everything' (B 114 = 23 M; cf. B 80 = 28 M); and it is analogous to, or identical with, the single divine law which 'nourishes' all human laws (B 114).[10] Alas, we do not possess (and perhaps Heraclitus never gave) a single luminous statement of this law: four muddy fragments contain the nearest we can get to a general account.

> Conjunctions are wholes and non-wholes: what is converging, what is diverging; what is consonant, what is dissonant: from everything one, and from one thing everything (34: **B 10** = **25 M**).[11]

> Listening not to me but to my account it is wise to agree that everything is one (35: **B 50** = **26 M**).[12]

> They do not understand how what is diverging is converging with itself: there is a back-stretched connexion, as of a bow and of a lyre (36: **B 51** = **27 M**).[13]

> One should know that war is common, and justice strife; and that everything comes about in accordance with strife and what must be (37: **B 80** = **28 M**).

These four fragments have suggested three abstract theses. First, there is the notorious Theory of Flux: all the furniture of the world is in constant, if imperceptible, change; the cosmos is a battleground, and its pacific façade hides the endless victories and defeats of an interminable internecine strife. Second, there is the Unity of Opposites: behind the coherent surface of things there is a tension of incompatibles; every object, however firm and enduring, is subject to contrary strains, and is constituted by opposing features. Third, there is a doctrine of Monism: in some fashion the diversity of appearances is underpinned or colligated by some single thing or stuff; at bottom, all is one.

Monism appears to be explicitly asserted in 35, and to be implicit in 34. The Unity of Opposites has been found in 36, and also in 34. Flux allegedly flows from 37, and perhaps from 36 and 34. The four fragments, taken alone, are difficult; and all the interpretations I have indicated have been disputed. Nevertheless, I think that all three theses can be ascribed to Heraclitus; and that together they form a metaphysical system.

(b) *Nature's bonfire*

The abstract monism of 35 is given a fiery and substantial nature by other fragments:

> This world neither any god nor man made, but it always was and is and will be, an ever-living fire, kindling in measures and being extinguished in measures (**38: B 30 = 51 M**).

> Everything is an exchange for fire, and fire for everything—as goods for gold, and gold for goods (**39: B 90 = 54 M**).

Fire is the prime stuff of the world. The thesis has a traditional Milesian ring; and on his monism Heraclitus constructed, perhaps not in conscientious detail, a physical science of a standard Milesian type. He also advanced an idiosyncratic theory of man and of the human soul; and the fragments contain the remnants of an unusual theology. Heraclitus attacked the empty polymathy of his predecessors (see below, p. 146); but there is evidence enough that he was a polymath himself; and he takes his place on the board of Ionian scientists—a rebel, perhaps, but not a revolutionary. The details of Heraclitus' science are as controversial as anything in his thought; and I shall not attempt to expound them. Instead, I shall look more generally at the nature and grounds of Heraclitus' monism.

'From everything one; and from one thing everything' (**34**): it is fire, as **38** makes clear, which is the one stuff from which everything comes; and **B 31 = 53 M** elaborates on the bald hypothesis:

> Turnings of fire: first, sea; and of sea, half earth and half burning (*prêstêr*). . . . Sea is dispersed and is measured in the same proportion as there was before (**40**).[14]

Fire turns into water; and water eventually reverts to fire, the proportions remaining constant.

The Stoics, some of whom claimed Heraclitus as their ancestor, subscribed to a doctrine of *ekpurôsis* or cosmic conflagration, according to which the whole universe is periodically consumed by fire to rise again, phoenix-like, from its own ashes (see *SVF* II 596–632). The doxographers ascribe such an *ekpurôsis* to Heraclitus (e.g., Clement, *ad* **B 31**; Simplicius, **A 10**): some scholars accept the ascription, others deny it; and there is large controversy. I incline to agree that Aristotle and the Peripatetics made the ascription; and that nothing in the secondary sources stands against it. Yet **38** says flatly that 'this world . . . always was and is and will be': that is a brusque rejection both of cosmogony and of cosmophthory—'this world (*kosmos*)' did not begin and will not end. And that, as far as I can see, is incompatible with a doctrine of *ekpurôsis*.[15] The doxography, even if Aristotle is its patron, must yield to the evidence of the fragments.

The point is worth stressing: **38** does not merely rule out *ekpurôsis*; it rules out any form of cosmic disintegration, and equally any form of cosmogony. Heraclitus surely knew of the Milesian cosmogonists: why, we may wonder, did he reject their enterprise? and why, for that matter, had the Milesians imagined a beginning to the world, and supposed that one of the tasks of a natural scientist was to supply an account of the world's birth-pangs? Our texts give us no answers. Perhaps the Milesians simply did not entertain the possibility that the present cosmos was sempiternal: their mythological predecessors had fabled a genealogical account of the world's origins, and they conceived it their duty to replace genealogy by science. Every thinker has some unquestioned starting points, and the necessity of cosmogony was perhaps such a starting point for the Milesians.

However that may be, no analogous explanation is available for Heraclitus' case: his rejection of cosmogony was no tacit assumption but a self-conscious piece of polemic; and he must surely have expected a request to explain and justify his innovatory suggestion. He may have preserved a discreet silence (I have already commented upon the curious lack of critical concern among the Presocratics: above, pp. 50–2); but that is an unflattering and an implausible guess. The Atomists, and later Aristotle, rejected cosmogony; but we cannot project Aristotle's highly Aristotelian arguments back on to Heraclitus, and we do not really know how the Atomists argued (vol. 2, pp. 128–9). Speculation may invent a variety of reasons to support Heraclitus' stand: I leave the reader to exercise his own fancy here.

The monistic formula, 'Everything is from X', can be read cosmogonically. So read, it implies that at some time all things were X. That reading, I have just argued, is not possible for Heraclitus; but the formula admits a different interpretation, on which it implies only that everything at some time was X. On the first, cosmogonical, reading, at some time everything was X; on the second reading, everything was, at some time, X. The notation of quantificational logic brings out the distinction clearly. '$(\exists x)\ \phi x$' means 'Something is ϕ' '$(\forall x)\phi x$' means 'Everything is ϕ'. Let the variable x range over physical objects, and let the variable t range over times or instants. Then the cosmogonical interpretation of monism can be expressed by:

(1) $(\exists t)\ (\forall x)\ (x\ \text{is}\ X\ \text{at}\ t)$—'At some time every physical object is X'. And the second reading of monism is given by:

(2) $(\forall x)\ (\exists t)\ (x\ \text{is}\ X\ \text{at}\ t)$—'Every physical object is at some time X'.

Here (1) entails (2); but (2) does not entail (1). It seems to me that the analogy Heraclitus draws in **39** fits well with (2) and ill with (1); and that this makes it probable that Heraclitus had (2) fairly clearly in mind.

According to Simplicius,

> Heraclitus ... made fire the principle, and derives the things that exist from fire by condensation and rarefaction, and resolves them again into fire, taking this as the single underlying nature; for Heraclitus says that everything is an exchange for fire (**41: A 5**).

Fire on this view is the 'material principle' of everything. The view is ubiquitous in the doxography; and it is found in Aristotle (*Met* 984a7 = **18 A 7**).

Simplicius adverts to **39**; and scholars have been quick to point out that the fragment does not require an Aristotelian interpretation. Nor do the two main fragments on fire, **38** and **40**, embody an Aristotelian view; and the assertion in **38** that fire is 'extinguished in measures' has been taken to imply that fire does not, like a substrate, persist through its 'turnings'. Thus in Heraclitus' world things were made from, but are not made of, fire.[16]

Three frail reasons stand against this conclusion. First, Simplicius' reference to condensation and rarefaction supports an Aristotelian interpretation. (But Simplicius may only be reporting a Peripatetic conjecture, or making a conjecture of his own.) Second, 'everything is one' (**35**); and we may say, without abuse of language, that 'everything is fire' only if we mean that everything actually *is*, at bottom, fire. (But Hippolytus, who quotes **35**, suggests a different interpretation of the phrase.) Third, the sort of inference required to reach the Aristotelian view from a thesis like (2) is, as I shall shortly show, characteristically Heraclitean. (But need Heraclitus have made the inference here?) I incline to accept the Aristotelian interpretation; but the evidence is thin, and I put no weight on the matter.

How, then, did Heraclitus argue for his monism? Some scholars would say that this question was misconceived: Heraclitus' statements are oracular, and their production has little to do with argument; 'his conclusions are based on intuition rather than on observation and analysis of data'; or again: 'the content of [Heraclitus'] very general formula seems to have been filled in by a coherent chain of statements linked together not by logical argument but by interlocking ideas and verbal echoes, with an elaborate use of imagery, word-play and enigma'.[17] And those scholars who do perceive argument in Heraclitus regard his chief logical tool as analogy; and they talk of a 'thought pattern' rather than of ratiocination in any inferential sense.[18] Who, in any case, would expect a quick flame from hydropical Heraclitus?

There are certainly analogical statements in Heraclitus; but their number has been overestimated, and where they do occur they seem, to me at least, more a stylistic device than an argumentative mode. Again, there is certainly imagery and word-play in the fragments; but this too is a stylistic embellishment rather than a substitute for logical procedure. The fragments, I think, are consistent with, and indeed positively suggest, the view that Heraclitus, like any good Presocratic, was ready to support his statements by argument and evidence. I hope to make this claim plausible when I turn to Flux and Unity: for Monism the fragments are less helpful.

We might, indeed, imagine (consistently with the hypothesis of a rational Heraclitus) that his monism was an unargued postulate: like the Milesians, Heraclitus saw it as scientifically virtuous to construct his system on the simplest foundations; and like them again, he saw that monism provided the greatest degree of simplicity. Many scholars do not like unargued postulates; and of those, some have taken Heraclitus' monism as an inference from the Unity thesis. Heraclitus, they imagine, offered an *a fortiori* argument: 'If opposites form a unity, then everything forms a unity; hence everything is one.' There is a temptation to see just such an argument in 34, where the last clauses present Monism, and the first clauses expound the Unity thesis. But the reconstruction is implausible; for the inference it offers Heraclitus is gross: from Unity there is no reasonable path to Monism.

There is, in any case, a better line of reasoning which we can ascribe to Heraclitus. We may suppose, first, that he posited a monistic theory to explain the generation of things; second, that he picked on fire as his fundamental material on the basis of observations of the same vague and general sort which influenced Anaximenes; third, that he understood his fiery monism as a special, cosmic, case of the Theory of Flux; and fourth, that he applied the general argument from Flux to Unity which I shall shortly expound, in order to derive an Aristotelian monism. This reconstruction is wholly speculative: it has the twin merits of ascribing arguments to Heraclitus which we have some reason to think him capable of using, and of placing the three main components of his account of the world in some sort of logical relation to one another.

(c) *All things are a flowing*

Panta rhei, 'Everything flows', is the most familiar of Heraclitus' sayings; yet few modern scholars think he said it, and many think he never had a Theory of Flux at all.[19]

That view is perverse. It is true that the particular phrase '*panta rhei*' first occurs in Simplicius (**40** (c⁶) **M**); but the Theory itself is ascribed to Heraclitus by a horde of authorities.[20] Plato is explicit enough:

> Heraclitus, I think, says that everything moves (*panta chôrei*) and nothing rests (**42**: *Cratylus* 402A = **A 6**).

And there is earlier evidence yet: the Hippocratic treatise *de victu* is a silly farrago of ill-digested Presocratic opinions: one particularly Heraclitean chapter of the work, §5, opens with the phrase *chôrei panta*. The treatise probably dates from about 500 BC; and it thus contains a pre-Platonic reference to Heraclitean Flux.[21] The doxography consistently ascribes Flux to Heraclitus; and here, at least, we can trace it beyond the Peripatetic writers.

The doxographers are, I think, supported by the fragments themselves: Heraclitus' remarks on the rule of War and Strife (especially **37**) strongly suggest a dynamic and changing world of the sort envisaged by the Theory of Flux. And several fragments, which I shall shortly consider, offer what are reasonably taken as arguments for, or at least illustrations of, the Theory.

In sum, I think that Flux is Heraclitean; indeed I am disposed to take Plato's *panta chôrei* as an actual quotation from Heraclitus: there is as much reason for accepting this as there is for accepting many of the lines which orthodoxy prints as *ipsissima verba*.[22]

Some of those scholars who accept the Theory as Heraclitean are inclined to see nothing very original in it: the Milesians, after all, had held a similar view. The Milesians, like all observant men before Parmenides, had indeed noticed that things change: the world is patently not a static *tableau*. Yet it is far from a patent truth that *everything* changes, still less that everything *always* changes; and the Milesians, like ordinary men before Heraclitus, seem to have thought that within the changing world there was room for a number of stable and relatively permanent objects: the stars do not change in their courses, and the earth does not move from its place. There is no reason to deny Heraclitus the novelty of generalizing the natural view of a changing world to the more pugnacious thesis that everything changes; whether there was more to his innovation than such a generalization remains to be seen.

THE NATURAL PHILOSOPHY OF HERACLITUS

Discussion must start from the notorious 'river fragment' which has been associated with the Theory of Flux at least since Plato's time. The *Fragmente der Vorsokratiker* present us with not one but three quotations:

> On those who step into the same rivers, different and different waters flow (**43: B 12 = 40 M**).

> We both step and do not step into the same rivers; we both are and are not (**44: B 49a = 40 (c²) M**).

> It is not possible to step into the same river twice (**45: B 91 = 40(C³) M**).

These three passages have sustained a massive commentary.[23] Are all three fragments genuine? Are two genuine and the third a paraphrase? Is one genuine, the other two paraphrases? Are all paraphrases of some single, lost, original? What, if anything, did Heraclitus actually say about rivers? and what did he mean?

These controversial, and perhaps unanswerable, questions have, I think, acted as a smoke-screen: behind them the chief, and answerable, question has sailed on unheeded. That question is: What doctrine might the river fragments, whatever their original form, suggest, or seem to support? The common core of the fragments is the observation, trite and true, that rivers, on which common parlance and the nomenclature of the geographers impose a permanence and stability, are all the while changing in at least one essential respect: the waters of which they are constituted are never the same from one instant to the next. Plainly, this observation exemplifies, and therefore in some measure supports, the Theory of Flux. The superficial stability of rivers masks a continuous and essential change: things look, but are not, the same. We need not take Heraclitus' river allegorically, as Plato apparently did; but once we have granted Heraclitus a Theory of Flux, it is silly not to take his river to exemplify it. The obvious and the natural message of rivers is this: stability may cover constant change. That message can hardly have been misunderstood by a proponent of Flux.[24]

A less celebrated fragment offers a second piece of evidence:

> The barley drink disintegrates if it is not stirred (**46: B 125 = 31 M**).

Here the moral is less impressively instanced but more easily drawn: cocktails must be shaken or stirred; a glass of stuff whose contents are not continuously changing cannot be a cocktail but will disintegrate into separate layers of barley, honey and wine. Change is essential to the identity and existence of the drink (cf. Themistius, **A 3b**).

A further fragment makes the same point in more general terms:

> Cold things grow warm; warm grows cold; wet grows dry; parched grows moist (**47: B 126 = 42 M**).

A farmer looking at his land will refer to the fields and the soil which he cultivates; his way of thinking and speaking assumes a constancy and stability in nature. Yet momentary reflexion is enough to remind him that the fundamental properties of his farmland, on which its appearance and its powers depend, are changing from day to day and hour to hour. Or again, a man's body is constantly changing its temperature and humidity, as he breathes and digests: the surface stability of the human shape hides a hubbub of operations without which men would soon cease to be.

Fire, like water, evidently flows; and **38** indicates that Heraclitus saw Flux on a cosmic scale: 'This world . . . is an ever-living fire, kindling in measures and being extinguished in measures.' Similarly, **40** presumably points to certain familiar but grand meteorological changes: the sea is always losing its substance, parts being drawn up in vapour by the sun, parts being filtered out as silt and adding to the land. Such observable changes indicate that the world as a whole, though apparently divided with some permanence into the great and stable masses of fire, water and earth, is subject to a continuous transformation: even at a cosmic level, reality is essentially changing.

Other fragments can more doubtfully be adduced as pointing to the same conclusion (see, e.g., **B 67 = 77 M; B 36 = 66 M**); and one crucial remnant, which I shall discuss in the next section, makes the connexion between Flux and Unity (**B 88 = 41 M**). But the fragments I have already quoted appear to me sufficient to establish a certain rationality to Heraclitus' procedure: the Theory of Flux was no *a priori* intuition or piece of fanciful imagery; it was a general thesis about the nature of reality, founded upon and supported by a series of empirical observations.

The same fragments give us a clearer view of the nature of the Theory, and enable us to scotch two popular interpretations whose intrinsic absurdity may partly account for the reluctance some scholars feel at ascribing the Theory to Heraclitus.

The first interpretation pictures Heraclitus as an early Wittgensteinian who 'visualized the world . . . not as the sum-total of all *things*, but rather as the totality of events, or changes, or facts'. 'Heraclitus' problem' was 'the *problem of change*—the *general* problem: *How is change possible?* How can *a thing* change without losing its identity—in which case it would no longer be *that thing* which has changed?' And Heraclitus' answer was that there are no changing things, but only changes: since nothing changes, the 'problem of change' is dissolved. For 'to Heraclitus the truth is to have grasped the essential being of nature, i.e. to have represented it as implicitly infinite, as process in itself'.[25]

This diverting interpretation does at least take Heraclitus' Theory as a serious philosophical proposition; but it is a fantasy, and a confusion. First, I protest against the widely accepted *dictum* that 'if you want to explain Heraclitus you must first show where his problem lay'.[26] Heraclitus, like his predecessors, did not focus his attention on some one 'problem': he wanted to give a general account of nature or the world. (Moreover, we are in no position to identify any 'problem' he found independently of his 'answers'.) Second, there is no evidence that Heraclitus posed 'the general problem of change': change for him was in particular cases a datum, and in general a theory; it was not a 'problem'. Third, the Theory of Flux does not imply the Wittgensteinian thesis that 'the world is the totality of facts, not of things'. Nor does it imply the different theory that the world is the totality of changes. Rather, it suggests that the world is a mass of things—stuffs and substances—which are subject to constant change. And such a suggestion does not approach, let alone dissolve, the 'general problem of change'.

The second interpretation of the Theory of Flux comes from Plato's *Theaetetus* (179D–183B): it takes the Theory to assert that all things are at every moment changing in every respect. Aristotle gives the following report:

> Again, seeing that the whole of nature is in motion, and that nothing is true of what is changing, they supposed that it is not possible to speak truly of what is changing in absolutely all respects. For from this belief flowered the most extreme opinion of those I have mentioned—that of those who say they 'Heraclitize', and such as was held by Cratylus, who in the end thought one should say nothing and only moved his finger, and reproached Heraclitus for saying that you cannot step into the same river twice—for he himself thought you could not do so even once (**48**: *Met* 1010a7–15 = **65 A 4**).

The surviving evidence on Cratylus the Heraclitean is sparse and puzzling: our two chief sources, the *Metaphysics* and Plato's *Cratylus*, are not easily harmonized; nor, for that matter, are they easily interpreted. I assume that the *Metaphysics* is reliable; and that the main burden of Cratylus' argument is this: 'If the water in the pot is changing temperature, you cannot truly ascribe any temperature to it; if the door is being painted, you cannot truly ascribe a colour to it; and in general, if *a* is changing in respect of some continuum of qualities *S*, then you cannot ascribe any position on *S* to *a*. But everything is always changing in every respect; hence you can say nothing truly about anything.'

The argument assumes the strong version of Flux found in the *Theaetetus*. Plato argues that Flux of that strength is incoherent. To state the theory, it is necessary to refer to subjects of change, to identify objects, or at least areas of space, that are undergoing change; but reference and identification require a certain minimal stability in the object referred to or identified: I cannot refer to *a* unless I can truly assign *some* property to it. The extreme Cratylan theory of Flux thus denies one of its own presuppositions: if the theory is true, it cannot even be stated. Hence it is necessarily false. Cratylus' own argument is an adumbration of Plato's. For, according to Cratylus, Flux implies that nothing can truly be said of any object. Cratylus inferred that one can refer, or point, to objects (if that is why he 'moved his finger') but that one can predicate nothing of them; Plato inferred that one could not even refer to objects, since reference implies predication.

There are interesting hares trembling here for pursuit; but I shall not chase them. For there is no reason at all to ascribe a strong Cratylan Flux to Heraclitus. Cratylus did not sit at Heraclitus' feet, nor did he parrot Heraclitean doctrine: his theory is explicitly presented as a development, not a restatement, of Heraclitean Flux. Cratylus is described as a Heraclitean, and that is intelligible enough: his doctrine, that everything is always flowing in *all* respects, is evidently a child of Heraclitus' doctrine, that everything is always flowing in *some* respects.

(d) *A world of contradictions*

According to Aristotle, 'Heraclitus' account says that everything is and is not' (*Met* 1012a24); at least, this was a view of Heraclitus current in Aristotle's day, even if Aristotle himself, for philosophical reasons, was sometimes reluctant to accept it (cf. *Met* 1005b24–5 = A 7). The context of Aristotle's remark allows us to give it a fairly precise interpretation: 'Take anything you like, there is some property which it both has and lacks'; in symbols:

(1) $(\forall x)(\exists \phi)(\phi x \ \& \ \text{not-}\phi x)$.

Aristotle does not mean that Heraclitus propounded (1) in so many words; and of the fragments only 44 (above, p. 66) explicitly states a case of (1), and that is of dubious authenticity. On the other hand, the fragments do make frequent play with 'opposites' or contrary predicates; and if we jib at (1) we might allow Heraclitus the view that 'opposites belong to the same thing' (Sextus, *Pyrr Hyp* I.210; cf. II.63). Thus, letting 'ϕ'' mark a predicate contrary to 'ϕ' we can state the Heraclitean thesis as follows:

(2a) $(\forall x) (\exists \phi) (\phi x \,\&\, \phi' x)$.

In Aristotle's view (1) follows at once from (2a) (cf. *Met* 1011b15–22), and that will explain his ascription of (1) to Heraclitus.

Heraclitus did not, of course, say anything quite like (2a): that formula uses the artifices of a later logical notation. Hippolytus, who reports **35**, says that by 'all things are one' Heraclitus meant 'all opposites are one'. If he is right we possess, perhaps, one part of Heraclitus' own formulation of the Unity thesis. In modern notation, that amounts not to (2a) but to:

(2b) $(\forall \phi) (\exists x) (\phi x \,\&\, \phi' x)$.

We may conclude that the Unity of Opposites is properly expressed by the conjunction of (2a) and (2b): every pair of contraries is somewhere coinstantiated; and every object coinstantiates at least one pair of contraries:

(2) $(\forall \phi) (\exists x) (\phi x \,\&\, \phi' x) \,\&\, (\forall x) (\exists \phi) (\phi x \,\&\, \phi' x)$.

Many scholars will object to this interpretation of the Unity of Opposites: it ascribes an anachronistically precise thesis to Heraclitus, and thereby makes his view absurdly and trivially false. I shall say something about the absurdity of Heraclitus' thesis later; here I want to answer the charge of anachronism.

The charge is in effect twofold. First, Heraclitus did not use the categories of formal logic which (2) foists upon him; in particular, the subject-predicate structure of (2) has metaphysical implications which are quite alien to Heraclitus' thought. One part of this criticism is misguided: it is true that (2) states matters with greater precision than any sentence Heraclitus used; but to make a fairly precise statement of a philosopher's loosely expressed thought is not to misrepresent him; rather, it is a necessary preliminary to any adequate interpretation. Another part of the criticism is less clearly erroneous: perhaps (2) is precise in the wrong way? perhaps a different formulation of the Unity Thesis is possible? It is easy to invent other formulations; the only one which has any interest, or any plausibility as an interpretation, is:

(3) $(\forall \phi) (\phi = \phi')$.

White is black; heaviness is lightness; and the light is darkness itself: contrary properties are strictly identical with one another.[27]

Now some of Heraclitus' fragments do suggest something like (3);

but others are much more naturally taken to illustrate (2). And those which suggest (3) can be treated, without great strain, as rhetorical essays at (2). Again, (3), together with the harmless assumption that all the opposites are instantiated, entails (2); and on any interpretation what is most puzzling about Heraclitus' thesis is his apparent 'violation of the Law of Contradiction', which is most clearly brought out in (2). Finally, I cannot really believe that Heraclitus subscribed to (3): can anyone have seriously supposed that, say, being wet and being dry was one and the same thing? It is one thing to persuade oneself that one and the same thing is both wet and dry; another to imagine that there is no difference between being wet and being dry.

Thus in answer to the first charge, I say first that the precision of (2) is entirely proper, and indeed necessary; and second, that (2) is probably precise in the right way. Now for the second charge: (2) comes from Aristotle; but Aristotle may have got Heraclitus wrong. In particular, Aristotle may have taken Heraclitus' utterances too literally; by his assertions of 'unity' Heraclitus only means that things 'are "one" . . . in that they all have a common component . . . and because they all connect up with one another *because of* this common structure'.[28] Heraclitus observed that things, even opposites, are connected in far more complex and manifold ways than we incline to imagine; and he expressed this interesting but logically innocuous observation with rhetorical exaggeration. 'All things,' he said, 'are one'; but he meant: 'All things are interconnected'.

Can Heraclitus have meant that? It is small beer; indeed the thesis that 'all things are interconnected' is almost certainly a truism. Heraclitus saw himself as a vendor of novelty and paradox; he can hardly have intended to peddle such dullard truths as that. In any case, there are fragments in which Heraclitus clearly commits himself to instances of (2); and there are explicit statements to the effect that '*X* and *Y* are one'. We can take these as heightened tropes if we choose; but such a choice ignores the obvious sense of Heraclitus' remarks. Moreover, the mild interpretation confuses the grounds of Heraclitus' Unity Thesis with the Thesis itself: it is true, I think, that Heraclitus argues for this Thesis from various observations about 'common structures' and the like. But if the Unity Thesis is supported by such facts, it follows not that the Thesis is constituted by those facts, but rather that the Thesis is *not* constituted by them.[29]

The Unity Thesis, if it is expressed by (2), is bizarre and outrageous: it will constitute the core of Heraclitus' idiosyncratic 'account' of the way things are. The ancient critics concurred in this judgment: of the thesis that 'everything in the world is by nature pretty well opposite', Philo asked (*quis rer div her*, 43, 214),

Is it not this which the Greeks say that their great and celebrated Heraclitus set up as the high-point of his philosophy and paraded as a new discovery? (**49**: Diels-Kranz, I.491. 39–42).

What could have impelled Heraclitus to so strange a view? Part of the answer is, I think, given in **B 88 = 41 M**:

> [i] The same thing is living and dead, and what is awake and what sleeps, and young and old; [ii] for these, having changed about, are those; and those, having changed about, these (**50**).

The fragment is textually controversial; and the illustrative examples it adduces are somewhat obscure in themselves—how does youth follow age or life death?[30] But the obscure story offers a plain moral: sentence [i] states three instances of the Unity Thesis and sentence [ii] grounds these instances, as its introductory particle shows, on the Theory of Flux.

Roughly speaking, Heraclitus argues thus: 'Being awake and being asleep succeed one another; therefore, the same things are awake and asleep.' It is plausible to find a similar argument in at least one other fragment:

> Hesiod is a teacher of most men: they are convinced that he knew most things—he who did not know day and night (for they are one) (**51**: **B 57 = 43 M**: cf. Hesiod, *Theogony* 123).

Thus: 'Night and day are mutually successive; hence the same thing is both night and day'. Text **46**, quoted in illustration of the Theory of Flux, may well have continued by inferring a case of the Unity Thesis; and the wretchedly difficult **B 58 = 46 M** perhaps contained a further argument of this sort.

But do such things deserve the name of argument? They are, at least when soberly expressed, palpably and scandalously invalid. How can Heraclitus have come to accept them? At least three explanations offer themselves. First, the Greeks were, as we are, prone to say that X and Y form a unity, or 'are one', if they are in some way continuous (*sunechês*). Heraclitus observed the continuity of night and day; he perhaps expressed this by saying to himself that night and day 'are one', and then inferred that night and day are identical. So understood, his argument commits a 'fallacy of equivocation': '. . . are one' means both '. . . form a unity' and '. . . are identical'; and Heraclitus' argument moves silently from the first sense to the second.[31]

Again, the succession of X and Y can be expressed by 'X is *ek* Y'; and from 'X is *ek* Y', in a different sense of '*ek*', the Greeks were often prepared to infer 'X is Y' (see above, p. 42). Perhaps, then, Heraclitus expressed the succession of day and night by means of the phrase 'day is *ek* night'; and then, improperly interpreting '*ek*', inferred the identity of day and night.

The third path of fallacy follows a different route. Flux—the change from one property to its contrary—can be expressed schematically by the following formula:

(4) ϕx at t_1 & $\phi' x$ at t_2.

Heraclitus' inference, then, passes in effect from (4) to:

(5) ϕx & $\phi' x$.

The fallacy lies in dropping the temporal qualifiers, 'at ti', or in passing from 'P at t_i' to 'P' without qualification. The Aristotelian Greek for 'P' without qualification is 'P *haplôs*'; and in the *Sophistici Elenchi* Aristotle warns against the fallacy of 'dropping the qualification' or of inferring P *haplôs* from some modified version of P (166b37–167a20; for an explanation of *haplôs*, see *Top* 115b29–35).

It is not anachronistic to suppose that Heraclitus fell for a fallacy of this sort: Aristotle makes it clear that such fallacies were still rife, and still perplexing, a century and a half after Heraclitus' day.[32] In many cases, of course, qualifiers can be validly dropped: 'Brutus stabbed Caesar' certainly follows from 'Brutus stabbed Caesar with a dagger'; and that may have encouraged a certain insouciance towards adverbial modifiers in general. Moreover, temporal indications are often concealed in ordinary discourse: watching the barber we may chronicle the change in his victim by the successive utterances 'He's hairy', 'He's bald'. Time is marked only by the present tense; and the logic of conjunction may seduce us to the conclusion: 'He's hairy and he's bald'.

That there is an inference in **50**, and that the inference is fallacious, are certainties. It is less clear how the fallacy is to be diagnosed. If I guess that the third diagnosis is Heraclitean, that is because there is some evidence that fallacies of that sort marred other bits of his reasoning. For the Unity of Opposites did not rest simply on inference from the Theory of Flux: it was also supported, as Flux itself was, by a collection of particular cases. And in some at least of these cases the fallacy of the dropped qualification is again visible.

Some twenty fragments in all may plausibly be construed as illustrating the Unity of Opposites. Most of them are controversial; many of them are too vague or too obscure to be worth adducing; and one of the most celebrated is no more than a pun.[33] Of the remainder, one group can be collected about **B 61 = 35 M**:

> Sea is purest and foulest water: for fish it is drinkable and salutary; for men it is undrinkable and lethal (**52**).

There are similar 'relativist' observations in **B 13** = **36 M**, on the pleasures of the pig (cf. Democritus, **68 B 147**); in **B 9** = **37 M**, on the values of the donkey; and in **B 4** = **38 M**, on the eating habits of oxen.

Observations of a generally relativistic type are common enough outside Heraclitus: the Sicilian comedian Epicharmus, who will take the stage in later chapters, provides an example:

> It is no wonder that we talk like this
> and please ourselves, and seem to one another
> to be so fair; for to a dog a bitch
> seems the most fair—and to a bull a cow,
> to an ass an ass, and to a pig a pig (54: 23 B 5).

Epicharmus propounded relativism to raise a laugh: Heraclitus' aim is philosophical; for from relativistic observations he could infer cases of the Unity thesis.

In **52** the inference is explicit; it proceeds from:
(6) Seawater is good for fish and bad for men
to:
(7) Seawater is good and bad.

The argument is closely parallel to that from (4) to (5): the omission of two qualifying phrases—'for fish', 'for men'—allows a common truth to yield a paradoxical conclusion. Here at least it is clear that Heraclitus committed the fallacy of the dropped qualification; and it is reasonable to imagine that the collection of propositions of which (7) is my exemplar were all derived by way of that fallacy, and then advanced in support of the Unity Thesis.[34]

Another type of argument lies behind **B 26** = **48 M**. The text of this fragment is hopelessly corrupt; but its shell in all probability reads:

> Man . . . while living touches death . . . and while waking touches sleep (54).

The metaphor of touching is susceptible to more than one interpretation. A plausible construe glosses 'touch' by 'resemble'[35] and ascribes to Heraclitus the following argument: 'There is no clear distinction between such opposites as life and death: we cannot say of a sleeping man that he is alive (for he exhibits few of the features of vivacity), nor yet can we say that he is dead (for sleepers and corpses are in many ways distinct). Thus life and death are strictly indistinguishable, and one and the same man is both alive and dead.' This type of argument is surprisingly popular: we are all familiar with the ploy forbidding us to say that a is ϕ rather than non-ϕ, on the grounds that there are numerous cases in which we are unwilling or unable to predicate either ϕ or non-ϕ. The argument is silly, and its invalidity is patent once it is stated; yet I think Heraclitus may have fallen for it.

Here, finally, are a few more illustrations of Heraclitean Unity. In **B 60 = 33 M**:

> The road there and back is one and the same (55).

Heraclitus observes correctly that we apply the predicates 'going to Thebes' and 'coming from Thebes' to a single subject; and he surely thinks he is providing us with a clear exemplification of (2).[36] **B 103 = 34 M** reads:

> Beginning and end on a circle are common (56).

One and the same point is describable both as the first point and as the last point of the circle's circumference. According to **B 59 = 32 M**:

> The path of the carding roller is straight and curved (57),

as it rolls over the wool. **B 15 = 50 M** is often read as an attack on popular mystery religions:

> If they did not make a procession to Dionysus and sing a hymn to the organs of shame, they would act most shamefully (58).

But I suspect that the phallic hymns are adduced primarily to illustrate the Unity of Opposites: they are reverent (for failure to sing them would be a shameful act); and they are also shameful (for they are paeans to the penis).[37]

The Unity of Opposites thus has twofold support: first, it is inferred from the Theory of Flux and thus has whatever support that Theory lays claim to; second, it rests upon a wide variety of observations, some of them direct instantiations of the Unity thesis, others requiring a small argumentative step to bring out their significance. Even at his most paradoxical, Heraclitus remained a rational thinker: his extraordinary thesis of Unity, no less than his traditional monism, was based on evidence and arguments.

(e) *Sage Heraclitus?*

Empirical observation and bold generalization led Heraclitus to the Theory of Flux: that all things constantly change is a well confirmed scientific hypothesis. Change is between opposites; and the logic of change seemed to draw Heraclitus irresistibly to the Unity of

Opposites: opposites are coinstantiated. Common observation, supported by a further application of the fallacy of the dropped qualification, confirmed the thesis of Unity. The commonplaces of Milesian science gave reason for accepting a Monism: everything was made from, and is made of, one stuff. The continuous cosmic changes provide a grand illustration of Flux; and the inference from Flux to Unity permits the Aristotelian conclusion that fire is the material substrate of the universe.

Of the three interlocking theories which constitute Heraclitus' account of nature, monism is the least important. The Theory of Flux is a bold development of earlier speculation. The Unity of Opposites is an extraordinary innovation. Monism on the Milesian model is tacked on to these theories to show how Heraclitus can provide any enlightenment which his predecessors could provide, and provide it on a sounder and deeper basis. At all events, it is Flux and Unity which will seem most original and most shocking to modern readers.

And yet both these theories seem idiotic in themselves, and rest upon idiotic arguments; they are not worth a moment's attention from a rational man. Large objections are immediately to hand, and appear to destroy the whole Heraclitean account with ease and finality.

Flux and Unity are open to obvious empirical objections. Some things, no doubt, are in a state of Flux; and some things, perhaps, own perplexingly contrary properties; yet it is evident to the most cursory glance that not all things are in a state of Flux, and that not all things are bound to contrariety: a few careless observations have encouraged Heraclitus to propound a theory which our whole waking life constantly disproves.

Heraclitus anticipated this elementary objection:

Nature likes to hide itself (**59: B 123 = 8 M**).

The unevident connexion is stronger than the evident (**60: B 54 = 9 M**).

He illustrated his claim by a little parable:

Men are deceived with regard to knowledge of what is evident, like Homer who was the wisest of all the Greeks. For he was deceived by some boys who were killing lice and said: 'What we saw and caught, we are leaving behind, what we neither saw nor caught, we are taking with us' (**61: B 56 = 21 M**).

The parable and the Heraclitean claim supply two important glosses on the Theory of Flux and the Unity of Opposites.

First, Heraclitus maintains that scientific truths are not all patent to casual observation: the truth is often hidden, and the fact that common experience suggests stability and coherence rather than flux and contrariety indicates not the falsity of Heraclitus' account but the superficiality of common experience. According to Aristotle, 'some say that it is not the case that some of the things that exist are changing and others not, but that everything always changes although this escapes our perception' (*Phys* 253b9–11). Aristotle does not name Heraclitus; but it seems certain that he had Heraclitus in mind.

The second point embellishes the first. Heraclitus is interested in the 'nature' or *phusis* of things: this emerges both from 59 and also from the various examples of Flux and Unity which have survived; and it was plainly stated at the very beginning of Heraclitus' work: he is concerned to 'divide up each thing in accordance with its nature, and say how it is' (33). But what is a thing's 'nature'? According to an ancient doctrine, things—or rather sorts of thing—have a 'real essence'. Locke explains the notion thus: 'By this *real Essence*, I mean, that real constitution of any Thing, which is the foundation of all those Properties, that are combined in, and are constantly found to coexist with the *nominal Essence* [i.e., with the complex *idea* the word stands for]; that particular constitution, which every Thing has within itself, without any relation to any thing without it' (*Essay* III. vi. 6). The real essence of a sort is given by its fundamental constitution, by those features or that structure which explains the remaining properties of items of the sort and without which nothing is an item of that sort.

Real essences have been much derided, but to my mind derision is wrong-headed: one main task of many sciences is to isolate the fundamental structure or features of a thing or stuff (its atomic or its genetic structure) in order to explain its remaining powers and qualities. The theory of real essence is an attempt to describe that scientific enterprise; and Heraclitus' 'nature', I suggest, is an attempt to get at real essence: a thing's 'nature' determines 'how it is'; it is customarily 'hidden' and its discovery requires a penetrating mind; it is 'stronger' than any superficial properties in that it explains and supports those properties.

Heraclitus is thus offering a large scientific theory, comparable to the atomist hypothesis: Flux and Opposition are features in the nature of every sort of thing; they are essential to it and explanatory of its properties. The theory is in principle falsifiable, as atomism is; but it is not refuted by everyday observation, as atomism is not.

This conclusion is, I hope, enough to raise Heraclitus from the ranks of the mystery-mongers and to place him among the great philosopher-scientists; and that is what makes his account the completion and perfection of Milesian science. Flux and the Unity of Opposites are twin horses, bred and nourished on wholesome empirical food, possessed of a deep strength, and harnessed to the old monistic chariot which Heraclitus inherited from his predecessors.

So much for the objection that Heraclitus' theories are empirically absurd. A second objection is this: the theories of Flux and Unity are criminally vague; and the most charitable attitude to real essences hardly raises them to precise hypotheses. I doubt if any precise account will cohere with all the fragments; and to that extent the objection succeeds. Nevertheless, I am inclined to think that the following sketch is both moderately clear and roughly Heraclitean. 'All identifiable things have an identifiable constitutive stuff or amalgam of stuffs: rivers are made of water; fields, of earth; men, of flesh and blood; the universe itself, of earth, water and fire. These stuffs form the 'nature' of what they constitute, in that all the powers and properties of the things—'how the things are'—are determined by their stuffs. Rivers support boats because of the properties of water; the fertility of a field depends on its constitutive earth; the barley-drink revivifies in virtue of its ingredients; men owe the powers and capacities they exhibit to their fleshy make-up. (Ultimately, no doubt, all those properties will be shown to depend upon the intrinsic character of the ultimate constituent of the world, fire.) Observation supports the hypothesis that those constituent stuffs are in a constant flux: they are always changing in one respect or another. And those changes are no chance contingencies. They are essential to the being of all that the stuffs constitute; for those things would cease to exist, and hence to exercise any of their powers, if their natures ceased to change: there is no river if the waters cease to flow; the barley-drink is destroyed as soon as its parts settle; men die when their temperature and humidity becomes constant and they are no longer being nourished; the world itself will fall apart if the cycle of stuffs ever ceases. The changes involved are of different sorts—qualitative, quantitative and locomotive. (No doubt some natures undergo more than one change of more than one sort.) But they all qualify as changes in virtue of one common feature: if a changes between t_1 and t_2, then there is a pair of contrary predicates ϕ and ϕ' such that a is ϕ at t_1 and a is ϕ' at t_2. From this feature of Flux a simple inference leads us to the Unity of Opposites, a thesis which in any case concords happily with experience.'

If such considerations give Heraclitus' theories a somewhat sharper definition, they are only the better prepared to be struck down by the third objection. That objection alleges logical inconsistency: Heraclitus' central contention, the Unity thesis, is inconsistent; it flagrantly violates the Law of Contradiction; hence it is false, necessarily false, and false in a trivial and tedious fashion. It is empty to praise for his scientific insight a thinker whose main and innovatory tenet is a straightforward self-contradiction.

It will not do to admit the charge and try to brazen it out.

> Do I contradict myself?
> Very well then, I contradict myself.
> (I am large, I contain multitudes.)

No one is large enough for that: contradiction implies falsity; and that is that.

It will not do to suggest that 'we need not expect Heraclitus' thought to be by our standards completely logical and self-consistent',[38] and to intimate that by Heraclitean logic the Unity thesis is consistent. The standards of logic are not 'our' standards: they are the eternal standards of truth; and any statement which fails by those standards fails to be true whether its utterer spoke in knowledge or in ignorance of the standard he flouted.

It will not do to observe that Heraclitus never *clearly* violates the Law of Contradiction, and to insinuate that an obscurely stated inconsistency is only a peccadillo. On the contrary, that suggestion adds the vice of obscurity to the sin of inconsistency, and doubles the offence.

It will not do to argue that, as Heraclitus never used the term 'opposites', so he never regarded his thesis as concerned with opposites at all. The 'opposites' Heraclitus adverts to are patently contrary, and patently thought of as such; and the metaphors of war and strife which sound in the fragments are Heraclitus' way of speaking of opposition.

It will not do, finally, to interpret the Unity thesis as saying that *apparent* opposites are not in reality opposed. Some of Heraclitus' examples admittedly adduce properties whose opposition is only apparent; but others adduce plain contraries. And, again, Heraclitus clearly means to shock us: his warfare and strife are not shadows thrown onto the world by the incapacity of the common mind to discern false from true opposition. War and strife—contrariety and opposition—are essential features of reality.

How, then, can we explain Heraclitus' adoption of a self-contradictory thesis? We might begin by asking why Aristotle found his thesis trivially inconsistent. The answer is straightforward: if ϕ and ϕ' are contrary predicates, then '$\phi'x$' entails 'not-ϕx'; the entailment is a necessary (though not a sufficient) condition of contrariety—the logical notion of a contrary predicate is defined by way of the entailment. Given the entailment, 'ϕx & $\phi' x$' immediately and evidently yields the explicit contradiction 'ϕx & not-ϕx', and the absurdity of Heraclitus' view is patent.

Now this logical notion of contrariety was certainly not available to Heraclitus: it is improbable that he even had a word for contrariety as such,[39] let alone excogitated an Aristotelian analysis of the concept. Rather, he was working with a fairly loose, intuitive notion of what 'opposites' were; he would, I imagine, have presented a list, not a definition, if asked to explain himself: wet, dry; up, down; straight, crooked; sweet, sour; hot, cold; male, female; and so on. The list would no doubt be long, and its items would, to our eyes, be logically diverse: some pairs seem logical contraries; some express physically incompatible properties; some are elliptically expressed relations between which no true incompatibility exists.

Heraclitus intended his list to present opposing pairs: each pair was locked in internecine strife, and their harmonious compresence is not a thing to be expected. Yet his list allowed him to see the opposition as, so to speak, a contingent one: some of the pairs in the list plainly do coexist, despite their opposition (they are not genuinely incompatible, as we should say); and that suggests that all the pairs may be found together. Moreover, the lack of an explicit definition of opposition meant that Aristotle's easy inference was never brought to Heraclitus' notice. The examples Heraclitus adduces do not shout incompatibility with a unanimous tongue; the metaphors of war and strife do not lead at once to thoughts of affirmation and contrary negation: with such resources, Heraclitus might well have failed to see the necessary falsity of his position. What is in fact an impossibility had in his eyes the status of a paradox; and the paradoxical is often true.

Some may wonder whether Heraclitus' thesis is properly denominated a Unity of Opposites if he had no clear, Aristotelian, notion of contrariety. There is something in this thought; but it cannot bring Heraclitus an eleventh hour reprieve. For if we refuse to introduce the notion of contrariety into our elucidation of Heraclitus, we leave him without a thesis at all. The Aristotelian notion is simply a precise formulation of the intuitive conception with which Heraclitus was working. Deny him the notion, and he has no thesis to propound; make the notion explicit, and his thesis lapses into inconsistency.

Heraclitus was indubitably a paradoxographer; and his account of the world is fundamentally inconsistent. That, however, does not make him a mystical figure, standing aloof from the young rationalism of Miletus; nor, I submit, does it make him a silly or a shallow philosopher. Evidence and argument are no strangers to the surviving fragments, and their presence places Heraclitus firmly in the Ionian tradition. And he offered a philosophy of science which exhibits an admirable articulation, and foreshadows one of the most influential of Aristotle's doctrines, the doctrine of real essence. A certain conceptual inadequacy doomed his fine system to the fires of contradiction; but that is a fate which more than one great metaphysician has suffered.

V

The Divine Philosophy of Xenophanes

(a) *A wandering minstrel*

Xenophanes of Colophon was a four-square man, remarkable for the breadth of his interests, the depth of his thought, and the length of his life. He was a poet and satirist of note, an erudite and versatile polymath, and a considerable philosopher. The range of his accomplishments, and his unflinching devotion to the gods of reason, make him a paradigm of the Presocratic genius.

His longevity deserves a paragraph. By his own account a nonagenarian (**21 B 8**), he may have achieved a century (Censorinus, **A 7**). In all probability his life fell within the period from 580 to 470 and thus overlapped with the life-spans of most of the major Presocratic thinkers. He travelled widely; he was a celebrated and controversial figure in his life-time; he was familiar with, and often highly critical of, the thoughts of his predecessors and contemporaries (**B 7**; **B 19**; Diogenes Laertius, IX. 18 = **A 1**; Plutarch, *apud* Proclus, **A 20**); and it can hardly be doubted that his opinions influenced and were influenced by those of his peers. Yet those influences cannot be charted with any certainty, and that for a simple reason: with two uninteresting exceptions (**B 2**; **B 8**), we do not know at what point in his life Xenophanes formulated or made public his views. If his birth and his death can be dated with modest precision, his intellectual biography is a tract of darkness some eighty years across.

What holds of Xenophanes holds of the other Presocratics: they did not usually date their works, and they left behind them no *Nachlass* from which busy scholars might reconstruct their spiritual careers; even where the gross, corporeal chronology of their births and deaths is discoverable, the finer dating of their mental histories remains perfectly unknown.¹ Scholars have combed the surviving fragments for internal evidence of influence and reaction; in a few cases they have produced results commanding general assent; more often the assessment of one scholar nicely balances the contradictory assessment of another. But even where some influence is indubitable, the direction of influence can hardly be discovered in the absence of a detailed external chronology. Thus Xenophanes is often thought to have influenced Parmenides; but the opposite influence is chronologically possible, and has been staunchly maintained. Again, the relation between Parmenides and Heraclitus is as controversial as it is obscure. And later it will emerge that the mutual connexions between the later Eleatics (Zeno and Melissus) and the early neo-Ionians (Empedocles and Anaxagoras) are beyond our grasp.

Any account of Presocratic thought will impose some overall pattern on the material; and at a very high level of abstraction some pattern is indeed discernible. Details, however, escape us; and detail is the stuff of history.

Xenophanes' long life produced a large *oeuvre*. The extent of his enquiries is unquestionable: Heraclitus marked, and scorned, his polymathy (**A 3** = **22 B 40**); and the documents testify to a vast knowledge. There is evidence for a detailed cosmology on the Milesian model (e.g., **B 17–33**; pseudo-Plutarch, **A 32**; Hippolytus, **A 33**);[2] there are social and political comments which might be dignified into a political theory (e.g., **B 2–3**); there is contemporary history (Diogenes Laertius, IX.21 = **A 1**); and there are substantial pieces of a more strictly philosophical nature.

Of this *oeuvre* some forty-odd fragments are all that survives;[3] and the most considerable of these have a literary rather than a philosophical interest. Moreover, the origin of the scientific and philosophical remnants is disputed. Some scholars imagine a fairly formal treatise *Concerning Nature*; others suppose a systematic set of beliefs expressed piecemeal in a variety of poems; the majority view maintains that 'Xenophanes expressed such scientific opinions as he had incidentally in his satires', and had no systematic thoughts to present—that intellectually he was a thing of shreds and patches.[4]

The majority view has no intrinsic merits and is supported by no ancient testimony. Against it there stands the doxography, which recognizes Xenophanes as a well-rounded thinker, and which thrice refers to a work *Concerning Nature*. Furthermore, one fragment (**B 43**, which I shall analyse in a later chapter) appears to have the form of a prologue, or to come from a poem or a passage introducing Xenophanes' philosophical reflexions. In it Xenophanes mentions 'the gods and everything about which I speak': I shall argue later that the phrase refers to theology and natural philosophy; and I believe that **B 34** implies the existence, if not of a poem *Concerning Nature*, at least of a fairly systematic and comprehensive parcel of scientific and philosophical verses. If that is so, then Xenophanes was a professional and self-conscious thinker, and not a poet and satirist whose polemical whims occasionally led him to paddle in philosophical ponds.

As a philosopher, Xenophanes has not received a universally appreciative audience: he is dismissed as unoriginal, 'a poet and rhapsode who has become a figure in the history of Greek philosophy by mistake'.[5] There is, it is true, an ancient error about Xenophanes' philosophical achievement: in the *Sophist* (242DE = **A 29**) Plato, jesting, makes Xenophanes the first Eleatic monist; Aristotle repeated the point (*Met* 986b21 = **A 30**); Theophrastus felt obliged to refer to it; and the doxographers slavishly follow their master (Cicero, **A 34**; pseudo-Galen, **A 35**).[6] The doxographical tradition has no value here; and Xenophanes cannot qualify as a philosopher by pretensions to a monistic ontology. There are, however, other opinions which are securely attributed to Xenophanes on the basis of his own words and which, in my opinion at least, indicate a brilliant, original and sophisticated talent. Those opinions concern epistemology and natural theology. I shall reserve Xenophanes' remarks on the nature and extent of human knowledge for a later chapter; here I deal with his theology.

(b) *Summa theologiae*

At a symposium, Xenophanes says, 'first of all, pious men should hymn the god with decent stories and pure words' (**B 1**, 13–14). It is as a theologian that Xenophanes is most celebrated; for even if it is true, in general, that 'when one reads the Presocratics with an open mind and sensitive ear, one cannot help being struck by the religious note in much of what they say',[7] nevertheless, in the majority of Presocratic writings the note forms part of the harmony: in Xenophanes alone is it thematic.

Xenophanes was, as I have said, an accomplished satirist; and many of his divine *dicta* are negative and polemical in form. Most scholars deny him a systematic theology, and we may readily concede that Xenophanes was no Aquinas, his writings no formal *Summa*. For all that, the various theological sayings which have come down to us can be fitted into a coherent and impressive whole.

I start by listing the divine dogmas whose ascription to Xenophanes

is secured by actual fragments of his poems. They are seven in number:
(1) God is motionless.
(2) God is ungenerated.
(3) 'There is one god, greatest among gods and men.'
(4) God is not anthropomorphic.
(5) God thinks and perceives 'as a whole'.
(6) God moves things by the power of his mind.
(7) God is morally perfect.

If we have in (1)–(7) the bones of a theology, is it a natural or a revealed theology? According to Nietzsche, Xenophanes was merely 'a religious mystic'; and modern scholarship concurs: '... in Xenophanes we find a new motif, which is the actual source of his theology. It is nothing that rests on logical proof, nor is it really philosophical at all, but springs from an immediate sense of awe at the sublimity of the Divine.' In Xenophanes a 'mystical intuition' replaces the 'pure speculation' of his Ionian predecessors.[8] If that is true, then Xenophanes is the progenitor of that pestilential tribe of theological irrationalists, whose loudest member is Martin Luther and whose recent aspirations to philosophical respectability have been encouraged from the grave by the palsied shade of the late Wittgenstein. Must Xenophanes really incur such profound and posthumous guilt?

There is, I think, no evidence in the fragments to support a mystical or irrational interpretation of Xenophanes' theology: there is no appeal to sublime intuition, no descent to mere enthusiasm. And there is evidence that tells in the opposite direction.

The immobility of God, dogma (1), is thus stated in **B 26**:

> Always he remains in the same state, in no way changing;
> Nor is it fitting for him to go now here now there (62).

For the moment I ignore the first line of the couplet. The second line both states and justifies (1); the justification is conveyed by the word 'fitting (*epiprepei*)'. Some scholars take the notion of what is 'fitting' to be an aesthetic one: locomotive gods are not pretty, hence god does not move. It is incredible that any thinker should have advanced such a fatuous piece of reasoning. Fortunately, the word 'fitting' need not be held to a strictly aesthetic sense; it is readily interpreted in a logical fashion: the phrase 'it is not fitting' is Xenophanes' archaic and poetical version of 'it is not logically possible'. It does not 'fit' the essential nature of god, or our concept of what it is to be divine, to imagine that divinities locomote: that is to say, 'God moves' is self-contradictory. That interpretation does not, I think, strain the Greek; and it will turn out to be consonant with the general tenor of Xenophanes' theological reasoning.

The logical aspect of Xenophanes' theology is further exhibited by dogma (2), divine ungenerability.[9] Here the fragments fail us; **B 14** reads:

> Mortals opine that gods are born,
> And have their clothes and voice and form (63).

We may safely infer (2) from **63**; but for argument we must apply to the doxography. And in fact we are offered three reasonings.

The first argument is found in Aristotle:

> Xenophanes used to say that 'those who assert that the gods are born are as impious as those who say that they die', for in both cases it follows that the gods at some time fail to exist (**64**: *Rhet* 1399b6–9 = **A 12**).

Gods are essentially sempiternal (cf. Cicero, **A 34**): even in Homer they are 'the gods who always exist' (*theoi aei eontes*: e.g., *Iliad* I. 290). Everyone recognizes that the gods cannot therefore die; yet the theogonies nonchalantly tell of divine births.[10] Xenophanes points out that birth and death are analogous in that each entails a denial of sempiternity: a consistent Homer or a clear-eyed theist will reject divine generation for precisely the same reason for which he rejects divine destruction.

The argument is pointed but not profound: perhaps there is an asymmetry between birth and death; perhaps divine death is ruled out not because it conflicts with sempiternity, but because it implies that something can get the better of the gods and force them out of existence. Thus it is divine power which precludes divine death; and divine power does not similarly preclude divine birth.

That objection is in effect answered by the second and third arguments for (2) which our sources ascribe to Xenophanes. Of the three relevant doxographical reports—in Simplicius, in pseudo-Plutarch, and in the pseudo-Aristotelian treatise *de Melisso, Xenophane, Gorgia* (**A 31**; **A 32**; **A 28**)[11]—the fullest is the last:

> And he says that it is impossible, if anything exists, for it to have come into being—stating this in the case of god. For it is necessary that what has come into being should have come into being either from like or from unlike. But neither is possible; for it is not suitable (*prosēkein*) that like should be sired by like rather than sire it (for things that are equal have all their properties the same and in similar fashion as one another); nor that what is unlike

should come into being from unlike (for if the stronger came into being from the weaker, or the greater from the less, or the better from the worse—or the reverse: the worse from the better—what is would come into being from what is not, which is impossible) (**65**: 977a14–22 = **A 28**).

This report is contaminated by later Eleatic logic; yet that it contains a Xenophanean core is proved not only by certain turns of phrase but also by a striking fragment of Epicharmus.

Epicharmus was a Sicilian playwright, active at the beginning of the fifth century BC. The surviving fragments of his works exhibit an interest, satirical but not superficial, in the philosophical issues of his day; in particular, Epicharmus knew Xenophanes' poems, and parodied them more than once.[12] Fate has preserved a fragment in dialogue form on the birth of the gods; it is evidently a pastiche of Xenophanes:

> —But the gods were always about and never off the scene; and they are always about in the same way and always with the same habits.
> —But Chaos is said to have been first born of the gods.
> —How so? if he didn't have anything from which or to which he could be the first to come?
> —Then nothing came first?
> —No—and nothing second either of the things we're now talking about; but they always existed (**66: 23 B 1**).

In this fragment Epicharmus is tilting at Hesiod (*Theogony* 116–17); but the thought it contains was influential (it drove Epicurus to philosophy: Sextus, *adv Math* X.18); and from it and **65** we can construct two Xenophanean arguments for (2). The nerve of each argument is the claim that a generated god must have something to 'come from'. (I ignore the jocular suggestion in Epicharmus that a generated god must also have something to 'come to'). More generally:

(8) If a comes into being, then for some x a comes into being from x.

I have noted, in another connexion, the ambiguity of the phrase 'from x' (above, pp. 39–40). How is it to be glossed in (8)? Epicharmus uses the colourless verb *gignesthai* for 'come into being'; in the *MXG* the word *teknoun*, 'to sire', is employed: it is tempting to suppose that this represents Xenophanes' original thought. If that is so, then 'come into being' in (8) means 'be born'; and (8) states the necessary truth that everything that is born has a parent. But, so construed, (8) supports not (2) but the weaker assertion that gods are not *born*: may not a god come into being without being born? may not divine generation be spontaneous generation? Perhaps Xenophanes would have replied that coming into being cannot be simply inexplicable: a divine generation, like any other, requires a moving cause; and what could a cause of divine generation be but a parent or quasi-parent? Thus divine generation is either divine birth or something logically equivalent to divine birth; and there is no room to drive a wedge between the generation in (8) and the generation in (2).

However that may be, we still have to link (8) to (2). Epicharmus suggests the following supplementary premiss:
(9) If a comes into being from b, then b existed before a existed.
That is surely a tautology; and (2) follows from (8) and (9), in conjunction with:
(10) If a is a god, then nothing existed before a existed.
Now if gods are essentially creative beings, and if nothing exists except as a result of divine creativity, then (10) suggests itself. But the suggestion is hasty: for all that has been said so far, gods may be created, provided that their creators are themselves divine. And the traditional theogonies do, of course, give generated gods divine parents. Thus (10) must be weakened to:
(10*) If a is a god, then if b exists before a, b is a god.
I now anticipate myself and call upon Xenophanes' dogma (3), which I shall argue is a statement of monotheism: if there is at most one god, and (10*) is true, then (10) is true too. Thus by tacitly assuming (3), Xenophanes may properly argue from (10), (9), and (8) to (2). That exegesis is undeniably contorted; yet I can see no other way of extracting a decent argument from Epicharmus.

The *MXG* presents a different set of considerations. I shall here draw from the text what I think is its Xenophanean kernel, though I confess that my account has a somewhat arbitrary air. The crucial premiss is:
(11) If a comes into being from b, then b is at least as great as a.
What might commend (11) to Xenophanes? There is a general theory of causation which asserts that 'There is as much reality in the cause as in the effect'. We tend to associate the theory with the name of Descartes; but in fact it is much older. Indeed in the next chapter I shall suggest that the Synonymy Principle, as I call it, has a Presocratic origin (below, p. 119); and it is, I think, possible that Xenophanes implicitly rested premiss (11) upon it: if b gives greatness to a, then b must itself possess greatness. But a less general argument suggests itself: if I am able to make a powerful product, then I must surely have as much power as that product possesses; for a product, which owes its power to its producer, can hardly have more power than that

producer. Indeed, the power enjoyed by my products is, in a sense, enjoyed by me; for the labour exerted by the products of my labour is itself, at one remove, my labour. The argument will not, and should not, convince the thoughtful reader; but it may suffice to give an air of plausibility to (11).

Now I shall shortly argue that Xenophanes subscribed explicitly to:
(12) If a is a god, then a is greater than anything else.
From (8), (11) and (12) the conclusion (2) follows deductively.

Thus we have three *a priori* arguments for (2), one from Aristotle, one from Epicharmus, and one from the *MXG*, the two latter arguments using a common premiss. Did Xenophanes use any or all of these arguments? It would be gratuitously sceptical to deny all three arguments to Xenophanes; and since I can see no good reason for singling out any one of them as peculiarly Xenophanean, I conclude that all originate with him.

I turn now to the most notorious, and the most interesting, of Xenophanes' theological tenets: monotheism. The doxographical tradition generally makes Xenophanes a monotheist (e.g., *MXG*, **A 28**; Simplicius, **A 31**; Hippolytus, **A 33**; Cicero, **A 34**; pseudo-Galen, **A 35**; but pseudo-Plutarch, **A 32**, implies polytheism). Most modern scholars have followed the doxographers, finding monotheistic hints in various fragments (especially **B 24–6**), and an explicit assertion in the first line of **B 23**, of which the orthodox translation reads:

There is one god, greatest among gods and men (67).

Some, however, are unhappy with this; and they attack the monotheistic stronghold itself: How, they ask, can **B 23** state monotheism in its first two words (*heis theos*), when the very next phrase ('greatest *among gods*': *en . . . theoisi*) is unequivocally polytheistic? It is customary to answer this by saying that the phrase 'gods and men' is a 'polar expression', and that such expressions may be used in Greek even when one pole, in this case the divine one, is wholly inapposite. Thus, 'greatest among gods and men' means no more than 'greatest of all'; and the phrase carries no polytheistic baggage.[13] But that suggestion leaves Xenophanes with a verse that is inept, to say the least; and if that is the best that can be done for him on the standard translation, then there is much to be said for a different translation.

The Greek has been thought to allow the following version: 'The one greatest god among gods and men is . . .'. This translation turns Xenophanes into a polytheist, and a polytheist of the traditional Homeric type: there is a hierarchy of divinities ruled by a greatest god, as the Homeric Zeus rules, with uncertain sway, the Olympian pantheon.[14] The suggestion restores consistency to the first line of **B 23**: no monotheistic claim opposes the plural *en . . . theoisi*. But consistency is purchased at a high price: the translation is strained (Xenophanes' Greek-speaking admirers and detractors never conceived of it); it flouts the doxography; it is obliged to ignore the monotheistic hints of the other fragments; and it replaces a polemical thesis by a traditional platitude.

Perhaps further reflexion will allow us to keep the orthodox translation without falling into elementary inconsistency. Let us approach the question by asking what argument Xenophanes could have advanced in favour of monotheism. Again, the fragments give no help, and we are forced back upon the doxography. First, the *MXG*:

> And if god is most powerful of all, he [sc. Xenophanes] says that it is suitable (*prosêkein*) for him to be unique. For if there were two or more, he would no longer be most powerful and best of all. For each of the several, being a god, would equally be such. For this is what a god and a god's capacity is—to have power and not to be in someone's power (*kratein alla mê krateisthai*), and to be most powerful of all. Hence, in so far as he is not more powerful, to that extent he is not a god (**68**: 977a24–9 = **A 28**).

Second, Simplicius:

> . . . [Xenophanes] proves that [god] is unique from his being most powerful of all; for if there were several, he says, having power would necessarily belong to them all alike; but god is what is most powerful of all and best (**69: A 31**).

Third, pseudo-Plutarch:

> And about the gods he says that there is no leadership among them; for it is not holy for any of the gods to have a master (*despozesthai*), and none of them stands in need (*epideisthai*) of anything at all (**70: A 32**).

The three reports presumably go back to Theophrastus. A happy chance allows us to trace their argument into the fifth century: in his *Hercules Furens* Euripides has Theseus say:

> But *I* do not believe that the gods love beds
> which right denies them, and that they manacle one another
> I have never credited, nor shall I be persuaded;
> nor that one is by nature master (*despotês*) *of another*.

> For god—if he is genuinely a god—needs (*deitai*)
> nothing: these are the wretched tales of poets (71: 1341–6 = **C 1**)[15]

The last three lines of this passage contain our argument: their context is Xenophanean, and the verbal coincidences between Euripides and pseudo-Plutarch make it probable that the *Hercules* is here paraphrasing a poem of Xenophanes.

The four passages I have just quoted differ in two minor ways and in one major. First, pseudo-Plutarch grounds god's mastery or power on holiness ('for it is not holy'), while Simplicius and the *MXG* make mastery a conceptual requirement of divinity ('but god is . . .'; 'for that is what a god is. . . .'). My prejudice in favour of the latter reading is supported by Euripides ('if he is genuinely a god'[16]). Second, pseudo-Plutarch conjoins divine mastery with divine independence: gods lack nothing; and in Euripides, independence grounds god's mastery. I shall soon return to divine independence; but it is not immediately relevant to the present argument, and the *MXG* and Simplicius have not ignored anything of importance in their presentation of the matter.

The major difference between our reports concerns the premiss expressing divine mastery. In pseudo-Plutarch and in Euripides we find something that can be paraphrased by:
(13) If a is a god, then nothing is greater than a.
(Note, first, that I treat power and mastery as identical, using the general notion of greatness; and second, that in Euripides' version the consequent of (13) reads: '. . . then no god is greater than a'. But since it goes without saying that no non-god can be greater than a, (13) can be deployed without qualms.) In Simplicius and the *MXG*, on the other hand, we get not (13) but:
(14) If a is a god, then a is greater than everything else.

Now (13) and (14) are not equivalent: (14) entails (13), but (13) does not entail (14). Which premiss is to be preferred? The textual evidence inclines us to (13); for Euripides is our earliest and perhaps our most faithful source. (13) does not support monotheism: it is compatible with a plurality of potent divinities, each of which is at least as great as anything else in existence. And since pseudo-Plutarch does not present (13) as part of a monotheistic argument, we might conclude that Simplicius and the *MXG*, misrepresenting Xenophanes' premiss by (14), have falsely fathered on him an argument for a monotheism which he never recognized.

I am not content with that conclusion. If we reject (14), we must accept one of two positions: either Xenophanes asserted monotheism in **B 23**, but did not argue for it by way of (14); or else **B 23** is polytheistic. The latter position imports an inconsistency; for the only polytheism with which (13) is compatible is egalitarian, and the only polytheism with which **B 23** is compatible is hierarchical. The former position has Xenophanes assert a novel creed, come within an ace of arguing for it, and then rest content with (13). For these reasons, I prefer to believe that Xenophanes uttered (14). He may, I suppose, have uttered (13) as well (if pseudo-Plutarch is reporting a distinct argument from that in Simplicius and the *MXG*); but it is easier to believe that pseudo-Plutarch has misrepresented (14) by (13).

From (14) it is easy to infer:
(15) There is at most one god.
And this, together with the premiss that there *are* gods (a premiss to which I shall return) amounts to monotheism.

How, finally, is all that to be reconciled with the first line of **B 23**? In 67 that line was translated: 'There is one god, greatest among gods and men.' It is, I think, not implausible to see here a highly concise epitome of the argument I have just developed; for the line may be paraphrased: 'There is one god, since (by definition) a god is greater than anything else, whether god or man.' The paraphrase seems remote when the line is taken in isolation; but if we imagine **B 23** to have followed an exposition of the argument from (14), then I do not think that the paraphrase imposes an unbearable intellectual strain.

Xenophanes, I conclude, was a monotheist, as the long tradition has it; and he was an *a priori* monotheist: like later Christian theologians, he argued on purely logical grounds that there could not be a plurality of gods.

The next three dogmas, (4), (5) and (6), go together; for we may reasonably take (5) and (6) as partial explanations of (4), which simply says, in general and negative terms, that god is

> not at all like mortals in form or even in thought (72: **B 23**.2).

Some have found an argument for (4) in Xenophanes' assertion that worshippers make their gods in their own image: the dark and hook-nosed Ethiopians, he observes, pray to dark and hook-nosed gods: the gods of the auburn, blue-eyed Thracians are blue-eyed redheads (cf. **B 16**: see below, p. 142). More caustically:

> If cows and horses or lions had hands,
>   or could draw with their hands and make the things which men can,
> then horses would draw pictures of gods like horses,
> and cows like cows, and they would make bodies

in just the form which each of them has itself
(73: B 15; cf. Aristotle, *Pol* 1252b24–7)

The actual practice of human worshippers and the hypothetical practice of animal statuaries show that ordinary beliefs about the gods are entirely determined by the nature of the believer; hence, Xenophanes implies, those beliefs cannot pretend to the status of knowledge. I shall consider this splendid argument when I turn to Xenophanes' epistemology: here I content myself with the elementary point that **73** and **B 16** do not license a conclusion to (4): if the common belief in the anthropomorphic nature of god does not amount to knowledge, it does not follow that the belief is mistaken, and that the gods in fact are non-anthropomorphic; for the belief, irrational and ill-based though it is, may yet accidentally enshrine the truth.

If we require an argument for (4) we may better look to (5) and (6). Doctrine (5) comes from **B 24**:

He sees as a whole, he thinks as a whole, and he hears as a whole (74).[17]

That does not imply, as commentators from Clement onward have asserted, that god is incorporeal, nor even that he perceives without the use of sensory organs; it need mean no more than that any divine organs are, so to speak, spread evenly over the divine body: god is, as Hippolytus says, 'perceptive in all his parts' (**A 33**; cf. *MXG* 977a37 = **A 28**; Simplicius, **A 31**). Why should that be so? It is probable that Xenophanean gods were omniscient: direct evidence is flimsy (see **B 18**; **B 36**; Arius Didymus, **A 24**), but divine omniscience is both traditional (e.g., *Iliad* II.485; *Odyssey* IV. 379, 468), and a plausible corollary of divine mastery.[18] If god is omniscient, his organs of perception can hardly be localized: he needs eyes in the back of his head.

Dogma (6) comes from **B 25**:

Without effort, by the will of his mind he shakes everything (75).

We may imagine that Xenophanes moved readily enough to (6) from (1) and the fundamental assertion of god's mastery.

(5) and (6) are enough to prove (4): since god's sensory organs are not localized, he is not like mortals 'in form'; since he can move things 'by the will of his mind', he is not like mortals 'in thought'.

Finally, we have god's moral perfection. That Xenophanes upheld (7) is an inference from **B 11**:

> Homer and Hesiod ascribed to the gods everything
> that brings shame and reprobation among men—
> theft, and adultery, and mutual deception (76: cf. **B 12**).

Plainly, Xenophanes is appalled by the brazen assertion of divine peccation; and it is, I think, quite reasonable to infer that he himself was devoted to divine decency. The texts offer no explicit statement of (7); but Simplicius and the *MXG* say that god is essentially 'best'.[19]

Xenophanes' theology is a rational construction, relying on logic and not on mystical intuition: he has earned the title of natural theologian. It remains to be shown that a simple systematic pattern can be discovered in, or imposed upon, his thoughts.

Suppose, with Euripides, that god lacks nothing, or is perfect, and lay this down as an axiom of theology.[20] The axiom first yields the two pivotal theorems found in the *MXG* and Simplicius: god is all powerful, and god is all good. The second pivotal theorem amounts to (7). The first pivotal theorem yields uniqueness (3), ungenerability (2), and the attribute of being creator and sustainer of all things (6). Next, the axiom of perfection implies immutability (as line 1 of **62** perhaps states),[21] and hence motionlessness (1). Thus god's sustaining actions must be effected by the mere exercise of his will. Third, perfection implies omniscience; and this in turn requires a peculiar mode of perception (5). Given (5) and (6), we must deny anthropomorphism and assert (4).

I do not suggest that any Xenophanean poem set out a theology in that systematic fashion (though I am strongly tempted to think that Xenophanes' thoughts were arranged with a moderate degree of clarity and coherence in his mind). I do not suggest that the propositions I have discussed constitute the sum of Xenophanes' theology (I shall shortly mention two other candidates from the doxography). I do not suggest that Xenophanes' theology is a logically coherent system (for I doubt if any natural theology of this sophisticated kind is strictly coherent). But I do suggest that Xenophanes' theology is a remarkable achievement; and that its author managed to attain an astounding level of abstraction and rationality in a field where abstract thought frequently produces only high-sounding vacuity and reason rapidly gives place to ranting.

(c) *Theology and science*

Strictly speaking, Xenophanes' natural theology does not establish monotheism: *a priori* argument leads to the conclusion that there is at most one god; but it does not supply the further proposition that there is at least one god. Why, then, was Xenophanes a theist? On what grounds did he assert that there exist gods? In order to answer this question I shall digress briefly and discuss the evidence for early Ionian theological beliefs.

Aristotle distinguishes the *phusiologoi* who offer argument (*apodeixis*) in support of their opinions from the *theologoi* who simply tell stories or speak *muthikôs* (*Met* 1000a9–20). The decisive innovation of the *phusiologoi* was not that they abandoned the gods and eschewed theology, but that they replaced stories by arguments. Nonetheless, their general cast of mind may well seem not merely rationalistic but also hostile to any form of theism. Science and theology are, after all, natural antagonists: the Darwinian controversy was one unusually violent campaign in an extended war. Poseidon once stirred the sea and Zeus the air; but, taught by science, we no longer expect reference to those divinities in the meteorological forecasts.

> Shall gods be said to thump the clouds
> When clouds are cursed by thunder?
> Be said to weep when weather howls?
> Shall rainbows be their tunics' colours?

Well might Bishop Hermias mutter to himself that 'philosophy took its start from the fall of the angels'.

The antagonism between science and religion was as vivid in the Greek as in the English mind: Aristophanes' Socrates asserts, in the *Clouds*, that 'gods are not currency with us' (247), and he explains at length how physical science has ousted the old divinities from their seat (365–411). In about 430 BC Diopeithes persuaded the liberal democrats of Athens to impeach 'those who disbelieve in things divine or teach doctrines about the heavens (*ta metarsia*)' (Plutarch, *Pericles* 32). Anaxagoras is said to have been caught by this decree (see vol 2, p. 4); and the accusers of Socrates conjoined in their charge atheism and the study of astronomy (Plato, *Apology* 23D). The same conjunction is found in Euripides (fr. 913).

The matter is clearly stated by Plato:

> [Most people] think that those who apply themselves to astronomy and the other arts associated with it become atheists when they see that things can come about by necessity and not by an intelligent will concerning the accomplishment of good things (77: *Laws*, 967A).[22]

Science substitutes natural necessity for divine efficacy: the gods, put out of work, drop out of existence. Hippo, who mined the old Milesian veins in the mid-fifth century, was nicknamed 'the Atheist' 'because he assigned the cause of everything to nothing else beside water' (Philoponus, **38 A 8**; cf. Simplicius, **A 4**; Alexander, **A 9**). A later epigram puts it neatly (**B 2**):

> This tomb is Hippo's whom the fates, 'tis said,
> Made equal to the immortal gods—he's dead.

Atheism is not an invariable effect of science: on the contrary, Plato argues that a proper appreciation of astronomy leads men to god (*Laws* 886AE), and his argument has Presocratic antecedents (below, p. 99). Again, a naturalistic science may restrict the scope of divine activity without reducing it to nothing. Thus Xenophanes says of the rainbow:

> What men call Iris, that too is by nature a cloud,
> purple and red and green to see (**78: 21 B 32**).

and he said something similar of at least one other such phenomenon, namely St Elmo's fire 'which some men call the Dioscuri' (Aëtius, **A 39**). In strictness of logic, those sentences do not entail that meteorological occurrences have no spark of divinity in them; but it is plain that by talking of 'what men *call*' Iris or the Dioscuri Xenophanes implies that there is, in reality, nothing divine about those phenomena: rainbows have a purely natural explanation; divine interference is an unnecessary hypothesis. For all that, Xenophanes is no atheist.

Again, though you expel god with a pitchfork, *tamen usque recurret*: if nature or the stuff of the world usurped the function of god, why then nature or the stuff of the world was thereby shown to *be* god. Socrates, having declared an uncompromising atheism at line 247 of the *Clouds*, asserts eighty lines on that his clouds are gods (329); and natural divinities figure frequently in the ensuing scene.

In sum, the advance of science may affect theism in at least three ways: it may seem to abolish the gods entirely, replacing their agency by purely natural operations; it may appear to limit but not to annihilate their realm, taking some phenomena from their control and leaving others within it; and it may give a new twist to our conception of the divine nature, ousting anthropomorphism and introducing a more abstract notion of divinity. In a later chapter I shall return to this theme; here I ask what attitude the Milesians adopted to religion. The answer must rely on a doxography whose evidence is scant and brittle.

According to Diogenes, Thales said that

The universe is alive and full of spirits (**79**: I: 27 = **11 A 1**).

But this report derives ultimately from a conjecture of Aristotle's:

> And some say that a soul is mingled in the whole universe—which is perhaps why Thales thought that everything is full of gods (**80**: *An* 411a7 = **A 22**).

If Thales did say that everything is full of gods or spirits, he probably only adverted to his belief in the ubiquity of animation (above, p. 8): there is no good reason to make him a pantheist. Again, according to some, Thales said that 'god is the mind which makes everything from water' (Cicero, **A 23**; cf. Aëtius, **A 23**; pseudo-Galen, 35); according to others, water itself was Thales' god (Hippolytus, *Ref. Haer.* I. 3). Both reports are in all probability late guesses.

The evidence for Anaximander is not much better. A controversial tradition ascribes to him belief in innumerable worlds; and the doxographers make those worlds gods (Cicero; Aëtius, **12 A 17**; pseudo-Galen, 35). The reports are not probative. Text **16** speaks not of the worlds but of Anaximander's principle: 'And this [i.e. the unlimited body] is the divine; for it is immortal and deathless, as Anaximander and most of the *phusiologoi* say' (Aristotle, *Phys* 203b13-5 = **A 15**; above, p. 31). Aristotle does not explicitly say that Anaximander made 'the Unlimited' a divinity. Some scholars ascribe to Anaximander Aristotle's inference from immortality to divinity; others reject the ascription.[23] I see no way of deciding the issue.

Finally, in the case of Anaximenes there are a few weak and disparate reports. Cicero and Aëtius say that Anaximenes called his principle a god (**13 A 10**). Hippolytus' text contains the following absurdity:

> He said that the principle was unlimited air, from which what comes about and what came about and what will be and gods and divine things come to be, and the rest from the offspring of this (**81**: **A 7**; cf. Augustine, **A 10**).

Hippolytus is garbled; Cicero and Aëtius carry little weight.

It would not require a very ardent scepticism to conclude that the Milesians had no theology at all. If they were not atheists in the sense of positively denying the existence of any gods, at least they were negative atheists: they left no room in their systems for gods, and were not perturbed by the omission. And even if we are disposed to accept the little evidence we have, we shall scarcely imagine that the Milesians were profoundly interested in gods and the divine; at most they said, unemphatically and uninterestedly, that their principles—or some of the things produced therefrom—were gods or godlike.

The case of Heraclitus is quite different. His system was, as I have already argued, scientific in the Milesian manner; and it was also self-consciously deterministic (below, pp. 131–5). Yet Heraclitus had a developed, if idiosyncratic, theology. I shall not expound or examine the material here; for Heraclitus, so far as we know, had nothing of Xenophanes' subtle and complex interest in natural theology. But there are important points of contact both with Xenophanes and with the Milesians: Heraclitus was, probably, a monotheist; his god, like that of Xenophanes, in some fashion or other governed the world; and it is at least possible that this theology was in some sense pantheistic: God and Fire, are, if not identical, at least closely assimilated to one another.

Science and theism are uneasy bedfellows, and the Milesians may have sensed the fact; yet they did lie together, in the thought of Heraclitus and possibly in that of his Milesian models. And they lay together in the mind of Xenophanes. We might expect Xenophanes, the logical theologian, to have said something about the nature of their union. Did he do so?

The doxography adds two further propositions to the seven from which Xenophanes' theology was reconstructed: his god is said to have been spherical (Diogenes Laertius, IX.19 = **21 A 1**; *MXG* 977b1 = **A 28**; Simplicius, **A 31**; Hippolytus, **A 33**; Cicero, **A 34**; Sextus, **A 35**); and he is identified with the universe (Simplicius, **A 31**; Cicero, **A 34**). These reports are generally dismissed as late fabrications; but the dismissal is not indisputable.[24]

The sphericality of god is supposed to be due to an Eleatic interpretation of Xenophanes: his god foreshadowed the 'Eleatic One'; 'the One' was a sphere; hence Xenophanes' god must have been a sphere. A different story can be told. The *MXG* and Simplicius take the fact that god is 'similar in every respect (*homoion hapantêi*)', and infer sphericality from that. A fragment of Timon says that Xenophanes made his god 'equal in all ways (*ison hapantêi*)' (fr. 60 = **A 35**); and there is something to be said for the view that this phrase, like the rest of the fragment, echoes Xenophanes. For Timon was an avid admirer and imitator of Xenophanes; he had access to his poems; and he is unlikely to have been influenced by any disreputable Peripatetic inventor who insinuated *ison hapantêi* into the Xenophanean corpus in order to make his own account of Xenophanes' god seem more authentic. Thus Xenophanes may well have said that god is *ison hapantêi*, 'equal in all ways'; and the only reasonable interpretation of that phrase is the traditional one—his god was a sphere.

The identification of god and the universe derives from Aristotle. Xenophanes, he reports,

> looking at the whole heaven, says that the One is god (**82**: *Met* 986b24 = **A 30**).

A second fragment of Timon makes Xenophanes speak as follows:

> For wherever I turned my mind, everything was reduced to one and the same thing; and everything that exists, however it was twisted, always came to rest in one similar nature (**83**: fr. 59 = **A 35**).

Aristotle may be indulging his imagination; and Timon is writing satire, not history. Yet there is something to be said for the conjecture that Aristotle and Timon each allude to a lost line of Xenophanes; for both reporters, independently of one another, ascribe to him a view for which we find no evidence in the extant fragments. In some lost verses, I suggest, Xenophanes grounded his belief in god on a contemplation of the vast and ordered wonders of the heavens; and Aristotle and Timon each reflect those verses.

If there is anything in these two suggestions, we may add to our picture of Xenophanes the natural theologian: science and astronomical speculation led Xenophanes to god; the starry vastness convinced him not of a divinity but of their divinity, and he came to adopt a spherical pantheism. Observing the world in the light of Ionian science, and with a clear and unconventional reasoning power, Xenophanes remained a theist while rejecting the traditional forms of theism. Pure logic moulded his conception of god; science gave his conception substance and matter.

On this view, Xenophanes' thought assumes a sort of unity: science and theology are not dissociated elements in a jackdaw production; rather, science grounds theology, and theology frees science from the shadow of atheistical mechanism. The Milesians may have paid lip-service to the gods, and Heraclitus certainly paid heart-service: Xenophanes used his head; he attempted to construct a new Ionian theology that might be a fitting partner to the new Ionian science. It is clear that Xenophanes failed, and that his pantheism is hardly intelligible or consistent; but his project as a whole, and the execution of many of its parts, are sufficiently remarkable to prove that the initiator of natural theology was by no means its least practitioner.

VI

Pythagoras and the Soul

(a) *Ipse dixit*

The ancient historians of philosophy distinguished between the Ionian and the Italian tradition in Presocratic thought. Something of the early Ionian achievement has been sketched in the preceding chapters; and I turn now to Italy. Although the Italian 'school' was founded by *émigrés* from Ionia, it quickly took on a character of its own: if the Ionians followed up Thales' cosmological speculations, the Italians, I judge, had more sympathy for his inquiry into psychology and the nature of man. But that estimate of the scope of early Italian thought is controversial; and before I look more closely at the Italian doctrines, I must indulge in a brief historical excursus.

The prince of the Italian school was Pythagoras, who flourished in the last quarter of the sixth century, a younger contemporary of Anaximenes.[1] The Pythagorean doxography is of unrivalled richness. We are told more about Pythagoras than about any other Presocratic thinkers; and Pythagoras is one of the few Presocratics whose name has become a household—or at least a schoolroom—word.

Pythagoras himself had the wisdom to write nothing.[2] His numerous sectarians, eager to repair his omission, generously ascribed their own views to their master, or even wrote works in his name.[3] Those pious offerings portray an impressive figure: Pythagoras, discoverer and eponym of a celebrated theorem, was a brilliant mathematician; by applying his mathematical knowledge, he made great progress in astronomy and harmonics, those sister sirens who together compose the music of the spheres; and finally, seeing mathematics and number at the bottom of the master sciences, he concocted an elaborate physical and metaphysical system and propounded a formal, arithmological cosmogony.[4] Pythagoras was a Greek Newton; and if his intellectual bonnet hummed at times with an embarrassing swarm of mystico-religious bees, we might reflect that Sir Isaac Newton devoted the best years of his life to the interpretation of the number-symbolism of the book of *Revelations*.

If Greek science began in Miletus, it grew up in Italy under the tutelage of Pythagoras; and it was brought to maturity by Pythagoras' school, whose members, bound in fellowship by custom and ritual, secured the posthumous influence of their master's voice.

What are we to make of this pleasing picture of a Newtonian Pythagoras? It is, alas, mere fantasy: the shears of scholarship soon strip Pythagoras of his philosophical fleece.[5] The evidence for Pythagoras' life and achievements is late. In this he is not extraordinary; but he does suffer from two peculiar disadvantages: first, the survival of Pythagoreanism as a living force, with a strong sense of its own tradition, guaranteed anachronistic ascription of views and discoveries to the founder; second, our sources for the Newtonian Pythagoras are not the careful doxographers of the Lyceum, but later, feebler and more partial men, men of the stamp of Iamblichus and Porphyry.[6]

Scholarly huffing and puffing has blown this chaff from the heap of history; and it has left few grains on the floor. There were two important episodes in the early history of Pythagoreanism. Plato and his followers were to some extent influenced by Pythagorean speculations in science and metaphysics. Their interest led to a syncretism of Platonism and Pythagoreanism, in which a sophisticated Platonic metaphysics was grafted on to a more primitive stock. The syncretic view, which can be traced back to Plato's nephew Speusippus, dominated the later philosophical tradition, and came to be regarded as Pythagoreanism pure and simple. Pythagoras the systematic metaphysician does not antedate Speusippus. We know from Aristotle, who was unimpressed by the Platonizing account, a certain amount about Pythagorean doctrine before it was Platonized.

The other episode occurred about a century earlier: Iamblichus, here drawing on Aristotle, reports the existence of two rival sects of Pythagoreans, the *mathematici* and the *acousmatici*; the schism is tied to the name of Hippasus of Metapontum, and may thus be dated to the middle of the fifth century.[7] The *mathematici*, scientifically-minded Pythagoreans, naturally claimed to be the genuine followers of Pythagoras; and some scholars accept the claim and mark Pythagoras himself as a *mathematicus*. The evidence does not support this view. Pythagoreanism was not a peculiarly scientific sect until the second half of the fifth century: Pythagoras the *mathematicus* is a fiction.

Metaphysical Pythagoreanism is largely a fourth-century product; scientific Pythagoreanism is not found before the fifth century: there remain the *acousmatici*, devotees of the Pythagorean *acousmata* or *sumbola*. The surviving lists of *acousmata* go back in nucleus to the time of Pythagoras himself; they consist of a number of aphorisms (What are the Isles of the Blest?—The Sun and the Moon; What is wisest of all?—Number), and a large mass of rules and prohibitions of a detailed ritualistic nature: the celebrated injunction to abstain from the eating of beans is a typical *acousma*. Some of the *acousmata* are tricked out with reasons; and I shall have something to say about Pythagorean ethics in a later chapter. But by and large there is nothing in the *acousmata* to captivate the philosophic mind.[8]

The Newtonian Pythagoras is thus displaced by a figure more reminiscent of Joseph Smith: a hierophant; something of a charlatan; the leader of a Freemasonry, united by prescriptions and taboos—a religious society, not a scientific guild, which dabbled in South Italian politics but did not contribute to the history of Greek philosophy.[9]

If that were all we could say, Pythagoras might justly be banished from the philosophy books. But Joseph Smith is, like Isaac Newton, an exaggeration. The early sources leave no doubt that Pythagoras had intellectual as well as political and religious pretensions: Heraclitus railed at his polymathy (**21 B 40; B 129**); Ion of Chios praised his wisdom (**36 B 4**); to Herodotus he seemed 'not the weakest wise man among the Greeks' (IV.95 = **14 A 2**). The philosophical system later erected in his name was not designed by him; but it does not follow that he had no philosophical ideas: we do not know anything he believed, but we do not know that he did not believe anything.

Our ignorance is not total; one ray of light shines through the clouds, and there is one doctrine, or set of doctrines, that we can ascribe with some confidence to Pythagoras. Aristotle's pupil Dicaearchus gives the following report:

> What [Pythagoras] used to teach his associates, no one can tell with certainty; for they observed no ordinary silence. His most universally celebrated opinons, however, were that the soul is immortal; then that it migrates into other sorts of living creature; and in addition that after certain periods what has happened once happens again, and nothing is absolutely new; and that one should consider all animate things as akin. For Pythagoras seems to

have been the first to have brought these doctrines into Greece (**84: 14 A 8a**).[10]

The doctrine of metempsychosis,[11] or the transmigration of souls, is on any account characteristic of Pythagoreanism; on Dicaearchus' account, to which I assent, it is the chief constituent of that small body of theory which we are justified in ascribing to Pythagoras. And it is enough, as I shall attempt to show, to secure a place for Pythagoras among the philosophers.

(b) *The progress of the soul*

Dicaearchus wrote two centuries after Pythagoras: what earlier evidence is there for metempsychosis as a Pythagorean doctrine?

Aristotle, a serious student of Pythagoreanism, refers to metempsychosis as a Pythagorean 'myth' (*An* 407b20 = **58 B 39**). Plato more than once advances transmigratory theories; but though we may guess that he was adopting Pythagorean thoughts, he never expressly says that he is.[12] Half a century earlier, Herodotus penned a tantalizing paragraph:

> The Egyptians were also the first to advance the theory that the soul of man is immortal, and that when the body perishes it enters into (*eisduesthai*) another living creature which comes into being at that moment; and when it has gone round all the land animals and all the sea animals and all the birds, it enters again into the body of a man who is coming into being; and this circumambulation goes on for three thousand years. Some of the Greeks adopted this theory—some earlier, some later—as though it were their own; I know their names, but I do not write them down (**85: II.123 = 14 A 1**).

Herodotus is wrong about the Egyptian origins of metempsychosis; and he is wickedly teasing in concealing the names of its Greek advocates. Yet we can hardly fail to believe that among the 'earlier' thinkers the most celebrated was Pythagoras.[13]

Herodotus' 'later' men will have included Empedocles, who flourished in the earlier part of the fifth century (see vol. 2, p. 4); and it is in the fragments of Empedocles' *Katharmoi* or *Purifications* that we find the fullest account of metempsychosis. Empedocles himself says:

> For already have I once been a boy, and a girl,
> and a bush, and a fish that jumps from the sea as it swims (**86: 31 B 117 = 34 Z**).[14]

Empedocles had thus undergone both animal and vegetable incarnations (cf. **B 127** = **16 Z**); and he indicates more than one appearance in human form (**B 146** = **17 Z**). A long fragment tells of a cycle of transmigrations, lasting 30,000 seasons, imposed by Necessity on spirits who 'sully their dear limbs with bloodshed' (**B 115** = **3 Z**). The cycle was by and large woeful (see **B 115–127**); and Empedocles drew the salutary moral that one should avoid bloodshed and stick to a vegetarian diet (**B 135–141**).

It is often asserted that Empedocles ascribes a transmigratory doctrine to Pythagoras; but the fragment in question (**B 129** = **28 Z**) attributes, to an unnamed 'man of extraordinary knowledge', the ability to 'see with ease each and every thing that happens in ten and in twenty human lifetimes': the connexions with transmigration and with Pythagoras are alike dubious.[15] Again, the ancient assertions that Empedocles was himself a Pythagorean are of little worth. The most we can say is that Empedocles' environment was Pythagorean: he came from Acragas in Sicily; and it was in Sicily and South Italy that Pythagoras spent most of his life, and that his doctrines especially flourished. In 476 BC, when Empedocles was a boy, Pindar addressed his second *Olympian* ode to Theron, the ruler of Acragas, and in the poem depicted the delights of transmigration as to an audience familiar with and enamoured of the doctrine.

A final witness takes us back to Pythagoras himself:

> and about [Pythagoras'] having been different men at different times, Xenophanes bears witness in an elegy that begins:
>   Now I shall set out another account, and
>   show another way.
> and what he says goes like this:
>   And once they say he passed a dog that was being whipped;
>   and he took pity on it and uttered this word:
>   'Stop—don't beat it. For it is the *psuchê* of a friend of mine—
>   I recognized him by his voice (**87**: Diogenes Laertius, VIII. 36 = 21 B 7).

Xenophanes' story is a jest, not a piece of doxography; but the jest has no point if its butt was not a transmigrationist.[16]

Numerous questions arise about the content of Pythagoras' theory: Do all creatures, or all men, or only a favoured few, undergo transmigration? Are all living things potential recipients of human souls? Is transmigration cyclical? and is there a fixed hierarchy of incarnations? Are there gaps between incarnations? and do these involve some sort of Judgment Day? Is metempsychosis tied to a moral theory, or to a way of life, or to a theology?

To most of those questions we can only conjecture answers; and it is, I think, likely enough that different thinkers held different views. I shall return in a later chapter to the question of the connexion between metempsychosis and morals; for the rest it is enough to say that, whatever their anthropological interest, such peripheral questions have little philosophical bearing. It is the hard centre of the theory which gives it philosophical importance; and that centre consists simply in the contention that, at death, a man's soul may leave his body and animate another.[17]

There is nothing strikingly novel in the view that we somehow survive our earthly deaths; and the view was widespread in Greece from the dawn of history. Nor was there anything new in the supposition that the soul of my grandam might haply inhabit a bird: 'theriomorphism' is a commonplace in Greek mythology. The gods, with tedious frequency, dress themselves in bestial garments; and Circe turned Odysseus' crew to swine.[18] The novelty in Pythagoras' doctrine (if novelty it was[19]) consisted in its conjunction of those two old superstitions: men survive death by virtue of their *psuchê*'s taking on a new form. Survival and transmogrification add up to metempsychosis.

What sort of a *psuchê* does the doctrine of metempsychosis presuppose? I shall advert later to some of the things which the Pythagoreans and Empedocles said, or implied, about the human *psuchê*; here it is only necessary to observe the central fact about metempsychosis: that it proclaims a *personal* survival of bodily death. Pythagoras, in Xenophanes' story, recognized the dog as his friend; Empedocles, on his own account, had himself been a boy, a girl, a bush and a dolphin; when my *psuchê* moves, I move with it, and if my *psuchê* is incarnate in *a*, then I am *a*. Now the transmigration of my liver, or the transplantation of my heart, is of no personal concern to me: my entrails do not constitute myself. If transmigration of the *psuchê* is to do its Pythagorean duty, that can only be because the *psuchê*, unlike the entrails, is intimately connected with the self. John Locke put this very clearly: if soul does not carry self or consciousness, then a man will not be Nestor or Thersites 'though it were never so true, that the same Spirit that informed *Nestor*'s or *Thersites*'s Body, were numerically the same that now informs his. For this would no more make him the same Person with *Nestor*, than if some of the Particles of Matter, that were once a part of *Nestor*, were now a part of this Man, the same immaterial Substance without the same consciousness, no more making the same Person by being united to any Body, than the same Particle of Matter without consciousness united to any Body, makes the same Person' (*Essay* II.

xxvii. 14).

The early history of the notion of *psuchê* is obscure, the texts bearing on it sparse. I do not claim either that Pythagoras had a clearly articulated concept of *psuchê*, or that there was a single and uniform notion of *psuchê* common to the early Greek philosophers. But for all that, the essence of the business is neither dark nor debatable: metempsychosis anchored a personal survival; and the mode of survival was a transmigration of the *psuchê*. Those two facts suffice to show that Pythagoras' *psuchê* was the seat of personality.[20]

Thus the Pythagorean *psuchê* is more than Thales' animator: it is the seat of consciousness and of personality; a man's *psuchê* is whatever makes him the person he is, whatever is responsible for his particular self and personality. Metempsychosis is the doctrine of the transcorporation of the self; and the *psuchê* is the self. It is this which gives Pythagoras' theory a potential philosophical interest; for ever since Locke's discussion of the case of the Prince and the Cobbler, transmigratory fantasies have been a stock element in the discussion of personal identity.

(c) *Metempsychosis, mysticism and logic*

It may be thought fanciful to connect the obscure superstitions of Pythagoras with modern studies on personal identity: 'In Pythagoras' time', it will be said, 'no one knew or cared about the problems of personal identity; and Pythagoras himself was promulgating an eschatological dogma, not propounding a philosophical thesis.' A piece of Epicharmus will refute that sceptical suggestion: a debtor has been hauled to court for failing to pay his creditor; here is his defence:

DEBTOR. If you like to add a pebble to an odd number—or to an even one if you like—or if you take one away that is there, do you think it is still the same number?

CREDITOR. Of course not.

D. And if you like to add some further length to a yard-measure, or to cut something off from what's already there, will that measure still remain?

C. No.

D. Well, consider men in this way too—for one is growing, one

declining, and all are changing all the time. And what changes by
nature, and never remains in the same state, will be something
different from what changed; and by the same argument you and I
are different yesterday, and different now, and will be different
again—and we are never the same (**88: 23 B 2**).

Thus the defendant in court is not the same person as the borrower of
the cash; and it is consequently quite unjust for him to be dunned for
money which *he* never borrowed.[21]

This *jeu d'esprit* contains several remarkable features. It discusses
personal identity in a legal and moral context; and, as Locke
observed, 'person' is primarily 'a Forensick Term appropriating
Actions and their Merit' (*Essay* II. xxvii. 26). Second, Epicharmus'
debtor clearly takes continuity of consciousness as irrelevant to his
case: he is not denying that he has memories of incurring the debt,
only that he himself was the man who incurred it. Again, bodily
identity is taken as a necessary condition for personal identity: it is the
debtor's physical alterations which absolve him from his debt. And
finally, the conditions for bodily identity are very strict: any physical
change, any increase or decrease in size, disrupts identity.

All that would stand further investigation; but my purpose in
quoting Epicharmus is to prove that the problem of personal identity
was not alien to Pythagorean critics in the early fifth century.
Epicharmus' debtor presents a 'theory' of personal identity that
stands at the opposite pole to that implicit in metempsychosis;
Epicharmus, if not a Pythagorean himself, was certainly aware of the
philosophy preached in his homeland; and I suppose that his play is
evidence of a lively debate on matters of personal identity in early
Pythagorean circles.

Was the debate a matter of assertion and counter-assertion? or did
the Pythagoreans employ argument? Was metempsychosis a rational
theory or a religious dogma?

It has been held that 'a doctrine like that of metempsychosis,
which transcends normal human ways of knowing, can find a
guarantee only in supernatural experience, in the world of the divine
or quasi-divine';[22] and the multitude of miraculous stories told of
Pythagoras were narrated, according to Aristotle, in an attempt to
supply that transcendental guarantee (fr. 191 R^3 = **14 A 7**). But if
Pythagoras did display a golden thigh, that would hardly constitute a
reason for accepting his doctrine of transmigration. Supernatural
experience or an unnatural constitution are not to the point.

It is also false that 'the prophet [of transmigration] must be able to
refer to his own example':[23] *any* example will constitute evidence for

the thesis; and there is nothing logically superior about Pythagoras' own case. Nonetheless, it is very likely that Pythagoras did refer to his own case; and it is probable that he based his theory on his own experience. Antiquity provides several lists of Pythagoras' incarnations; though they vary in detail they collectively represent an old, and I think an authentic, tradition. Here is the version given by Heraclides Ponticus, a pupil of Plato's who was noted for his interest in the occult (and also for his historical imagination):

> Heraclides Ponticus says that [Pythagoras] says about himself that he was once Aithalides, and was deemed a son of Hermes; and that Hermes told him to choose whatever he wanted except immortality, and so he asked that both alive and dead he should remember what happened. So in his life he remembered everything, and when he died he retained the same memory. Some time later he passed into Euphorbus, and was wounded by Menelaus. (And Euphorbus used to say that he had once been Aithalides, . . .) And when Euphorbus died, his soul passed into Hermotimus. . . . And when Hermotimus died, he became Pyrrhus the Delian diver; and again he remembered everything—how he had been first Aithalides, then Euphorbus, then Hermotimus, then Pyrrhus. And when Pyrrhus died, he became Pythagoras, and remembered everything that has been said (**89**: fr. 89 W = Diogenes Laertius, VIII.4–5 = **14 A 8**).

Pythagoras thus claimed a series of incarnations for himself; and he supported his claim by his *mémoires d'outre-tombe*.

Heraclides' insistence on Pythagoras' memories is no accidental embellishment of his story. The later Pythagoreans were devoted to mnemonics: 'a Pythagorean does not get out of bed before he has recalled the previous day's happenings', and he makes use of a detailed recipe for reminiscence (Iamblichus, **58 D 1**, §165). It is plausible to connect this practice with the theory of metempsychosis: an acute memory will break the bonds of time, and give a Pythagorean vastly increased knowledge, both of the world and also of his own early biography.[24]

Nor, of course, is memory alien to the problems of personal identity; but 'memory' is a term with more than one application, and it is important to single out the appropriate one. Pythagoras is relying on what might be called 'experiential' memory. 'Experiential' memory is typically expressed by way of the formula '*a* remembers ϕing'; and the object of such memory is an experience, and an experience of the rememberer's. I may remember *that* I had a certain experience without having any 'experiential' memory: I remember that I lived in Colyton during 1943, but I cannot remember living there; I remember that I visited the Festival of Britain in 1951, but I remember little or nothing of the visit. I am inclined to think that experiential memory is a fundamental sort of remembering; and that it necessarily involves mental visualizings. (If that is so, then the much-despised empiricist account of memory may be less disreputable than it seems.) But those are obscure and difficult issues; and the present argument is independent of them.

John Locke's account of personal identity is properly expressed in terms of 'experiential' memory; it amounts, I think, to a conjunction of the following two theses:

(M1) If a is the same person as b, and b ϕed at time t and place p, then a can remember ϕing at $t\,p$.

(M2) If a can remember ϕing at $t\,p$, and b ϕed at $t\,p$, then a is the same person as b.

Of these two theses, (M1) seems open to immediate counter-example: the examiner who conscientiously forgets the questions he has set does not lose responsibility for setting them; the criminal may plead amnesia as a mitigating factor, but he cannot advance it as a proof of innocence; and in general we forget many of our past actions without forfeiting our identity with their agent. Locke was well aware that such an objection would be raised against him; and he anticipated it by a characteristically blunt negation (*Essay* II. xxvii. 22). I shall not attempt to say anything in his defence.

(M2), on the other hand, is immediately plausible. Indeed, if we take the notion of place narrowly, so that at most one person can be at p at any given moment, and if we construe 'remember' in a veridical sense, then (M2) is a necessary truth; for if a remembers ϕing, then a ϕed; and if a ϕed and b is the ϕer, then a is identical with b. And it is (M2) which Pythagoras requires. The argument which Heraclides implicitly ascribes to him is simple enough:

(1) Pythagoras remembers being killed by Menelaus at Troy at noon on 1 April 1084 BC.

(2) Euphorbus was killed by Menelaus at Troy at noon on 1 April 1084 BC.

Hence:

(3) Pythagoras is identical with Euphorbus.

The argument is valid; and its validity rests on (M2).

Any Lockean who is committed to (M2) is committed, not of course to Pythagoreanism, but to the possibility of Pythagoreanism. And Locke himself, though he has ironical words for one account of metempsychosis (*Essay* II. xxvii. 6), explicitly allows as much: '*personal Identity* consists ... in the Identity of *consciousness*, wherein, if *Socrates* and the present Mayor of *Quinborough* agree, they are the same Person' (ibid., 19). According to Locke, we are simply ignorant as to 'whether it has pleased God, that no one such Spirit shall ever be united to any but one such Body' (ibid., 27).

Yet even if Pythagoras' argument is valid, and has the blessing of John Locke, no one, I suppose, will be very impressed by it: premiss (2) we may pass (it is easily replaced by historically more acceptable propositions); but premiss (1) invites challenge: Pythagoras no doubt *says* he remembers being killed—but *does* he? People's memories often play them up; the Trojan War took place a long time ago; and it is, in any case, a touch unusual to remember being killed. Moreover, the Greeks had 'often seen wise men dying in verbal pretence—then, when they come home again, they get the greater honour' (Sophocles, *Electra* 62–4). Perhaps Pythagoras was another of those charlatans?

Pythagoras was well prepared for such appalling scepticism; and he provided an answer to it:

> They say that, while staying at Argos, he saw a shield from the spoils of Troy nailed up, and burst into tears. When the Argives asked him the reason for his emotion, he said that he himself had borne that shield in Troy when he was Euphorbus; they did not believe him, and judged him to be mad, but he said he would find a true sign that this was the case; for on the inside of the shield was written in archaic lettering EUPHORBUS'S. Because of the extraordinary nature of the claim, they all urged him to take down the offering; and the inscription was found on it (**90**: Diodorus, X. 6. 2).

Later Pythagoreans dismissed the story as a vulgarization; and modern scholars agree that it is a confection dreamed up by a fourth-century fabulist. I cannot prove that it is an old tale; yet I hope that it is. For though it may be false, it is certainly *ben trovato*: logically, it is precisely what Pythagoras needs. For of the several ways of defending a disputed memory claim, one is the exhibition of present and indisputable knowledge which can plausibly be derived from the experiences allegedly remembered.

If you show scepticism at my reminiscences of lunching royally in the *Tour d'Argent*, I may describe to you the menu, the decoration and the staff of the restaurant, and show myself capable of recognizing photographs of it. Similarly, but more cogently, by recognizing Euphorbus' shield, Pythagoras exhibited knowledge that could well be explained on the hypothesis that he had indeed fought at Troy. Of course, such facts do not *demonstrate* the truth of memory claims, in the sense that they are logically incompatible with their falsehood. But that is not to the point: the feats provide evidence—more or less good evidence—for the truth of the claims; and evidence is what Pythagoras is asked to supply. If Pythagoras did indeed pick Euphorbus' shield, the Argives will have suspected him of cheating; and if they were convinced that no cheating occurred, they may have shrugged their shoulders and spoken of chance or coincidence. Pythagoras' action does not prove his claim, still less his theory (what action can prove anything?); but it does provide some evidence—and, I suggest, fairly good evidence—for the truth of what he asserts.

That completes the account of metempsychosis. The whole matter is put briefly and neatly in Ovid's *Metamorphoses*; Pythagoras speaks:

> For soules are free from death. Howbeet, they leaving evermore
> Theyr former dwellings, are receyvd and live ageine in new.
> For I myself (ryght well in mynd I beare it too be trew)
> Was in the tyme of Trojan warre *Euphorbus*, *Panthewes* sonne,
> Quyght through whoose hart the deathfull speare of *Menelay* did ronne.
> I late ago in Junos Church at Argos did behold
> And knew the target which I in my left hand there did hold.
> (**91**: XV. 158–64; trans. Golding)

Metempsychosis is no rough dogma: it is a rational theory, capable of rigorous statement and implying a respectable account of the nature of personal identity; and it was advocated by Pythagoras on solid empirical grounds. We are far from mystery-mongering.

(d) *Selves and bodies*

Epicharmus' debtor still has his appeal: are there not cogent and widely accepted objections to a Lockean account of personal identity? Has it not been shown that bodily identity is a necessary condition of personal identity? And can we not thence infer the impossibility of metempsychosis?

Some philosophers may object to metempsychosis and side with Epicharmus' debtor because they do not feel happy with the prospect of disembodiment: *psuchai*, they suspect, cannot exist apart from a physical body. Now metempsychosis does not, in logic, require disembodiment; and I doubt if the theory was regularly associated with the survival of disembodied *psuchai*.

You might think that metempsychosis involved at least momentary disembodiment, on the strength of the following argument: 'It is a necessary truth that if the *psuchê* which animates a at t_1 is the same as the *psuchê* which later animates b at t_2, then a is the same person as b. Suppose, then, that a dies at t_3, a moment falling between t_1 and t_2. Well, b must have some birthday, t_4, between t_3 and t_2. But t_4 cannot be identical with t_3 (for then the *psuchê* would inhabit two distinct bodies at the same time); nor can t_4 be contiguous with t_3 (for no two instants of time are contiguous). Hence there must be a gap between t_3, and t_4 during which the *psuchê* is disembodied.'[25]

I reject the argument for two reasons: we have no cause to assign a birthday to b or to suppose the existence of a birthdate t_4; and even if there is a gap between t_3 and the alleged t_4, we need not suppose that the *psuchê* exists during that gap. (I shall have more to say on the former of these objections when I discuss Zeno: below, pp. 270–1).

The argument from birthdays fails; and I can think of no other feature of metempsychosis that might appear to commit Pythagoras to disembodiment. Nor does anything commit him to dualism: he need not suppose that bodies are made of 'matter' and *psuchai* of that completely different substance, 'spirit'. Metempsychosis is transcorporation of the *psuchê*: that implies nothing about the status of the *psuchê*'s constituent stuff.

If I am right so far, the philosophical opponent of transmigration must do more than deny the hypothesis of an immaterial, spiritual substance; and more than reject the possibility of disembodied persons. He must, in effect, maintain that the *psuchê* and the body are identical; for only if a's *psuchê* actually is a's body does metempsychosis become impossible; only if I am the person I am by virtue of having the body I have, can I be prevented, by logic, from changing bodies.

I know of only one serious *a priori* argument which purports to prove the identity of *psuchê* and body. It is the duplication argument, and it runs like this.

Suppose that, on the day after Pythagoras made his startling identification of Euphorbus' shield, Xenophanes visited Argos. On being told the hot news of Pythagoras' identity, he claimed that not Pythagoras but he was Euphorbus: *he* could remember being killed by Menelaus; and what is more, *he* could pick out the shield to prove it. And suppose further that Xenophanes successfully picked out Euphorbus' shield, and indeed succeeded in duplicating *every* feat that Pythagoras had performed. There are now two candidates for identity with Euphorbus: each can marshal exactly the same facts in his favour as the other can; yet both cannot be Euphorbus, for then they would be identical with one another, and one candidate not two. Hence to identify either with Euphorbus is strictly unreasonable. And since anyone with Pythagorean pretensions must always be prepared to face a rival Xenophanes, it can never be reasonable to accept any Pythagorean claim. The theory of metempsychosis is consequently vain.

The duplication argument is impressive; but it has its chinks. First, observe that it does not yield the conclusion that neither Pythagoras nor Xenophanes is Euphorbus: it concludes only that we can have no reason for preferring either candidate to the other. If that conclusion is correct, it indicates that the doctrine of metempsychosis is in a certain sense empty; but it does not show that Pythagoras was wrong.

Second, notice that the argument applies in all cases of 'experiential' memory. I remember sitting in seat K 5 of the Playhouse last night; and if you care to doubt my word I can produce, perhaps, a ticket stub and a sworn affidavit from a *soi-disant* occupant of seat K 6. Now it is perfectly possible that a *Doppelganger* should appear and claim that *he* remembered occupying seat K 5; and that he should produce a ticket stub as informative as mine, and a sworn statement from an alleged neighbour. Moreover, any further efforts I may make to support my claim will immediately be imitated by my *Doppelganger*. Thus there are two rival claimants to one seat: neither of us produces any evidence not immediately matched by the other; and though it does not follow that neither of us occupied the seat, it does follow that for you to believe one of us rather than the other is strictly unreasonable.

I and my *Doppelganger* are in all relevant respects analogous to Pythagoras and Xenophanes; *any* memory claim can be disputed; *any* evidence can be matched; *any* reminiscent raconteur may find his duplicate, reminiscing with equal plausibility and recounting with equal sincerity. Duplication is not restricted to metempsychotic memories: it applies impartially to all.

But what does the possibility of duplication prove? If my *Doppelganger* actually arrives and mimics my claims in that monstrous way, then you will be right to credit neither of us. Similarly, if Xenophanes had actually turned up at Argos and mimicked Pythagoras, the Argives would have done well to retreat into a bewildered scepticism. But it does not follow from this that the mere possibility of such a *Doppelganger* is evidence against my claim to have sat in seat K 5, or that the mere possibility of Xenophanes' appearance is evidence against Pythagoras. Schematically, the case looks like this: a set of propositions, P_1, counts as reasonable evidence for a claim C_1; and a rival set, P_2, counts as reasonable evidence for an incompatible claim, C_2. P_1 and P_2 are logically compossible. If both

P_1 and P_2 are known to be true, then it is unreasonable both to believe C_1 and to believe C_2. But it is absurd to infer that if P_1 is known to be true, then it is unreasonable to believe C_1 because P_2 is compatible with P_1.

These considerations evidently need deeper probing; but they seem to me enough to throw doubt upon the strength of the duplication argument, at least as a refutation of the possibility of metempsychosis. C. S. Peirce once asserted that 'Pythagoras was certainly a wonderful man. We have no right, at all, to say that supernal powers had not put a physical mark upon him as extraordinary as his personality'; indeed, we have for this 'far stronger testimony than we have for the resurrection of Jesus'. Peirce was speaking of Pythagoras' golden thigh; but his remarks apply equally to Pythagoras' incarnations. Peirce's credulity is charming; and his comparison is apt: if we reject Pythagoras' claim, it must be on the same grounds that we reject the miraculous stories of the early Christians. The materialist enemies of John Locke cannot shoot Pythagoras down with *a priori* arrows; if their failure leaves us with a disagreeable feeling, we may hope that the notorious shafts of Hume will drop him along with other miracle-mongers. But however that may be, it seems to me that the doctrine of metempsychosis does indeed have 'a rigour and a speculative power that is the mark . . . of a bold and original thinker'.[26]

(e) *Intimations of immortality*

According to Dicaearchus, Pythagoras taught the immortality of the *psuchê* (above, text **84**).[27] Metempsychosis does not in itself entail immortality: a feline *psuchê* enjoys nine transmigrations but no more. And we may ask how Pythagoras and his followers justified their immortal pretensions. We may ask; but we receive no answer. And other Presocratic psychologies are no more informative. According to Diogenes,

> Some say—among them Choirilus the poet—that [Thales] was also the first to hold that *psuchai* are immortal (**92**: I. 24 = **11 A 1**; cf. Suda, **A 2**);

but the report does not inspire much confidence, and no trace of an argument survives. Heraclitus may have subscribed to the doctrine of immortality; but again, no argument, and no clear assertion, survives. And other early thinkers did not greatly bother their heads about their *psuchai*.

There is one bright exception to that generalization. Alcmeon of

Croton, an eminent physician and an amateur of philosophy, both believed in and argued for psychic immortality; and his argument so impressed Plato that he adopted it for his own.

Alcmeon probably worked at the beginning of the fifth century, a younger contemporary of Pythagoras. According to Diogenes, 'most of what he says concerns medicine, but he sometimes treats of natural philosophy' (VIII. 83 = **24 A 1**). His philosophical interests included astronomy (e.g., Aëtius, **A** 4); and he offered some metaphysical reflexions which seemed vaguely Pythagorean in tone to Aristotle (*Met* 986a27–34 = **A 3**). He also touched upon epistemological matters (see below, pp. 136, 149). But his main interest appears to have lain in what may loosely be called the philosophy of man—and in particular, in human psychology. It is here that his argument for the immortality of the *psuchê* belongs.

We know the argument by report, not by quotation; but before turning to the reports it will be well to quote one of the few fragments of Alcmeon's own writings:

> Men perish for this reason, that they cannot attach the beginning to the end (**93: B 2**).

There have been many attempts to elucidate this enigmatic apophthegm, but none is particularly satisfactory.[28] Whatever the fragment may mean, it shows that Alcmeon made a distinction between a man and his *psuchê*. Men are mortal, perishing things; but *psuchai*, as the argument we are to examine pretends, are immortal and deathless. Now it is tempting to argue thus: 'If men are mortal and Socrates is a man, then Socrates is mortal. But men, according to **B 2**, perish; so Socrates will perish, and the immortality of his *psuchê* will not secure his own survival. Alcmeon and the Pythagoreans part company: for Alcmeon, psychic immortality is not personal immortality; my soul may go marching on, but I shall not.' To avoid that conclusion we must divorce the notions of *man* and *person*, and maintain, with Locke, that the term 'man' connotes a being of a certain form and physical constitution: to be a man is to be an animal of a determinate type. Persons, then, are not necessarily men: Socrates may cease to be a man without ceasing to be. Plato probably took Alcmeon to be arguing for personal immortality; for when he adopts Alcmeon's reasoning, he does so in the conviction that it supports a doctrine of individual immortality. Again, the Pythagorean doctrine of metempsychosis, with which Alcmeon was indubitably acquainted, closely associated psychic and personal survival, and thus implicitly distinguished between persons and men. Finally, the Lockean distinction between person and man, which some modern philosophers find outlandish and absurd, was familiar to every Greek schoolboy: when Odysseus' companions were turned into swine by Circe they ceased to be men, but did not lose their personal identity. Circe did not kill Odysseus' crew: she transmogrified them.

I thus suppose that according to Alcmeon men die but people do not: the survival of the *psuchê* does not guarantee 'human' survival; but it does hold out the promise of personal survival. Alcmeon's argument may indeed have been intended to give philosophical respectability and rational support to the plain assertions of the Pythagoreans.

I turn to Alcmeon's argument. There are five reports to be mentioned. First, Aristotle:

> Alcmeon . . . says that [the *psuchê*] is immortal because it is like the immortals; and that this holds of it in virtue of the fact that it is always moving. For all divine things are always moving continuously—moon, sun, the stars, and the whole heavens (**94**: *An* 405a29–b1 = **A 12**).

Second, a fragment of Boethus:

> Looking at this [sc. the similarity of our *psuchê* to god], the philosopher from Croton said that, being immortal, it actually shuns by nature every form of rest, like the divine bodies (**95**: Eusebius, *PE* XI. 28. 9).

Third, Diogenes:

> He says that the *psuchê* is immortal, and that it moves continuously like the sun (**96**: VIII. 83 = **A 1**).

Fourth, Aëtius:

> Alcmeon supposes [the *psuchê*] to be a substance self-moved in eternal motion, and for that reason immortal and similar to the divine things (**97: A 12**).

The fifth text does not name Alcmeon; it is the section of the *Phaedrus* in which Plato transcribes and adapts Alcmeon's argument. I quote the beginning and the end of the passage:

> Every *psuchê* is immortal. For what is ever-moving is immortal. And what moves something else and is moved by something else, having a respite from movement has a respite from life; thus only that which moves itself, in so far as it does not abandon itself, never stops moving. . . . Every body whose movement comes from

without is inanimate (*apsuchos*) and every body whose movement comes from within is animate (*empsuchos*), this being the nature of an animator (*psuchê*). And if this is so, and if what moves itself is nothing other than an animator, then from necessity animators will be both ungenerated and immortal (**98**: *Phaedrus* 245C–246A).

Plato's text is disputed at crucial points;[29] and the structure of his argument is controversial: he appears to have grafted Alcmeon's reasoning onto a distinct set of considerations (they appear in the passage I have omitted), and the grafting is uncharacteristically crude. Moreover, we cannot be sure how far Plato is embellishing Alcmeon, and how far he is simply following him.[30] We must, therefore, rely primarily on Aristotle and the doxographers for the reconstruction of Alcmeon's argument.

Those reports ascribe three propositions to Alcmeon:
(1) *Psuchai* are always moving.
(2) *Psuchai* are like the divine heavenly bodies.
(3) *Psuchai* are immortal.
Diogenes lets the three propositions stand without any clear inferential linking. Boethus appears to present an argument from (3) to (1). Aristotle and Aëtius, more plausibly, make an argument from (1) to (3).

According to Aristotle, Alcmeon inferred (2) from (1), and (3) from (2). His argument is thus a hideously feeble analogy: *psuchai* are like the heavenly bodies in one respect—they move continuously; hence they are like the heavenly bodies in another respect—they are immortal. As well infer that *psuchai* are flat discs—for the sun is so shaped (Aëtius, **A 4**).

According to Aëtius, Alcmeon inferred (2) from (1), and also inferred (3) from (1). (3) does not require the analogical mediation of (2): it follows directly from (1). Plato supports Aëtius here; and I am inclined to accept his report. Alcmeon, I suppose, originally said something like this: 'Animators, like the divine denizens of the heavens, move continuously; hence, like those divinities, they are immortal.' Aristotle misread the illustrative comparison with the heavenly bodies as an analogical premise; but Aëtius preserves the true deductive character of the argument. To make the argument fully explicit we need to add a further premiss:
(4) Anything that always moves is immortal.
From (1) and (4), (3) follows.

Premiss (4) is a necessary truth. According to Aëtius, Alcmeon's *psuchai* were 'self-moving';[31] and 'self-motion' occurs in Plato's version of the argument. Some scholars opine that the introduction of that notion into the argument was the work of Plato; but there is no reason to deny the notion to Alcmeon: the belief that living things—men, animals, and heavenly bodies—are 'self-moving', in the sense that they move without being impelled from outside, is not a deeply philosophical opinion. Since anything that has the power to cause motion is alive (above, p. 7), any self-mover is alive. Hence anything that is moving itself at t is alive at t; and anything in continuous self-motion is eternally alive. And to assert that is to assert (4).

There is more difficulty in premiss (1): in what way can *psuchai* move? Why should we suppose that they *do* move? And why should we agree that they *always* move?

There is a temptation to connect the animator's motion with its cognitive function: it might be suggested, in a Cartesian vein, that animators cogitate, and that cogitation is a species of 'motion', in a relaxed sense of that term. Then Alcmeon's premiss that *psuchai* always move will parallel the notorious Cartesian thesis that the soul always thinks.

The suggestion is attractive; but I fear we must be content with a far cruder account of psychic locomotion. In one of the more bizarre portions of that most bizarre work, the *Timaeus*, Plato explains how the minor gods in their creation of men 'imitated the shape of the universe, which is round, and confined the two divine revolutions in a spherical body, which we now call the head, and which is the most divine part of us and rules over everything in us' (44D). The 'two divine revolutions' are the whirling circles of the Same and the Other, which constitute our *psuchê*. The human skull is thus an orrery, representing the heavens; and the soul, revolving within it, mimics the revolutions of the heavenly bodies. This strange conception is full of obscurities which I am happy to ignore; it is enough to say that so many of its features are reminiscent of Alcmeon that the whole theory, in outline at least, may plausibly be ascribed to him. In the *Timaeus*, as in the *Phaedrus*, Plato draws on Alcmeon. As far as premiss (1) of Alcmeon's argument is concerned, the moral is this: the movements of the *psuchê* are, quite literally, locomotions—circular revolutions in the space of the skull.

Why should Alcmeon have felt drawn by so strange an hypothesis? According to Aristotle, 'some say that an animator is first and foremost what gives motion. And, believing that what is not itself in motion cannot move anything else, they supposed the animator to be something moving' (*An* 403b28–31). What moves other things must itself move; hence the animator, being a motor, is in motion. The argument did not appeal to Aristotle; but it is, I think, a particular application of the Synonymy Principle of causation (above p. 88); and that principle can be found in Aristotle's own works. 'Causation is by synonyms': who breeds fat oxen must himself be fat. The fire warms me only if it is itself warm; ice cools gin because ice itself is cold; this ink, which is black, renders this paper black; sweet-smelling lavender makes the sheets smell sweet. In general: if a brings it about that b is ϕ, then a is ϕ.

The principle is supported by numerous examples; and it helps to explain the occult property of causality: causes produce changes in the objects they effect by transferring or imparting something to those objects; when the fire makes me warm, it bestows heat upon me; and the lavender, we say, gives the sheets their sweetness. Now since I cannot give you what I do not myself possess, causes must themselves be endowed with the properties they impart. This emerges plainly from a passage in which Descartes employs a particular instance of the principle: 'Now it is manifest by the natural light that there must be at least as much reality in the efficient and total cause as in its effect. For, pray, whence can the effect derive its reality if not from its cause? And in what way can this cause communicate this reality to it, unless it possesses it itself?' (*Meditation* III).

If some examples commend the principle, many more stand against it; and it is not difficult to see that the principle both is false in itself and conveys a misleading notion of the causal process. Berkeley was characteristically abrupt: 'Nihil dat quod non habet or the effect is contained in ye Cause is an axiom I do not Understand or believe to be true' (*Philosophical Commentaries* A § 780). And indeed it is easier to show the inadequacy of the principle than to explain its popularity and longevity.

The origin of the principle is, I think, unknown: it is found, as I have said, in Aristotle, and it is traceable in Plato's *Phaedo*; I do not doubt that it is Presocratic, and I see no reason to question Aristotle's implication that it lay behind Alcmeon's argument for the immortality of the *psuchê*: a *psuchê* causes locomotion; therefore it must itself move.

If animators must move, why need they be moving continuously? Why is sporadic or temporary motion not sufficient? After all, the bodies they move do not move continuously or for ever. The *Phaedrus* suggests alternative answers to this question. First, Plato observes that 'that which moves itself, in so far as it does not abandon itself, never stops moving' (245C). The point is obscure to me; perhaps Plato means this: 'Self-movers are autonomous agents, whose movement is not dependent upon external forces; consequently the moved thing, being always attached to—since it is identical with—an autonomous motor, will always move.' That is an uncompelling argument: the heavenly motions in my head may, I suppose, be autonomous in the sense that no external mover causes my cerebral motor to move; but it does not follow that my *psuchê* is entirely indifferent to the outside world, or that my psychic revolutions will survive a sharp crack on the skull.

A passage from the end of Plato's argument suggests a different type of explanation for the eternity of psychic motion. It is, Plato says, 'the nature of an animator' to move the body; 'what moves itself is nothing other than an animator'; so that 'from necessity' animators are immortal. These phrases hint at the following argument: 'An animator is, by definition, a motor; motors, of necessity, themselves move. Hence of necessity animators move. Hence an animator cannot at any time not be moving. Hence animators are always moving.' Psychic motion, in short, is a matter of logical necessity; and evidently what happens of necessity happens always.

Alcmeon's argument for the immortality of the *psuchê* can now be set out fairly explicitly. It runs, I suggest, thus: 'I am animate, and hence, trivially, contain an animator. My animator is, by definition, a motor; for it is, *inter alia*, whatever is the source of my various locomotive efforts. The analysis of causation shows that of necessity motors move. Thus my animator moves of necessity; and hence it moves always and continuously. Now anything in autonomous movement is alive, so that anything always in motion is always alive, and thus immortal. *Ergo*, my animator is immortal.'

That is a complex and a sophisticated argument. Indeed, in certain respects it bears comparison with St Anselm's notorious Ontological Argument: both proofs start from a definition, and both end with an eternal existent. Both proofs are unsound; and Alcmeon's is both less perplexing and less philosophically fecund than Anselm's. But I shall leave criticism of Alcmeon to the reader, and end this chapter on a note of mild commendation: I do not know of any argument for the immortality of the soul one half so clever as Alcmeon's, the very first argument in the field.

VII

The Moral Law

(a) *First steps in ethics*

One of the more delicious prerogatives of the philosopher is that of telling other people where their duties and obligations lie, and what they ought to do. Ethics is a traditional branch of philosophy; and, with the exception of a few modern heretics, all professors of ethics have been primarily concerned to discover the rules of right and wrong, and to disseminate their discoveries. Of course, not every preacher is a philosopher; and if philosophers have a pre-eminent claim to our attention when they choose to moralize that is in large part because they do not, professionally at least, offer piecemeal and dogmatic injunctions, but are prepared to provide some general prescriptions for conduct which are systematic, rational, and analytic. The natural tendency of the human mind to proffer advice and instruction might lead us to expect that ethics was a subject of interest to the earliest Presocratic philosophers. Their historical circumstances, and their known practical bent, support that expectation. A potent drive to ethical reflection has always been given by observation of the radical differences in moral outlook from country to country and from age to age. Such observation was made by quick-minded Greek travellers of the sixth century; and if Xenophanes was moved by his acquaintance with different religious beliefs to advance a rational theology, surely acquaintance with different moral beliefs would move him and his peers to investigate the grounds of morality?

Again, the Presocratics did not live as anchorites or academics, far from the madding crowd's ignoble strife. On the contrary, they strove. Plutarch, defending philosophy against the charge of irrelevant other-worldliness, lists and applauds the political cares and achievements of its practitioners. Even Parmenides, that most abstract of intellects, took sufficient time off from metaphysics to 'arrange his own country by excellent laws, so that the citizens still make their officials swear each year to abide by the laws of Parmenides' (Plutarch, *adv Col* 1126A = **28 A 12**). The Seven Sages—those early Greek heroes distinguished by their capacity for political wisdom and brisk aphorism—included Thales in their number; and the tales of Thales' practical prowess are not unique: stories of a similar nature and content are told, not incredibly, of most of the Presocratics.

Nonetheless, ethics was not a central interest for the majority of the early philosophers: the Milesians offered no moral philosophy at all. Xenophanes evinces various ethical sentiments: his strictures on Homeric theology imply a conventional morality (**21 B 11–12**); he has some caustic remarks about the degenerate and effeminate dress of his contemporaries (**B 3**); and he makes a pleasingly heterodox assessment of the relative worth of philosophers and Olympic victors (**B 2**). Yet there is nothing particularly philosophical about those opinions. As a moralist, Xenophanes works in the tradition of the didactic poets of old Greece: Hesiod, Theognis, Solon.

I do not know why the early Presocratics were largely silent about ethics: they will hardly have thought it a subject too serious or too slight for philosophizing. Perhaps they said nothing for the reason, as rare as it is commendable, that they had nothing to say. However that may be, the silence was broken only by two men, Heraclitus and Empedocles. Their views are not vastly impressive; yet they have a fascination, if only because they represent the first tottering steps ever taken in the still tottering subject of ethics.

(b) *Eating people is wrong*

Whether or not Empedocles was a Pythagorean, the moral views which he vociferously advocates plainly rest upon those elements in his philosophy which are most Pythagorean in their nature. The question arises whether he is not a mouthpiece for an earlier Pythagorean ethics.

We possess a long account of Pythagorean views on ethics, politics and education; the account is, in a loose sense, systematic; and it is also in most respects sensible, wise and humane (**58 D**). But its author is the fourth-century philosopher Aristoxenus; and there is no reason to treat it as a document bearing on Presocratic Pythagoreanism. The Pythagorean *sumbola*, on the other hand, are in nucleus early; but they do not pretend to systematic organization or philosophical backing. Some of the rules and rituals are indeed tricked out with reasons; but those reasons, like the allegorical interpretations which sometimes accompany them, are evidently embellishments, designed by later devotees whom the primitive taboos of the early Pythagoreans offended and embarrassed. Pythagorean ethics, so far as we know, first became a philosophical morality in the hands of Empedocles. For all that, it is, I think, appropriate to discuss Empedocles' ethical views out of their chronological context; for they depend on the Pythagorean eschatology I have already sketched, and they do not (so far as I can see) make use of any later philosophical contentions.

Aristotle remarks that 'there is, as everyone divines, by nature a common standard of justice and injustice, even if men have made no society and no contract with one another' (*Rhet* 1373b6); by way of illustration he quotes some celebrated lines from Sophocles' *Antigone*, and a couplet from Empedocles. The couplet runs thus:

> But that which is lawful for all stretches endlessly through the broad
> aether and through the vast brightness (**99: 31 B 135 = 22 Z**).

Evidently, as Aristotle implies, Empedocles wanted to contrast a law of morality, universal and absolute, with those temporal and changing laws which vary from state to state: the couplet implies a staunch rejection of moral relativism.

And, taken in isolation, the couplet might appear to indicate a fairly comprehensive system of morality. But if we hope to find in Empedocles a wide-ranging and absolute code of conduct, that hope is soon dashed: Aristotle says that **99** is concerned with 'not killing living creatures'; and the surviving fragments of Empedocles' ethics bear him out. We are enjoined to abstain from 'harsh-sounding bloodshed' (**B 136 = 29 Z**), and in particular to avoid sacrifice (**B 137 = 31 Z**); moreover, we must not eat meat (**B 138 = 33 Z**); nor, for that matter, beans or bay leaves (**B 140 = 36 Z**). And that, so far as the fragments go, is that: Empedocles' universal law amounts to a prohibition on bloodshed, and a modified vegetarianism.[1] The high intimations of **99** are not borne out: no one will maintain that Empedocles' ethics supplies answers to more than a minuscule proportion of our moral questions.

For all that, Empedocles' injunctions were both revolutionary and rational. Acragas was 'a rich town and a devout town'. Animal sacrifice was a normal part of Greek religious practice, and the streets of Acragas 'must have resounded with the shrieks of dying animals, its air reeking with the stench of blood and burning carcases'.[2] To advocate bloodless liturgy in such circumstances will have seemed both impious and absurd.

Why, then, did Empedocles dare to be so shocking? The answer starts from his theory of metempsychosis, and his conception of the long series of incarnations to which people were necessarily bound. The descent from a divine to a terrestrial life begins, indeed, by bloodshed:

> When any one defiles his dear limbs with bloodshed
> —one of the spirits who have been allotted a long-lasting life—
> he is to wander thrice ten thousand seasons away from the blessed ones . . . (**100: B 115. 3–6 = 3 Z**)[3]

Bloodshed, the cause of our woeful sojourn on earth, is evidently an unwise operation; yet if murderous spirits were imprudent, it does not follow that murderous men are immoral. Why, we may still ask, should we now abstain from the delights of the butcher's knife?

A further fragment from the *Katharmoi* reads as follows:

> The father lifts up his own son in a different shape
> and, praying, slaughters him, in his great madness, as he cries piteously
> beseeching his sacrificer; but he, deaf to his pleas,
> slaughters, and prepares in his halls an evil feast.
> Just so does son take father, and children mother:
> they tear out their life and devour their dear flesh. (**101: B 137 = 31 Z**)[4]

The sheep you slaughter and eat was once a man. Once, perhaps, your son or your father: patricide and filicide are evidently wrong; to avoid them you must avoid all bloodshed. And to avoid dining off your late relatives you must avoid eating meat or any of those select members of the vegetable kingdom which may receive once-human souls. The doctrine of transmigration, in short, shows that killing animals is killing people, and that eating animals is eating people; and eating people is wrong.

The ancient doxographers all agree that metempsychosis thus grounded Empedoclean ethics. Theophrastus and Xenocrates applauded the moral inference; and modern scholars concur: 'the self-evident corollary of the doctrine of metempsychosis would have to be complete vegetarianism'.[5] The inference from metempsychosis to vegetarianism is far from self-evident to me; but that, I fear, is because I can see nothing very reprehensible in eating people: *chacun à son goût*. The inference from metempsychosis to the prohibition on killing animals is a different matter; and there Empedocles seems, at first blush, to be on firmer ground. Killing animals is killing people, and killing people gratuitously (as in sacrifice), or for our own enjoyment (as in butchery), is surely a morally objectionable practice.

101, it must be admitted, does not itself prove that Empedocles found it objectionable to kill a person as such: the fragment suggests that the wickedness in killing animals derives from the danger of killing a close relative; and it is consistent with this to suppose that if you could be sure that a sheep was no kinsman of yours, you might with propriety wield the knife. **B 136**, however, appears to state a more general thesis:

> Will you not cease from harsh-sounding bloodshed? Do you not see that you are slaughtering one another in the thoughtlessness of your mind?
>
> (**102**: B 136 = 29 Z)

The commentators tacitly suppose that **101** merely gives a peculiarly dramatic instance of **102**, in order to underscore the horror of animal sacrifice. And they are surely right.

Nonetheless, it is not clear why Empedocles should have found killing people objectionable. There was, I am told, an early sect of Christians who took the promise of Heaven seriously and threw themselves off cliff-tops to expedite their journey to Paradise. If death marks not the cessation of life but rather the transformation to a different vital form, death will often be a boon for the victim; and a metempsychotic killer might well reason that the slaughter of a sheep was a deed of moral worth, in that it removed a person from the tedium of ovine existence and accelerated his return to the divine status from which his psychic peregrinations began. I cannot see why Empedocles should have disapproved of that humane practice.

However that may be, such Empedoclean concerns may seem entirely remote from us. It is true that in Oxford, as in Acragas, we daily consume monstrous quantities of flesh; and in our academies, as in the Acragantine temples, the blood runs freely on the sacrificial altars: the modern scientist, like the Sicilian seer, kills in the hope of gaining knowledge. Yet we do not believe in metempsychosis; and Empedocles' fulminations may therefore leave us unmoved.

That is a hasty conclusion. Late authorities ascribe to the Pythagoreans a doctrine of the kinship of all living creatures; Sextus, in his introduction to **102**, speaks of a relationship (*koinônia*) which we have 'not only to one another and to the gods, but also to brute creatures' (*adv Math* VII. 127); and it is on that relationship that he grounds Empedocles' prohibition on killing. If animal souls are identical with human souls, then, trivially, animals and humans are psychically akin. And since it is not the physical form or constitution of a man, but rather some feature of his psychic make-up, which makes killing people wrong, what is wrong for men is by the same token wrong for animals.

Modern defenders of the rights of animals are, I think, essentially Empedoclean in their stance. In their view, the orthodox morality which condones vivisection and animal experimentation and fails even to discern a moral issue in the eating of meat, is a form of 'speciesism'; and speciesism, if less imprudent than racism, is no less obnoxious: any argument against racism is, *mutatis mutandis*, an argument against speciesism; and the pragmatic question '"Is a vegetarian diet nutritionally adequate?" resembles the slave-owner's claim that he and the whole economy of the South would be ruined without slave labour'.[6]

Psychologically, we are all Aristotelians: we do not believe, with Empedocles, in the formal identity of all souls. But the opponents of speciesism will happily accept this; for Aristotelianism assigns to men and animals alike the faculty of sentience, and it is the possession of sentience (more particularly, of the capacity to suffer) which gives men a title to moral consideration. We cannot adopt one moral rule for human killing and another for animal slaughter; for the feature which makes human killing morally wrong is common to all animal life. Jeremy Bentham put it best: 'The French have already discovered that the blackness of the skin is no reason why a human being should be abandoned without redress to the caprice of a tormentor. It may come one day to be recognized, that the number of legs, the villosity of the skin, or the termination of the *os sacrum*, are reasons equally insufficient for abandoning a sensitive being to the same fate. What else is it that should trace the insuperable line? Is it the faculty of reason, or, perhaps, the faculty of discourse? But a full-grown horse or dog is beyond comparison a more rational, as well as a more conversable animal, than an infant of a day, or a week, or even a month, old. But suppose the case were otherwise, what would it avail? The question is not, Can they *reason*? nor, Can they *talk*? but, Can they *suffer*?' (*Introduction to the Principles of Morals and Legislation*, ch. XVII, n.)

Metaphysically, Bentham and Empedocles are poles apart; morally, Bentham (unlike some of his modern disciples) never indulged in the wholesale and passionate condemnations which flowed from Empedocles' Sicilian pen. Yet for all that, the comparison I have just marked is not far-fetched: both Empedocles and Bentham find a psychic element common to man and beast; both Empedocles and Bentham rest a moral doctrine on that common element. The appeal which the two men make to us is, at bottom, the same; and it is, I think, an appeal to which many of us assent in our hearts. But we lie in our teeth.

(c) *Heraclitus and the laws of God*

We generally treat Heraclitus as a metaphysician, not as a moralist. Diodotus, a Stoic teacher of Cicero, held the opposite view: Heraclitus' book, he argued, 'is not about nature, but about government, and the remarks about nature have an illustrative function' (Diogenes Laertius, IX.15 = 22 A 1).[7] Diodotus is hardly right; yet he errs in the right direction: there is evidence enough that Heraclitus was a moralist as well as a metaphysician, and that he attempted to found an idiosyncratic ethical code upon his idiosyncratic metaphysical system.

The surviving fragments contain several utterances which are, or probably imply, specific moral judgments; and many of these can be loosely attached to features of Heraclitus' non-moral views. Thus his austere and apparently monotheistic theology accounts for **B 5b = 86 M**:

> they pray to these statues, as though a man were to chat with his house (**103**).[8]

The metaphysical thesis that strife is essential to existence comports with **B 53 = 29 M**:

> War is father of all, king of all; and it has shown some as gods, some as men; it has made some slaves, some free (**104**).

(The fragment is usually and plausibly read as an approval of things martial.) Again, Heraclitus' psychological and eschatological views, obscure though they are,[9] evidently lie behind such judgments as **B 25 = 97 M**:

> Greater deaths receive greater shares (**105**)

or **B 96 = 76 M**:

> Corpses are more to be thrown out than dung (**106**).[10]

Some of Heraclitus' *dicta* are trite, some are shocking; some are plain, others dark; but none, I think, has any great intrinsic interest.

Behind those detailed judgments, and doubtless in some sense supporting them, there lie a few remarks of a more general and systematic nature; and it is these which I shall consider. It is best to approach them obliquely.

The doxographers made Heraclitus a determinist in the Stoic mould: he says that 'everything happens according to fate (*heimarmenê*), and that this is the same as necessity (*anankê*)' (Aëtius, A 8). The report presumably derives from 37 (**B 80 = 28 M**), which asserts that 'everything comes about in accordance with strife and what must be'.[11] Since, according to 33 (B 1 = 1 M) 'everything comes about in accordance with [Heraclitus'] account', his account or *logos* expresses a law under which all events are subsumed: bound by law, the world and everything in it is governed by necessity.

Necessity is orderly. Heraclitus more than once points to the regularity of things: the world itself is a *kosmos* or ordered arrangement (38: B 30 = 51 M); fire, the basic constituent of everything, is exchanged for things as gold is exchanged for goods (39: B 90 = 54 M), and the exchange rate was fixed in certain 'measures' or *metra* (38, 40: B 31 = 53 M); celestially, the sun has its 'measures' which it will not overstep (B 94 = 52 M); and the coming and going of human generations is marked by a numerically specifiable periodicity.[12] Order and regularity permeate the harmonious Heraclitean universe.

Universal regularity suggests a universal regulator:

> The thunderbolt steers everything (107: B 64 = 79 M).

> The one wise thing has the knowledge by which everything is steered in all ways (108: B 41 = 85 M).

There is a single divine law (*nomos*) which 'controls as much as it wishes' (B 114 = 23 M). The world is governed by God; and if

> Time is a child, playing, moving its pawns—the kingdom is a child's (109: B 52 = 93 M),

then perhaps that government is a divine whimsy, and we are little chessmen, pushed about on the board of the universe at the pleasure of a god.[13] As flies to wanton boys are we to the gods: they kill us for their sport.

Heraclitus' theology, and his view on the relation between god and the world, are matters of profound scholarly controversy; and the account which I have just sketched is far from universally accepted. But its central feature, that the events in the world are all governed by law, is, I think, beyond serious dispute; and it is that feature on which the rest of my argument turns.

There is a vulgar and perennial confusion induced by the equivocity of the English word 'law'. In the language of science, a law is a general description of natural phenomena; scientific laws state how things are, or perhaps how, by a kind of 'natural necessity', things must be. Such laws cannot be broken or violated: if Kepler's 'laws' of planetary motion ascribe a certain orbit to Neptune, and Neptune is observed to stray from that orbit, it is not Neptune but

Kepler who is at fault. Kepler's laws are not broken but falsified, they are shown to be inadequate descriptions of the celestial phenomena; they are not laws of nature after all. In the language of legislation, which moralists and politicians professionally pillage, a law is a general prescription for human behaviour; legislative laws state how things are to be or how they ought to be. Such laws cannot be falsified: if Dracon's laws lay down that Athenians are not to abstract one another's purses, and Cleonymus steals my purse, then it is not Dracon but Cleonymus who is at fault; Dracon's laws are not falsified but violated. They are shown, perhaps, to be inadequately policed; they are not shown to be invalid, or to be no laws at all.

The distinction between the descriptive laws of the scientist and the prescriptive laws of the legislator is obvious enough; yet it is blurred or ignored with tedious frequency. Moral laws are construed as accounts of what must be; scientific laws are read as injunctions to natural phenomena.

The English word 'law' is closely paralleled in this unfortunate respect by the Greek word *nomos*.[14] '*Nomos*' has a long history, and it is applied in many contexts; only two of those applications are of moment here. First, a *nomos* may be a custom or a regularity: if all A's are B, or if A's are, as a general rule, B, then it may be said to be a *nomos* that A's are B. Second, a *nomos* may be a law or a rule: if A's are enjoined or urged to be B, by implicit rule or explicit ordinance, then it may be said to be a *nomos* for A's to be B. These two distinct applications are neatly confused in a passage from Hesiod's *Works and Days*:

> The son of Cronos ordained this *nomos* for men:
> that while fish and beasts and winged birds
> eat one another (for there is no justice among them),
> to men he gave justice, which is by far the best—
> for if anyone is prepared to say just things from knowledge, to him
> far-seeing Zeus gives riches;
> but whoever in bearing witness willingly swears an oath
> and lies, and violating justice does an evil deed,
> he leaves behind him a feeble offspring—
> and the offspring left behind by the faithful man is better
>   (**110**: 276–85).

Zeus' *nomos* for brutes is that they eat one another; his *nomos* for men is that they should deal justly with one another. The animal *nomos* is a law of nature; the human *nomos* is a law of morality. The word *nomos* occurs but once; its changing application is shown not only by the sense of what Hesiod says, but also by his fluttering syntax.

In English, 'justice' does not have the same ambivalence as 'law'. We do not speak of the 'justice' of nature in the way we speak of the laws of nature; 'justice' remains a purely prescriptive term. The Greek word '*dikê*' is often correctly translated as 'justice'; but '*dikê*' is also used outside prescriptive contexts: '*dikê*' may mark the way things are as well as the way things ought to be. In that respect, '*dikê*' and '*nomos*' run parallel courses.

I do not know whether or not we should say that '*nomos*' and '*dikê*' are ambiguous terms, each having at least two distinct senses; so far as I know, no ancient text distinguishes descriptive from prescriptive senses of the words, and it may be that in the notions of *nomos* and *dikê* description and prescription are merely confused. What is clear is that both prescriptions and descriptions are expressed by the words *nomos* and *dikê*.[15] I shall shortly exhibit a Heraclitean example; and I am inclined to believe that this feature of the Greek language played a part in forming one of the most obvious and familiar features of early Greek science: 'The early Greek notion of justice'—and of law—'lends itself with seductive ease to application far beyond the bounds of politics and morals'.[16] The first thinker to be seduced was Anaximander: 'The things from which is the coming into being for the things that exist are also those into which their destruction come about, in accordance with what must be;[17] for they give justice and reparation to one another for their offence, in accordance with strife and what must be (37: **B 80** = **28 M**). formulated, appropriately enough, in terms of natural necessity: things come about 'in accordance with what must be'; they happen as they are bound to happen. But Anaximander then explains that grand fact in terms of crime and punishment, of offence and reparation, of transgression and justice. The language of prescription improperly replaces the language of description, and the lawyer invades the province of the scientist.

Heraclitus echoes Anaximander: 'one should know that war is common, and justice strife; and that everything comes about in accordance with strife and necessity' (37: **B80** = **28 M**). Characteristically, Heraclitus corrects Anaximander: where Anaximander sees in the 'strife' of things an offence which must be corrected, Heraclitus sees justice in this very strife; but the fundamental insight of the two men is the same: natural phenomena are bound by law and are subject to a cosmic justice. A striking fragment illustrates Heraclitus' general thesis:

> The sun will not overstep its measures; otherwise the Furies,
> ministers of justice, will find it out (**111: B 94 = 52 M**).

The natural laws of celestial motion are backed by sanctions: why else would the sun consent to its tedious diurnal round? Keplerian descriptions are confused with Draconian prescriptions; what is and what ought to be are confounded.[18]

To ascribe such a gross confusion to Heraclitus may seem at best uncharitable: '37, after all, glosses "justice" by "what must be"; and 111, with its Homeric echo (*Iliad* XIX. 418), may be no more than a colourful metaphor. Cosmic justice is a figure of speech, not a theory; a piece of harmless rhetoric, not a logical confusion.' Charity is always tempting; but it rarely comports with the harsh facts of history: let us consider the two main theses in Heraclitus' moral theory.

Christianity has hardened us to the absurd; and there are, I believe, those who can contemplate with serenity the assertion that we live in a *nonpareil* world.

> All Nature is but Art, unknown to thee;
> All Chance, Direction, which thou canst not see;
> All Discord, Harmony, not understood;
> All partial Evil, Universal good;
> And, spite of Pride, in erring Reason's spite,
> One truth is clear, 'Whatever IS, is RIGHT'.

Since God is both all-good and all-potent, the natural theologians, those metaphysical estate agents, must market the world as a desirable residence. Their contemptible claims have won the approbation of numerous great men; and their professions were not wholly unknown in the ancient world. In a later chapter I shall consider some late-fifth-century assaults on theodicy: here I limit attention to Heraclitus.

For Heraclitus was a Presocratic Pangloss. He says clearly enough that whatever is is right:

> To god everything is fine and good and just; but men have taken some things to be unjust and others to be just (**112: B 102 = 91 M**).

This fragment does not illustrate Heraclitus' thesis of the Unity of Opposites; it does not, as some scholars think, urge that 'just and unjust are one and the same'. On the contrary, it avers that nothing is unjust: despite ordinary human judgments, everything that happens is, in God's eyes and hence in reality, a just and good happening. After all, if 'everything happens in accordance with strife' and 'justice is strife', it is an easy inference that all events are just, and that our world is a perfect world.

Why did Heraclitus espouse that belief? Consider the following pair of syllogisms: 'Everything happens in accordance with *nomos* (*logos*); what happens in accordance with *nomos* happens justly: *ergo*, everything happens justly.' 'Everything occurs *kata dikên*; what occurs *kata dikên* occurs justly: *ergo*, everything occurs justly.' Both arguments are valid; in each the first premiss is Heraclitean, and the second premiss seems tautological. Yet the arguments are evidently unsound: they trade on the confusion between prescriptive *nomos* and descriptive *nomos*, between prescriptive *dikê* and descriptive *dikê*. The first premiss in each argument uses its keyword descriptively, asserting the regularity of cosmic phenomena. The second premiss in each argument is true and tautological only if its keyword is taken prescriptively. Both arguments are examples of the 'fallacy of equivocation'. I do not suggest that Heraclitus consciously advanced those arguments; I do incline to believe that the confusions which they brazenly exhibit helped to ease Heraclitus into his absurd position.

I turn finally to the second main thesis of Heraclitean ethics. Fragments **B 114** and **B 2** are plausibly conjoined to read as follows:

> Those who speak with sense (*xun nôi*) must put their strength in what is common (*xunôi*) to all, as a city in law—and much more strongly. For all human laws are nourished by one, the divine [law]; for it controls as much as it wishes, and it is sufficient for all, and is left over.
>
> For that reason one should follow what is common (*xunôi*); yet though the account is common, most men live as though they had a private understanding (**113: B 114 + B 2 = 23 M**).[19]

The importance of law was clear in Heraclitus' mind:

> The people should fight for their law as for their city-wall (**114: B 44 = 103 M**).

Those terrestrial laws are nourished by the one divine law, which is the content of Heraclitus' 'account'; consequently, men should pay heed to that great law, follow it, and obey its ordinances.

Heraclitus' argument in **113** is obscure; for it relies on an uncertain metaphor. He is, I take it, arguing to the conclusion that we should act in accordance with the common *logos*; and his premiss is the content of **114**, that we should obey our political laws. His argument is *a fortiori*: our human laws are 'nourished' by the divine law; if we should follow them, plainly we should follow it.

The metaphor of nourishment is difficult; and it is not explained by the statement that the divine law 'controls, is sufficient and is left over'. I offer the following tentative exegesis: 'Human *nomoi* owe what validity they have to the divine *nomos*: since that *nomos* governs everything, the human *nomoi* are valid only in so far as they coincide with, or translate into particular terms, the divine injunction; hence if human *nomoi* are to command obedience, that can only be in so far as they mirror the divine law; and since, by 114, human *nomoi* are valuable, the divine *nomos* is to be followed.'

However that may be, the main burden of 113 is plain enough. Like Empedocles, Heraclitus contrasts human laws with an overarching injunction; like Empedocles, he enjoins assent to that universal ordinance. But whereas Empedocles' great law relates only to one aspect of life, Heraclitus' law is all-embracing. We must regulate our lives in accordance with the general account which describes the total workings of nature and the world; and those particular regulations which Heraclitus saw fit to emphasize are simply some of the possible specifications of the ultimate moral injunction to 'follow what is common'. If anyone doubts the wisdom of 'following what is common', let him remember the Furies who await an aberrant sun; for

> How might anyone escape the notice of that which never sets? (115: B 16 = 81 M).

> Justice will catch up with the fabricators and purveyors of lies (116: B 28a = 19 M);

> There awaits men when they die what they do not expect or imagine (117: B 27 = 74 M).[20]

Thus:

> It is wisdom to speak the truth and to act knowingly in accordance with nature (118: B 112 = 23 (f) M).

The sentence is a paraphrase, not a quotation; but it summarizes Heraclitus' doctrine well enough. The Stoics adopted and developed the view: like Heraclitus, they were determinists; and like Heraclitus, they stated the ultimate moral injunction as *oikeiôsis*: Zeno of Citium 'said that the end is to live in agreement with nature (*homologoumenôs têi phusei*), which is to live virtuously' (Diogenes Laertius, VII. 87 = *SVF* I. 179). Similar views have been enunciated more recently.

John Stuart Mill opined that 'the fundamental problem of the social sciences is to find the law according to which any state of society produces the state which succeeds it and takes its place'; and by the aid of such a science 'we may hereafter succeed not only in looking far forward into the future history of the human race, but in determining whatever artificial means may be used, and to what extent, to accelerate the natural progress in so far as it is beneficial, to compensate for whatever may be its inherent inconveniences or disadvantages, and to guard against the dangers or accidents to which our species is exposed from the necessary incidents of its progression' (*System of Logic* VI. 10). Here the *bourgeois* Mill borrows from the aristocratic Heraclitus, and lends to Karl Marx.

Holders of such a Heraclitean position have three theses to maintain: first, that every event, and consequently every human action, occurs in accordance with some universal law or set of laws; second, that men ought, therefore, to give destiny a helping hand and accommodate their actions to the demands of the universal legislature; and third, that those law-breakers and malingerers, who are inevitably to be found, will suffer discomforts, either terrestrial or eschatological, for their temerarious disobedience. As you will act, so you should act—and if you don't God help you.

The position is patently muddled; and it is frequently denounced as ridiculously and irretrievably confused. It contains a grand inanity and a simple inconsistency.

The inanity is the conjunction of the first and second theses: 'if all men *will* act in accordance with the universal law, then it is fatuous to urge them that they *ought* to act in accordance with it. If they will act so, then they will act so whether urged or not; and moral injunction is a futile form of language.'

The ramifications of that line of argument are multitudinous and familiar; and I cannot here be more than dogmatic: the fact that all men will act in accordance with the universal law does not make Heraclitus' injunction pointless. His utterance of the injunction in 113 will, of course, itself be determined by the universal law; yet it may for all that form a link in the causal chain—or one of the causal chains—which shackle future actions to the past. Heraclitus' injunction may have causal efficacy in a deterministic world: had he (*per impossibile*) not so enjoined, men would not so have acted. His injunction is neither fatuous nor futile. Indeed, he may comfort himself with the thought that he is after all playing a bit part in the universal comedy; and the comfort will only dissolve when he reflects that the comforting thought is itself determined by the universal law, a line written into the script of a play whose actors are forbidden to *ad lib*.

The inconsistency of the Heraclitean position resides in its first and third theses. Here the matter is simple: the first thesis says that everyone *does* act by the law; the third implies that some men do *not*. And that is the simplest form of contradiction one can hope to find, even in a Presocratic text.

The contradiction emerges from a strict reading of certain fragments; in particular, it requires us to take the word 'everything' in 33 and again in 37 in the strongest possible sense. Perhaps that is unjust: 'everything', after all, is regularly used hyperbolically or loosely; and in any case, the larger context of its Heraclitean use is lost to us. Thus Heraclitus might be extricated from inconsistency, and in more than one way. 'Everything' might be restricted to inanimate phenomena: the world of heartless, witless nature runs according to the universal law, by necessity; we do not—but since we cannot fly to Venus or to Mercury we are well advised to temper our acts to that law. Or again, 'everything' might be interpreted weakly, implying a general but not a strictly universal law: there is a *nomos*, a general rule or regularity; but it allows exceptions—if we are prudent, we shall conform to it rather than taste the delusory joys of unconventionality.

We do not possess enough remnants of Heraclitus' book to know if either of those suggestions fits his thought; other suggestions are possible. Yet if we take the surviving fragments at their face value—a reasonable procedure, in all conscience—we shall return, reluctantly, to the conclusion that Heraclitus admitted human renegades to a cosmically determined world. And we are also obliged to credit Heraclitus with the crude command 'There is a universal law—obey it', wherein descriptive and prescriptive laws are confused. Thus Heraclitus initiated two perennial confusions in philosophical ethics: if it takes a great philosopher to originate a great error, Heraclitus has a double grandeur.

VIII

The Principles of Human Knowledge

(a) *The origins of scepticism*

The sceptical philosophers of Hellenistic Greece held that no one at all could know anything at all; and with commendable consistency they proceeded to deny that they themselves knew even that distressing fact. Their splendid doctrine, or antidoctrine, had, they believed, been adumbrated in the epistemological reflexions of the early Presocratics; for although scepticism had not flourished until the late fifth century, Parmenides' predecessors had reflected, at least casually, on epistemological matters, and some of them had emitted pronouncements of a sceptical tone. And that, after all, is hardly surprising: the first philosophers had propounded theories of unprecedented scope and presumption. Their utterances must have aroused wonder and amazement; and wonder, as Aristotle observes, is the father of thought. Having wondered that the Milesians knew so much, men might wonder how they knew so much; and having wondered how, it was but a short step to wondering whether they knew quite everything that they professed:

> all ignorance toboggans into know
> and trudges up to ignorance again.

The uphill trudge is the natural successor to the heady slide.

At all events, the early Presocratics did, I believe, invent epistemology or the science of knowledge; and they brought a form of scepticism to birth. We may start from Alcmeon of Croton. According to Diogenes Laertius, Alcmeon's treatise *Concerning Nature* opened as follows:

> Alcmeon of Croton, son of Peirithous, said this to Brotinus and to Leon and to Bathyllus: concerning things unseen the gods possess clear understanding (*saphêneia*); but in so far as men may guess [... I say as follows ...] (**119**: 24 B1).

The text of the fragment is controversial:[1] on any account **119** is sceptical in tone; but different versions give radically different sorts of scepticism.

With the text I adopt, Alcmeon is no Pyrrhonian; he does not absolutely deny the possibility of knowledge and the rationality of belief. First, he ascribes knowledge, even of 'things unseen', to the gods; only men are deprived of knowledge: it is the human candle whose illuminatory powers are feeble. Second, it is only 'things unseen' which escape human knowledge: what we see, Alcmeon implies, we can indeed know. Alcmeon is thus closer to the urbane scepticism of Locke than to the hyperbolical doubt of Pyrrho and his followers. And that, perhaps, is to the good; for while Pyrrho's views are ostentatiously incredible, Lockean scepticism is both plausible enough to be persuasive and sufficiently removed from our unreflective thoughts to be disconcerting.

Lockean scepticism was endemic in the Greek mind. Its *locus classicus* is in the second book of the Iliad, where the poet seeks help from the Muses:

> for you
> Are goddesses, are present here, are wise, and all things know,
> We only trust the voice of fame, know nothing. . . .

There are numerous imitations and parallels;[2] and the melancholy sentiment is of a piece with that 'modest assessment of the importance of mankind in the universe'[3] which is characteristic of early Greek writings. Such effusions express a mournful emotion rather than enunciate a philosophical belief; and we might be tempted to regard Alcmeon's sceptical proem as no more than a bow to a Greek convention: a decent modesty is expected of a man who is about to describe the history and nature of the universe. But Alcmeon has philosophical as well as poetical predecessors; and it is to them that I now turn.

Xenophanes, according to pseudo-Plutarch, 'says that the senses are false, and together with them he also delivers a general attack on reason itself' (**21 A 32**). Sotion, more briefly, makes him 'the first to say that everything is unknowable' (Diogenes Laertius, IX. 20 = **A 1**). Timon, who was of a sceptical turn of mind, evidently found a kindred spirit in Xenophanes; for his poetical dialogues on the history of philosophy are feigned to have occurred between himself and his predecessor (Diogenes Laertius, IX. 111). Sextus places Xenophanes at the head of the sceptical sect (*Pyrrh Hyp* II. 18; *adv Math* VII. 48–52).[4]

Four of the surviving fragments of Xenophanes' poems bear on epistemological matters; and the longest of them, amounting to no more than four lines, was certainly the chief and perhaps the sole source of his sceptical reputation. It runs thus:

> And the clear truth (*to saphes*) no man has seen nor will anyone
> know, about the gods and concerning everything of which I speak.
> For even if he should actually manage to say something that is the case,
> nevertheless he himself does not know. But for all there is belief
> (**120**: B 34).[5]

The lines are prefatory in character; and I accept the suggestion that they come from an exordium to Xenophanes' philosophical *oeuvre* (see above, p. 83). Antiquity read **120** in a sceptical fashion: by modern scholars the sense of the fragment is hotly disputed.

First, it has been argued on philological grounds that **120** has nothing whatever to do with scepticism. Xenophanes, the argument goes, asserts not that no one *knows*, but that no man has *seen*, the truth about the gods; and the phrase which I have translated 'nor will anyone know' (*oude tis estai eidôs*) is more properly rendered by 'nor will anyone see'—for the verb *eidenai*, of which *eidôs* is the participle, is originally a verb of perception. **120** does not, then, advocate scepticism: it states that on certain subjects *perceptual* knowledge is unattainable, thereby implying that a non-perceptual form of knowledge is appropriate there, a perceptual form elsewhere. **120** classifies knowledge, it does not attack knowledge; and Xenophanes the sceptic slopes off into the populous limbo of historical fantasy.

The argument has, I think, now been conclusively refuted. Careful research does indeed show that, etymologically, *eidenai* is a perceptual verb; but further extensive researches have incontrovertibly shown that even in Homer the verb bears the general sense of 'know', and that this sense was normal by Xenophanes' time: in Xenophanes, as in classical texts, *eidenai* simply means 'know'.[6] Moreover, *eidôs* in line 2 contrasts with *dokos* in line 4; and since *dokos* can only mean 'belief', *eidôs* will naturally be translated by means of the verb 'to know'. Thus, **120** does after all enunciate some sort of sceptical thesis: it asserts that no man has known or will know certain things.

Second, we may ask whether Xenophanes' scepticism is, like Alcmeon's, a thesis about the capacities of human cognition. That question is easily answered. **120** talks explicitly of men; **B 18** and **B 36**, which I shall shortly quote, imply that the gods have knowledge which men lack; and Arius Didymus explicitly says that, according to Xenophanes, 'god knows the truth, but for all there is belief' (**A 24**): the second clause comes from **120**; and it is a happy suggestion that the first clause, which is metrical, is also a quotation from Xenophanes.[7]

Third, what is the scope of Xenophanes' scepticism? Is he denying all knowledge to men, or only certain areas of knowledge? **120** specifies the scope by the phrase 'about the gods and concerning everything of which I speak'. If, as I believe, **120** prefaced a scientific poem in the Milesian tradition, then Xenophanes means to say that knowledge about things divine and knowledge about natural science, lie beyond our human grasp.

That interpretation is confirmed by a passage from a justly celebrated treatise in the Hippocratic *corpus*: the treatise is *On Ancient Medicine*, and it was probably composed towards the end of the fifth century. Alcmeon specified the scope of his scepticism by the phrase 'the things unseen (*ta athêêta*)'; the Hippocratic treatise takes up Alcmeon's notion, if not his phrase, to pillory those pretentious disciplines which deal with 'what is invisible and puzzled over (*ta aphanea te kai aporeomena*)'. The pretentious scientists are men who study 'the things in the air (*ta meteôra*) and the things underground'. Those words pick out the main areas of early scientific interest;[8] and an attack on the students of *ta aphanea* is an attack on the pretensions of Ionian science. The stars are visible, and the rocky substance of the earth is not unseen; for all that, the early scientists could be said to apply their minds to *ta aphanea* and *ta athêêta* inasmuch as their astronomical and geological theories advanced far beyond the bounds of perception.

On Ancient Medicine criticizes its scientific opponents in the following terms:

> If one should state and declare how these things are, it would be clear neither to the speaker himself nor to his hearers whether they were true or not; for there is nothing by referring to which one can know the clear truth (*to saphes*) (**121**: §1).

The connexions between this passage and **120** are close; I think they are too close to be coincidental, and I suggest that in *Ancient Medicine* we find an early and favourable exegesis of Xenophanes' fragment. Thus in **120** Xenophanes advocated a limited, and not a general scepticism: it is theology and natural science, not knowledge in general, that must elude our human grasp.[9]

Three further fragments bear on the question. **B 18** reads thus:

> Not from the beginning did the gods show everything to mortals; but in time by inquiring they find things out better (122).

The fragment is complemented by **B 36**:

> Whatever they have revealed to mortals to be seen . . . (123).

122 shows that 'they' in **123** refers to the gods; and **123** in turn indicates that **122** should be glossed as follows: 'The gods did not reveal everything to men at once; but their few revelations, aided by patient inquiry, will lead to progress.' It is a plausible inference from the two fragments that Xenophanes does allow some knowledge to men: patient inquiry will increase the small stock of god-given knowledge. Finally, **B 35**:

> Let these things be believed (*dedoxasthô*) as being similar to what is true (124).

Belief and verisimilitude, not knowledge and truth, mark the goal of man's cognitive journey. The reference of 'these things' is determined by **120**: as **120** formed part of a prologue to Xenophanes' *oeuvre*, so **124** comes from its epilogue; and as the scepticism of **120** is limited to theology and science, so too is the injunction of **124**.

The conclusion, that Xenophanes advocated a limited and not a general scepticism, is again confirmed by *Ancient Medicine*. Immediately after his echo of **120**, the author announces that in the art of medicine knowledge is not only attainable, but has, to some extent, been attained; and that, he says, was achieved 'by inquiring for a long time' (§2). That surely is an echo of **122**; indeed, it is possible that Xenophanes himself mentioned medicine as a potential field for knowledge and progress; and it is probable that doctor Alcmeon did so.

Xenophanes did not merely assert a scepticism; he argued for it. The second couplet of **120** begins with an inferential particle:

> For (*gar*) even if he should actually manage to say something that is the case,
> nevertheless he himself does not know.

The reference to saying is, I take it, insignificant: and the antecedent of the couplet glosses as: 'even if *a* truly believes that *P* . . .'. Pretty clearly, Xenophanes is implying that knowledge consists of true belief and something more; the implication was developed in Plato's

Theaetetus; and it has stood as a central problem in modern epistemology. Knowledge is more than true belief; but what must be added to true belief to attain knowledge? and how can the addition be secured?

Xenophanes' answer to those questions has been sought in **120**. Sextus glosses the consequent of the second couplet as follows: '... *a* does not know that *a* truly believes that *P*'.[10] So construed, **120** argues thus: '*a* does not know that *P*; for even if *a* truly believes that *P*, he cannot know that he does'. The principle behind the argument is:

(1) If *a* knows that *P*, then *a* knows that *a* truly believes that *P*.

The principle has some initial attractions: it suggests, on the one hand, a thesis about knowing that one knows that has been much canvassed in recent philosophical literature, and on the other hand, it hints at the danger of an infinite regress of the type Plato was so concerned to avoid.

A closer inspection proves (1) less attractive. If '*a* knows that *a* truly believes that *P*' is equivalent to '*a* knows that *a* believes that *P* and *a* knows that *P* is true', then (1) is equivalent to:

(2) If *a* knows that *P*, then *a* knows that *a* believes that *P* and *a* knows that *P* is true;

and (2) is equivalent to:

(3) If *a* knows that *P*, then *a* knows that *a* believes that *P*.

Now even if (3) is true, as on some interpretations of 'know' perhaps it is, it is not a proposition with any seriously sceptical implications. In the context of Xenophanes' argument, it implies that the additional element required to turn true belief into knowledge is the knowledge that you hold the belief in question. And such knowledge is surely not peculiarly elusive: of all things, our own beliefs are most accessible to us.

In short, Sextus' interpretation imputes the following argument to Xenophanes: 'we cannot aspire to knowledge of theology and science, for such knowledge presupposes knowledge of our own beliefs'. Such an argument is feeble, and I therefore incline to reject the Sextan interpretation. For a simpler interpretation is possible: the consequent of the couplet reads simply '*a* does not know that *P*'; and **120** argues thus: 'you cannot know that *P* for though you may attain true belief, that is not knowledge'. The argument turns on the fact that knowledge is not just true belief. It immediately raises the question of why the additional component in knowledge, whatever it may be, is so hard to come by; but it does not answer the question or even identify the extra component. For that we must look beyond the confines of **120**, and reconsider some of the fragments of Xenophanes' theology.

The gods are commonly supposed to be anthropomorphic (**63: B 14**), yet a little imagination will indicate that cows and horses, had they the wit to conceive of gods at all, would make them theriomorphic (**73: B 15**); and observation shows that:

> Each group of men paint the shape of the gods in a fashion similar to themselves—as Xenophanes says, the Ethiopians draw them dark and snub-nosed, the Thracians red-haired and blue-eyed (**125: Clement, B 16**).[11]

With these fragments we should compare **B 38**;

> If god had not made golden honey, men would say that figs are much sweeter (**126**).

There is, I think, an epistemological moral here: our beliefs—or many of them—are explicable in terms of our circumstances; they do not, therefore, amount to knowledge.

Let me expand upon that. A Thracian believes that the gods are red-haired. His belief is explicable in a way which has no connexion with the actual nature of the gods: because the Thracian is himself red-haired, he believes the gods to be red-heads too. The causal hypothesis is supported by the findings of comparative anthropology; for everywhere men's gods are themselves writ large. The hypothesis does not show the Thracian's belief to be false; but it does show it to fall short of knowledge. Again, an Athenian nurtured on honey from Hymettus holds that figs are only moderately sweet. His belief is explicable in a way which has no connexion with the intrinsic nature of the figs: because the Athenian has had a taste of honey, he believes figs to be mildly sweet. The causal hypothesis is supported by the findings of comparative sociology; for men's gustatory judgments vary according to their gustatory experience. The hypothesis does not show the Athenian's belief to be false; but it does show it to fall short of knowledge. And in general, for a very large and important class of beliefs, if a believes that P, then there is some causal hypothesis, quite unconnected with the content of his belief, which explains why he believes that P. 'For all there is belief': some lucky men may 'actually manage to say something that is the case'; but for all that, 'the clear truth no man has seen, nor will anyone know'.

It is important to see what Xenophanes is not saying here. First, he is not commenting on the disreputable origins of most of our beliefs: many of my beliefs about Roman history were first fixed in my mind by the novels of Robert Graves and Julian Green; yet for all that, some at least of my beliefs have been turned into knowledge. Thin opinions, illicitly imbibed, may later be transformed by an intellectual digestion into red-blooded knowledge. Xenophanes does not deny that. Second, Xenophanes is not objecting to causal explanations of knowledge as such. My present belief that Caesar was murdered on the Ides of March is, I suppose, causally explicable by reference to my avid reading and memorizing of the accounts of his death in various ancient texts. It does not follow—nor does Xenophanes imply that it does—that my belief falls short of knowledge.

Rather, Xenophanes' point is that many of my beliefs are explicable by a causal hypothesis which has no direct connexion with the content of those beliefs. I believe that P, and P is true: yet there is a causal chain explaining my belief which was neither originated nor at any stage supplemented by the fact that P. And that is why my belief is not knowledge.

Xenophanes' thesis requires a more careful statement and a lengthier consideration than I can give it here. I am confident, however, that the philosophical part of it is true: *if* my belief that P was caused by events having no suitable connexion with the fact that P, then I do not know that P. The non-philosophical part of Xenophanes' thesis, that very many of our beliefs do have defective causal antecedents of that sort, cannot be assessed in general terms: to test it, we must take believers and their beliefs piecemeal. I shall, however, indulge myself to the extent of offering an unsupported judgment that here too Xenophanes is probably right.

Men's beliefs do not amount to knowledge because they have unsatisfactory causes. The conclusion suggests that true belief will amount to knowledge if its causal antecedents are reputable. The extant fragments give no clue to Xenophanes' canons of respectability, if indeed he ever formulated any. He implies, if my interpretation is correct, that in some areas at least knowledge is attainable by men; and it is therefore reasonable to ask what features of those favoured areas make them open to human cognition, and to require of Xenophanes, if not a general account of causal respectability, at least an indication of certain cases in which the causal chain leading to belief has the strength and direction to turn that belief into an item of knowledge.

(b) *The foundations of empirical knowledge*

The key is again to be found in *Ancient Medicine*:

> You will find no measure or number or balance by referring to which you will know with certainty—except perception (**127**: § 9).

THE PRINCIPLES OF HUMAN KNOWLEDGE

An elaboration of that blunt assertion will produce an empiricist theory of knowledge. The first attempt to sketch such a theory is to be found in the writings of the early Presocratics.

Heraclitus certainly had the makings of a cynic; and some see him as a sceptic. He denounces the claims to knowledge made by his great predecessors, Hesiod, Hecataeus, Pythagoras, and even Xenophanes;[12] and he regularly rails at the folly of mankind:

> Most men do not understand what they meet with, nor when they learn do they gain knowledge—but they seem to themselves to do so (**128:22 B 17 = 3 M**).

> What understanding or intelligence have they got? They put their faith in folk-singers, and they use the multitude as a teacher, not knowing that 'the many are bad and few are good' (**129: B 104 = 101 M**).[13]

Again, there are several fragments of a relativist bent, reminiscent of Xenophanes' comment on the sweetness of honey:

> Disease made health sweet; famine, satiety; exhaustion, rest (**130: B 111 = 44 M**).

> A man is held foolish by a spirit, as a child is by a man (**131: B 79 = 92 M**).

And several fragments suggest scepticism more directly:

> Nature likes to hide itself (**59: B 123 = 8 M**).

> Human character has no insights (*gnômai*), divine character does (**132: B 78 = 90 M**).

If you seek knowledge, you will be like gold-diggers who 'dig over much earth and find little' (**B 22 = 10 M**); and if you had the temerity to study psychology,

> you would not find in your journey the limits of the *psuchê*, even if you travelled the whole road—so deep is its account (*logos*) (**133: B 45 = 67 M**).

A narrow inspection, however, does not support that interpretation of Heraclitus: the scornful attacks on other men's pretensions and on the ignorance of the multitude do not suggest scepticism but the reverse; for the attacker claims a superiority. The relativistic fragments served a metaphysical rather than an epistemological purpose (see above, p. 74). The sceptical fragments, with the exception of **132**, are designed only to stress the important platitude that knowledge is not easily won; and **132** may carry a moral rather than an epistemological message.

Certain optimistic philosophers have embraced a doctrine of Manifest Truth. According to Spinoza: 'Truth at once reveals itself and also what is false, because truth is made clear through truth—that is, through itself—and through it also is falsity made clear; but falsity is never revealed and made manifest through itself. Hence anyone who is in possession of the truth cannot doubt that he possesses it, while one who is sunk in falsity or in error can well suppose that he has got at the truth' (*Short Treatise on God, Man and his Well-Being*, ch. 15).[14] That curious and confused view would certainly have been rejected by Heraclitus: truth does not 'reveal itself'—it lies hidden at the bottom of the well, and only an accomplished workman will have skill enough to draw it up. To say that is to be a realist, not a sceptic.

A difficult fragment has indeed been read as an explicit rejection of Xenophanean scepticism:

> For the most trustworthy man (*ho dokimôtatos*) knows how to guard one from what seems to be the case (*ta dokeonta*). And indeed justice will catch up with the inventors and purveyors of lies (**134: B 28 = 20 M + 19 M**—see above, p. 133).

According to Xenophanes, we must be content with belief (*dokos*); according to Heraclitus, a clever man (*dokimôtatos*) can preserve us from *dokeonta* and lead us to genuine knowledge.[15] Whether or not that is the right reading of **134**, its import is undeniably Heraclitean.

The path to preservation requires a sturdy independence: we must not behave like 'children of parents', accepting what we are told on the mere authority of the teller (**B 74 = 89 M**); and if

> eyes are more certain witnesses than ears (**135: B 101a = 6 M**),

that is partly because our ears bring us hearsay evidence and are responsible to a greater extent than our eyes for the inculcation of second-hand opinions. We are not to accept things even on the authority of Heraclitus himself: we must listen not to him but to what he says (**35: B 50 = 26 M**); and his *logos* is to be accepted for its intrinsic merits, not on the say-so of its first discoverer. Diogenes says of Heraclitus that 'he studied at no one's feet, but he says that he searched for himself and learned everything by himself' (IX. 5 = **A 1**). A knower must be able to say, with Heraclitus,

> I searched for myself (**136: B 101 = 15 M**).[16]

The fragments indicate that Heraclitus was true to his own prescription: 'he learned at the feet of no philosopher but was educated by nature and by industry' (Suda, **A 1a**).

It is to this context, I suspect, that two celebrated fragments on 'polymathy', or the learning of many things, belong. The fragments read thus:

> Polymathy does not teach understanding (*nous*)—otherwise it would have taught Hesiod and Pythagoras, and again Xenophanes and Hecataeus (**137: B 40 = 16 M**).
>
> Pythagoras, son of Mnesarchus, practised inquiry most of all men, and excerpting those writings he claimed for himself wisdom—polymathy, malpractice (**138: B 129 = 17 M**).[17]

A vulgar Baconianism holds that science advances by first amassing countless pieces of particular information and then inferring a universal law: understanding, on this view, is the product of polymathy; and it is tempting to regard Heraclitus' dismissal of polymathy as a deliciously modern protest against a precocious form of Baconianism.

I doubt that interpretation. It seems to me that it is the second and not the first half of the word 'polymathy' which arouses Heraclitus' scorn. Pythagoras' fault is not that he learned a lot, but that he stole his thoughts from others: he claimed wisdom, when he had indulged only in malpractice and polymathy. *Manthanein* means 'to learn', and in particular 'to learn from another'; and polymaths are men who have acquired a large stock of opinions from other men. Learning and discovery are opposed.[18] Learners have not 'sought for themselves'; and it is for that reason that, however much they may have learned, they cannot lay claim to understanding or knowledge. John Locke urged that testimony, or the word of other men, could support a probable opinion but could never sustain knowledge. Keats expressed the same view in another terminology:

> knowledge dwells
> In heads replete with thoughts of other men;
> Wisdom in minds attentive to their own.

Heraclitus, I suggest, is the originator of that epistemological tradition.

And like Locke, Heraclitus was an empiricist; indeed, our evidence suggests that he was not only an empiricist but a sensationalist: knowledge must be built on experience, and specifically on sense-experience.

> The things we learn of by sight and hearing, those do I prefer (**139: B 55 = 5 M**).[19]

> If all things became smoke, the nostrils would discern them (**140: B 7 = 78 M**).

In our familiar world, eyes and ears give the basis for knowledge; and even in a radically different world the appropriate senses would be our only ultimate guide. An ill-attested fragment says that according to Heraclitus the sun has 'the breadth of a human foot' (**B 3 = 57 M**). Some scholars take this to make the banal assertion that the sun looks about a foot across; others find in it a metaphorical expression of some psychological theory.[20] But if the fragment is not a mere forgery, we must take it to mean what it says: it is a crude piece of astronomy, and it evinces a strict and severe sensationalism. Our eyes tell how big the sun is; and they are the best witnesses we could have.[21]

A further fragment remarks that

> we must be knowers of very many things (**141: B 35 = 7 M**).

There is, of course, no incompatibility between that prescription and Heraclitus' rejection of 'polymathy';[22] and **141** immediately suggests the second stage in the classical empiricist recipe for attaining knowledge: the senses give us particular information; frequent and diverse inquiry amasses an organized quantity of such information; it only remains to transmute that mass of dross into the gold of knowledge.

How is the transmutation to occur? Some scholars find a hint in **B 107 = 13 M**:

> Bad witnesses for men are the eyes and ears of those who have barbarous *psuchai* (**142**).

Sextus, who reports the fragment, takes it to 'refute perception' (**A 16**); but he misconstrues the Greek. The fragment should rather be compared with **128** ('Most men do not understand the things they meet with . . .') and with **61: B 56 = 21 M** ('Men are deceived with regard to knowledge of what is evident . . .'): the truth is not manifest; only a practised eye will discern what is presented to it; the senses need direction by a mind that is not 'barbarous'.

Can we press the notion of a 'barbarous mind' into epistemological service? The Greeks used the word '*barbaros*' to denominate, rudely, foreigners. Etymologically it is connected with the idea of twittering or babbling: *barbaroi* are men who cannot talk intelligibly. (I do not know if *barbaros* means 'foreign' or 'non-Greek'; the lexicons offer both translations as if they were synonymous.) It is usually, and plausibly, supposed that 'barbarous minds' belong to men with some sort of linguistic deficiency; yet what deficiency can Heraclitus have in mind in 142?

Heraclitus is hardly advancing the chauvinist thesis that non-Greek speakers cannot attain knowledge; nor is he anticipating those delightful Frenchmen of the seventeenth century who held that the ancient tongues were peculiarly appropriate to the expression of scientific and metaphysical truth. Again, Heraclitus is hardly expressing the insight that scientific knowledge is available only to men who can speak a language; for 142 tilts against the ignorant masses and Heraclitus will hardly have supposed that the majority of his contemporaries were literally incapable of speech.

Some scholars connect 142 with Heraclitus' alleged interest in the subtle metaphysical implications of some linguistic turns; and they suggest that the fragment means that 'your senses will deceive you if you do not have an accurate understanding of your own language'[23]—such understanding being the key to the Heraclitean thesis of the Unity of Opposites. But Heraclitus' main 'metaphysical' tenets derive not from a consideration of language but from a contemplation of the evidence of the senses. Heraclitus, as I read him, was not *un homme entre les choses et les mots*: he had, no doubt, a lively interest in language, and a keen nose for a pun; but language and a deep study of linguistic modes did not guide him in his philosophical endeavours, and he has no reason to require linguistic study from others.

I incline, therefore, to a more metaphorical reading of '*barbaros*' in 142: barbarous *psuchai* are ignorant, uncomprehending *psuchai*; they are characteristic of men who have no intellectual grasp of things, men who, in a neighbouring metaphor, cannot read the great Book of Nature. For 'the phenomena of Nature', as Berkeley quaintly observed, 'form not only a magnificent spectacle, but also a most coherent, entertaining, and instructive Discourse.... This Language or Discourse is studied with different attention, and interpreted with different degrees of skill. But so far as men have studied and remarked its rules, and can interpret aright, so far they may be said to be knowing in nature. A beast is like a man who hears a strange tongue but understands nothing' (*Siris* §254).

It is a pleasant metaphor; but it is a metaphor. And it is not clear what literal point lies behind it. Perhaps Heraclitus is merely insisting on the need for attentive and selective observation: in order to see that the road to Thebes is the road from Thebes, that the course of the carding-roller is straight and crooked, that the river is constantly changing its waters, and all the other detailed facts which are metaphysically significant, no ordinary or casual inspection is sufficient; unless you are well-acquainted with the ways of nature, her secrets and their significance will elude you. No doubt that is true and important; but it does not answer the question of how our many observations are to be turned into universal knowledge. The remaining fragments of Heraclitus' book do not shed any further light on the question: either Heraclitus ignored it, or fate has deprived us of his answer.

Another source supplements that deficiency. In the *Phaedo* Socrates recounts his early infatuation with natural philosophy; one of the questions that entranced him concerned the nature of thought:

> and is it blood with which we think? or air? or fire? Or is it none of these, but does the brain rather supply the senses of hearing and seeing and smelling, and memory and belief come from them, and then, when memory and belief come to rest, in this way knowledge comes about? (**143**: 96B = **24 A 11**).

Socrates is referring to Presocratic theories: Empedocles has us think with blood; Anaximenes, and Diogenes of Apollonia, with air; Heraclitus with fire. Who, then, propounded the more complicated theory which Socrates mentions after these brief accounts? and what exactly does that theory state?

According to Theophrastus, Alcmeon says that

> man differs from the other animals because he alone has understanding (*sunesis*), while the others perceive but do not understand (**144**: *Sens* §25 = **24 A 5**).

Alcmeon was singular among Presocratics in making such a sharp distinction between perceiving and understanding, sensation and knowledge; and the author of Socrates' theory made just such a distinction. Again, Alcmeon gave a detailed physiological account of perception. In it he argued that 'all the senses are in some way connected to the brain' (Theophrastus, *Sens* §26 = **A 5**). The theory in the *Phaedo* contains precisely that thesis. Those two facts make it plausible to ascribe Socrates' theory to Alcmeon. Plato, as we know, was acquainted with Alcmeon's work, and apparently fond of it; it is no surprise that a theory of Alcmeon's should be accorded some little pre-eminence in the short intellectual biography of Socrates.[24]

What, precisely, was Alcmeon's theory? It is the first statement of a view familiar to us from Aristotle's *Metaphysics* (A1) and *Posterior Analytics* (B19); and those passages are the twin origins of modern empiricism. The theory presupposes that full-blooded 'scientific' knowledge is expressible in universal propositions of the form 'Every *F* is *G*'. And it offers a causal explanation of how such knowledge is possible: I perceive an *F* which is *G*; opine that this *F* is *G*; and store that opinion in my memory. As time passes, I perceive many more *F*'s which are *G*; and store many more opinions in my memory. At this stage, according to Aristotle, I have 'experience' or *empeiria*, but not yet knowledge. Knowledge comes about when these various memories 'come to rest' (*ēremein*: *Phaedo* 96B; *APst* 100a6) and somehow coalesce into a universal proposition. In the *Metaphysics* Aristotle illustrates his theory, in tacit tribute to Alcmeon, by a medical example: I observe that hellebore helps Socrates when he is feverish, and that it helps Callias when he is feverish, and so on in many cases, until those multitudinous particular opinions, collected in my memory, unite into the knowledge that all feverish men are helped by hellebore.

Universal knowledge is thus possible. If I believe that all *F*s are *G* then my belief amounts to knowledge, provided that it was acquired in the way the theory specifies; and a careful attention will ensure that, in some cases at least, the proper path to acquisition is narrowly followed. I suppose that this theory was roughed out by Heraclitus in answer to Xenophanean scepticism; and that it was first formulated in something like its Aristotelian guise by Alcmeon.

How successful was the theory? Xenophanes, if my interpretation is right, required beliefs to have a respectable causal ancestry if they were to amount to knowledge; Heraclitus and Alcmeon attempted to specify an ancestry which could command respect. If their specification were accepted, then we could say that some at least of Heraclitus' major claims were preserved from Xenophanean criticism; for his major thesis—the elements of his *logos*—were, I argued earlier, intended to have their basis in perception.

Yet Alcmeon and the Hippocratic author, empiricists both, still maintained a Xenophanean scepticism. They must have felt, for reasons which we cannot now divine, that Heraclitus' bold theories simply outflew his modest epistemology. They played Locke to Heraclitus' Boyle: empiricism was the only hope for scientific endeavour; yet it did not permit those profound searchings into the very nature of things which Heraclitus desired to justify. I doubt if this critical attitude to Heraclitus is wholly correct; but to discuss its credentials would be both tedious and speculative. In any case, such considerations may well seem petty. Later philosophers would question this early empiricism in a far more severe fashion. The theory has us pass from a host of particular opinions to a universal belief; but that inductive move, as a later age insisted, is of dubious validity; and an empiricism which ignores sceptical doubts about perception and induction is a weak theory. But it would be absurd to disparage Alcmeon for ignoring problems which no one had yet raised, and to deny him the signal credit of sketching out the first rough draft of an empiricist epistemology.

THE SERPENT

IX

Parmenides and the Objects of Inquiry

(a) *Parmenides' journey*

Parmenides of Elea marks a turning-point in the history of philosophy: his investigations, supported and supplemented by those of his two followers, seemed to reveal deep logical flaws in the very foundations of earlier thought. Science, it appeared, was marred by subtle but profound contradictions; and the great enterprise undertaken by the Milesians, by Xenophanes and by Heraclitus, lacked all pith and moment. The age of innocence was ended, and when science was taken up again by the fifth-century philosophers, their first and most arduous task was to defend their discipline against the arguments of Elea. If their defence was often frail and unconvincing, and if it was Plato who first fully appreciated the strength and complexity of Parmenides' position, it remains true that Parmenides' influence on later Presocratic thought was all-pervasive. Historically, Parmenides is a giant figure; what is more, he introduced into Presocratic thought a number of issues belonging to the very heart of philosophy.

Parmenides' thoughts were divulged in a single hexameter poem (Diogenes Laertius, I.16 = **28 A 13**) which survived intact to the time of Simplicius (**A 21**). Observing that copies of the poem were scarce, Simplicius transcribed extensive extracts; and thanks to his efforts we possess some 150 lines of the work, including two substantial passages. It is hard to excuse Parmenides' choice of verse as a medium for his philosophy. The exigencies of metre and poetical style regularly produce an almost impenetrable obscurity; and the difficulty of understanding his thought is not lightened by any literary joy: the case presents no adjunct to the Muse's diadem.[1]

The poem began with a long allegorical prologue, the interpretation of which is for the most part of little philosophical importance. Its last four lines, however, call for comment; for they present one of the strangest features of Parmenides' work. The prologue is a speech to the poet from the goddess who leads him on his intellectual journey and describes his philosophy to him and to us. At the end of her speech she promises thus:

> And you must ascertain everything—
> both the unmoving heart of well-rounded truth,
> and the opinions of mortals in which there is no true trust (*pistis*).
> But nevertheless you will learn these too (**145: B 1.28–31**).[2]

The words are echoed near the end of the long central fragment:

> Here I stop the trustworthy (*pistos*) account and the thought
> about truth; henceforth learn mortal opinions,
> listening to the deceitful arrangement of my words (**146: B 8.50–2**).

The goddess has two stories to tell: the truth, and mortal opinions. And Parmenides' poem, after its exordium, falls into two corresponding parts, the first recounting the Way of Truth, and the second the Way of Opinion.

The Way of Opinion is paved with falsity: 'there is no true trust' along it, and its description is 'deceitful'. It could hardly be stated more plainly that the Way of Opinion is a Way of Falsity. Many scholars have found themselves incapable of believing that one half of Parmenides' work should have been devoted to the propagation of untruths; and they have accordingly advanced the palliative thesis that the Way of Opinion is a way of plausibility or verisimilitude or probability, and not exactly a way of falsehood. That conciliatory effort has origins in antiquity; and the dispute between its proponents and those sterner scholars who see no Truth in Opinion, is ancient (Plutarch, **A 34**; cf. Simplicius, **A 34**; *in Phys* 38.24–8). Yet Parmenides' own words decide the contest: he says unequivocally that the Way of Opinion is a path of falsehood and deceit; he says nothing of any probabilities lying on the road; and we are bound to take him at his word. Nor, after all, is it unusual for a philosopher to describe, at length, views with which he vehemently disagrees.

Moreover, the goddess tells us why she troubles to chart the Way of Opinion:

> I tell you all this appropriate arrangement
> in order that no thought of mortals may ever drive past you
> (**147: B 8.60–1**).

The metaphor of 'driving past (*parelaunein*)' is not transparent. Some gloss it by 'outstrip', or the like, and explain that knowledge of the Way of Opinion will enable Parmenides to hold his own in argument with any old-fashioned cosmologists he may meet. A better gloss, perhaps, is 'get the better of' or 'convince': the goddess, by describing the Way of Opinion and thereby indicating its flaws, will ensure that Parmenides does not succumb to its meretricious temptations. However that may be, the Way of Opinion does not express Parmenides' own convictions. Only a few fragments of that Way survive: it seems to have paraded a full scale account of natural philosophy in the Ionian tradition; but the details are controversial and for the most part unexciting.[3] In a later chapter I shall discuss one fragment from the Way of Opinion (vol. 2, p. 184); here I ignore that primrose path and struggle instead up the steep and rugged road of well-rounded Truth.

(b) *At the crossroads*

Before leading him up the Way of Truth, the goddess instructs Parmenides about the nature of the different ways that face the neophyte philosopher; and she provides him with a proof that the Way of Truth is alone passable. He not only should follow that Way—he must follow it; for no other way leads anywhere. The goddess's exposition and argument are difficult. I shall begin by setting out the relevant texts: if my English translation is in places barely intelligible, that is partly because Parmenides' Greek is desperately hard to understand.

> Come then, I will tell you (and you must spread the story when you have heard it)
> what are the only roads of inquiry for thinking of:
> one, both that it is and that it is not for not being,
> is the path of Persuasion (for Truth accompanies it);
> the other, both that it is not and that it is necessary for it not to be   5
> —*that*, I tell you, is a track beyond all tidings.
> For neither would you recognize that which is not (for it is not accomplishable),
> nor mention it. (**148: B 2**).

> The same thing is both for thinking of and for being (**149: B 3**).[4]

> What is for saying and for thinking of must be;[5] for it is for being,
> but nothing is not: those things I bid you hold in mind;
> for from this first road of inquiry I restrain you.
> And then from that one, along which mortals, knowing nothing,
> wander, two-headed; for helplessness in their   5
> breasts directs a wandering mind; and they are carried about
> deaf alike and blind, gawping, creatures of no judgment,
> by whom both to be and not be are thought the same
> and not the same; and the path of all is backward turning (**150: B 6**).
>
> For never will this be proved, that things that are not are.
> But do you restrain your thought from this road of inquiry (**151: B 7. 1–2**).

(Note that my translations of **149** and **150**.1 are not universally accepted. **150**. 8–9 is also controversial: see below, p. 168.)

Let us begin with **148**: what are 'the only roads of inquiry'? and what does the goddess mean when she says that they 'are for thinking of'?

The phrase 'are . . . for thinking of' (line 2) renders '*esti noêsai*'. The verb '*noein*', of which '*noêsai*' is the aorist infinitive, plays a central role in Parmenides' subsequent argument, where it is standardly translated as 'think of' or 'conceive'. Some scholars, however, prefer the very different translation 'know', and thereby change the whole character of Parmenidean thought.[6] I think that the standard translation makes better sense of Parmenides' argument; and I doubt if the heterodox translation is linguistically correct. It is true that in certain celebrated Platonic and Aristotelian passages, the noun '*nous*' is used to denote the highest of cognitive faculties; and there are passages in those philosophers, and in earlier writers, where 'intuit', 'grasp' or even 'know' is a plausible translation of '*noein*'. But against those occurrences (which are fairly uncommon and usually highflown) we can set a host of passages where '*noein*' simply means 'think (of)': '*noein*' is the ordinary Greek verb for 'think (of)', and 'think (of)' is usually its proper English equivalent. Moreover, the linguistic context in which the verb occurs in Parmenides favours (indeed, to my mind requires) the translation 'think (of)'. For '*noein*' is thrice conjoined with a verb of saying: with '*legein*' at **150**.1; and with '*phasthai*' twice in **B 8**.8 (cf. '*anônumon*' at **B 8**.17). '*Legein*' and '*phasthai*' mean 'say', not 'say truly' or 'say successfully' (the Greek for which is '*alêtheuein*'); and the contexts of their occurrence imply that 'say' and '*noein*' share at least one important logical feature: they both stand in the same relation to 'being'. In this respect it is 'think that *P*' and 'think of *X*', rather than 'know that *P*' and 'know *X*', which parallel 'say that *P*' and 'mention *X*'; and that fact, I think, establishes the traditional translation of '*noein*'.

So much for the meaning of '*noêsai*'. All, however, is not yet plain; for the syntax of '*esti noêsai*' is disputed. Phrases of the form *esti* + infinitive recur later in the poem, and their presence is indicated in my translation by phrases of the rebarbative form 'is (are) for ϕing'. The usage, which is not uncommon in Greek, has connexions with the 'potential' use of '*esti*'. (*Esti* with infinitive often means 'it is possible to . . .'. In that case '*esti*' is 'impersonal', whereas in our locution it always has a subject, explicit or implicit.) Indeed, it seems to me reasonable to gloss '*a* is for ϕing' either by '*a* can ϕ' or by '*a* can be ϕed'—the context will determine whether active or passive is appropriate. Thus in **148**.2 'are for thinking of' means 'can be thought of'.[7] Observe that the gloss differs from its original in one important feature. The grammatical form of the phrase '*a* is for ϕing' may seduce us into making a fallacious deduction: from '*a* is for ϕing' it is easy to infer '*a* is'. The grammatical form of the gloss does not provide the same temptation. The point may assume significance later.

Then what roads of enquiry can be thought of? **148** mentions two roads: Road (A) is described in line 3, and proved by line 4 to be the Way of Truth; Road (B) is the 'track beyond all tidings', delineated in line 5. **150**. 3–4 also mentions two roads: Road (C), described in lines 4–9, is that 'along which mortals . . . wander', and it is therefore the Way of Opinion. The 'first road' of line 3 also has pitfalls (for the goddess 'restrains' Parmenides from it); and it cannot therefore be identical with Road (A), the Way of Truth. Now lines 1–2 contain the end of an argument concerned with this 'first road'; and, as I shall show, it is plausible to find the beginning of the argument in **148**. 7–8, which starts to recount the horrors of the 'track beyond all tidings'. If that is so, then the 'first road' of **150** is identical with Road (B); and in consequence Road (B), the 'track beyond all tidings', is not the Way of Opinion.

148 and **150** show Parmenides at a crossroads, faced by three possible paths of inquiry: (A) the Way of Truth; (B) the 'track beyond all tidings' and (C) the Way of Opinion.[8] The first duty of the goddess is to characterize those three roads in a logically perspicuous fashion. Road (A) maintains 'both that it is (*esti*) and that it is not for not being' (**148**. 3);[9] Road (B) maintains 'both that it is not and that it is necessary for it not to be' (**148**. 5); Road (C) is not explicitly described in comparable terms, but must have maintained 'both that it is and that it is not' (cf. **150**. 8).

The three roads are thus distinguished by means of the word '*esti*', 'it is'. Both the sense of the verb and the identity of its subject are matters of high controversy. Since they are also vital to any interpretation of Parmenides' argument, we cannot burke the issue. I begin by asking what is the sense of the verb '*einai*' as Parmenides uses it here. The classification of the different 'senses', or 'uses', of the verb '*einai*' is a delicate task, abounding in linguistic and philosophical difficulties;[10] and my remarks will be crude and superficial. Nevertheless, something must be said.

We can distinguish between a complete and an incomplete use of '*einai*': sometimes a sentence of the form '*X esti*' expresses a complete proposition; sometimes *esti* occurs in sentences of the form '*X esti Y*' (or the form '*X esti*' is elliptical for '*X esti Y*'). In its complete use, '*einai*' sometimes has an existential sense: '*ho theos esti*' is the Greek for 'god exists'; '*ouk esti kentauros*' means 'Centaurs do not exist'. In its incomplete use, '*einai*' often serves as a copula, and the use is called predicative: '*Sôkratês esti sophos*' is Greek for 'Socrates is wise'; '*hoi leontes ouk eisin hêmeroi*' means 'Lions are not tame'. Many scholars think that Parmenides' original sin was a confusion, or fusion, of the existential with the predicative '*einai*'; and they believe that the characterization of the three roads in **148** catches Parmenides *in flagrante delicto*. If we ask what sense '*esti*' has in line 3, the answer is disappointing: '*esti*' attempts, hopelessly, to combine the two senses of 'exists' and 'is *Y*'.[11]

Now I do not wish to maintain that Parmenides was conscious of the distinction between an existential and a predicative use of '*einai*'; credit for bringing that distinction to philosophical consciousness is usually given to Plato. But I do reject the claim that **148** fuses or confuses the two uses of the verb. I see no reason to impute such a confusion to the characterization of the three roads; for I see no trace of a predicative 'is' in that characterization. The point can be simply supported: Road (B) rules out '*X* is not'; if we read 'is' predicatively, we must suppose Parmenides to be abjuring all negative predications. to be spurning all sentences of the form '*X* is not *F*'. Such a high-handed dismissal of negation is absurd; it is suggested by nothing in Parmenides' poem; and it is adequately outlawed by such lines as **B 8**.22, which show Parmenides happy to accept formulae of the form '*X* is not *F*'.[12] '*Esti*', in the passages we are concerned with, is not a copula.

Then is '*esti*' existential? Aristotle distinguishes what has been called a 'veridical' use of '*esti*'; '*X esti*', in this use, is complete, and '*esti*' means '. . . is the case' or '. . . is true'. If Socrates asserts that cobblers are good at making shoes, his interlocutor may reply '*Esti tauta*', 'Those things are' or 'That's true'. It has been suggested that Parmenides' complete '*esti*' is veridical, not existential.

That suggestion can be accommodated, I think, to **148** and **150**; but the accommodation is not easy, nor (as far as I can see) does it have any philosophical merit. In any event, the suggestion breaks on the rocks of **B 8**: in that fragment, Parmenides sets himself to infer a number of properties of X from the premiss that X *esti*. None of those properties consists with the veridical reading of '*esti*': the very first inference is that X is ungenerated; and if it is not, strictly speaking, impossible to take 'X' in 'X is ungenerated' to stand for the sort of propositional entity of which veridical '*esti*' is predicable, it is grossly implausible to do so, and the implausibility mounts to giant proportions as the inferences of **B 8** proceed. Since the inferences in **B 8** are tied to the '*esti*' of **148** and **150**, the veridical reading of *esti* in those fragments can only be maintained at the cost of ascribing to Parmenides a confusion between veridical and non-veridical *einai*. And I see no reason for making that derogatory ascription.[13]

Existential '*einai*' remains. The obvious and the orthodox interpretation of '*esti*' in **148** and **150** is existential; and that interpretation is felicitous: it does not perform the impossible task of presenting Parmenides with a set of doctrines which are true, but it does give Parmenides a metaphysical outlook which is intelligible, coherent and peculiarly plausible. I shall continue to translate Parmenides' '*einai*' by 'be'; but I shall paraphrase it by 'exist'.

Road (A) thus says that 'it exists', *esti*. Scholars have naturally raised the question of what exists: what is Parmenides talking about? what is the logical subject of '*esti*'? Some have denied the appropriateness of the question, urging that we need no more ask after the subject of '*esti*' than we do after '*huei*', 'it is raining'. I find that suggestion perfectly incomprehensible.[14] Nevertheless, the spirit behind it is sound: '*esti*' need not have a logical subject. For in general, we can make sense of a sentence of the form 'it ϕs' in either of two ways: first, we may find a determinate reference for 'it', so that 'it ϕs' is understood as '*a* ϕs'. ('How is your motor car?'—'It's working again'.) Here we do look for a logical subject and we expect to find it, explicit or implicit, in the immediate context. Second, 'it ϕs' may be the consequent of a conditional or a relative sentence: 'If you buy a machine, look after it'; 'Whatever machine you buy, something will go wrong with it'. In ordinary discourse, the antecedent is often not expressed: 'What will you do if you catch a fish?—Eat it'. Here there is no question of finding a logical subject for the predicate 'ϕs': 'it' does not name or refer to any particular individual.

One standard view gives '*esti*' in **148**.3 a logical subject: that subject is 'Being'; and Road (A) asserts, bluntly, that Being exists. I am at a loss to understand that assertion; what in the world can be meant by 'Being exists'? Nevertheless, behind abstract Being there lurks a more concrete candidate for the post of logical subject: '*to eon*', 'what is': should we gloss '*esti*' as 'what is, is'?[15]

Phrases of the form 'what ϕs' do not always serve as logical subjects: 'what ϕs' may mean 'whatever ϕs' ('What's done cannot be undone'); and then 'what ϕs ψs' means 'for any x: if x ϕs, x ψs'. Thus we might gloss Parmenides' '*esti*' by 'what is, is', and yet deny that 'what is' is a logical subject; for we might explain the phrase by 'what*ever* is, is'. Road (A), on that view, maintains that whatever exists exists and cannot not exist. It has been objected to that interpretation that Parmenides attempts to prove that Road (A) is right, and Roads (B) and (C) mistaken; but that the interpretation makes (A) tautologous, and hence in no need of proof, and (B) and (C) contradictory, and hence in no need of disproof. But the objection is doubly mistaken: first, tautologies can, and sometimes should, be proved; and contradictions can, and sometimes should, be disproved. Second, Road (A) does not turn out tautologous; since it is far from a tautology that what exists *cannot not exist*.

'What ϕs' may mean 'the thing that ϕs', and serve as a logical subject. Thus '*to eon*' may mean 'the thing which exists'. Then Road (A) maintains that the thing that exists—'the One' or 'the Whole' or 'Nature'—exists and cannot not exist. It has been objected to that interpretation that Parmenides proceeds in **B 8** to prove that the subject of his poem is One; and that he can hardly have intended to prove the tautology that 'the One is one'. Again, the objection is weak: first, Parmenides may have tried to prove a tautology; second, it is far from clear that Parmenides ever does try to prove that the subject of his poem is One; and thirdly, it is not clear that it is tautologous to say that 'the Whole' or 'Nature' or 'Reality' is one.

Nevertheless, I do not believe that '*to eon*', on either interpretation, is a likely supplement to Parmenides' '*esti*'. The reason is simple: nothing in the context of **148** could reasonably suggest to even the most careful reader that by 'it is' Parmenides meant 'what is, is'. The term 'what is' does not appear in **B 1** or in **148**; and it is not the sort of term a reader would naturally supply for himself.[16]

A close investigation of the context of **148** has supplemented '*esti*' in a different way: instead of 'what is', supply 'what can be thought of' or 'what can be known'. Road (A) then says that 'what can be thought of exists'; and 'Parmenides' real starting-point is . . . the possibility of rational discourse' or of thought.[17] My objection to that suggestion is a weaker version of my objection to '*to eon*': nothing in the introductory context of **148** suggests such a supplement for '*esti*' at line 3; reflexion on the subsequent argument may indeed lead us to 'what can be thought of', but it will also lead us to berate Parmenides for a gratuitously roundabout and allusive way of expressing himself; for the most careful reader, on this view, will only understand the crucial lines of **148** after he has read a quantity of later verses.

Nonetheless, the philosophical advantages of the interpretation are considerable; and we may well be loth to abandon the spectacle of a Parmenides who investigates, in Kantian fashion, the implications of rationality. We can retain the advantages and avoid the objection by modifying the interpretation slightly. I suggest the following paraphrase for lines 1–3: 'I will tell you . . . the different conceivable ways of inquiring into something—the first assumes that it exists and cannot not exist . . .' In the paraphrase, 'it' has an explicit antecedent, and 'inquiring into' has an explicit object: viz. the word 'something'. In the Greek text there is no explicit subject for '*esti*' and no explicit object of '*dizêsios*' ('inquiry'). Subject and object must both be supplied, and nothing is easier than to make this double task one: the implicit object of '*dizêsios*' is the implicit subject of '*esti*'. 'Of the ways of inquiring [about any given object], the first assumes that [the object, whatever it may be] exists.'

Thus Road (A) says that *whatever we inquire into* exists, and cannot not exist: Parmenides' starting-point is the possibility, not exactly of rational thought, but of scientific research. The immediate context of **148**, and the general atmosphere of **B 1**, make that an intelligible way of understanding the goddess's roads; the argument about the relative merits of the three roads is, as we shall see, thoroughly consonant with the interpretation; and we find Parmenides, in a historically appropriate fashion, investigating the logical foundations of the programme of the early Greek philosophers.

If the '*esti*' of **148** is now explained, the characterization of the three roads is still not completely clear: two uncertainties remain. First, are the objects of inquiry to be specified by singular or by general terms? does road (A) say that if anyone studies things of a given sort (stars, winds, horses) then there must exist things of that sort? or does it say that if anyone studies any individual object (the sun, Boreas, Pegasus) then that object must exist? Philosophers' attitudes to Parmenides' argument may differ according to which alternative we choose; but nothing in the poem indicates that Parmenides saw two alternatives here, and had he done so he might, I think, have decided to embrace their conjunction.

Second, how are we to interpret the modal operators in the second half of lines 3 and 5? Road (A) maintains that what is inquired into 'is not for not being' or 'cannot not be'; Road (B) holds of what is inquired into that 'it is necessary for it not to be'. Road (A) states that objects of inquiry necessarily exist, Road (B) that they necessarily do not exist; does 'necessarily' here mark *necessitas consequentis* or *necessitas consequentiae*? does Road (A) state:

(1) If a thing is studied, it has the property of necessary existence, or rather:

(2) It is necessarily true that anything studied exists?

I cannot tell if Parmenides' Greek favours either (1) or (2); and I suppose that Parmenides did not see that two distinct propositions were on view: confusion between *necessitas consequentis* and *necessitas consequentiae* is distressingly common.

Let me now try to characterize Roads (A) and (B) a little more formally: I use '$\Box P$' to abbreviate 'necessarily P'. Each Road has four possible formulations:

(A1) $(\forall x)$ (if x is studied, $\Box x$ exists).
(A2) $(\forall \phi)$ (if ϕs are studied, $\Box$ there exist ϕs).
(A3) $\Box (\forall x)$ (if x is studied, x exists).
(A4) $\Box (\forall \phi)$ (if ϕs are studied, there exist ϕs).
(B1) $(\forall x)$ (if x is studied, $\Box$ x does not exist).
(B2) $(\forall \phi)$ (if ϕs are studied, $\Box$ there exist no ϕs).
(B3) $\Box$ $(\forall x)$ (if x is studied, x does not exist).
(B4) $\Box$ $(\forall \phi)$ (if ϕs are studied, there exist no ϕs).

If we ignore the distinction between 'x exists' and 'there exist ϕs', we may limit ourselves to two versions of Roads (A) and (B); how, then, are we to formulate road (C), the Way of Opinion?

There are three aids to formulation: Road (C) is the road of ordinary mortals; it is expressible, vaguely enough, by the phrase 'it is and it is not'; and the triad of (A), (B) and (C) includes all the conceivable paths of thought. The first version of (A) and (B) gives:

I   (Ai) $(\forall X)$ (if X is studied, $\Box$ X exists).
    (Bi) $(\forall X)$ (if X is studied, $\Box$ X does not exist).

For (C) we might perhaps imagine:

   (Ci1) $(\forall X)$ (if X is studied, $\Box$ X exists & $\Box$ X does not exist).

or else:

   (Ci2) $(\exists X)$ (X is studied & $\Box$ X exists) &
         $(\exists X)$ (X is studied & $\Box$ X does not exist).

If the triad of roads is to be genuinely exhaustive, we need rather:

(Ci3) (∃X) (X is studied & not-□ X exists)
      & (∃X) (X is studied & □ X exists).

The second version of (A) and (B) yields:

II (Aii) □(∀X) (if X is studied, X exists).
    (Bii) □(∀X) (if X is studied, X does not exist).

And then for Road (C) we may offer:

(Cii1) □(∀X) (if X is studied, X exists & X does not exist).
(Cii2) □(∃X) (X is studied & X exists) &
        (∃X) (X is studied & X does not exist)
(Cii3) ◇(∃X) (X is studied & X does not exist)
        ◇(∃X) (X is studied & X exists).

(In (Cii3), '◇' abbreviates 'possibly'.)

I state these possibilities neither to bemuse the reader nor to exhibit my own virtuosity: their statement is a necessary preliminary to any examination of Parmenides' metaphysics; and if we are to treat his argument with the respect it deserves, we must be prepared to analyse its components with a rigour that Parmenides himself was not equipped to supply. I turn now to the argument itself.

(c) *The paths of ignorance*

The argument against Road (B) begins in **148**, 6–8. Line 8 is a half line, and so is **149**: the two halves make a metrical and a rational whole, and I assume that **149** is in fact continuous with **148**. Finally, **150**, 1–2 completes the case against the track beyond all tidings.

Let us take a student, *a*, and an object of study, *O*; and suppose that *a* is studying *O*. Now first, Parmenides observes, 'neither would you recognize that which is not ... nor mention it'; i.e.

(1) (∀X) (if X does not exist, then no one can recognize X and no one can mention X).

From (1) we infer:

(2) If *O* does not exist, then *a* cannot recognize *O*, and *a* cannot mention *O*.

But why should we credit (1)? It is not, after all, a particularly plausible thesis on the face of it. **149** comes next in our text; and it amounts to: 'Whatever can be thought of can exist, and vice versa'; i.e.

(3) (∀X) (X can be thought of if and only if X can exist).

Now (3) yields:

(4) If *a* can think of *O*, then *O* can exist.

But (4) does not offer us any immediate help.[18]

Let us, then, try **150**, 1–2. 'What is for saying and for thinking of must be': a plausible translation is:

(5) □(∀X) (if X can be mentioned or X can be thought of, then X exists).

Now (5) gives:

(6) If *a* can mention O or *a* can think of O, then O exists.

Let us ascribe another premiss to Parmenides, viz:

(7) (∀X) (if X can be recognized, X can be thought of);

and let us infer from (7) to:

(8) If *a* can recognize O, then *a* can think of O.

Now we have an argument for (2); for (6) and (8) together entail (2).

So far, (3) has done no work, and (5) is unsupported. **150.**1 continues: 'for it is for being'; i.e., 'for what is for saying and for thinking is for being', or:

(9) (∀X) (if X can be mentioned or X can be thought of, then X can exist);

whence:

(10) If *a* can mention O, O can exist.

There remains the first clause of **150.**2, 'but nothing is not'. That means, of course, 'But nothing is not for being', i.e., 'nothing cannot exist'. Now 'nothing (*mêden*)' is used as a synonym for '*to mê on*', 'what is not' (cf. **B** 8.10); so that we have:

(11) (∀X) (if X does not exist, X cannot exist);

whence:

(12) If O does not exist, O cannot exist.

Proposition (3) can now be put to use; for (4), (10) and (12) together entail (6).

Let us now suppose that Road (B) is the one *a* chooses to follow in his inquiry; whether we pick (Bi) or (Bii) we can infer:

(13) If *a* studies O, O does not exist.

Now it is evidently true that students must be able to say what they are studying, or at least to recognize the objects of their inquiries; i.e.

(14) (∀X) (if X is studied, then X can be mentioned or X can be recognized).

Hence:

(15) If *a* studies O, then *a* can mention O or *a* can recognize O.

But if *a* studies O, we can now infer, from (6), (15) and (13), that O exists and O does not exist. But that is impossible; hence if *a* is a student, (13) is false; and, in general, no student can proceed along Road (B). And that completes Parmenides' argument: Road (B) is indeed a track beyond all tidings.

My reconstruction has been laborious; and it may be of use if I state more briefly the train of argument it ascribes to Parmenides. First, premiss (9) [= **150.**1] gives (10), and premiss (3) [= **149**] gives (4). Then premiss (11) [= **150.**2] gives (12); and (4), (10) and (12) together yield (6) [cf. **150**.1]. A new premiss, (7), gives (8); and (6) and (8) entail (2). A further new premiss, (14), gives (15). Assume that there are students, and that they follow Road (B). Then via (13), we meet with an explicit contradiction. And that licenses the rejection of our assumption.

The argument is, I claim, subtle and ingenious. (I offer a formal version in the Appendix to this chapter.) I suppose that it convinced Parmenides of the pointlessness of Road (B). Yet as it stands, in naked rigour, it shows at least one ugly blemish: premiss (11) is false, and obviously false. Not all nonentities are *impossibilia*: many things might, but do not, exist. So obvious and so offensive a flaw may be thought to show that the argument I have constructed cannot have been propounded by a thinker of Parmenides' calibre. But to say that is to ignore the seductive powers which certain falsehoods may have when they are stated informally in ordinary English or in ordinary Greek. Premiss (11) is conveyed by some such sentence as 'what doesn't exist can't exist'; and that sentence is an 'untruism'; that is to say, it is an ambiguous sentence expressing, on one interpretation, a trivial truth and on another, a substantial falsity. 'Nothing is not for being', or 'What doesn't exist can't exist', may mean either:
(16) It is not possible that what does not exist exists;
or else:
(17) If a thing does not exist, then it is not possible for it to exist.
Either:
(16a) $\Box$ (if a does not exist, a does not exist),
or
(17a) If a does not exist, $\Box$ (a does not exist).
If Parmenides' sentence is interpreted as (16) it is true; but it does not yield (11). If it is interpreted as (17) it yields (11); but it is false. Parmenides, I suggest, was blind to the ambiguity of the sentence he used: he supposed that he could, as it were, take advantage in one and the same proposition, both of the truth of (16) and of the logical implications of (17). Parmenides' philosophy rests, if I am right, on an untruism; it is some slight consolation that his was by no means the last system to be built on such a sandy foundation.

I turn now to Road (C). Scholars have given **150** a quantity of attention; for some have found in it evidence that Parmenides was attacking Heraclitus. The evidence is weak—an alleged verbal echo or two—and since Road (C) is the Way of Opinion, which most mortals tread, Heraclitus is at best one of its travellers and not a lone rambler. If Parmenides has Heraclitus in mind at all (which I doubt), it is only as a particularly striking representative of all that is bad in mortal opinions.[19]

However that may be, my present interest centres on the reasons for Parmenides' rejection of (C) rather than on the protagonists of the rejected view; and **151** provides a better starting-point than **150**.

'For never will this be proved—that things that are not are'. No doubt; but what is that to the travellers on Road (C)? A very simple argument suggests itself: (C) is committed to the view that at least some objects of inquiry do not, or may not, exist. Suppose that O is such an object: then by **151**.1, since O does not exist, it will never be shown that O does exist; but the argument against Road (B) showed precisely that O, if it is an object of inquiry, does exist. Thus Road (C) leads to contradiction and must be abandoned.

In short, Road (C) leads nowhere for the same reasons that (B) leads nowhere; and the argument against (B) applies immediately to (C). That does not imply, as some scholars have feared, that (B) and (C) somehow fail to be genuine alternatives: if a mine wrecks two bridges at once, it does not follow that the bridges only offered one way across the river. And anyone who has argued against (B) in the Parmenidean mode will hardly fail to see that his argument can be deployed against (C).

What, then, of **150**? Most of the fragment is abuse; yet the last three lines appear to offer an argument against Road (C) which is distinct from the one I have just extracted from **151**.1-2. In **150**.7 Parmenides asserts that men wander about 'deaf alike and blind, gawping, creatures of no judgment'; and in line 9 he concludes that 'the path of all is backward turning (*palintropos*)'.[20] To say that a man's path turns backward is presumably to say that he contradicts himself; and we should expect to find in line 8 something which is, or directly implies, a contradiction. Our expectations are not disappointed: line 8 brims with contradictory-looking phrases. The problem is to determine which of them Parmenides meant to saddle mortals with: we need not suppose that, in Parmenides' view, ordinary men are given to uttering explicit contradictions; he means only that men are committed to contradictions. But committed to what contradictions? and why?

The Greek of line 8 has been deemed to allow at least three translations:
(i) 'By whom both to be and not to be are thought to be the same and not the same';
(ii) 'By whom it is thought both to be and not to be both the same and not the same';
(iii) 'By whom it is thought both to be and not to be, both to be the same and not to be the same'.

Translation (i) ascribes to mortals the compound contradiction:

(18) (Being = not-being) & (Being ≠ not-being).
But (18) is a strange proposition; and I cannot concoct any line of reasoning that plausibly produces it from mortal opinions.

Translation (ii) has often suggested a simple interpretation: according to ordinary folk, many things change and yet retain their identity; thus, in an obvious sense, men are committed to the view that things are and are not the same (hence, equivalently, that they are and are not not the same). Translation (iii) may well be construed in a similar fashion: by allowing generation and destruction, mortals commit themselves to propositions of the form '*a* is and *a* is not'; by allowing alteration, they commit themselves to '*a* is the same and *a* is not the same'.

Grammar, I think, favours (iii) over (ii);[21] and (iii), on this interpretation, offers a thicker sense. But a weighty argument tell against (ii) and the interpretation of (iii) in terms of change: the interpreters will have it that Parmenides finds contradiction in men's ordinary talk of change. Now fragment **B 8** contains a long and intricate argument against the possibility of change and generation; and that argument rests upon the foundation of Road (A). Are we to suppose that in his attack on Road (C), in a fragment which only prepares the ground for the major deductions of **B 8**, Parmenides can have anticipated, without apology, the main and most striking conclusion of those deductions? Parmenides was not so cack-handed a fellow: the abolition of change is the business of **B 8**, and it cannot have been presupposed in **150**.

Translation (iii) does not have to be interpreted in terms of generation and change. I quote a sentence from the *Dissoi Logoi* (see vol. 2, p. 215):

> And the same things exist and do not exist; for the things that exist here do not exist in Libya, and those in Libya do not exist in Cyprus; and the same goes for everything else. Thus things both exist and do not exist (**152:90A5**, §5).

Ask a man in Libya if there exist any lions, and he will give you a fearful affirmative; ask the same man in the peaceful streets of Athens 'Are there any lions?'—he will answer 'By the dog, no'. Conjoin his replies, each of which seems ordinary and respectable, and the result is contradiction: 'There are and there are not lions'. Again, it is the same things that are and are not; for it is lions which are said to be, and lions which are said not to be. But evidently the lions which *are*, the Libyan lions, are beasts of a far tougher character than those Athenian animals which do not exist. Lions, in sum, 'are and are not, are the same and not the same'.

That interpretation of line 8 seems to me the least implausible. But the reasoning it ascribes to Parmenides will stand no weight; and it is fortunate that Parmenides need set no weight on it. For, as I have argued, in rejecting Road (B), Parmenides has said quite enough to reject Road (C) too: Road (A) alone is left for intellectual travellers.

Parmenides draws a moral from his rejections of Road (C):

> Do not let much-experienced habit force you along this road,
> to let run an aimless eye and an echoing ear
> and a tongue; but judge by argument (*logôi*) the much-
> contending refutation uttered by me (**153**: **B** 7. 3–6).

I shall return later to the attack on sense-perception allegedly contained in these lines (below, p. 297). Here I wish to point out the positive part of Parmenides' moral: we are to judge his 'refutation' of Road (C) by 'argument' and not by appealing to experience. The request is as sound as it is simple: no amount of assertion, however well grounded on sensory evidence, can show where Parmenides' reasoning fails; if we want to refute Parmenides, we must attack argument with argument, *logos* with *logos*.

This sane request was ignored by most of Parmenides' successors. I have already remarked upon the fact that the Presocratics rarely gave any critical examination of the arguments whose conclusions they opposed (above pp. 50–2). That failure is nowhere more evident than in the reaction to Parmenides: later thinkers knew that his conclusions were unacceptable; but they could not, or would not, say where his arguments broke down. Parmenides saw where his opponents' task lay better than they did themselves. And in attempting to analyse Parmenides' argument, and to show where it goes wrong, I have done no more than follow Parmenides' own advice.

Parmenides' attack on Road (B) fails, and with it his attack on Road (C); consequently, he fails to show that Road (A) is the only traversable road. Can we perhaps come to Parmenides' support and offer him more powerful weapons from our own logical arsenal? We might attempt to save him at any of three points. First, we might attempt to support proposition (5) of his argument: what can be mentioned or thought of exists. Of modern philosophers, only Berkeley would dare to defend Parmenides here; for Berkeley held that whatever is thought of exists. I quote his notorious argument: 'But say you, surely there is nothing easier that to imagine trees, for instance, in a park, or books existing in a closet, and nobody by to perceive them. I answer, you may so, there is no difficulty in it: but what is all this, I beseech you, more than framing in your mind certain ideas which you call *books* and *trees*, and at the same time omitting to frame the idea of any one that may perceive them? *but do not you yourself perceive or think of them all the while*? this therefore is nothing to the purpose; it only shows you have the power of imagining or forming ideas in your mind; but it does not show that you can conceive it possible the objects of your thought may exist without the mind: to make out this, *it is necessary that you can conceive them existing unconceived or unthought of, which is a manifest repugnancy.*' (*Principles of Human Knowledge*, § 23). Berkeley's argument is in direct line of descent from Parmenides. It is fallacious (though the fallacy is interestingly elusive); and Berkeley's Parmenidean conclusion will not stand. 'For Scylla and Chimaera, and many non-entities, are', as the Sophist Gorgias said, 'thought upon' (**82 B 3**, § 80). We do think of unicorns and centaurs, of Zeus and Jehovah, of phlogiston and the luminiferous ether; and such objects do not exist. Existential questions can be sensibly entertained; I can wonder whether Homer existed or whether there really ever were any dodos. And the fact that such questions can be posed is sufficient to show that non-entities can be thought upon.

If proposition (5) is indefensible, perhaps we can take a stand on (1), and agree that anything that can be recognized or mentioned must exist? Surprisingly many philosophers will defend Parmenides at that point: perhaps we can think of non-entities; but we certainly cannot mention them or discourse about them. If I am to mention an object, then I must be able to predicate things of it, to identify it, to refer to it; but we cannot ascribe properties to non-entities; we cannot identify the non-existent; we cannot refer to things which are not there for referring—what is for speaking of, must be.

That popular argument is, I think, mistaken; but it requires more consideration than I can give it here.[22] We do, in our unphilosophical moments, imagine that we can talk about non-entities: mythographers refer felicitously to Scylla and Chimaera; scientists will talk dismissively about phlogiston; and literary critics will write you a book about Hamlet at the drop of a hat. And if it is allowed that we can *think* of non-entities, surely it must follow that we can *identify* and *refer to* non-entities? In order to think about Pegasus, I must somehow pick out that mythical beast for myself; and if I can pick him out, mentally, for myself, why can I not pick him out, linguistically, for you? I do not pretend that talking about the non-existent is easily analysed; but it is easily done. And that is enough to dispose of Parmenides' proposition (1).

If we can salvage none of Parmenides' argument, may we save his conclusion, that Road (A) is the only traversable path? that objects of enquiry, at least, must exist? Again, many philosophers, allowing thought of and reference to the non-existent, might finally agree that the non-existent cannot be the object of scientific research: 'a thing must exist if we are to study it or institute inquiries concerning its nature and properties'.[23] Aristotle, in whose view science started from the *ousia* or essence of things, held that only entities have an essence, so that scientific inquiry is restricted to the things that really exist. According to Locke, 'real' knowledge must bear upon real objects; otherwise it is vain and alchimerical (*Essay* IV.iv). And if Locke argues not that knowledge of non-entities is impossible but only that it is fatuous and footling, nevertheless it is not hard to find a stricter, Parmenidean thesis below the surface of his text: zoologists study horses, not unicorns; chemists study oxygen, not phlogiston; historians study Shakespeare, not Hamlet.

But surely mythologists study unicorns, not horses; historians of science study phlogiston before oxygen; and literary men may inquire into the character of Hamlet rather than of Shakespeare? A tough-minded Parmenidean may argue that mythologists are really investigating not the nature of non-existent beasts but the beliefs of once-existent men, and that literary critics inquire into the intentions of Shakespeare and not the character of his fictions; and he might further suppose that historians really study the present traces of past ages and not those ages themselves. The argument deserves lengthy development; but in the end it is, I think, unconvincing. Nor can it account for the efforts of the paradigmatic inquirers; for natural scientists regularly study idealized entities: the objects of their theories are not the rough and ready physical bodies of our mundane world, but ideal approximations to them; they study frictionless surfaces, not ordinary tables or desks; they talk of an isolated system, not of a piece of our messy world. Physics is the most unreal of sciences.

We can and do think of things that do not exist; we can and do talk of things that do not exist; we can and do study things that do not exist. Such thoughts, such discourses and such studies are not always fatuous. Parmenides has given us no good reason to reject those ordinary opinions; and in consequence his metaphysics is based upon a falsehood and defended by a specious argument. But for all that, Parmenides' views on the objects of inquiry are not merely antique exhibits in the roomy museum of philosophical follies: the arguments he adduces, though unsound, are ingenious and admirable; their conclusion, though false, has a strange plausibility and attractiveness. Many eminent philosophers have struck Parmenidean attitudes, and have done so for essentially Parmenidean reasons.

(d) *Gorgias on what is not*

Gorgias of Leontini 'in his book entitled *Concerning What Is Not or Concerning Nature* establishes three points—first, that nothing exists; second, that even if anything exists, it is incomprehensible to mankind; third, that even if it is comprehensible, at all events it is incommunicable and inexpressible to a neighbour' (Sextus, *adv Math* VII.65 = **82 B 3**). Gorgias was active in the last third of the fifth century; he was, at least primarily, a rhetorician; but his bizarre tract *Concerning What Is Not* has close connexions with Eleatic philosophy, and those connexions win it a place in a book on Presocratic argument.[24]

Some scholars make Gorgias a profound thinker, a nihilist and a sceptic; others treat *What Is Not* as a serious and witty *reductio* of Eleatic metaphysics; others again take it for a rhetorical *tour de force* or a sophisticated joke. A similar problem arises in connexion with Gorgias' *Helen*, which I discuss in a later chapter (in vol. 2, pp. 221–8). I do not know what Gorgias intended me to think of his two pamphlets; nor do I lament that ignorance. Whatever Gorgias may have thought, his writings contain matters of some interest, and I shall take his writings (if not their author) seriously.

We do not possess the original text of *What Is Not*; instead, we have two paraphrases, one by Sextus (*adv Math* VII.66–86 = **82 B 3**) and the other in the *MXG* (979a10–980b22). I shall follow Sextus' account both because the text of the *MXG* is wretchedly corrupt and because Sextus' presentation and argument are, in my view, regularly superior to those of the *MXG*.[25]

Here I quote without comment the second part of Gorgias' treatise. The first and the third parts will be found on later pages (below, p. 182). Passages in square brackets are Sextan comments; and Sextus' paragraph numbers are included for ease of reference.

(77) [It must next be shown that even if anything exists it is unknowable (*agnôston*) and unthinkable (*anepinoêton*) by mankind.] If what is thought of (*ta phronoumena*) [says Gorgias] is not existent, then what exists is not thought of. [And that is reasonable; for just as, if being white belongs to what is thought of, then being thought of belongs to what is white, so if not being existent belongs to what is thought of, of necessity not being thought of will belong to what exists. (78) Hence 'If what is thought of is not existent, then what exists is not thought of' is sound and preserves validity.] But what is thought of [for we must take this first] is not existent, as we shall establish. What exists,

therefore, is not thought of. Now that what is thought of is not existent is evident: (79) for if what is thought of is existent, then everything that is thought of exists—and that in the way in which one thinks of them. But that is not sensible. For it is not the case that if anyone thinks of a man flying or chariots running over the sea, a man thereby flies or chariots run over the sea. Hence it is not the case that what is thought of is existent.

(80) In addition, if what is thought of exists, what does not exist will not be thought of. For opposites belong to opposites, and what does not exist is opposite to what exists. And for this reason if being thought of belongs to what exists, then not being thought of will certainly belong to what does not exist. But this is absurd; for Scylla and Chimaera and many non-existent things are thought of. What exists, therefore, is not thought of.

(81) And just as what is seen is called visible because it is seen, and what is audible audible because it is heard, and we do not reject the visible because it is not heard or the audible because it is not seen (for each must be judged by its own sense and not by another), so too what is thought of will exist even if it is not seen by sight or heard by hearing, because it is grasped by its proper criterion. (82) If, then, someone thinks that chariots run over the sea, even if he does not see them, he must believe that chariots running over the sea exist. But this is absurd. What exists, therefore, is not thought of and apprehended (**154**).

Appendix: *A formalization of Parmenides' argument*

'$M\alpha\beta$' abbreviates 'α mentions β'; '$T\alpha\beta$', 'α thinks of β'; '$R\alpha\beta$', 'α recognizes β';'$S\alpha\beta$', 'α studies β'; '$E\alpha$', 'α exists'. Numerals in square brackets pair lines of the formalization with the steps in the informal presentation of section (c).

1	(1)	$(\forall x)(\forall y)(Sxy \to {\sim}Ey)$	A [(Bii)]
2	(2)	$(\exists x)(\exists y)Sxy$	A
3	(3)	$(\exists y)Say$	A
4	(4)	Sab	A
5	(5)	$(\forall y)(((\exists x) \Diamond Mxy \vee (\exists x) \Diamond Txy) \to \Diamond Ey)$	A [(9)]
6	(6)	$(\forall x)(\forall y)(\Diamond Txy \leftrightarrow \Diamond Ey)$	A [(3)]
7	(7)	$(\forall y)({\sim}Ey \to {\sim}\Diamond Ey)$	A [(11)]
8	(8)	$(\forall x)(\forall y)(\Diamond Rxy \to \Diamond Txy)$	A [(7)]
9	(9)	$(\forall x)(\forall y)(Sxy \to \Diamond Mxy \vee \Diamond Rxy)$	A [(14)]
1	(10)	$Sab \to {\sim}Eb$	1,UE [(13)]

PARMENIDES AND THE OBJECTS OF INQUIRY

1, 4	(11)	$\sim Eb$	4, 10, MPP
9	(12)	$Sab \to \Diamond Mab \vee \Diamond Rab$	9, UE [(15)]
4, 9	(13)	$\Diamond Mab \vee \Diamond Rab$	4, 12, MPP
8	(14)	$\Diamond Rab \to \Diamond Tab$	8, UE [(8)]
4, 8, 9	(15)	$\Diamond Mab \vee \Diamond Tab$	13, 14 T
5	(16)	$(\exists x) \Diamond Mxb \vee (\exists x) \Diamond Txb \to \Diamond Eb$	5, UE
6	(17)	$\Diamond Tab \leftrightarrow \Diamond Eb$	6, UE [cf. (4)]
18	(18)	$\Diamond Mab$	A
18	(19)	$(\exists x) \Diamond Mxb$	18, EI
5, 18	(20)	$\Diamond Eb$	16, 19, T
21	(21)	$\Diamond Tab$	A
6, 21	(22)	$\Diamond Eb$	17, 21, T
4, 5, 6, 8, 9	(23)	$\Diamond Eb$	15, 18, 20, 21, 22, v E
7	(24)	$\sim Eb \to \sim \Diamond Eb$	7, UE
4, 5, 6, 7, 8, 9	(25)	Eb	23, 24, MTT
1, 4, 5, 6, 7, 8, 9	(26)	$Eb \& \sim Eb$	25, 11 & I
4, 5, 6, 7, 8, 9	(27)	$\sim(\forall x)(\forall y)(Sxy \to \sim Ey)$	1, 26 RAA
2, 5, 6, 7, 8, 9	(28)	$\sim(\forall x)(\forall y)(Sxy \to \sim Ey)$	3, 4, 27 EE; 2, 3, 27 EE

The argument is, I think, formally valid. ('T' stands for 'tautology'; the other rules are standard.) It is not elegant; but I blame its lack of beauty on Parmenides.

X

Being and Becoming

(a) *Parmenidean metaphysics*

According to Aristotle, metaphysics or 'first philosophy' is the study of 'being *qua* being'. The Aristotelian metaphysician, in other words, attempts to discover, to elucidate and to analyse the properties which must belong to every existent thing as such. And Aristotle's notion of metaphysics, in a somewhat relaxed and sophisticated form, is still the modern notion. The first full-blooded metaphysician was Parmenides; and the first systematic metaphysics was the Eleatic philosophy. We have two accounts, both almost complete, of Eleatic metaphysics. The first is contained in fragment **B 8** of Parmenides, the second occupies the several fragments of Melissus; the two accounts differ in important detail, but their overall structure and their general intellectual *nisus* is one and the same; and it is, I think, helpful as well as convenient to consider them side by side.

Having argued that every object of inquiry must exist, Parmenides proceeds to consider the properties that objects of inquiry, as existent, must possess—the properties of beings *qua* being. Parmenides' consideration is strictly deductive: 'he agreed to nothing if it did not seem necessary, while his predecessors used to make assertions without demonstration' (Eudemus, fr. 43W = **28 A 28**). The point has often been repeated; and it is borne out by the fragments of Parmenides' poem. **B 8** is an intricate and concise argumentation, continuous in form and some fifty lines long. Simplicius, who preserves the fragment for us, implies that it contains the whole of Parmenides' metaphysics (cf. **A 21**); and its self-contained form corroborates the implication.[1] Thus we have, in these few compact lines, a complete deductive metaphysics.

On the strength of **B 8** Parmenides has been hailed as the founder of logic. The title is not wholly apposite, for Parmenides does not theorize about logic, and he was not the first thinker to propound deductive arguments; but it happily underlines the fact that in **B 8** we have a deduction far more complex and far more self-conscious than anything the Presocratics have yet offered us. Melissus' argument is as complicated as his master's, and Zeno's paradoxes are as sophisticated as anything in Parmenides; but Melissus is essentially a derivative thinker, and Zeno does not show the logical stamina of Parmenides. We meet nothing comparable to **B 8** until the middle dialogues of Plato.

Further subtlety is sometimes sought. In **B 5** the goddess announces:

> It is indifferent to me
> whence I begin; for I shall come back there again (155).

The announcement has been attached to **B 8** and given a logical sense: the order of the 'signposts' along the Way of Truth is indifferent; we may begin at any one of them and proceed to deduce all the others. In other words, the various properties of existents are all mutually implicative: truth is indeed 'well-rounded' (**B 1**. 29). I do not think that this interpretation of 155 can be ruled out; and it is possible to invent arguments, similar to those of **B 8**, which would support the thesis it ascribes to Parmenides. But as it stands **B 8** does not attempt to establish the mutual implication of all the 'signposts'; and 155 is certainly capable of different interpretations. Whether Parmenides' metaphysics contains the subtlety of circularity may be left an open question.[2]

A different subtlety has recently been found in **B 8**: 'to repeat that memorable image of Wittgenstein, Parmenides' argument is a ladder to be climbed up and thrown away. Such arguments are not, [to] put it picturesquely, horizontal deductions; if they parade as deductions they are patently self-defeating.'[3] Parmenides' arguments certainly do parade as deductions: the language of **B 8** leaves no doubt about that. Whether and in what sense they are self-defeating are questions which must wait upon a detailed examination of their successive steps. Here I consider only the suggestion that the deductive parade is somehow a sham: the arguments are not really deductive and self-defeating; they are something else—not deductions at all, or at least not 'horizontal' deductions.

I find myself unable to understand the suggestion. The adjective 'horizontal' is no doubt picturesque; but the picture tells no story: I do not know what a non-horizontal deduction might be. Equally, the notion that Parmenides' argument might not be deductive at all escapes me: how can there be an argumentative sequence that is not, or is not equivalent to, a deductive train? Parmenides' arguments are hardly inductive or analogical. Thus I shall ignore the finer niceties of logic which have been read into **B 8**, and treat it as an ordinary deduction. Such a conventional treatment is in any case quite hard enough.

Here, first, is a translation of the whole of **B 8**. The fragment contains textual problems, to some of which I shall later advert; and its obscurities are deliberately left dark by my fairly literal rendering. For all that, some of the character of the piece may come across.

> A single story of a road
> is left—that it is. And on it are signs
> very many in number—that, being, it is ungenerated and
>   undestroyed,
> whole, of one kind and motionless, and balanced.
> Nor was it ever, nor will it be; since now it is, all together,   5
> one, continuous. For what generation will you inquire out for it?
> How, whence, did it grow? Neither from what is not will I allow
> you to say or think; for it is not sayable nor thinkable
> that it is not. And what *need* would have aroused it
> later or sooner, starting from nothing, to come into being?   10
> In this way it is necessary either for it to be altogether or not.
> Nor ever from what is will the strength of trust allow
> it to become something apart from itself. For that reason neither to
>   come into being
> nor to perish has justice allowed it, relaxing her chains;
> but she holds it. And judgment about these things lies in this: 15
> it is or it is not. And it has been judged, as is necessary,
> to leave the one [road] unthought and unnamed (for it is not a true
> road) and to take the other, whereby it is, actually to be real.
> And how might what is be then? And how might it have come into
>   being?
> For if it came into being, it is not, nor if it is about to be at some
>   time   20
> Thus coming into being is extinguished, and destruction is
>   unheard of.
>   Nor is it divided, since it is all alike
> And neither more here (which would prevent it from holding
>   together)
> nor less, but it is all full of what is.
> Hence it is continuous; for what is neighbours what is.   25

>   And motionless in the limits of great chains
> it is, beginningless, endless; since coming into being and
>   destruction
> have wandered far away and true trust has driven them off.
> And the same, remaining in the same state, it lies in itself
> and thus firmly remains there. For a strong necessity   30
> holds it in chains of a limit which fences it about,
> because it is not right for what is to be incomplete;
> for it is not lacking—otherwise it would want everything.
>   And the same thing are to think and a thought that it is.
> For not without what is, on which what has been expressed
>   depends,   35
> will you find thinking; for nothing is or will be
> other than what is—since *that* has Fate fettered
> to be whole and motionless. Hence all things are a name
> which mortals have laid down, trusting them to be true—
> to come into being and to perish, to be and not,   40
> and to change place and to alter bright colour.
>   And since there is a furthest limit, it is complete
> from all directions, like the bulk of a well-rounded ball,
> equally balanced from the centre in all directions. For neither any
>   more
> nor any weaker can it be here or here.   45
> For neither is there anything that is not, which might stop it from
>   reaching
> its like; nor is there anything that is, so that there might be of what
>   is
> here more and there less—since it is all inviolable.
> Hence, equal from all directions, it meets the limits alike.
>   Here I cease the trustworthy account and thought   50
> about the truth . . . (**156**).

The logical articulation of the fragment is, I think, less clear than is sometimes claimed. And a preliminary statement of my view of its structure may not come amiss: support for this statement must wait upon detailed discussion.

The fragment begins with a prospectus, listing the 'signs' along the Way of Truth; in other words, summarily stating the properties of being *qua* being which **156** is to demonstrate.[4] The prospectus occupies lines 3–4. Line 3 gives a pair of properties, ungenerability and imperishability: they are argued for in lines 5–21. The beginning of line 4 presents a textual *crux*: I follow the modern orthodoxy, and read *oulon mounogenes te*.[5] *Oulon* ('whole') is taken up in lines

22–5. I incline to associate *mounogenes* closely with *atremes* ('motionless'), and I suppose that 'monogeneity' and immobility are jointly advocated in lines 26–33. At the end of line 4 the manuscripts, with trivial exceptions, read *êd' ateleston* ('and incomplete'). I agree with those scholars who find that reading incompatible with what is said in lines 32 and 42. Of the several conjectures, I have hesitatingly preferred *êd' atalanton*.[6] And I suppose that this last announcement in the prospectus is answered in lines 42–9. Lines 34–41 remain: I cannot associate them with anything in the prospectus; and I have sympathy with the proposal to place them after line 49, and to read them as a sort of summary of the Way of Truth. The plausibility of that suggestion may be assessed later on.

(b) *Melissus' metaphysics*

Melissus of Samos presents a melancholy aspect in the official portrait: his one book *Concerning Nature or What Is* (Simplicius, **30 A 4**) is no more than a cheap edition of Parmenides' poem, full of misprints and misunderstandings, to be purchased only by the intellectually impoverished. Aristotle initiated that *damnatio memoriae*: Melissus was 'a trifle crude' (*Met* 985b26 = **A 7**), his reasoning 'uncouth' (*Phys* 186a9 = **A 7**). Aristotle's magisterial judgment was elaborated by the author of *MXG* (**A 5**) and generally parroted by the later Peripatetics (**A 10a R**).[7] An amateur philosopher (and an amateur admiral), Melissus has a certain historical and personal interest; yet his fragments will hardly divert or detain us if we can listen to his master's voice.

Aristotle's judgment should be contested. Melissus was not despised by Plato (*Theaetetus*, 183E = **A 7a R**); and there is some evidence that he was for a time regarded as the authoritative spokesman of Eleatic thought.[8] His plain prose has an admirable lucidity, and a certain naive charm: it abandons the tortuous expression of Parmenides, but retains the conscientious intricacy of his logical argumentation. The Eleatic system is stated with strength, and also with clarity. Nor is Melissus wholly derivative: if one of his aims was the exposition and defence of the Parmenidean position, at several points he deliberately rejects his inheritance and advances views entirely his own. Perhaps he is a trifle crude; certainly he cannot be held innocent of logical blunders. (What philosopher can?) But his fragments are, to my mind, as interesting as those of Parmenides, and equally deserving of sympathetic study.

The ten surviving fragments are all preserved by Simplicius; with perhaps two exceptions they form part of a systematic deduction parallel to Parmenides' Way of Truth. The fragments themselves are sufficient to establish the general outline of Melissus' progress; and corroboration is available from the running paraphrases in the *MXG* (**A 5**), in Simplicius (*ad* **B 1–7**), and in Philoponus (**A 10a R**). Here, then, is a sketch of Melissus' system.

If we can think and talk about any object O, then it is axiomatic that
(A) O exists.
Melissus lays down (A) and then asks what follows from it;[9] he argues first, in **B 1**, that:
(T1) O is ungenerated,
and then infers from (T1), in **B 1** and **B 2** that:
(T2) O is eternal,
or in other words (**B 2**, **B 4**) that:
(T3) O is temporally unlimited.
An analogous argument (**B 3**, **B 4**) yields:
(T4) O is spatially unlimited.
From (T4) we are next to infer (**B 5**, **B 6**) that:
(T5) O is unique.
It seems certain (cf. **B 7**.1) that Melissus proceeded from (T5) to:
(T6) O is homogeneous.
The long fragment, or pair of fragments, **B 7**, passes from (T6) to:
(T7) O does not alter,
and hence to:
(T8) O is not destroyed,
(T9) O does not grow,
(T10) O is not rearranged,
(T11) O does not suffer pain,
and:
(T12) O does not suffer anguish.
Next,[10] Melissus proceeds to:
(T13) O is not empty,
and hence to:
(T14) O is full.
And from (T14) he infers both:
(T15) O does not move,
and:
(T16) O is not dense or rare.
Finally **B 10** infers from (T15) to:
(T17) O is not divided up.

That, so far as we know, is the end of Melissus' metaphysics. Two fragments remain: **B 8** contains an interesting argument against the validity of sense-perception, which came from, or perhaps formed, a polemical appendix to Melissus' work; and **B 9** is a controversial remark about incorporeality. I shall deal separately with these two fragments (below, pp. 298, 227).

As a coda to this section I quote the first part of Gorgias on *What is Not*. The passage is not an exposition of Eleatic metaphysics and does not stand in any sense as a parallel to **B 8** of Parmenides or the fragments of Melissus; but I shall on occasion refer to it, and it is pertinent and strange enough to warrant transcription. Again, I follow Sextus' version (above, p. 173).

(66) [That nothing exists, he argues in this fashion:] If something exists, either what exists exists or what does not exist exists or both what exists and what does not exist exist. But what exists does not exist, as I will establish, nor does what does not exist, as I will show, nor do both what exists and what does not exist, as I will teach. It is not the case, therefore, that something exists.
(67) Now that which does not exist does not exist. For if what does not exist exists, at the same time it will exist and it will not exist—in so far as it is conceived of as not existing, it will not exist; in so far as, not existing, it exists,[11] it will again exist. But it is utterly absurd that anything should at the same time both exist and not exist. What does not exist, therefore, does not exist. Again, if what does not exist exists, what exists will not exist; for these are contrary to one another, and if existence holds of what does not exist, non-existence will hold of what exists. But it is not the case that what exists does not exist; nor, then, will what does not exist exist.
(68) But neither does what exists exist. For if what exists exists, it is either eternal or generated or at the same time eternal and generated; but it is neither eternal nor generated, nor both, as we shall prove; what exists, therefore, does not exist. If what exists is eternal (for we must begin here), it does not have any beginning.
(69) For everything that comes into being has a beginning, but what is eternal, being ungenerated, has no beginning. But not having a beginning, it is unlimited. And if it is unlimited, it is nowhere. For if it is anywhere, that in which it is is different from it, and thus what is, being contained by something, will no longer be unlimited; for the container is greater than the contained, but nothing is greater than what is unlimited; so that what is unlimited will not be anywhere. (70) Nor is it surrounded by itself. For then that in which it is and that which is in it will be the same, and what exists will become two, place and body (for that in which

it is is place and that which is in it is body). But that is absurd. Nor, then, is what exists in itself. Hence if what exists is eternal, it is unlimited and if it is unlimited, it is nowhere; and if it is nowhere, it does not exist. Hence if what exists is eternal, it is not existent at all. (71) But neither can what exists be generated. For if it was generated, it was generated either from an existent or from a non-existent. But it was not generated from an existent; for if it is existent, it was not generated but already exists. Nor from a non-existent; for what does not exist cannot generate anything because, of necessity, that which generates anything must partake in subsistence. What exists, therefore, is not generated. (72) And by the same token it is not both together, eternal and generated at the same time. For these are destructive of one another, and if what exists is eternal it was not generated; and if it was generated, it is not eternal. Thus if what exists is neither eternal nor generated nor both together, what exists will not exist.

(73) Again, if it exists, it is either one or many. But it is neither one nor many, as will be established; what exists, therefore, does not exist. If it is one, it is either a quantity or continuous or a magnitude or a body. But whichever of these it is, it is not one—but if it is a quantity it will be divided; if continuous, it will be split; and similarly if it is conceived as a magnitude it will not be indivisible; and if it is a body, it will be threefold, for it will have length and breadth and depth. But it is absurd to say that what exists is none of these; what exists, therefore, is not one. (74) Nor is it many. For if it is not one, it will not be many. For the many too are taken away with it. That neither what exists nor what does not exist exists is clear from these considerations.

(75) That both together—what exists and what does not exist—do not exist is easy to argue for. If what does not exist exists and what exists exists, what does not exist will be the same as what exists, as far as existence goes; and because of that, neither of them exists. For that what does not exist does not exist is agreed; and what exists has been proved to be the same as this; it too, then, will not exist. (76) But if what exists is the same as what does not exist, it is not possible for both to exist. For if both do, they are not the same; and if they are the same, not both do. From which it follows that nothing exists. For if neither what exists nor what does not exist nor both exist, and if nothing apart from these is conceived of, then nothing exists (**157**).

(c) *On generation and destruction*

Melissus' fragment **B 1** stood at or near the beginning of his book: I doubt that he offered a preliminary paragraph justifying axiom (A), that O exists;[12] rather, he assumes the success of Parmenides' attack on the two false roads of inquiry, or else he is uninterested in any alternative hypothesis to (A). **B 1** contains only the briefest argument for (T1), the theorem of ungenerability:

> Whatever is[13] always was and always will be. For if it came into being, it is necessary that it was nothing before coming into being; now if it was nothing, in no way might anything come into being from nothing **(158)**.

The *MXG* (975a3 = **A 5**) pertinently asks why we should accept Melissus' brusque assertion that 'nothing comes from nothing'. Melissus has no explicit answer; but it is evident that here too he is relying on Parmenidean precedent. And indeed, in Melissus' presentation of Eleatic philosophy, (T1) has little intrinsic importance: it is only adduced in the course of an argument for (T2)—(T5).

In order to grasp the Eleatic attack on generation, therefore, we must undertake the arduous task of elucidating the opening argument in Parmenides' deduction. It will emerge, however, that Melissus is not wholly useless: there are two features of **B 1** which throw light on Parmenides' argument and confirm two otherwise controversial items of interpretation.[14]

I turn, then, to Parmenides, 156, lines 5–21. I leave lines 5–6a aside for the moment, and begin with the questions of 6b–7a: 'For what generation will you inquire out for it? How, whence, did it grow?' Some scholars distinguish between the question of generation and the question of growth;[15] but I find nothing in the subsequent lines that reflects such a distinction, and I take 'grow' as a picturesque synonym for 'come into being'. On the other hand, 'how' and 'whence' do not appear to be synonymous: we appear we have two questions: How could O have come into being? Whence did O come into being?

Most commentators focus their attention on the latter question; and they find that Parmenides argues for it by way of a dilemma: 'Suppose that O comes into being from O'; i.e., that O' generates O. Then either O' is non-existent or O is existent. But O' cannot be non-existent (lines 7b–11); nor can it be existent (lines 12–13a). Hence O cannot come into being at all.'

That interpretation seems to me to be mistaken on two counts. (It also requires an emendation in line 12; but I do not cite that as an objection; for, on different grounds, I accept the change of text.)[16]

First, I do not find a dilemmatic argument in Parmenides' poem; nor do I find one in Melissus, who summarily repeats Parmenides' argument against generation; nor yet in Empedocles, who makes self-conscious use of the same argument. Both of Parmenides' followers assert simply that O cannot come into being from what is not; they do not add 'or from what is'.[17] Second, I dislike the importation of generators into Parmenides' argument; for that importation burdens him with a patent *non sequitur*: having urged that O is not generated by O' he is made to conclude that O does not come into being at all. The interpretation has him use the tacit, undefended, and unevident premiss that whatever comes into being is *brought* into being by something. An interpretation which does not insinuate that premiss is preferable.

Let us take a closer look at Parmenides' phrase 'from what is not' (*ek mê eontos*). Phrases of the form 'from X' (*ek X*) take more than one paraphrase: I have already listed several different 'senses' of 'from' in connexion with Milesian monism. One such 'sense' (sense (v) of p. 40) has us gloss '*Y* comes into being from *X*' by: 'What was formerly *X* is now *Y*'. The stock Aristotelian example is 'the musical comes into being from the unmusical' (*Phys* 190a23), i.e. 'what was unmusical is now musical'. The hypothesis which Parmenides rejects is: 'What is comes into being from what is not'. I suggest that we interpret that hypothesis thus: 'Something that was non-existent is now existent'. Nothing speaks against this interpretation; and two texts speak for it. First, in **158** Melissus says that 'if it came into being, it is necessary that it was nothing (*mêden*) before coming into being'. That is Melissus' version of the hypothesis that 'what is came into being from what is not' (for *mêden* is synonymous with *to mê on*: above, p. 166); and he plainly understands the hypothesis as I have interpreted it. Second, Empedocles' account of Parmenides' argument presupposes the same interpretation: in **31 B 11** he berates those who 'expect that what formerly is not comes into being'; and he explains that 'it is impossible to come into being from what in no way exists' (**B 12**). Melissus and Empedocles interpret '*O* comes into being from what is not' as '*O*, which formerly did not exist, now exists'; and their interpretation is authoritative.

The generative dilemma disappears from Parmenides' text. In its place, we find the following taut argument: 'If O exists, then O cannot have come into being. For if O comes into being at *t*, then prior to *t* O did not exist. But, by the argument in **148–150** against Road (B), it is impossible for O not to exist.'

Is that a good argument? There are at least three objections to it.

First: 'Parmenides says in lines 8b–9a that "it is not sayable nor thinkable that it is not"; and that is taken as a reference to the rejection of Road (B). But in 148–150 Parmenides only urged that if O does not exist, you cannot think of O; he did not urge that you cannot think that O does not exist.' The objection is not fatal; if I can think *that* O is something or other, then presumably I can think of O; hence if I cannot think of O I cannot think that O does not exist.

The second objection follows immediately: 'Parmenides says that it is unthinkable that O does not exist; he needs the premiss that it is *impossible* that O should not exist. How can he bridge the gap between inconceivability and impossibility?' Parmenides himself makes no attempt to bridge the gap. He is content to observe that the judgment 'O does not exist' cannot be true. If it makes sense, it is false; and if it makes no sense, it is of course neither true nor false. And perhaps this is all that he needs; for an opponent cannot intelligibly say that although the *judgment* that O does not exist cannot be true, nevertheless O may not exist: such a retort is simply contradictory. The opponent might reply that some facts are ineffable and unjudgeable; but again Parmenides has an answer: If there are unjudgeable facts, O's non-existence cannot be among them; for if it were a fact that O does not exist, then the judgment that O does not exist would be true. If we drive a wedge between facts and judgments, then the facts must be utterly unspecifiable: the opponent wants, impossibly, a fact that is *both* specifiable *and* unjudgeable.

The third objection is more severe. The Parmenidean connexion between thought and existence, as I have presented it so far, has not carried any explicit reference to time. Yet in the context of a discussion on generation such reference must be made; and the result of making it surely yields:

(1) $(\forall t)$ (if at t a thinks that O exists, then O exists at t).

Now the suggestion that O comes into being 'from what does not exist' amounts to:

(2) O exists at t and at some t' prior to t O did not exist.

But no contradiction can be won from (1) and (2): the first conjunct of (2) guarantees the thinkability of O; and that seems enough to sustain the thought that O did not exist. The time of the thought and the time of O's putative non-existence are different: Parmenides has at most shown the absurdity of 'O does not exist'; he has not yet shown any absurdity in 'O did not exist'. And (2) requires only the latter judgment.

Now Parmenides might counter that argument by appealing to a general and plausible thesis about the relation between truth and time, viz:

(3) $(\forall t)(\forall t')$ (if at t a truly says that [P at t'], then if at t' a says that [P at t'] he speaks truly).

What is now truly said to have happened yesterday could yesterday have been truly said to be happening then. Hence if at t I can truly say that O did not exist at t', at t' I might truly have said 'O does not now exist'. But, by (1), I cannot truly say at t' 'O does not now exist'; hence at t I cannot truly say 'O did not exist at t''.

Of course, anyone who accepts both (1) and (3) will be obliged to infer that no true propositions at all can be made about beings whose existence has temporal limits. That conclusion may seem absurd, yet it is not a conclusion to make an Eleatic shudder; and I am inclined to think that Parmenides' argument in lines 6–9 has considerable force. If I reject it, that is because I have already rejected (1). I suspect, indeed, that some who are sceptical of (1) will still feel some force in Parmenides' first argument against generation; I shall return briefly to this point at the end of my discussion of lines 5–21.

The next argument occupies lines 9b–10: it takes up the question of *how* O might come into being 'starting from nothing'. (*Tou mêdenos* again means *tou mê eontos*.) '... what *need* would have aroused it later or sooner . . .?' The phrase *husteron ê prosthen* is sometimes translated 'later rather than sooner', or 'at one time rather than at another'. Thus Parmenides is applying the Principle of Sufficient Reason, and his argument runs as follows:

(4) If O does not exist during a period T, then for any two points t, t' in T, O has a property P at t if and only if it has P at t'.

(5) If O comes into existence at t, then for some P, O comes into existence at t because O has P at t.

Suppose, then:

(6) O comes into existence at t_1.

Then:

(7) O comes into existence at t_1 because O has P at t_1.

Hence:

(8) O has P at t_1,

and so, by (4):

(9) O has P at t_2.

But from (9) and (7) we can infer:

(10) O comes into existence at t_2.

And that is incompatible with (6).

The Principle of Sufficient Reason operates at step (5) and at step (10): (5) is an application of the requirement that all happenings have *some* explanation; and the inference from (9) and (7) to (10) assumes that the explanation must be *sufficient* for what it explains. Compare Anaximander's argument about the stability of the earth (above, pp. 23–6).

There is a fairly obvious weakness here: (4) is, at best, true only if P is restricted to non-relational properties of O; yet it is precisely in terms of its relational properties that we would hope to explain the generation of O: O may not change intrinsically during T; but at t_1 something may hold of it which does not hold of it at t_2—the demiurge may have determined upon t_1 as the appropriate time to create O.

That may encourage us to seek a simpler argument in the text; and scholars have doubted the propriety of ascribing (4)—(10) to Parmenides, both on linguistic and on historical grounds.[18] If we revert to the earlier translation, 'later *or* sooner', and gloss that by 'at any particular time', we need only ascribe to Parmenides the blunt assertion that if O does not exist prior to t, then there is no reason why O should come into existence at t, or at any other time. Unfortunately, that simple argument is open to a simple version of the objection to the sophisticated argument: why ever should we suppose that an intelligent agent might not pick upon t as the time for exercising his creative powers on O?

The objection raises interesting issues; but I think that Parmenides would be unmoved by it. For his line of thought is, I suspect, simpler than is usually supposed: if O does not exist at t, then nothing can 'rouse' it into existence, for it is not there to be 'roused'. And if we soften 'rousing' into creating we are no better off: a cannot create O at t unless he can think of O at t. And since, *ex hypothesi*, O does not exist at t, then by (1) a cannot think of O. Thus construed, Parmenides' second argument has as much force as his first.

The two arguments are summarized in line 11; but the line is puzzling. '*Pampan*' ('altogether') must bear a temporal sense; and '*houtôs*' ('in this way') should mean something like 'as far as the considerations so far broached take us'. Thus I gloss the line as follows: 'As far as generation goes, O either exists at all times or not at any'.[19] The case against generation is now concluded: unless we can make out a case for the destructibility of what exists, we must allow its sempiternity.

We therefore expect an argument against destruction; and line 14 implies that the expectation has been satisfied. But lines 12–13 are desperately difficult: they contain a textual *crux*, and two ambiguities.

I have translated an emended version of line 12: the manuscripts read '*ek mê eontos*': 'Nor from what is not will the strength of trust allow *gignesthai ti par' auto*'. In the last phrase, '*ti*' may be either subject or complement of '*gignesthai*', and '*auto*' may refer either to 'what is' or 'what is not'. Thus the manuscript text yields four readings: (i) 'From what is not, it is not possible for anything to come into being apart from what is'; (ii) 'From what is not, it is not possible for anything to come into being apart from what is not'; (iii) 'From what is not, it is not possible for it to become anything apart from what is'; (iv) 'From what is not, it is not possible for it to become anything apart from what is not'.

None of (i)—(iv) is satisfactory: (iii) and (iv) make no decent sense at all; (i) is impotent as an argument against generation and cannot constitute an argument against destruction. If we construe 'from' in the generator sense, then we can conjure an argument out of (ii): 'If O' does not exist and O' generates O, then O does not exist; hence if O exists and is generated from O', it is not the case that O' does not exist.' But I doubt if that argument is Parmenidean: first, the very notion of the generation of non-entities is remote from Parmenides' thought; second, (ii) interprets 'from' in the fashion which raises problems for the rest of lines 5-21; and third, (ii) has no bearing upon destruction.

Several scholars, for different reasons, have emended '*ek mê eontos*' in line 12 to '*ek tou eontos*' or some equivalent phrase.[20] With that text '*auto*' can only pick up 'what is'; and there are thus just two readings: (v) 'From what is, it is not possible for anything to come into being apart from what is'; (vi) 'From what is, it is not possible for it to become anything apart from what is'.

Reading (v) yields the gloss: 'If O exists, and O generates O', then $O = O''$. There is an argument against generation here if we add the plausible premiss that a thing cannot generate itself: 'If O exists and generates something, it generates itself; but nothing generates itself; hence nothing can be generated from what exists'. But I find it hard to impute that argument to Parmenides: the thesis that existent generators could only generate themselves is bizarre, and can hardly stand unsupported in the text; nor does that reading yield an argument against destruction.

I therefore turn to reading (vi); and my translation is designed to fit that reading. Given (vi), the word 'from' has the same sense as I have given it earlier; and Parmenides offers us an implicit argument against destruction. I paraphrase: 'Nor from a state of existence can O become something other than what is'; i.e., O cannot change from existing to not existing, O cannot be destroyed. That offers a statement, not an argument. Yet it is obvious what argument we are to supply: if O is destroyed at t, then O exists before t and O does not exist after t. But 'it is not sayable nor thinkable that it is not.' The objections and replies that I rehearsed in connexion with lines 6–9 will bear equally on lines 12–13; I shall not march them out again. It is worth saying, however, that those philosophers who sympathize with lines 6–9 are unlikely to extend their sympathy to 12–13: Parmenides sees an exact symmetry between generation and destruction, past and future: the neo-Parmenideans feel an important asymmetry here. That feeling will be discussed later.

We can now conclude that either O exists 'altogether'—is sempiternal, or else it exists not at all. And lines 13b–18, relaxing the tight stays of Parmenides' argument, remind us that the second alternative is already ruled out; for we are travelling along the Way of Truth.

(d) *Being and time*

By now, then, 'coming into being is extinguished and destruction is unheard of'; but before he states that conclusion Parmenides interposes two more lines of argument. Line 19 offers two theses, in the form of rhetorical questions; and line 20 offers two supporting reasons. Theses and reasons are arranged chiastically.[21]

The second reason is unambiguously expressed: 'it is not, . . . if it is about to be at some time'; i.e.:

(1) If O is going to exist in the future, O does not exist.

The first thesis is crabbed: 'how might what is be then?' We can extract an intelligible thought if we read 'then' (*epeita*) as 'in the future'; thus:

(2) If O exists, O will not exist in the future.

For (2) actually follows from (1); hence (1) may reasonably be advanced in support of (2). And Parmenides plainly means us to infer that O will not exist in the future.

The first reason reads: 'if it came into being, it is not'; i.e.:

(3) If O came into existence, O does not exist.

And the second thesis, correspondingly, should run:

(4) If O exists, O did not come into existence.

That, at least, is the natural construe; but it suffers from a severe disability; for the deliberately symmetrical form of Parmenides' verse turns out to mask an asymmetrical content: (1) talks about future being, (3) about past *becoming*. There are two ways of restoring symmetry. Some interpret '*genoito*' and '*egento*' in lines 19–20 as though they were past tenses of '*einai*': 'And how could it *have existed*? For if it *existed*, it is not'. Then (3) denies past existence to what is, just as (1) denies further existence to it. Alternatively, '*epeita peloi*' and '*mellei*' may be twisted to refer to future becoming: 'How might what is *come to be* in the future? . . . nor if it is going *to come to be*'. Then (1) denies future becoming to what is, just as (3) denies past becoming to it.

Neither of those suggestions fits the Greek easily; and neither fits the context peculiarly well: on the first reading we have a pair of thoughts which are inappropriate harbingers of the conclusion at line 21. On the second reading, we have a further otiose attack on generation. Moreover, on neither interpretation does Parmenides have a pellucid argument. On the second reading, the case against future generation is sound: if O is to come into existence at t, O does not now exist. But the case against past generation cannot be stated in a parallel fashion: from 'O came into existence at t' it does not follow that O does not exist now; in order to extract that conclusion we must pad the argument with Parmenidean premisses drawn from earlier parts of the attack on generation: 'if O came into existence at t, then before t O did not exist; and if O ever failed to exist, O always fails to exist'.

On the first reading, we cannot find a sound argument either for (1) or for (3). The first reading does, however, suggest a plausible explanation of why Parmenides should have thought (1) and (3) true. There is a distinction between what a man implies in stating something, and what his statement implies. Very roughly, in saying that P I imply that Q if it would be odd or unconventional or misleading for me, in those circumstances, to say that P, if I also believed that not-Q. P implies Q if it is impossible for P to be true and Q false. If you ask me how many hours a day I work, and I say 'At least four', I imply that I do not regularly work for ten hours a day; but my statement does not imply that. Similarly, if I say 'a is going to be F' or 'a was F', then I imply that (at least as far as I know) a is not yet, or no longer, F; but what I say does not have those implications. Now it is easy to confuse the implications of what I say with the implications of my saying it; and I suggest that Parmenides may have fallen into just such a confusion here: observing, correctly, that anyone who says 'O was' or 'O will be' implies that O is not now, he mistakenly inferred that 'O was' and 'O will be' both imply 'O is not', and hence concluded that O was not and O will not be.

On the whole, then, I incline to the interpretation of lines 19–20 which has them deny past and future existence to what now exists. Evidently, that interpretation raises severe difficulties of a logical and of a structural nature: how can Parmenides argue against the generation of what exists and yet hold that what exists did not exist in the past? Why does he interpolate lines 19–20 before his conclusion, in line 21, about generation and destruction? Before facing up to those difficulties, I shall attempt to elucidate lines 5–6a of **156**:

> Nor was it ever, nor will it be; since now it is, all together, one, continuous.

Textually the lines are far from certain; but, for once, the variant readings offer no serious variation in sense. I begin with three preliminary points. First, we should not take 5–6a as part of Parmenides' prospectus; for the lines overtly contain an argument. Second, we may not divorce 5–6a from 6b–21; for an explanatory particle unites them. Third, the three phrases *homou pan*, *hen* and *suneches* ('all together, one, continuous') are synonymous, or at least mutually explicatory. To say that O is 'one' is to say that it is a unity, and a prime way of being unitary is being continuous (cf. Aristotle, *Met* 1015b36–1016a3). Continuity here is temporal: O is continuous if there are no temporal gaps in its career. And to say that O is 'all together' is only to say that it is 'altogether' (line 11): there are no temporal periods which do not contain it.[22] Thus the conclusion expressed in line 5a is derived from a premiss asserting that O is temporally continuous; and that premiss, it seems, is in turn to be derived from the argument in lines 6b–21 that I have already analysed.

What conclusion does line 5a state? At least four interpretations are on the market. (a) Some say that line 5a merely denies generation and destruction, in a rhetorically elevated style; and that view has tidiness in its favour, for it leaves lines 5–21 with a single subject. Tidiness, however, is outweighed by two considerations: line 5a purports to offer a deduction from the ungenerability of what is, and not merely to assert its ungenerability; and only the wildest rhetorical fancy will read line 5 as expressing the same sentiment as lines 3 and 21.[23] (b) Others say that line 5a states the omnitemporality of what exists; and that view comports well with lines 6b–21; for if O is ungenerable and indestructible, it exists for ever. But I am unable to see how an assertion that O did not and will not exist can amount to an expression of the omnitemporality of O. (c) Third, it is said that line 5a sets O outside the boundaries of time: O is a timeless entity in the sense that no temporally tagged predications hold good of it. That interpretation sees Parmenides through Platonic eyes, and reads into line 5a an adumbration of the doctrine advanced in the *Timaeus* (37D–38A). There are attractions in the view; but again there is strong textual evidence against it: line 5 expressly says that O 'now is' (*nun estin*), and that is flatly incompatible with the thesis of atemporality. (d) Finally, it has been supposed that O exists in time and endures through time, but that all times are eternally present in a changeless now. Such a notion has had theological and poetical adherents; thus God, according to Plutarch, 'exists in no time, but in the changeless and timeless *aiôn* . . . being one, he has filled eternity in a single now' (*de E apud Delphos* 393AB). But that notion is hopelessly confused: there is no sense in the suggestion that time past and time future are all one in time present, that all moments are eternally present; for the idea of a plurality of times implies a past or a future distinct from the present. I am loth to ascribe such a vile thought to Parmenides.

What, then, does line 5a say? The message seems to be simple enough: '*O* exists now' is true; '*O* exists at *t*' is false whenever *t* is distinct from now, either past or future. Is that message coherently supported by lines 5b–6a? Is it coherent in itself? Does it cohere with the views expounded in lines 6b–21?

It is tempting to find a sophisticated and powerful argument in 5b–6a.[24] Parmenides may be thought to rely tacitly upon Leibniz' principle of the Identity of Indiscernibles, applied to temporal instants: 'Two instants in *O*'s career are distinct only if they are "discernible": only if something is true of *O* at one instant and not true of it at another. But *O* never changes in any respect—it is "all together" or alike in all respects—and so nothing could be true of it at any instant in its career which was not true of it at every instant. Hence there are no distinct instants in *O*'s career; and we cannot sensibly say of it that it was or that it will be.' That construction is attractive but misconceived. Parmenides does indeed argue that *O* cannot change in any respect at all; but his argument is not presented until lines 26–33. Thus the conclusion stated in line 5a is supposed to depend on an argument which is not advanced for another twenty lines. The gap is considerable, and nothing in the text of lines 26–33 invites us to think back to line 5a.

Let us take another look at the sweep of argument in lines 6–21. Consider the diagram:

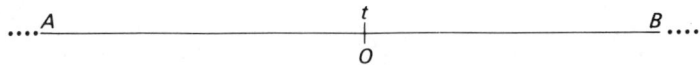

Here *t* is the present moment on the time-line *AB*. We know that *O* exists at *t*. Now the arguments of 6b–18, ruling out generation and destruction, show that *O* exists 'altogether'; in other words, that there is no point on *AB* at which *O* does not exist. And the argument in 19–20 shows that *O* does not exist at any point on *AB* except at point *t*. Those conclusions are not inconsistent: together they entail that every point on *AB* is identical with *t*. Not only is there no time like the present—there is no time but the present. *O*'s existence is not a beautiful atoll in the empty sea of eternity: there are no points in time not embellished by *O*, because time itself embraces no more than a point. Thus *O* is 'all together, one, continuous': it occupies every point of time at once; for time has only one point. The present moment's all its lot.

Is that view coherent? It is often believed that 'there is no time without change'. Take any two instants t_1 and t_2: if the state of the universe at t_1 is the same as its state at t_2, and if there is no instant t_3 between t_1 and t_2 such that the state of the universe at t_3 is different from its state at t_1, then $t_1 = t_2$. The Parmenidean universe is entirely changeless; consequently, if time implies change, that universe is punctual. *O*, and anything else there may be, exists only at *t*. I do not wish to defend that view of time here. I mention it only to indicate that the thesis I ascribe to Parmenides is not simply absurd; a later context will give an opportunity to return to the question.

Is that view of 5–6a consistent with the rest of Parmenides' philosophy? The punctual existence of *O* is not announced in the prospectus; it is not stated in line 21; it is not used to infer any of the other properties of *O*: it is, superficially at least, contradicted by lines 29–30, which appear to speak of a stable and enduring entity. Such facts will lead different readers to different conclusions. I incline to infer that Parmenides did not have a firm grasp of the inordinately slippery fish he held in his hand. Others may say that Parmenides simply contradicts himself; or that he changed his mind (perhaps incorporating lines 5–6 into a second edition of his poem); or that he never contradicted his punctual thesis but merely did not care to use it. Still others will infer that my interpretation of lines 5–21 is mistaken. Anyone who has given more than three minutes thought to those lines will recognize them as terrain in which true trust is impossible: the conclusion I offer here is not a thing I advocate; it is rather the view I am least often inclined to reject.

(e) *Eternity*

The first fragment of Melissus introduced my discussion of Parmenides' thoughts on generation. It is time to return to Melissus and to consider the second thesis of his philosophy: that *O* is eternal. With (T2)–(T4) Melissus leaves the safety of Parmenides' shadow, and strides forward on his own; at precisely this point, according to Aristotle, he walks into the quicksands of fallacy. First, here is the text of **B 2**:

Again, [i] since it did not come into being but it is, it always was and always will be, and it has no beginning and no end but is unlimited.[25] For [ii] if it had come into being, it would have had a beginning (for [iii] it would have begun coming into being at some time) and [ii^a] an end (for [iii^a] it would have ended coming into being at some time). But [iv] since it did not begin or end, it always was and always will be and it has no beginning or end; for [v] it is not accomplishable that what is not altogether is always (**159**).

As its first sentence shows, **159** intends to prove (T2) and (T3) on the basis of (T1): ungenerability grounds eternity and temporal infinity. (Propositions (T2) and (T3) are, I take it, equivalent; at all events, Melissus makes no attempt to distinguish between them.)

In presenting the argument of **159** I shall abbreviate '*O* always was and always will be, and has no beginning and no end but is unlimited' to '*O* is ϕ'. Thus, as sentence [i] shows, **159** is to prove:
(1) *O* is ϕ,
and to prove it by *modus ponens* from:
(2) If *O* is ungenerated, then *O* is ϕ.
Thus the burden of **159** is the establishment of (2).

(2) is derived from two propositions:
(3) If *O* is generated, then *O* has a beginning and *O* has an end.
(4) If *O* did not begin and did not end, then *O* is ϕ,
Proposition (3) is expressed in [ii] and [ii^a]; and it is supported in [iii] and [iii^a], which state:
(5) If *O* is generated, then *O* at some time began to be generated and *O* at some time ceased being generated.
Proposition (4) is expressed in [iv] and supported in [v] by:
(6) It is not possible that *O* is not altogether and *O* is always.

Each step in Melissus' argument is questionable. First, let us look at the inference from (6) to (4). The chief problem here is the obscurity of (6). Perhaps we should explain Melissus' phrase 'it is altogether (*pan*)' by Parmenides' phrase 'it is altogether (*pampan*)' (**156**. 11): *pampan* required a temporal explanation in Parmenides, and a temporal explanation of Melissus' *pan* will at least fit (6) into the context of **159**; moreover, it will make (6) a tautological truth.[26] Now it is possible to construe (4) as a tautology; and that construe is, I think, the one Melissus requires. Consequently, (4) follows trivially from (6).

Second, there is the inference from (5) to (3). The text in sentences [iii] and [iii^a] is uncertain: the canonical reading is not '*ginomenon*' (which I translate) but '*genomenon*'. That reading requires the following translation: '[ii] . . . had a beginning (for [iii], coming into being, it would have begun at some time) and [ii^a] an end (for [iii^a], coming into being, it would have ended at some time)'. But on that translation [iii] and [iii^a] merely restate [ii] and [ii^a]: they add nothing. The reading '*ginomenon*' is in any case better attested; and it gives an argument to Melissus. Unfortunately, the argument is feeble. Proposition (5) is indeed true: if *O* underwent a process of generation, then that process had a beginning and also had an ending. But (5) will yield (3) only by means of:

(7) If *O* began or ceased being generated, then *O* began or ceased.

Now the consequent of (7) must be read as '*O* began or ceased *to exist*'; and it is plain that (7) is false. We may imagine that Melissus gave his tacit assent to (7); for it involves just that move of 'dequalification' which we saw reason to ascribe to Heraclitus and which, on Aristotle's testimony, was a frequent and pervasive fallacy (above, p. 73). Certainly, Melissus' argument for (3) is fallacious; and it is hard to dream up any more plausible defence of (3).

What, finally, of the inference from (3) and (4) to (2)? Schematically, Melissus moves from propositions of the form:

(A) If *P* then *Q*,

and:

(B) If not-*Q*, then *R*,

to one of the form:

(C) If not-*P*, then *R*.

And that argument pattern is invalid. I suppose that Melissus took 'If *P* then not-*Q*' and 'If not-*P* then *Q*' to be equivalent: it is easy to see how that equivalence will license the move from (A) and (B) to (C). (In finding that false equivalence behind the argument of 159, I am, I think, agreeing with Aristotle, who accused Melissus of using illicit conversions on conditional propositions.[27]) Those who are schooled in formal logic, and acquainted with the complexities of the conditional, may despise Melissus for committing so gross a blunder. But the logic of conditionals is remarkably difficult to apprehend; in particular, it is easy to reason that if *P* implies not-*Q*, then not-*P* cannot also imply not-*Q* and so must imply *Q*. Plato and Aristotle were aware of the pitfalls surrounding conditional propositions; but they did not escape them all. Centuries later, Aulus Gellius delighted to find the Melissan fallacy committed by Pliny, 'the most learned man of his age' (IX.xvi). And if the modern logician is censorious of Melissus, let him reflect upon his own tiro entanglement with the logic of *if* and *then*.

Melissus' (T2) is not a Parmenidean thesis, if my interpretation of Parmenides as a punctualist is correct. Eleatic entities are ungenerable and incorruptible—that much is shared by Parmenides and Melissus. But while Parmenides' beings have no temporal duration, Melissan beings are sempiternal. The difference of view seems immense; but it reduces to a disagreement over the relation between time and change. Melissus' entities, like Parmenides', are immutable. Melissus, however, thought (tacitly, no doubt) that an immutable world might sensibly be said to endure; Parmenides implicitly denied that. Both philosophers agree that for any instant t, O exists at t. Parmenides believes and Melissus does not believe that all instants are identical.

(f) *The logic of becoming*

The theory that all genuine entities are sempiternal has had a remarkable popularity in the history of philosophy: it is a Platonic doctrine; it appears in Aristotle in the view that form and matter cannot be created or destroyed; the seventeenth-century rationalists held that substances are sempiternal; today we vaguely talk of the Conservation of Matter, and imply a belief that the basic stuff of the world has an Eleatic stability. I shall have a little to say about that theory in a later chapter; I end this chapter with a few notes on generation.

Most philosophers would agree that neither Parmenides nor Melissus proved the impossibility of generation; but many, I guess, will think that a finger plunged into the Eleatic pie will pull out a sweet philosophical plum.

Consider the logic of generation. 'If O comes into being at time t, then before t O does not exist, and after t O exists'. Generation, it seems, is a species of change or alteration. To put it roughly, O alters at t if and only if for some property P, before t O lacks P and after t O has P. Let P be existence; then the formula I have just used to express generation is only trivially different from one expressing a type of alteration. Aristotle is aware of this, or something like it: in *Physics* A 7-9 he first offers an analysis of 'absolute becoming' or generation which makes it a special case of alteration; and then he states that only in that way are Eleatic doubts about generation surmountable. Aquinas, reporting the Aristotelian position, puts it succinctly: *Omne fieri est mutari*, all becoming is changing (*Summa Theologiae* Ia, q.45, 2).

Aquinas did not like it: it follows, he says, that 'creation is a changing; but every changing depends on a subject [i.e., is the alteration of some pre-existing subject matter]. . . . Therefore it is impossible for anything to come into being from nothing by God's action.' Now the first chapter of *Genesis* proves that argument to be unsound; for God created the world *ex nihilo*. The Aristotelians, attending only to the present world, observed no sublunary creation and felt no misgivings about the thesis that becoming is changing. Aquinas agreed with their sublunary observations, but he accused them of ignoring the cosmic and original act of creation.

But Aquinas does not think that Aristotle is simply in error; he has a subtler thing to say: 'Creation is not a changing, except only in respect of our way of understanding. In creation, by which the whole substance of things is produced, you cannot find some one thing which is differently qualified now and before—except only in respect of our understanding, since some object is understood first not to have existed at all, and afterwards to exist' (ibid., *ad* 2). We cannot understand generation unless we think in terms of an object's changing from non-existent to existent; but our thought fails, in an important way, to correspond to the facts.

There is surely truth in this: creating a table is not like painting a table red. When it is painted, my pre-existent and complete table loses one property and acquires another: what was green is now red. When it is made or constructed, the table does not undergo any comparable process; for there is no table there to undergo any process: there is no table off-stage, leaving the green room of non-being to wait in the wings of becoming for its cue to pirouette onto the boards of reality. The metaphysics of creation and generation is not like that: becoming is not altering. And a precisely analogous argument goes for destruction: when I die, I do not alter—I cease to be: I do not lose one and assume another property—there ceases to be any property-bearer at all.

That argument is impressionistic. To delineate it more precisely would require a digression both long and unwarranted; for even though the argument raises interesting problems about generation, they are not, I think, Eleatic problems. According to Elea (if I may state things crudely) the formula '*O* did not exist and now *O* exists' is untrue—and that is why generation is impossible. According to Aquinas, the formula is potentially misleading; but for all that it may be true. And indeed, it is surely consistent, and plausible, to maintain on the one hand that Socrates' birth is not a process undergone by Socrates in the way in which his growing pale is; and on the other hand that part of what we mean when we say that Socrates was born in 477 BC is that before 477 Socrates did not exist, whereas after 477 he did exist.

Thus I leave Aquinas and turn to two modern dogmas with an Eleatic flavour. The first dogma is contained in the slogan 'Existence is not a Predicate'. If '*O* comes into being' entails '*O* did not exist and now O exists', then generation is indeed impossible. For in 'O did not exist and now O exists', 'exist' is used as a predicate of O: since existence is not a predicate, that formula is ill-formed; hence 'O comes into being' cannot say anything true. The argument has an Eleatic conclusion; but it out-Herods Herod: it eliminates 'O does not exist', but it also eliminates the Eleatic axiom 'O exists'. The Eleatics are going to get no help from the dogma that existence is not a predicate; and I therefore leave the dogma, observing only that it commits its holders to an Eleatic denial of generation—and that it is perfectly false.

The second dogma relates to issues I have discussed in the previous chapter. It connects thought with existence, holding that if I am to judge that O has P, then I must be able to refer to O, but that I cannot, at any instant t, refer to O unless O exists at t or existed prior to t. It follows that no sentence of the form 'O will come into being' can be the object of a true judgment. For if I judge that O will come into being, O must already exist or have existed; and so my judgment is false.

That view is Eleatic, but not full-bloodedly so; for it countenances an asymmetry between past and future. Assume the dogma true and consider this diagram.

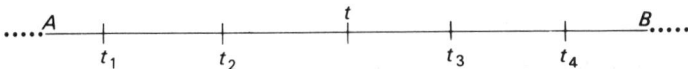

Take the following judgments, all made at t: (i) 'O came into being'; (ii) 'O will come into being'; (iii) 'O was destroyed'; (iv) 'O will be destroyed.' Suppose, first, that O in fact lasts from t_1 to t_2: then (i) and (iii) are true; (ii) and (iv) are false. Next, suppose that O in fact lasts from t_2 to t_3: then (i) and (iv) are true; (ii) and (iii) are false. Suppose, finally, that O in fact lasts from t_3 to t_4: then (i), (ii), (iii) and (iv) are all false. Thus (ii) alone is inevitably false; each of (i), (iii) and (iv)—which the Eleatics renounce along with (ii)—can be true.

The second dogma is thus Eleatic, but only to a low degree. In any event, the dogma seems to me to be false: I can, I think, judge that O has P even if O does not yet exist; I can judge that the Smiths' second child will be male, or that the Cup Final will be won by Arsenal. It is a difficult question to determine precisely under what conditions I can judge that O has P; and a question I shall not presume to broach here. But I end the chapter by saying, confidently, that neither the existence nor the pre-existence of O is a necessary condition for making judgments about O.

XI

Stability and Change

(a) *The limits of the world*

Following Melissus' account rather than that of Parmenides, I turn next to (T4), the theorem that O is spatially infinite. The Melissan texts read thus:

> But just as it is always, so it must always be unlimited (*apeiron*) in magnitude too (**160: B 3**).

> Nothing having both a beginning and an end is either eternal or unlimited (**161: B 4**).

I construe 'unlimited in magnitude' in **160**, and 'unlimited' in **161**, as 'spatially infinite'. The arguments against this orthodox position are unconvincing.

Some commentators suppose that Melissus infers (T4) from (T3), spatial from temporal infinity; and they point out the folly of the inference.[1] But **160** implies not that (T4) is inferred from (T3) but that the argument for (T4) is parallel to that for (T3); and **161** corroborates the implication. Thus I suppose that Melissus hoped to deploy the argument of **159** for a second time, concluding to (T4). And presumably the central proposition in his argument will therefore have run:

(1) If O is generated, then O at some place began to be generated and O at some place ceased to be generated;

and (1) will have been used to ground:

(2) If O is generated, then O has a spatial beginning and a spatial end.

The general thought behind (1) seems to be this: if O undergoes a process of generation, then O must come into existence in stages, and so there must be a first piece of O to be generated and also a last piece; and thus O cannot be spatially infinite. There are at least three flaws in that argument. First, why suppose (1) to be true? Why may not O spring fully-formed from Zeus' head? Second, (1) does not entail (2): suppose that O is generated in instalments, and that A is the first and Z the last piece of O to be generated; still, it does not follow that A and Z are on the edges of O or that O has edges at all. Third, (2) does not entail (T4): in inferring (T4) from (2) Melissus again confuses 'if P, then not-Q' with 'if not-P, then Q'. The Melissan fallacy is committed again.

Some scholars, appalled by the febrile appearance of this argument, have ascribed a different piece of reasoning to Melissus. Speaking of the Eleatic philosophy, Aristotle reports thus:

> They say that the whole is one and unmoved, and some that it is unlimited; for the limit would limit it against the void (**162**: *GC* 325a15–16 = **A8**).

Scholars say that 'some' refers to Melissus; and that Aristotle's argument here is the genuine Melissan attack on spatial finitude.[2]

I doubt it. First, **162** cannot represent the argument alluded to in **161**: if **162** is a Melissan argument for (T4), then Melissus had two arguments for (T4). Second, the argument in **162** rests on (T13) or something like it: the denial of the void. Now from (T13) we can only infer (T4) if we use (T5), the uniqueness theorem; and (T5), as we shall shortly see, is deduced from (T4). If **162** were Melissan, it would represent a simple circularity: its argument is as frail as that of **161**. Third, Aristotle does not mention Melissus by name in **162**; the passage, which is designed to explain the philosophical ambience of the birth of atomism, reads to me more like an Aristotelian *pot-pourri* than a piece of serious-minded historical doxography. The relation between **162** and Melissus is similar to that between **16** and Anaximander (see above, p. 35): the passage contains thoughts on an Eleatic theme, not reports of Eleatic pronouncements.

162 does not help (T4); and **161** remains impotent. Yet (T4) is an important theorem of Melissan metaphysics, and we might properly look to support it from the poem of Parmenides. What, then, did Parmenides have to say on the subject? The question is highly controversial. It rests on the interpretation of **156**. 42–9, to which I now turn.

The traditional and natural reading of those lines has Parmenides argue that what exists is finite and spherical; and if that reading is correct, then far from supporting (T4), Parmenides is committed to its negation. Aristotle observed that 'we should think that Parmenides spoke better than Melissus; for the latter calls what is infinite a whole, while the former says that the whole is limited, "equally balanced from the middle"' (*Phys* 207a15–17 = **28 A 27**; cf. Aëtius, **30 A 9**). The contrast between a finitist Parmenides and an infinitist Melissus is thus ancient; and a unanimous tradition repeats it. There is, however, a rival reading of lines 42–9; and on that reading Parmenides anticipates Melissus and argues for (T4). The reading requires attention; but first I shall expound a version of the traditional view.

The logical structure of lines 42–9 is fairly clear: a central core of argument in 44b–48 is preceded and followed by a statement of the thesis to be proved.[3] Let us look first at the central core.

The argument is supposed to establish the proposition stated in lines 44b–45: '... neither any more nor any weaker can it be here or here'. I take that Delphic utterance to announce the 'existential homogeneity' of O in space. By that revolting phrase I mean something like this:

(3) Every subvolume v_i of the volume of space determined by the boundaries of O contains some existent part, O_i, of O.

There cannot, in short, be any spatial gaps or holes in O. (3) is supported by two considerations. The first, lines 46–47a, is moderately clear, though the text of line 46 is uncertain: 'neither is there anything that is not, which might stop it from reaching its like'; i.e., if you start from some point in O you cannot come across any non-existent bit of O which will block your progress to 'its like', i.e., to another existent bit of O. You cannot do so for the simple reason that there can be no non-existent bits of O. The second consideration occupies lines 47b–48: 'nor is there anything that is, so that there might be of what is here more and there less—since it is all inviolable'. Conceivably Parmenides is saying that no part of O can be 'more' or 'less' existent than any other. That is true; for there is no sense at all in the notion of one part of a thing being 'more existent' than another (even if we can, in other contexts, graft some Platonic sense onto the odd notion of 'being more real'). But it is hard to see how Parmenides' assertion that 'it is all inviolable (*asulon*)' supports that.[4] Nor is it clear how the truth is related to (3).

From (3) we are to infer that '... equal from all directions, it meets the limits alike' (line 49). But (3) says nothing about spatial 'equality'; and it makes no mention of 'limits'. The second omission is explicable; for line 42a has already asserted that 'there is a furthest limit', and that is intended as a premiss for the argument of 42–9. Thus 42–9 first state that O has limits, and then establish (3); and from those two propositions they infer that O, 'like the bulk of a well-rounded ball', 'meets the limits alike'. In short, O is bounded (line 42); and O is spatially homogeneous (lines 44–5): therefore O is a sphere (line 49).

Parmenidean entities, unlike Melissan entities, are finite in extent; and they are spherical. That conclusion accords with a long-standing tradition.[5] Some scholars assert that Parmenidean spheres are geometrical, not physical entities; and they find in the contrast between the Way of Truth and the Way of Opinion an adumbration of the distinction between the abstract realm of pure mathematical entities and the mundane world of nature. But that assertion goes far beyond the evidence of the fragments.

The traditional interpretation of lines 42–9 has come under heavy fire.[6] I shall mention five objections to it. 'According to the traditional interpretation, the argument uses as a premiss the thesis that O has spatial boundaries; but nothing in **156** entitles Parmenides to that thesis. Rather, "limit" in line 42 must be taken in a metaphorical sense: it refers to the "invariancy" of O which (3) then articulates.' I cannot believe that: the language of lines 42 and 49 is resolutely spatial; and it is hard to take it all as a metaphor for invariancy. Parmenides has already argued that O is motionless, and his argument refers to 'limits' (lines 30–1). He assumed, I guess, that if O is motionless, then O must remain within fixed spatial limits. The assumption is highly plausible; and it is true provided that O is finite in magnitude.

'The move from (3) to "O is equal from all directions" is evidently invalid: Parmenides could not have meant to make it; and "equal from all directions" is only a metaphor.' I sympathize with the objection; but the remedy the objector proposes is less acceptable than the ill he seeks to cure. Parmenides, on any account, is not at his best in these lines. I suppose he thinks that if O is internally homogeneous it must have, so to speak, an externally homogeneous façade; and in that case it must be a regular solid, if not necessarily a sphere.

'The prospectus in lines 3–4 does not mention sphericity.' Line 4, on the common reading, does however say that O is 'complete'; and that is naturally connected with *tetelesmenon* in line 42, and hence with sphericity. On my reading, 'balanced', the prospectus picks out the feature with which most of lines 42–9 are occupied. The relation between prospectus and text is not tidy on that reading; but it is no worse than that between the prospectus and lines 5–21.

'The argument used to reject any internal gaps in O will equally show the impossibility of anything beyond O, and hence will show

that O is infinite. (Moreover, the importation into (3) of reference to *parts* of O is textually unwarranted: instead of (3) we require some proposition which eliminates external as well as internal non-entity).'
Again, I have only a weak reply: (3) is not the only interpretation of the text, but it is a plausible one; and Parmenides' argument, even if it could show the lack of any non-entity beyond O, does nothing to disprove the suggestion that O is surrounded and close-packed by other entities, and hence nothing to establish the infinitude of O.[7]

'Parmenides must surely have asked himself the question: What lies outside the Sphere? And he must have hit upon the celebrated dilemma of Archytas:

> Archytas, according to Eudemus, put the argument thus: 'Standing at the edge (e.g. at the heaven of the fixed stars), could I extend my hand or my cane outside it or not?' That I could not extend it is absurd; but if I do extend it, then what is outside will be either body or space (**163**: Eudemus, fr. 65W = **47 A 24**).

Anticipating Archytas, Parmenides cannot have believed in a finite spherical existent'. I answer: first, why should Parmenides have anticipated Archytas' subtle thought? Second, if he did, why should he have anticipated Archytas' dubious answer to his dilemma? Third, if the subject of Parmenides' deduction is not the Universe but any object of inquiry, then Archytas' argument is simply irrelevant.

It is certainly not the case that Parmenides clearly and explicitly argued for an infinite existent. Indeed, had such an argument been in his mind, he could hardly have found worse terms in which to expound it than those he uses in lines 42–9; for almost every reader of those lines has taken them to argue in precisely the opposite sense. On the other hand, if lines 42–9 do argue that any existent must be a finite sphere, they do so in an obscure and unsatisfying fashion. I conclude lamely: first, lines 42–9 contain no good or interesting argument; second, they are probably intended in the sense a long tradition ascribes to them. On any account, Melissus represents an advance over Parmenides here.

(b) *The Eleatic One*

The most celebrated of Eleatic doctrines is that of monism; and it is also the most shocking. After all,

> It is patent to the eye that cannot face the sun
> The smug philosophers lie who say the world is one.

But then those philosophers will retort, smugly but philosophically enough, that the eye is a bad purveyor of fact; and that pure reason bears out their solitary view. At all events, such is the retort that an almost unanimous tradition has ascribed to Parmenides, to Melissus, and to Zeno. From Plato onwards, students of philosophy have talked, in capitals, of the Eleatic One.

The Milesians, of course, were monists. But their 'material' monism was a milk-and-water affair compared to the heady Eleatic potion. Eleatic monism, or 'real' monism as I shall call it, does not say that everything is made of some single stuff; it says that there exists just one single thing: one reality, one entity. And that Melissus held and argued for such a strange thesis is indubitable.

Here is the relevant text:

> If it were [unlimited] it would be one; for if it were two, they could not be unlimited, but they would have limits against one another (164: B 6).[8]

Eudemus objected to the argument: 'Why is it one? Not because several things will somehow be limited against one another; for past time is thought to be unlimited, though it is limited against the present' (fr. 41 W = Simplicius, *ad* B 5; cf. *MXG* 976a31 = A 5). Convinced by Eudemus' argument, some scholars have saved Melissus by insisting that his 'real object was . . . to prove the infinity from its unity'.[9] But that scholarly suggestion gratuitously rearranges the train of Melissus' thought; and Eudemus' objection is in fact an irrelevancy. By (T3) and (T4) O has no temporal and no spatial boundaries. To infer monism from that we need only the weak auxiliary premiss that if O and O' have exactly the same spatio-temporal co-ordinates, then $O = O'$. Thus take any two entities, O and O': by (T3) and (T4) both O and O' are eternal and infinite; hence a spatial point p falls within O at t if and only if it falls within O' at t. Hence, by the auxiliary premiss, $O = O'$. The argument is valid: Melissus escapes Eudemus' objection because O is limitless in *all* directions, unlike past time which is 'limited' by the present.

Melissus' argument for monism is, I think, correct. What of Parmenides? If my tentative conclusions about lines 42–9 are right, he cannot have anticipated Melissus' argument for (T5), for he did not accept (T4). And in any event, there is no trace in the fragments or in the doxography of the Melissan argument. Then did Parmenides argue for monism? And if so, how?

There is doxographical testimony enough that Parmenides was a real monist; yet the fragments themselves, though they preserve the whole of the Way of Truth, offer very little that even appears to bear upon the matter. I shall avoid what would be a long and negative discussion, and concentrate on the only part of the Way which can reasonably be imagined to state or argue for a monistic thesis.

The lines are **156**. 34–41. According to Aristotle:

> Believing that what is not is nothing apart from what is, of necessity he [sc. Parmenides] thinks that what is is one and there is nothing else (**165**: *Met* 986b29 = **28 A 24**; cf. 1001a32).

Aristotle's remark is duly repeated by Theophrastus, Eudemus, and the doxography (see Simplicius, **A 28**). Its source, I think, is **156**. 36b–37a: 'for nothing is or will be other than what is'. If that is so, Aristotle does not report an argument for monism independent of anything in **156**, but he does give a monistic interpretation of two difficult lines.

The first thing to observe is that lines 36b–37a occur in the middle of an argument; they give neither the premiss nor the conclusion of the section. If they are intended as Parmenides' main statement of monism, they are placed in a strangely inconspicuous position. Second, note that the text of line 36b is corrupt. I have translated the generally accepted emendation; but I have no confidence in it, and I am strongly inclined to think that we do not even know what words Parmenides used at this critical point in his argument.

Still, the general drift of lines 34–41 is perhaps clear enough: 'Whatever exists is whole and motionless (line 38); hence nothing exists apart from what is (lines 36b–37a); hence there can be no thought apart from what is (line 35); hence thinking and thinking that something exists are the same (line 34); hence mortal language, which continually implies that things do not exist, cannot convey thoughts but is mere verbiage (lines 39–41).'

The premiss of the argument derives from lines 22–5 and 26–33, which attempt to prove that what is is continuous and motionless. How does that support the inference that 'nothing is or will be other than what is'? The thought, I take it, is this: what now exists is continuous—hence there is no room for there to be anything now apart from what now exists; and what now exists is motionless—hence there is no way in which present conditions might change and allow the insinuation of something other than what now exists.

The rest of the argument can be reconstructed on that base. For, given that the only things there are or ever will be are presently existing things, 'not without what is . . . will you find thinking'.[10] If anyone thinks, he thinks of something; everything now exists: hence if anyone thinks, he thinks of something now existing. That deals with line 35. Next, line 34: sense and syntax are hotly disputed; and only the argumentative context can provide a solution to the disputes: whatever it means, line 34 must be a plausible intermediary between 35 and 39–41. If line 34 is translated as I have translated it, viz. 'And the same thing are to think and a thought that it is', then a reasonable thesis can be extracted from it. 'The same thing' must be read loosely: Parmenides is not asserting the absurd proposition that the *only* thinkable items have the form '*O* exists'; nor need he be asserting that every thought has, as one of its explicit components, some item of that form. A charitable construction will allow him the more modest claim that any thinkable item carries an implicit rider of the form '*O* exists'. Thus construed, line 34 is plausible inference from line 35; and from line 34 we can infer the contents of 39–41; for if every thought implies '*O* exists', then those mortal utterances which imply the contradictory—'*O* does not exist'—cannot be deemed to carry coherent thoughts at all; they are 'a name', mere verbiage, unbacked by any intelligible content.[11]

Lines 34–41 do not introduce any new matter into the Way of Truth; and if those scholars who see them as a mere summary of what has already been said are not exactly right, the kernel of their claim is acceptable. If 34–41 import nothing new, they do not import the novel thesis of monism. And in fact my reconstruction gives no plausibility to the suggestion that monism is asserted or argued for in lines 36b–37a. The Peripatetic interpretation could only occur to scholars desperate to find monism in Parmenides, and prepared to gaze myopically at half a dozen words, taken out of their context. The lines say that nothing does or will exist apart from what now exists: quite evidently that does not state or imply any monistic thesis. It is worth repeating that the vital lines are corrupt; but I see no possibility of introducing a monistic sentiment by emendation—monism is simply irrelevant to the context.

Was Parmenides a monist? The surviving fragments do not make him one. Since we are fairly confident of possessing the whole of the Way of Truth, I incline to believe that Parmenides' poem was not monistic. And since we hear nothing of any Parmenidean doctrine not included in the Way of Truth, I suspect that Parmenides was not a monist. At all events, as far as our evidence goes, real monism was an invention of Melissus.

(c) *Homogeneity*

After arguing for monism, Melissus turned to homogeneity. The fragments fail us here, but their loss can be made good: **B 7** asserts and twice employs the homogeneity of the unique Melissan entity; and it implies that the homogeneity thesis (T6) was inferred from

(T5). That implication is confirmed both by Simplicius' paraphrase and by the *MXG*. In the *MXG* the argument runs as follows:

> And being one, it is in all respects homogeneous (*homoion*); for if it were heterogeneous (*anhomoion*), being several things it would no longer be one but many (**166**: 974a 12–14 = **A 5**).

I suppose that *homoion* means 'qualitatively uniform';[12] and I take it that (T6) can be written as:

(1) If O_1 and O_2 are parts of O, then O_1 and O_2 are qualitatively identical.

Melissus' argument is a *reductio*. Suppose (1) false, i.e.:

(2) For some P, O_1 has P and O_2 does not have P.

Then by Leibniz' law:

(3) $O_1 \neq O_2$.

Since any part of an existent object must itself exist, (3) implies that more than one thing exists. And that, by (T5), is impossible.

You may scoff at that: surely O may be unique and yet have differentiated parts; for 'O is unique' only makes sense if it is taken as elliptical for some proposition of the form 'O is the unique f'. Number, as Frege showed us, is parasitical upon concepts: 'O is one', 'O and O' are two', are nonsense if strictly construed; we are always obliged to ask 'One what?', 'Two what?' But if O is the unique f, that in no way rules out (3); for O_1 and O_2 may be a pair of gs. Moreover, if 'O is unique' makes no sense, we may well ask what happens to Melissus' monism. It appears that (T5) is senseless: real monism, far from being a thesis provable inside the Eleatic system, is an unthinkable confusion.

The generous reader will run to Melissus' aid: O, after all, is not completely uncharacterized—it is, essentially, existent. Real monism says not that O is unique, but that O is the unique entity; indeed (to anticipate some future revelations) we may take (T5) to say that O is the unique physical object. (3) will then assert that O_1 and O_2 are distinct entities or physical objects; and that will not consist with (T5). Melissus springs the Fregean trap.

Here we might call on Aristotle to support Frege. Aristotle insists that all counting presupposes some determinate unit (that is essentially Frege's point); and he adds that the unit must be 'indivisible'. What he means is this: if we are to count fs, then no part of an f may itself be an f; fs must be indivisible *into* fs. Thus we can count horses, for parts of horses are not horses; but we cannot count horse-parts, for parts of horse-parts are horse-parts. We can count hands, but we cannot count lumps of flesh; we can count tables and chairs, mice and men; but we cannot count physical objects, or things, or entities.

That view of Aristotle's is, I think, true. You cannot count 'homoiomerous' things because in their case there is no determinate answer to the question: How many fs are there? and there is no unique way of counting fs. If I point to the sea and ask how many bits of water you observe, my question has no answer; the sea is divisible into arbitrarily many bits: there are n gallons, m thimblesful, k barrels—but there is no number of bits. Similarly, you cannot say how many parts of the body there are, or how many lumps of flesh make up a mouse. (Convention does allow us to give sense to some questions of this sort: there is, in equestrian circles, a fixed number of 'points of the horse'; and if you show me five oranges and ask me how many orange things I see, you expect the answer 'five'. But that does not defeat the Aristotelian claim.)

Thus if the Fregean objection shows that real monism cannot be expressed by the formula 'O is unique', the Aristotelian objection rules out 'O is the unique entity or physical object'.

There is no appropriate f which will allow Melissus to state his thesis as 'O is the unique f'. Candidate terms that escape the Aristotelian objection are too specific to be interesting: it is a boring falsehood that there is at most one horse, a boring truth that there is at most one phoenix. Instead, Melissus might try something like:

(4) For every f: O is the unique f,

where f is restricted to terms of the appropriate countable sort. But (4) will not do; for it implies the absurdity that for every f, O is an f. Nor will an existentially quantified analogue to (4) fare any better. A more complicated formula is required:

(5) For some f: O is the unique f and everything that exists is the same f as O.

Is (5) strong enough to state monism? Might there not be one or more gs in addition to the unique f? Suppose that O is the unique f, and that O' is a g. Then by (5) O' is an f, and the same f as O. But then O is surely a g, and the same g as O'? That argument may be sound; but it is controversial. In any case, it is needlessly sophisticated; for by (T3) and (T4), O' and O share the same spatio-temporal co-ordinates; in such circumstances, I do not see how we could have any reason to say that O is the same f as O' but a different g, given that O' is a g.

Then let (5) stand as the revised and fortified version of monism. Can we argue from (5) to any form of (T6)? Does monism entail homogeneity? Suppose that (2) holds; then (3) follows, and O_1 is not the same f as O_2. But by (5) O_1 is the same f as O, and so is O_2. Hence

O_1 is the same f as O_2: the *reductio* goes through, and (T6) is established.

The trouble with Melissus' argument is strength, not weakness: it threatens to prove far too much. For the *reductio*, it seems, will work against the supposition that O has homogeneous parts as well as against the assumption of heterogeneity. It is partition, not heterogeneity, into which the argument fastens its teeth: we need only suppose that O_1 and O_2 are distinct parts of O to generate the contradiction. Then is the one Melissan entity partless, though infinite? At this point a notorious fragment clamours for consideration: since, however, a full discussion of that fragment, **B 9**, must wait on an account of **B 7**, I shall add a touch of suspense to the Melissan saga and postpone further probing of parts and partlessness until a later section.

(d) *Wholeness*

What of Parmenides? He asserts that what is is *homoion* (it is 'all alike': **6**. 22); and it is usually supposed that he was the first mover of (T6): homogeneity, like monism, is normally ascribed to the grand originator of Eleaticism. If Parmenides advanced (T6) then he did so either in lines 22–5 or else in the formally similar passage at lines 44–8. I have already offered some thoughts on the latter passage; and unless I am very much mistaken, there is no whiff of (T6) there: 'existential homogeneity', as I called it, by no means implies qualitative homogeneity. What then of lines 22–5?

The word 'whole' does not occur in 22–5; but it is scarcely to be doubted that 'continuous' (*suneches*) in line 25 answers to 'whole' (*oulon*) in the prospectus, line 4. What sort of 'wholeness' or 'continuity' Parmenides has in mind is less easy to settle. The orthodox view has Parmenides arguing for the spatial continuity of what is: O cannot be discontinuous, in the way in which a pack of cards or the United States of America is discontinuous; all its parts must be in spatial contact with one another. The language of the lines has been thought to impose that interpretation; and the lines do contain terms whose primary sense is spatial. But spatial terms are readily used with a temporal reference; and I do not think that Parmenides' language suffices in itself to rule out a temporal interpretation: O is certainly continuous in a temporal sense (unlike, say, a symphony that may have gaps between its movements) and temporal wholeness may be the message of 22–5. To decide on the sense of Parmenides' conclusion we must look first at the course of his argument. I quote the lines again:

>   Nor is it divided, since it is all alike
> and neither more here (which would prevent it from holding together)
> nor less, but it is all full of what is.
> Hence it is continuous; for what is neighbours what is.

The orthodox punctuation puts a heavy stop at the end of line 22, giving three separate tracts of argument: line 22, lines 23–4, line 25. In line 22 we then have the unsupported premiss that 'it is all alike'. Thus isolated, the phrase must be taken in the Melissan sense: 'it is qualitatively homogeneous'. But its presence is jarring: nothing in the earlier part of **156** suggests it, and we are left to suppose that Parmenides brazenly helps himself to a premiss on which he has no possible claim. But the orthodox punctuation is not sacrosanct: instead of a stop at the end of line 22, let us place a comma or indeed no punctuation mark at all;[13] 22b still expresses a premiss of Parmenides' argument, but that obscure expression is expanded and explained in lines 23–4. So construed, the structure of the section is this: *probandum* (22a); premiss (22b–24); restatement of conclusion (25a); intermediate step (25b). The logic is clear; and there is some hope that from 22b–24 we shall be able to drag out a proposition to which Parmenides is entitled. That, at any rate, is the supposition on which my translation and the following exegesis depend.

In 22a the *probandum* says: 'Nor is it *diaireton*'. Translators usually render this 'divisible'; and many scholars talk of 'theoretical indivisibility': O is not just undivided, it is not, even in theory, divisible into parts. But *diaireton* in 22a must be understood by way of *suneches* in 25a; for 'it is *suneches*' restates the conclusion of these four brief lines. And *suneches* ('continuous') does not imply indivisibility: the Mediterranean is *suneches*, but it is theoretically divided in atlases, and a cunning engineer might divide it physically by a causeway. In 22–5 Parmenides commits himself only to the view that O contains no gaps, not to the stronger view that gaps cannot be made in it, and still less to the very strong view that it does not admit of 'division in thought'.

The premiss for this conclusion is that 'it is all alike'; and the sense of that phrase is given by the gloss: '. . . neither more here . . . nor less'. The commentators think here, as they think at lines 44–5, of 'degrees of being': existence is not spread unevenly over O, like the butter on my morning slice of toast. But I cannot see how an uneven spread of existence would prevent it from holding together (*sunechesthai*, i.e., being *suneches*)—the butter on my toast is uneven but continuous. And I guess that Parmenides has a simpler thought in mind: 'If you take any two stretches of O, you will not find more existence in one than in the other. It is "all full of what is", "what is neighbours what is": at every point in every stretch of O, O exists; and thus O is indeed without gaps, continuous, undivided.'

Are the 'stretches' of O spatial or temporal? There is one strong argument against the spatial orthodoxy: lines 44-9 attempt to establish the spatial continuity of Parmenidean entities, and a brief but complete anticipation of that argument in 22-5 would be pointless, to say the least. On the other side, four short lines drawing an evident corollary of the denial of generation and destruction are apposite and intelligible: if O cannot be generated or destroyed (lines 5-21), then clearly it cannot have temporal gaps; the corollary is easily and appropriately drawn in lines 22-5.

There is an objection to the heterodox temporal interpretation: if Parmenides' entities are punctual, then how could he refer in 22-5 to temporal stretches in their careers? How can 'what is neighbours what is' in time, if whatever is is only now? Why did Parmenides not simply say: 'It is not temporally divisible, because it exists only now, and "now" is logically indivisible'? We might, I suppose, read my references to 'stretches' in O's career in a counterfactual way: 'if there *were* two temporal stretches in O's career, neither *could* "contain more existence" than the other'; and we might conjecture that Parmenides chose this way of demonstrating O's temporal continuity because he preferred to rest his argument on the fundamental and well understood notion of ungenerability rather than on its slippery partner, punctuality. After all, lines 22-5 *do* establish temporal continuity, given lines 5-21: the objection we are considering is merely that they do not do that in the most economical and telling fashion. But any reader who refrains from believing that explanation has my sympathy; and I readily concede that my interpretations of 5-21 and 22-5 do not unite in whole-hearted amity. If, for all that, I stick by them, it is because alternative interpretations seem to me to be still less congruous: again, I do not think that Parmenides—the first student of metaphysics—has fully grasped the implications of his own thoughts.

Lines 22-5 do not, I conclude, either argue for or state (T6); and I infer that Melissus was the first to maintain the thesis of homogeneity. For all that **156** says, Parmenidean entities may be qualitatively variegated.

As an appendix to this section, here is a further fragment of Parmenides:

Regard alike firmly in your mind things absent, things present;
for you will not cut off what is from holding to what is,
neither scattering everywhere in every way through the world,
nor gathering together (167: 28 B 4).

This is an utterly baffling quotation: its first line is, in the Greek, multiply ambiguous;[14] its position in Parmenides' poem defies determination.

The first line seems to envisage a plural world; and that has led some scholars to place 167 in the Way of Opinion. I do not accept the inference; but the conclusion is tempting. Simplicius, after all, implies that 156 represents the whole of the Way of Truth, and 156 cannot accommodate 167. On the other hand, the content of 167—to put the matter vaguely—smacks of Truth; and it has been cleverly suggested that 167 formed a tailpiece to the Way of Opinion: 'So much for the Way of Opinion: do not be misled along it, but "regard alike . . ."'.[15] If that suggestion is correct, what sense does 167 have?

The argument runs thus: '(i) What is can neither scatter nor coalesce; hence (ii) what is always holds to what is; hence (iii) you should regard absent and present alike.' Now (i) follows from the motionlessness of what is; Parmenides has argued for that in lines 26–33, and we may reasonably be expected to apply the moral in 167. Next, (ii) will follow from (i) on the supposition that at the present 'what is holds to what is'; and that supposition can be found either in line 25 (on a spatial reading of 22–5) or else in lines 42–9. This reading of (ii) has consequences for (iii): 'present' and 'absent' must refer to spatially present and absent parts of O, not to temporal presence or absence, and not to a plurality of individuals. For the inference from (ii) to (iii) must run: 'Since there can never be spatial gaps in O, you may safely treat present and absent bits of O alike'. And the underlying thought is merely this: no bits of O are non-existent; so you will run no danger of pseudo-thought by thinking of any bit of O, however remote.

167 on this interpretation is not peculiarly interesting or novel; but novelty is not wanted at the end of a poem. It is worth pointing out that my reading of 167 to some extent confirms my remarks about divisibility in line 22: 167 allows that O has parts that are at least notionally distinct; it denies that those parts may become physically separated from one another.

STABILITY AND CHANGE

(e) *Change and decay*

It was the Eleatic denial of change and motion which most troubled the philosophical and scientific world of the fifth century: generation and destruction the later scientists felt they could dispense with; sempiternity, too, could be accommodated to their designs, and monism was not perhaps felt as a very serious or persuasive thesis. But without change, and without locomotion, science was at a stand; and we shall see, in the later attempts to escape from the logical clutches of Elea, that the rehabilitation of locomotion, and with it of change, was the central and vital issue.

On this topic Parmenides, again, is dismally obscure; and I shall not look at his remarks on change and motion until I have examined Melissus' relatively clear and intelligible contribution. The theses in question are (T7)—(T12); they occupy the first part of **30 B 7**. That long fragment reads thus:

[i] In this way, then, it is eternal and infinite and one and all homogeneous. And [ii] it will not perish,[16] nor become greater, nor be rearranged, nor suffer pain, nor suffer anguish. For [iii] if it underwent any of these, it would no longer be one. For [iv] if it alters (*heteroioutai*), it is necessary that what is is not homogeneous, but that what was earlier perishes and what is not comes into being. Again, [v] if it were to become different (*heteroion*) by a single hair in ten thousand years, it will all perish in the whole of time.

But [vi] neither is it accomplishable that it be rearranged (*metakosmêthênai*); for [vii] the arrangement (*kosmos*) which was earlier is not destroyed, nor is that which does not exist generated. And [viii] since nothing is added or destroyed or alters, how might anything that is be rearranged?[17] For [ix] if it were to become different in any respect, it would thereby be rearranged. Nor [x] does it suffer pain. For [xi] it would not be altogether if it were in pain; for [xii] a thing in pain could not be always. [xiii] Nor does it have equal power with what is healthy. [xiv] Nor would it be homogeneous if it were in pain; for [xv] it would be in pain in virtue of something's passing from it or being added to it, and it would no longer be homogeneous. [xvi] Nor could what is healthy be in pain; for [xvii] what is would perish,[18] and what is not would come into being. [xviii] And about anguish there is the same argument as for being in pain.

Nor [xix] is it empty (*keneon*) in any respect; for [xx] what is empty is nothing, and it will not be nothing. Nor [xxi] does it move; for [xxii] it has no way to retreat, but it is full. For [xxiii] if it were empty, it would retreat into what was empty; but not being empty, it has not any way where it may retreat. And [xxiv] it will not be dense and rare. For [xxv] it is not accomplishable that what is rare is as full as what is dense, but what is rare thereby becomes emptier than what is dense. And [xxvi] one must make this distinction between what is full and what is not full: if it yields at all or receives, it is not full; and if it neither yields nor receives, it is full. [xxvii] Now it is necessary for it to be full, if it is not empty; and if it is full, it does not move (**168**).

Sentence [i] restates, without further argument, (T2), (T4), (T5) and (T6). Sentences [vii]–[xviii] are curiously convoluted, and I shall not attempt to unravel all their complexities.[19] Sentence [ii] asserts (T8)–(T12). [iii] supports this by observing that the negation of any of (T8)–(T12) entails the negation of (T5); and [iv] supports *this* by claiming that the negation of (T7) entails the negation of (T6). Thus: (T5) gives (T6); (T6) gives (T7); and (T7) gives each of (T8)–(T12). Monism gives homogeneity; homogeneity gives unalterability; and unalterability rules out destruction, growth, rearrangement, pain, and anguish.

I have already discussed the first of those inferences; and I suppose that a suitably generous understanding of 'alter' (*heteroiousthai*) will validate the third. The second inference may surprise: why, after all, should O not change from one homogeneous state to another? from being wholly red, say, to being wholly blue? Provided that the change occurred uniformly there would be no instant at which O was not homogeneous. But that reflection misses the full force of Melissus' argument for homogeneity: O_1 and O_2 were taken as 'parts' of O; but 'part' is not to be construed in a narrowly spatial sense: any spatio-temporal chunk of O will count as a 'part'. (If O is three-dimensional, then 'parts' of O are given by five co-ordinates, three spatial and two temporal.) As far as I can see, that gloss on 'part' does not affect Melissus' argument for (T6); and it renders immediately valid his inference from (T6) to unalterability (T7).

Sentence [iv] contains, however, a hint at a different argument for (T7). The hint lies in the phrase: 'what was earlier perishes, and what is not comes into being'. It is taken up again in [vii]; and it is important because it allows (T7) to by-pass (T5) and (T6), and to rest upon (T1) alone. Thus the denial of change need not depend upon monism. I turn, therefore, to [vii], remarking incidentally that sentence [v] is unintelligible to me.[20]

The sentence restricts itself to (T10), the denial of rearrangement;[21] and the full significance of (T10) will become clear at a later stage.

The argument of [vii] turns on the following principle:
(1) If O is rearranged at t, then at t O's earlier arrangement is destroyed and O's later arrangement comes into being.

Hence, since nothing can be destroyed or come into being, (T10) is established. As it stands, the argument makes use of (T8), the denial of destruction; and since (T8), in Melissus, is only established by way of (T5), (T10) is still, strictly speaking, dependent upon monism. But that dependence is easily broken. Replace (1) by:
(2) If O is rearranged at t, then at t O's later arrangement comes into being.

To get (T10) from (2) only (T1) is required: in brief, ungenerability rules out rearrangement.

The argument can be generalized: if O changes colour at t, then at t O's new colour comes into being; if O changes size at t, then at t O's new size comes into being. Generally:
(3) For any F: if O becomes F at t, then O's Fness comes into being at t.

Proposition (2) is a special case of (3); the phrase 'what is not comes into being' in [iv] points to a second case of (3); and in [xvii] there is something very close to a general statement of (3). Thus I do not hesitate to infer that some general principle such as (3) was in Melissus' mind.

The strength of (3) is great. In effect, (3) reduces all change to generation: every sentence of the form 'O becomes F' implies some sentence of the form 'O' comes into being'. But no sentence of the form 'O' comes into being' can express a truth; hence no sentence of the form 'O becomes F' can express a truth—since generation is extinguished, change cannot light our scientific path. And (3) is surely true: what does 'O's Fness comes into being' mean if it does not mean 'O becomes F'? Unless we rule out phrases like 'O's Fness' as ill-formed—a desperate and unconvincing stratagem—we are bound to concede that (3) is true.

Melissus has forged a powerful argument: from (T1) he can validly infer (T7), by way of (3); and (3) is true. If generation goes, then so does change of every sort. The value of his argument was never appreciated by Melissus' successors: they attempted to hold on to (T1) while rejecting (T7); yet they say nothing of (3). Aristotle, who despised Melissus and prided himself on his overthrow of the Eleatic arguments, nowhere faces up to (3). I do not wish to suggest that Melissus' argument is impregnable; but at this stage I leave it in control of the field—it deserves to enjoy at least a temporary victory.

The next sentences of **168** are curiosities. They attempt to establish that O is free from pain and free from anguish: (T11) and (T12). It is hard to believe that Melissus would have invented those strange theses off his own bat; yet scholars have unearthed no suitable opponent against whom they may have been enunciated. Again, what moral are (T11) and (T12) intended to suggest? Is Melissus denying the sensitivity of O, and implicitly rejecting an animate or divine being? For 'he used to say that one should say nothing about the gods; for there is no knowledge of them' (Diogenes Laertius, IX.24 = **A 1**). Or is he rather affirming the sensitivity of O, and hence implicitly its bliss and divinity? For according to other sources he made 'the One' a god (Aëtius, Olympiodorus, **A 13**). Or are (T11) and (T12) jokes?

(T11) is argued for in sentences [xi]–[xvii]. The structure of the passage is not clear to me. [xi]–[xii], I take it, rule out the possibility that O is permanently in pain: if O were in pain throughout its career, it would not 'be altogether' (*pan*: see p. 195), i.e., it would not exist for ever. I suppose that some fairly crude thought lies behind the argument: perhaps it is that pain weakens the sufferer, and in time will therefore destroy him. Sentences [xvi]–[xvii] rule out the possibility that O is sometimes in pain: O cannot pass from a healthy to a painful state; for O cannot change at all. Proposition (3) lies behind the argument. [xiv]–[xv] seem to have a more general scope: Melissus' point is that 'O is in pain' implies 'O is altering', for pain consists in the addition to or subtraction from the substance of the sufferer. There is presumably some sort of physiological theory behind this. Finally, sentence [xiii] is puzzling. Conceivably, it argues against the suggestion that O is both in pain and healthy, all the time, but in different parts of itself. Pain and health, Melissus avers, could not coexist in harmonious equilibrium as that suggestion requires; physiology, again, must be in the offing.

The argument in the first half of **168** is not set out with perfect grace; and parts of the paragraph are given over to Christmas-cracker philosophizing. That may explain the neglect of **168** in modern discussions of the Eleatic stand on change. At the risk of tedium, let me briefly restate the case: of all the Eleatic theses, (T7) and its companions are the most important; and of all the Eleatic theses, (T7) has the strongest support; for through the garish curtains of **168** there appears a fairy godmother of an argument: a touch of (3), and (T1) is magicked into (T7).

(f) *The void*

The remainder of **168** is concerned with local motion or change in place. In these paragraphs Melissus offers an argument which I think is original to him. The argument proved to be one of the most controversial in the history of philosophy, and indeed of physics. For the next two millennia every student of motion was obliged to take account of it; and the critics and defenders of Melissus' opinion are roughly equal both in numbers and in gravity. The logical articulation of the passage is given in [xxvii]: from (T13), absence of void, we get (T14), 'fullness'; and from (T14) there follows the denial of motion, (T15). The sentences about 'dense and rare', constituting (T16), muddy the waters of the argument.

We start, then, with 'the void'. Sentences [xix]–[xx] are standardly translated as follows: 'Nor is anything empty; for what is empty is nothing; so nothing will not be'. The particle 'so' (*oun*) is logical nonsense; the grammar of the third sentence strongly suggests the Polypheman fallacy of construing 'nothing' as a singular term (Odysseus tricked Polyphemus by giving his name as 'No one': the blinded Polyphemus then bellowed to his friends, 'No one has hurt me'); and the first sentence fits uneasily into the run of Eleatic theses, all of which have the form '*O* is *F*'. My translation[22] avoids all three difficulties, and yields the following argument:

(1) *O* is not nothing [sc. in any respect].
(2) What is empty is nothing.
Hence:
(T13) *O* is not empty in any respect.

Since 'nothing' is here, as often, used as a synonym of 'non-existent', (1) restates the Melissan axiom (A), with the tacit rider 'in any respect'. But (2) is a new and not a universally accepted proposition. That an object cannot have non-existent parts—be non-existent in some respect—seems evident enough; but does it follow that an object cannot have *vacuous* or empty parts? After all, a vacuum is an essential part of a vacuum flask. Part of the space occupied by my flask is empty; hence a part of my flask is vacuous—my flask is 'empty in some respect'.

That is a bad argument; and Melissus is right. His entity, O, is an occupant of space, an extended body. Let the volume of space O occupies be Vo. Now, trivially, every part of a volume of space occupied by an object is occupied by a part of that object. Suppose, then, that O is empty in some respect. That is to say, suppose that some part of Vo is not occupied by any body at all. Then that part is not occupied by any part of O. And hence Vo is not the volume occupied by O. But by hypothesis Vo is the volume occupied by O. The vacuum in my flask is not a part of my flask any more than the water in a bucket is a part of the bucket.

I conclude for Melissus. Moreover, from (T13) we can quickly infer the complete absence of void from the world. By (T4), O is infinitely extended, or occupies every region of space; by (T13) no part of O is vacant: hence no part of space is vacant, and 'the void does not exist'. This strong thesis is, of course, essential to Melissus' argument against motion; and that, I suspect, is why sentence [xix] receives the translation it ordinarily does. But the strong thesis is easily and obviously inferred, given the translation which I have adopted.

In [xxvii] Melissus indicates that (T15) follows from (T13) by way of (T14); and that, as we shall see, is not a casual hint. In [xxi]–[xxiii], however, (T14) is ignored; and the canonical Eleatic argument against motion, in its standard presentation, derives (T15) directly from (T13). For the moment I shall follow this tradition, postponing discussion of (T14) to the following section.

The argument for (T15) is sublimely simple: 'not being empty, it has not any way where it may retreat';[23] O, or parts of O, can move only if they have room for manoeuvre, and a full universe leaves no room at all. Locomotion is change of place, the transition from one locale to another. If an object moves, then it comes to occupy a new place; and that new place, prior to receiving its occupant, must be empty. Thus the general principle licensing the inference from (T13) to (T15) is something of the following sort:

(3) If O comes to occupy place p at time t, then immediately prior to t p is empty.

The principle has considerable plausibility; and Melissus may have taken it for self-evident: if p is occupied up to t, then O cannot get into it; for two things cannot occupy the same place at the same time. To make any headway, O's nose must be pointed at a vacuum: the parts of a rigid, close-packed, body do not and cannot move; for they leave no vacancies about them into which they can insert themselves.

Evidently, there are answers to that argument; and Melissus cannot be granted (3), or (T15), without more ado. Some at least of his successors exercised their ingenuities over (3) and proposed alternatives to it which apparently permit locomotion inside a *plenum*. I shall look at those proposals in their later historical setting and I shall not anticipate them here: for the extent of this chapter, let Melissus hold the field; his argument will shortly be reinforced by Zeno.

Before I turn to Parmenides' thoughts on motion and change, let me get Melissus' (T17) out of the way: O is not divided up. Fragment B 10 reads:

If what is has been divided (*diêirêtai*), it moves; but moving it would not be (169).[24]

The fragment infers from (T15) some denial of division. Simplicius (*ad* **B 10**) thinks that 'it has been divided' means 'it is divisible'; but the Greek will hardly bear that construction. Comparison with **167** suggests a different gloss: 'Since it cannot move, it cannot be split up into bits'. The argument is correct, and we may expect Melissus to have assented to it; but the past tense, 'it *has been* divided', is not explicable. A third suggestion wonders if '*O* has been divided' is supposed to entail that some parts of *O* are not in contact with one another. Then those parts are separated by a void; so *O* is in some respect empty, and 'if it were empty, it would retreat into what was empty'. I incline to think this the most probable interpretation of **169**; but I cannot say why Melissus should have decided to argue for (T17). However that may be, **169** introduces us to no new items of Melissan philosophy.

In **156**. 26–33 Parmenides attempts to show that what exists is *akinêton*, motionless:

And motionless in the limits of great chains
it is, beginningless, endless; since coming into being and
                                                                   destruction
have wandered far away, and true trust has driven them off.
And the same, remaining in the same state, it lies in itself
and thus firmly remains there. For a strong necessity
holds it in chains of a limit which fences it about,
because it is not right for what is to be incomplete;
for it is not lacking—otherwise it would want everything.

Lines 26–8 mean: 'since *O* cannot come into being or be destroyed, it is *akinêton*'. '*Kinêsis*' in philosophical Greek regularly carries wider connotations than 'motion' in English: it covers any form of change, alteration and change of size as well as locomotion. Line 41, which refers to locomotion and alteration as empty 'names', implies that Parmenides has rejected both locomotion and alteration; and the only passage where he might think to have done that is lines 26–33. Thus *akinêton* in line 26 rejects all forms of change. Lines 29–30a confirm that conclusion; for the words 'the same' contain a rejection of alteration; and 'firmly remains there' deny locomotion. ('remaining in the same state (*en tautôi*)' may refer either to alteration or to locomotion (see p. 322, n. 21). 'it lies in itself' presumably means 'it stays in the one place it occupies'.) I believe, too, that the prospectus prepares us for this combined treatment of alteration and locomotion: 'of one kind and motionless (*mounogenes te kai atremes*)' means 'unalterable and immobile'. *Akinêton* in line 26 thus denies both change and locomotion.

Being immobile, what is remains 'in the limits of great chains'. Modern scholars take 'limits' and 'chains' in lines 26 and 31 in a metaphorical sense: Parmenides has logical chains in mind; 'O is motionless in the limits of chains' means simply 'as a matter of necessity, O is motionless'. That is hard to believe: first, the phrase 'strong necessity' (line 30) gives, non-metaphorically, the sense of *a priori* immobility. Second, the literal sense of 'limits' is wholly appropriate: if O is immobile, what more natural than to infer that it stays forever within the spatial limits given by its original position? The point is not wholly niggling: as we have already seen, an important issue in the interpretation of lines 42–9 turns on the reading of the word 'limit' (above, p. 203).

One final point before advancing to the argument of the lines: if O has a purely punctual existence, how can it be said to 'remain' in limits? Remaining implies endurance; and O has no duration. The question is essentially the same as one raised earlier in connexion with **167** (above, p. 212). And again there are two answers: first, it is easy to suggest that Parmenides had not got the hang of his own punctuality thesis, and failed to see that although it does imply immobility, it is incompatible with an enduring immobility or 'remaining'. Second, we might gloss 'it remains at p' by 'For all t, if O exists at t, then at t O is at p'; and thus, at the price of a certain sophisticated artificiality, punctuality and 'remaining' are formally reconciled. I do not offer this second answer as an account of what Parmenides 'really thought'; I offer it to show that the objection to his using the verb 'remain' (*menein*) is a quibble.

Lines 26–33 contain two distinct arguments. The first occupies 26–28; it consists in the simple formula: 'No generation or destruction, so no *kinêsis*'. There is more than one way of expanding that into an argument, and I cannot see any internal evidence that points clearly in any particular direction. I surmise that Melissus' main argument against change, expressed in **168**, was intended as an elucidation of these brief lines; I do not intend to improve upon Melissus—though if he was offering his own argument to Parmenides he was a charitable man.

The second argument occupies lines 30b–33. Some scholars see no argument against motion here: they translate *houneken* ('because') in line 32 by 'wherefore' and find a self-contained piece of argumentation in lines 32–3.[25] I cannot understand 'wherefore' here; and in any case 'because' is linguistically preferable as a translation of *houneken*. With that translation Parmenides presents us with an argument for motionlessness starting from the premiss:

(4) If O is lacking, O wants everything.

Hence he infers:
(5) *O* is not lacking;
whence:
(6) *O* is not incomplete,
and so to '*O* is motionless'.

I find the argument baffling; and the text of line 33, from which the premiss (4) is drawn, is uncertainly transmitted and of uncertain sense.[26] Some scholars discover Melissus' canonical argument, supposing that Parmenides infers immobility from the lack of a void. The key to their interpretation is the construe of (5) as 'no space is not occupied by *O*', i.e., 'there is no vacuum'. (4) then means 'if there were a vacuum, *O* would occupy no space at all'; and the premiss which allows us to infer (5) from (4) is the proposition that *O* is a space occupier. It is hard to believe all that: it requires great faith to find any statement about vacuums in (5);[27] and why ever should Parmenides offer us (4)? What, again, is the function of (6)? Had Parmenides wanted to give the Melissan argument, he had the linguistic means at his disposal; I cannot believe that he would have disguised his intentions as thoroughly as this interpretation supposes.

I suspect that the argument has an element of teleology in it: 'If *O* moves—*kineitai* in the broadest sense—that could only be because *O* had not achieved some end or goal (was 'incomplete'); and that would only be true if *O* lacked something. But if it lacked anything it would lack everything. (Why? Perhaps the Principle of Sufficient Reason lurks behind the text: all of *O*'s properties are on a par—if it lacked a property P_1, then it would lack P_2 and P_3 and everything else.) But that is an absurd supposition, for it would make *O* into a propertyless non-thing.' That interpretation is perhaps preferable to the Melissan one; yet it hardly presents Parmenides with a decent argument, and I do not believe I know what he is saying in lines 32–3.

Once again, Melissus seems to me to be Parmenides' superior: in **156**. 26–33 little is clear and nothing is explicit and detailed; if those lines were all that Elea could muster in support of its case against *kinêsis*, then that case would not deserve a hearing. Melissus, on the contrary, presents reasonably lucid and relatively detailed arguments; and from his fragments it is possible to construct, without any special pleading and with surprisingly little polishing or pruning, two very respectable arguments, one against alteration and one against locomotion.

(g) *Corporeal being*

Matter, according to Descartes, is three-dimensional extension and nothing more. To see this, 'we have only to attend to our idea of some body, e.g., a stone, and remove from it whatever we know is not entailed by the very nature of body'. We 'remove' in this way hardness, colour, weight and temperature, and, in conclusion 'we may now observe that absolutely no element of our idea remains, except extension in length, breadth and depth'. Matter is thus identified with space, and the identification allows Descartes to reject the possibility of a vacuum: the notion of empty space, bodiless body, is a trivial contradiction.[28]

The Cartesian view might well have appealed to Melissus; but it was a heterodox view and there seemed to be overwhelming objections to it: how can Descartes distinguish between a geometrical 'solid' and a physical 'solid'? between a stereometrical sphere and a rubber ball? between an area of space and that area's occupants? He cannot, yet he must: geometrical bodies have no causal powers; geometry is a static subject, yet even if geometrical objects moved, they would not effect motion in one another—they have not the body to do so. A world of moving geometrical objects is like a world of images on a cinema screen: thin, unsubstantial, powerless, immaterial.

Three-dimensionality is perhaps necessary to materiality; but it is not sufficient. What more is needed? The classical answer is: Solidity, or impenetrability. And the *locus classicus* for that answer is in Locke's *Essay*: 'This of all other, seems the *Idea* most intimately connected with, and essential to Body, so as no where else to be found or imagin'd, but only in matter: and though our Senses take no notice of it, but in masses of matter, of a bulk sufficient to cause a Sensation in us; Yet the Mind, having once got this *Idea* from such grosser sensible Bodies, traces it farther; and considers it, as well as Figure, in the minutest Particle of Matter, that can exist; and finds it inseparably inherent in Body, where-ever, or however modified. This is the *Idea* belongs to Body, whereby we conceive it *to fill space*. The *Idea* of which filling of space, is, That where we imagine any space taken up by a solid Substance, we conceive it so to possess it, that it excludes all other solid Substances; and, will for ever hinder any two other Bodies, that move towards one another in a strait Line, from coming to touch one another, unless it removes from between them in a Line, not parallel to that which they move in' (II.iv.1–2). Solidity, impenetrability, resistance: physical objects, or 'bodies', do not merely have spatial location; they fill or occupy space. And if O fills a volume of space V, then O excludes from V any other physical object O', so that no two things can be in the same place at the same time (cf. *Essay* II.xxvii.1). Thus by filling V and excluding O' from it, O 'resists' O' and is 'impenetrable' to it.

The Atomists grasped this notion clearly enough: atoms, they said, are solid (*stereos*), massy (*nastos*), full (*plêrês*)—they are space occupants in the strong Lockean sense (see vol. 2, p. 43). The atomists took their view from Melissus; for in (T14) he expresses for the first time the thesis that substance is solid: 'O is full (*pleôn*)' means 'O is a space filler' or 'O is solid'.

At first sight, Melissus' explanation of 'fullness' in sentence [xxvi] of **168** does not suggest that gloss. More homely and familiar thoughts come to mind: a diamond, say, which neither 'yields' to pressure nor 'receives' other stuffs is 'full'; a squash ball, a wine bottle, and a loofah are not 'full'—the ball yields to the racquet, though it does not 'receive'; the bottle accepts the wine, though it does not 'yield'; the loofah both yields to the fingers and receives the bathwater. But on that account 'fullness' is an unhappy hybrid notion, compounded from hardness and non-porosity. (Locke carefully distinguishes solidity from hardness: *Essay* II.iv.4.) And in any case, the account cannot be correct. What is not full is, according to Melissus, empty, i.e. partially vacuous; and Melissus cannot have supposed that a rubber ball, an empty bottle and a dry loofah all contain vacuums. The bottle will 'receive'; but the 'received' wine displaces air, not a vacuum. The loofah will squash; but when squashed the water drips out of it.

A different account is required; and Lockean solidity is the only plausible alternative: when Melissus says that O is 'full', he means that it 'fills space'; when he says that O 'does not yield', he means that it has 'resistance'; when he says that O does not 'receive', he means that it is 'impenetrable'. The concept of solidity, delineated here with astonishing clarity and accuracy, was one of Melissus' most influential and valuable bequests.

Did he bequeath a truth or a falsity? Leibniz observed, correctly, that shadows and rays of light may interpenetrate (*Nouveaux Essais*, II.xxvii.1), and the same holds for smells and for sounds.[29] But such things are not primary substances, or physical objects. Again, a human body and a collection of cells will occupy the same place at the same time; yet they are distinguishable physical objects. But here the cells constitute the body; and evidently the Melissan principle does not rule out the interpenetration of a body and the sum of its parts or the sum of its physical constituents.

A third potential counter-example is more interesting. Science—

that unimpeachable and incomprehensible god—assures us that macroscopic physical objects are made up of a myriad atoms whirling about in a void: physical objects are not, in fact, solid; they are perforated and channelled by vacuous space. Perhaps, then, a certain correspondence and symmetry in the atomic sub-structure of physical objects might allow two bodies to interpenetrate; as an electric plug fits into a socket, so two electric plugs might fit into one another were their atoms and vacant interstices suitably arranged. Does this show that physical bodies are not essentially solid? or should we rather dissociate solidity from impenetrability so that physical objects are necessarily solid, but not necessarily impenetrable? Or is it not better still to infer that macroscopic objects are not in fact physical bodies, though they appear so to the untutored eye? The only genuinely physical objects in the world are the ultimate corpuscles of matter, microscopic objects which contain no vacancies. This third suggestion was made by the ancient Atomists; and I find it the least offensive of the three solutions. Necessarily, physical objects are solid and impenetrable; but it is a question for science to answer whether any of the macroscopic objects we daily observe are in actual fact physical objects.

However that may be, such atomist worries would not have moved Melissus; for he has already argued implicitly that atomism is false: substances contain no vacancies. From his denial of emptiness Melissus moves immediately to an assertion of fullness: 'it is necessary for it to be full if it is not empty' (sentence [xxvii]). (T14) is inferred at once from (T13): what has no vacancies is solid or impenetrable; what is in no respect empty is full—the inference seems trivial enough.

Yet is it sound? Leibniz, for one, doubted it: 'We see, for example, two shadows or rays of light which interpenetrate, and we might invent for ourselves an imaginary world wherein bodies would act in the same way' (*Nouveaux Essais* II. xxvii.1). Such an invention does not greatly tax the imagination: we are all familiar in childhood with men who walk through walls. But the imagination is a bad judge of the impossible: if we cannot, like the White Queen, believe five impossible things before breakfast, we can surely imagine them; and Leibniz' point is not that interpenetration is imaginable but that it is logically possible. Suppose we discover a new metal, and make a pair of billiard balls from it; the balls are hard and seem solid, they do not fall through the cloth of the table or disappear into the side cushions. Place ball a on one side cushion at point A, and cue it to the opposite cushion at A'; place b on the end cushion at B, and cue it to the opposite cushion at B'. The lines AA' and BB' intersect; call the point of intersection C. Now replace a at A and b at B. Strike a and b in such a way that each, if unimpeded, would reach C at the same time, t. Ordinary balls would clash and be diverted from their paths; but a and b, to the amazement of the spectators, continue through C to A' and B'. At t, then, a and b were in exactly the same place, C; at t a and b interpenetrated.

The case is imaginable: is it logically possible? I cannot show that it is; but equally I know of no argument that it is not. And the additional specification, that a and b are not 'empty in any respect', does not enable me to concoct an argument. I suppose that stories should count as logically innocent until they are proved guilty; and I therefore take the case of the curious billiard balls as setting up a *prima facie* refutation of Melissus' move from (T13) to (T14).

The matter is not indifferent to Melissus. For, contrary to the tradition which I have so far followed, Melissus' denial of motion in (T15) requires (T14) and not merely (T13): a body, a, may move into a location p even if p is already occupied by some other non-empty body b, provided that b, though not empty at all, is not impenetrable. Space may be, as it were, overfull: at no time is any volume of space unoccupied; but various volumes of space have several distinct occupants. Unless Melissus can establish (T14), in the strong sense of impenetrability, he cannot reach (T15). I shall, as I promised, consider objections to Melissus' argument against motion in a later chapter; but those objections are distinct from the one I have just canvassed. Nor are they otiose; for even if it is granted that (T14) does not follow logically from (T13), it may still be conceded to Melissus that if (T13) is true, then, as a matter of contingent fact, so is (T14).

From (T13) Melissus infers (T16): O is not 'dense or rare'. He means, of course, that O does not exhibit different degrees of density in its several parts. He clearly states that if O is rarer than O', then O must contain more void than O'; and given that, his inference holds. As far as I can see, it is not a logical truth that rare bodies contain more vacancy than dense bodies; and I do not know whether or not it is a scientific truth. At any rate, Melissus does not succeed in proving (T16). He might have done better to derive it from (T5); for homogeneity presumably excludes variation in density no less than in any other property. But (T16) is not a very interesting thesis, and I shall say no more about it.[30]

Whatever the value of Melissus' arguments in the latter part of **168**, they leave one point in no doubt: Melissus' entity, O, is a solid, physical body; it is 'full', a material occupant of space; and it is impenetrable, refusing to countenance any co-occupants.[31]

That conclusion was denied by Simplicius, who thought he could disprove it out of Melissus' own mouth:

> And that he wants it to be incorporeal (*asômatos*) is shown by his saying: 'If, then, it were, it must be one; and being one, it must not have body' (**170: B 9**).

Elsewhere Simplicius continues his quotation:

> And being one, it must not have body (*sôma*). But if it had mass (*pachos*), it would have parts, and it would no longer be one (**171**).[32]

It is worth setting the argument out explicitly. From:
(1) X is one,
Melissus infers:
(2) X has no parts.
Then to:
(3) X has no mass,
and finally to:
(4) X has no body.
It is only natural to identify X with O: then (1) is (T5); the move from (1) to (2) mirrors that from (T5) to (T6); and (4) implies that O is unextended—a geometrical point, perhaps.

That conclusion conflicts flatly with (T4); and those scholars, beginning with Simplicius, who consequently deny (T4) to Melissus fly in the face of the evidence.[33] Other scholars observe that (4) does not in fact require a purely punctual existence for X: X might be an infinitely extended geometrical solid. That conclusion fares no better: it conflicts flatly with (T14): O is physical, not geometrical.[34]

A bold answer to these difficulties rejects the identification of X with O: Simplicius wrongly took **171** to be about the Eleatic entity; in fact the fragment came from the polemical portion of Melissus' book and constitutes part of an attack upon the pluralist opponents of Elea. That there was such a portion to Melissus' work is made probable by **B 8**, which I examine in a later chapter; and **171** readily yields an argument of Zenonian stamp: 'Suppose that there are many X's. Then each must be a unity; hence it can have no parts; hence it cannot be corporeal.'

There are two powerful objections to this bold answer. First, it goes against Simplicius' express assertion that **171** is about 'the One'. But Simplicius' assertion is made in order to prove a contentious point; and, as his treatment of **160** and **161** shows, he is not at his best in dealing with Melissus. Moreover, the *MXG* implies, against Simplicius, that Melissus did not say that 'the One' is incorporeal.[35]

Second, even if **171** appeared in a polemical context, Melissus must surely have realized how close it stood to some of his positive remarks: how could he have argued for the incorporeality of pluralist units without seeing that the same argument applied to his own Eleatic entity? Perhaps he thought that the argument did not apply to his entity O. After all, if X is identified with O, then the argument from (2) to (3) is dismal: from the fact that O is partless, in the sense of homogeneous, it does not even seem to follow that O is incorporeal or unextended. On the other hand, if X is a pluralist unit, the inference can be given a passable complexion: Melissus doubtless held that the items in a plurality must be separated from one another (cf. Aristotle, *GC* 325a5; *Phys* 213b22); perhaps he maintained that any such free-floating item must, if it were divisible, in the course of time come to be divided and so cease to be a unity: pluralist units, being inherently liable to split, must be mere partless points if they are to be unitary; such reasoning does not apply to the Eleatic One.

I do not find the suggestion delicious. But it is less unpalatable than its rivals; for unless **171** is read as a piece of polemic, Melissus is left with a downright contradiction; and unless the polemic is read in the fashion I suggest, it will not yield any remotely reasonable argument.

I end this section by observing that **171**, as a polemical fragment, sheds no light on the question of the divisibility of O. **169**, as I have already observed, talks of being divided, not of being divisible. What, then, of the puzzle raised by Melissus' argument for (T6)? Did he go on to say that O is not even theoretically divisible, on the grounds that if you could notionally distinguish two parts of O (say in terms of co-ordinates based on an arbitrarily chosen point of origin in O) then there would exist at least three things, O and its two parts? There is no evidence that Melissus did make this move; nor is there any reason why he should have done: physically distinct or physically distinguishable parts of O are doubtless existent individuals, and such parts must therefore be denied by a monist. But the same does not obviously hold for notionally distinguishable parts. Aristotle would have assigned to such parts only 'potential' existence; and Melissus, I suggest, might (had he ever contemplated the question) have allowed notional divisibility to O on the grounds that such divisibility offends neither against uniqueness nor against homogeneity.

(h) *The philosophy of Elea*

Parmenides' Way of Truth is short, and the cluster of truths, or alleged truths, along it is small. What exists is ungenerated and without destruction; it forms a continuous whole in time and space; it is changeless and does not move. Probably it has a purely instantaneous existence; probably it is a finite sphere. Melissus adds little: what exists is full, it does not have degrees of density, it is homogeneous—those theses Parmenides might have accepted. Melissus also holds, in contradiction to Parmenides, that what is is spatially infinite and temporally eternal; and he maintains a real monism, where Parmenides was prudently silent.

The Eleatic system is brief, but powerful in its implications: those few properties which Eleatic beings have are, it seems, sufficient to bar them from the field of scientific investigation, and hence to leave the scientist with nothing but his own fantasies to contemplate: in a completely stable world the laws of physics will be trivial or dull.

That is not to say that the Eleatics leave absolutely nothing to science. It is often supposed that the Way of Truth, and Melissus' amended route, are both intended to be complete, that there is nothing to be said about the world which Parmenides and Melissus have not said. There is no warrant at all for that supposition in the case of Melissus, whose fragments nowhere pretend to completeness. Parmenides' goddess does indeed offer to tell him 'everything' (**28 B** 1.28) and his mares escort him 'as far as desire may reach' (**B 1**.1); but it is implausible to read those unsystematic remarks as an explicit claim to metaphysical completeness.[36]

I am inclined to think that the Eleatic system is, in theory at least, extendable: further metaphysical research might add further essential properties of *to on*. (It is a plausible conjecture that Parmenides discovered the punctuality of *O* after he had ordered the rest of his deduction: surely he would wish to leave open the way to further discoveries?) Moreover, I see nothing that positively excludes the scientific and experimental discovery of contingent properties of existents. One example must suffice: *O*, according to **156**. 41, cannot 'alter bright colour'. I infer that *O* has a 'bright colour', or perhaps a wash of different bright colours. Now **156** does not, and perhaps metaphysics cannot, infer the colour or colours of *O*; here, perhaps, is a little opening for scientific endeavour; and other openings, of a similar unexciting kind, are readily imagined.

It may be that this possibility is ruled out by Melissus: in **30 B 8** (below, p. 298), he lists as potential items in a plural universe 'earth and water and air and fire and iron and gold and living and dead and black and white and the other things which men say are real'. If 'black and white' are *not* real, as **B 8** implies, then perhaps *O* is neither black nor white nor any other colour: *O* has just those properties deducible from the fact that it exists; it has no contingent properties. I doubt the inference. Melissus' list divides into four groups of incompatibles; the reason is clear: if black *and* white are both real, then, since they are contraries, there must exist at least *two* things, contrary to monism. It does not follow that both black and white are unreal: Melissus could consistently allow that O was, say, black, and maintain the falsity of pluralism. He need not object to there being some one thing which is both gold and yellow: that does not infringe on the claims of monism; he need only object to there being both gold and iron, both yellow and grey. **B 8** is a polemical fragment, and Melissus is less explicit in certain parts of it than we might like. Nonetheless, I incline to think that he, like Parmenides, leaves open a narrow and fairly tedious path to the scientist.

I do not press these final remarks: Parmenides and Melissus were certainly not engaged in a conscious effort to point out the path of legitimate science; and it is absurd to praise them as the founding fathers of theoretical physics.[37] Indeed, had they observed the loopholes I have just indicated, they might, I suppose, have hastily closed them up: metaphysics will countenance no scientific tax-dodgers. My point is a gentle one: taken strictly, the surviving words of Parmenides and Melissus do not warrant the assertion that their Eleatic systems were intended to exhaust the whole well of human intellectual achievement. They could happily have encouraged further metaphysical speculation; they might not have frowned too severely upon a little elementary scientific research.

XII

Zeno: Paradox and Plurality

(a) *The Eleatic Palamedes*

According to Coleridge, 'the few remains of Zeno the Eleatic, his paradoxes against the reality of motion, are mere identical propositions spun out into a sort of whimsical conundrums'. Depreciatory judgments of that character excited a splendid retort from Russell: 'In this capricious world, nothing is more capricious than posthumous fame. One of the most notable victims of posterity's lack of judgment is the Eleatic Zeno. Having invented four arguments, all immeasurably subtle and profound, the grossness of subsequent philosophers pronounced him to be a mere ingenious juggler, and his arguments to be one and all sophisms.'[1]

Philosophers have been driven to repentance by Russell's lashes. Zeno now stands as the most celebrated of Presocratic thinkers; and his paradoxes are again vivacious philosophical issues. Yet of Zeno himself our knowledge is exiguous: the surviving fragments count barely two hundred words; the doxography is slight and repetitious; and the structure and impetus of Zeno's thought remain dark and controversial.

We know surprisingly little of Zeno's life and history;[2] and most of our information comes from the celebrated but suspect story in Plato's *Parmenides*. The passage is worth quoting at length; Pythodorus is describing the visit of Parmenides and Zeno to Athens:

> ... They came to Athens, as he said, at the great Panathenaea: the former was, at the time of his visit, about 65 years old, very white with age, but well favoured. Zeno was nearly 40 years of age, tall and fair to look upon: in the days of his youth he was reported to have been beloved by Parmenides. He said that they lodged

with Pythodorus in the Ceramicus, outside the wall, whither Socrates, then a very young man, came to see them, and many others with him: they wanted to hear the writings of Zeno, which had been brought to Athens for the first time on the occasion of their visit. These Zeno himself read to them in the absence of Parmenides, and had very nearly finished when Pythodorus entered, and with him Parmenides and Aristoteles who was afterwards one of the Thirty, and heard the little that remained of the dialogue. Pythodorus had heard Zeno repeat them before.

When the recitation was completed, Socrates requested that the first thesis of the first argument might be read over again, and this having been done, he said: What is your meaning, Zeno? Do you maintain that if entities are many, they must be both like and unlike, and that this is impossible, for neither can the like be unlike, nor the unlike like—is that your position?

Just so, said Zeno.

And if the unlike cannot be like, or the like unlike, then according to you, entities could not be many; for this would involve an impossibility. In all that you say have you any other purpose except to disprove the existence of the many? and is not each division of your treatise intended to furnish a separate proof of this, there being in all as many proofs of the non-existence of the many as you have composed arguments? Is that your meaning or have I misunderstood you?

No, said Zeno; you have correctly understood my general purpose.

I see, Parmenides, said Socrates, that Zeno would like to be not only one with you in friendship but your second self in his writings too: he puts what you say in another way, and would fain make believe that he is telling us something which is new. For you, in your poems, say The All is one, and of this you adduce excellent proofs; and he on the other hand says there is no many: and on behalf of this he offers overwhelming evidence. You affirm unity, he denies plurality. And so you deceive the world into believing that you are saying different things when really you are saying much the same. This is a strain of art beyond the reach of most of us.

Yes, Socrates, said Zeno. But although you are as keen as a Spartan hound in pursuing the track, you do not fully apprehend the true motive of the composition, which is not really such an artificial work as you imagine; for what you speak of was an accident; there was no pretence of a great purpose: nor any serious intention of deceiving the world. The truth is that these writings of mine were meant to protect the arguments of Parmenides against those who make fun of him and seek to show the many ridiculous and contradictory results which they suppose to follow from the affirmation of the one. My answer is addressed to the partisans of the many, whose attack I return with interest by retorting upon them that their hypothesis of the existence of many, if carried out, appears to be still more ridiculous than the hypothesis of the existence of one. Zeal for my master led me to write the book in the days of my youth, but someone stole the copy: and therefore I had no choice whether it should be published or not: the motive, however, of writing was not the ambition of an elder man, but the pugnacity of a young one. This you do not seem to see, Socrates; though in other respects, as I was saying, your notion is a very just one.

I understand, said Socrates, and quite accepted your account (**172**: 127A–128E, trans. Jowett).

The details of the story, and the chronology implicit in it, are not my concern. What matters is the central core of Plato's account, which most scholars accept as historical truth. According to that core, Zeno in his youth, incensed by the ignorant attacks on his master's monism, wrote a collection of arguments designed to reduce pluralism to absurdity and so to defend monism. The story thus ascribes a plan, an aim and a method to Zeno; let us take them in turn.

Zeno's tract contained many arguments (127E). Proclus, in his commentary on the *Parmenides*, says that there were forty *logoi* in all (**29 A 15**; so too Elias, **A 15**); and there is no reason to reject his testimony. All those *logoi* attacked the hypothesis of pluralism: of the eight Zenonian arguments that we possess, two certainly were numbered among those forty. The standing of the four paradoxes on motion is uncertain: they can be pressed into a suitable form for membership of the forty; but Elias (**A 15**) says that in addition to the forty *logoi* there were five arguments against motion.[3] Moreover, it is clear from Aristotle's account that the paradoxes of motion were customarily treated as a special unity; and that may reflect a special origin. For the rest, antiquity supplies four Zenonian book-titles;[4] but they do not enable us to say anything about the original format of Zeno's publications.

Some scholars are not content with the information that Zeno's tract contained forty *logoi*: they attempt to discern a grand architectonic structure uniting several of the *logoi* into a complex and sophisticated argument against pluralism. Thus Zeno is bent on attacking pluralism: if the world is divisible into parts, then it is finitely or infinitely divisible; if finitely divisible, then its parts are separated by other bodies or by gaps (which **B 3** rules out), or else they abut one another (which the Arrow rules out); if infinitely divisible, then either the division is completable (which **B 2** rules out) or it is not (which the Dichotomy and the Achilles rule out). By a happy chance, the *logoi* we possess form a single integrated construction.[5]

Such architectonic interpretations have a certain attraction. But closer inspection reveals gaps and botches in the building: if Zeno did build thus, he was not a particularly skilful builder. Moreover, those interpretations are wholly products of the scholarly fancy. There is not a jot of evidence in any ancient text that Zeno's *logoi* ever formed such an integrated and interdependent whole; no ancient author knows anything of Zeno the logical master-builder. On the contrary, there is some evidence against the interpretation; for Plato asserts that each *logos* itself constituted a proof against pluralism. And if the fragments and reports of Zeno's arguments have been supposed to suggest an overall structure, that supposition is, in my view, quite illusory; and my discussion of the paradoxes will give no hint of a systematic interdependence among Zeno's different arguments.

So much for the plan of Zeno's arguments. Their aim, according to the *Parmenides*, was to defend Parmenides against those who were attempting to make fun of him (128C). Modern scholars have tried to identify those anonymous mockers, but without success. Many have invoked the Pythagoreans: a curious philosophy, called 'unit-point-atomism', has been ascribed to the sect; the philosophy has been judged a consciously anti-Parmenidean invention; and Zeno's arguments have then been interpreted as a rejection of the philosophy and hence as a defence of Parmenides. But that account is the merest fantasy: 'unit-point-atomism', if it existed, would not constitute a peculiarly incisive and mocking rejection of Parmenides; it is pluralistic, but so is every non-Eleatic theory. And in any case, the doctrine never existed: there is no direct evidence for it; and in order to infer its existence from Zeno's paradoxes we must subject those arguments to a gratuitously tortuous interpretation. For many years scholars have campaigned for and against a Pythagorean opposition to Parmenides; by now the campaign should be over.[6]

Did Zeno defend Parmenides against philosophical attack from some other quarter? I doubt it. Plato implies that the attacks on Parmenides were satirical rather than philosophical, and the Eleatic position is an obvious target for satire and ridicule. We can be sure that Parmenides, like all later metaphysicians of any originality, was an object of popular mirth: where his doctrines were known—or half-known—they will have been jeered at. It is to such receptions, and not to philosophical opposition, that Plato refers.[7]

Was it Zeno's aim to defend Parmenides against mockery? I am inclined to doubt Plato's suggestion that it was. First, I doubt that Parmenides was a monist at all. Second, even in the *Parmenides* Zeno does not claim to have been defending monism in any straightforward way. He asserts that the defence of monism which Socrates has read into his *logoi* was only incidental; his aim was to show that pluralism suffers 'still greater absurdities' than monism. That is hardly the language of an ardent monist. Third, even if pluralism *is* absurd, monism is not thereby defended; Plato is wrong in saying that a proof of monism and a refutation of pluralism come to the same thing. Zeno's pupil Gorgias was well aware of that: he was, notionally at least, a nihilist.[8] Fourth, more than one of Zeno's arguments seem to bear with equal force against pluralism and against monism. I shall note these cases as I discuss the paradoxes; here I observe that they make it hard to envisage Zeno as a self-conscious monist.

These arguments seem to be supported by a strand in the doxographical tradition. The thesis that Zeno attacked 'the One' is discussed, and rejected, by Simplicius (*in Phys* 97.9–99.31; 138.3–139.23); and it originated with Eudemus.[9] Unfortunately, Eudemus offered only weak support for his opinion, citing an anecdote and preparing a collage of three Zenonian arguments. The arguments, as Simplicius observes, are taken from Zeno's *logoi* against pluralism, and I shall consider them later; whatever their force, they do not reveal Zeno as a formal opponent of monism. The anecdote runs like this:

> They say that Zeno used to say that if someone would tell him what on earth the one (*to hen*) is, he would be able to talk about the things that exist (**173**: Eudemus, fr. 37aW = **A 16** = **L 5**).[10]

Nothing can be based on this second-hand story: '*to hen*' may, I suppose, mean 'the [Eleatic] One', and Zeno may have meant to cast doubt on its credentials; but '*to hen*' may equally mean 'a unit', and refer to the units that construct the pluralist world.[11] Eudemus' evidence does not establish that Zeno overtly attacked monism; but the four preceding considerations do at least show that he was not greatly concerned to defend it.

I turn to the question of Zeno's logical method. In the *Parmenides* (127E), Socrates gets Zeno to agree that each of his arguments is intended to have the form of a *reductio ad impossibile*; and later writers dutifully expound them in that form (cf. Proclus, **A 15**). Aristotle called Zeno the father of 'dialectic', and 'dialectic' may mean 'logic'. Modern scholars often regard Zeno as the first self-conscious logician, or at least as the inventor of argument by *reductio*.[12]

A pinch of sceptical snuff will clear the mind. Zeno was not the first thinker to use *reductio*, nor was he the first logician to reflect upon *reductio*; others had argued reductively before Zeno, and no one studied logic before Aristotle. Moreover, it is improbable that Zeno himself used reductive arguments. Indeed Plato almost says as much; for he represents Socrates as extracting from Zeno the realization that his arguments are reductive and not as finding a reductive form in the *logoi* themselves. Socrates is bringing to fictional consciousness what was at best latent in historical reality. Zeno's surviving fragments contain no *reductio*: he takes an hypothesis and infers an absurdity from it; but he never makes the characteristic move of *reductio*, the inference to the falsity of the hypothesis. He argues 'If P, then Q', where Q states some absurdity; but he does not explicitly infer the falsity of P. In other words, he does not use *reductio ad absurdum* as a technique for disproof.

In the *Parmenides* Zeno presents himself, or at least his juvenile self,[13] as an eristic debater, a sophist out to impress an audience; and in the *Phaedrus* he is called an *antilogikos* or logic-chopper.[14] I do not suggest that Zeno was a charlatan, a purveyor of arguments which he knew to be fallacious; nor do I mean that he had no philosophical interest in Eleaticism. But I do suggest that Zeno was not a systematic Eleatic solemnly defending Parmenides against philosophical attack by a profound and inter-connected set of reductive argumentations. Many men had mocked Parmenides: Zeno mocked the mockers. His *logoi* were designed to reveal the inanities and ineptitudes inherent in the ordinary belief in a plural world; he wanted to startle, to amaze, to disconcert. He did not have the serious metaphysical purpose of supporting an Eleatic monism; and he did not adopt a ponderous logical precision in his method.

That conclusion has some slight importance. Many modern interpreters of Zeno have argued that such and such an account of a paradox is wrong because it attributes a silly fallacy to a profound mind. Zeno was not profound: he was clever. Some profundities did fall from his pen; but so too did some trifling fallacies. And that is what we should expect from an eristic disputant. If we meet a deep argument, we may rejoice; if we are dazzled by a superficial glitter, we are not bound to search for a nugget of philosophical gold. Fair metal and base, in roughly equal proportions, make the Zenonian alloy.

(b) *Large and small*

It is appropriate to begin with those of Zeno's surviving arguments which specifically attack pluralism. They account for all that we possess of Zeno's own words; they were certainly a part of his collection of *logoi*; and some of the issues they raise underlie the subtler paradoxes of motion.

The hypothesis under attack, pluralism, simply says that 'there exist many things'. I shall abbreviate this to *P*. It is, I take it, a moderately clear and unambiguous hypothesis. If Zeno is out to show the absurdity of pluralism, we may expect his attacks on *P* to conclude to propositions of the form:
(Z*) If *P*, then *Q* and not-*Q*.
That is equivalent to:
(Z) If *P*, then *Q*; and if *P*, then not-*Q*,
and the surviving evidence shows that, in some cases at least, Zeno did set himself to demonstrate a conjunctive proposition of the form (Z); and his procedure was the obvious one of arguing independently for each conjunct of the conjunction.[15]

According to the *Phaedrus*, Zeno made 'the same things seem like and unlike, and one and many, and at rest and in motion' (261D = **A 13**). To those three pairs of opposites we may add at least two others: large and small (**B 1-2**), and finite and infinite (**B 3**). Such pairs can all readily be accommodated to the schema (Z). Doubtless there were more pairs; but it is hardly likely that the forty arguments used forty distinct pairs of opposites.[16]

The first *logos* in Zeno's treatise used the pair 'like and unlike' (**172**: *Parm* 127D-E). Zeno's first conclusion, then, will have been:
(Z1) (a) If *P*, then everything is alike, and (b) if *P*, then everything is unlike.
We do not know how Zeno argued for (Z1), nor what he meant by 'everything is alike'.[17] The word for 'alike' is '*homoios*'. Perhaps: 'If *a* and *b* are distinct existents, then they are similar (*homoios*) in so far as each exists—hence they are alike; and they are dissimilar (*anhomoios*) in so far as each is different from the other—hence they are unlike.' Or perhaps rather: 'If *a* and *b* are distinct existents, then as existent each will be homogeneous (*homoios*)—hence they are alike; and yet being distinct, they are heterogeneous and hence unlike'.

Neither argument has any power; for neither conclusion is more than an apparent absurdity: the consequents of (Z1) do not together amount to anything of the damning form '*Q* and not-*Q*'. The first argument is sound and harmless; the second, even if it were sound, would cause no pluralist any loss of sleep. For all that, it is worth starting with (Z1), for two reasons. First, it may finally kill the desire to find a subtle argument behind Zeno's every *dictum*. Second, it exhibits an interesting feature of Zeno's technique: *P* contains the two notions of *existence* and of *plurality*. In (Z1), conjunct (Z1a) makes use of the notion of *existence* in *P*, and conjunct (Z1b) turns to that of *plurality*. *P* is absurd (Zeno urges) because it conjoins two notions with contradictory implications.

I turn now to the *logos* of 'large and small'; we know that it preceded the *logos* of 'finite and infinite' (Simplicius, *in Phys* 140.34), but we do not know its absolute position among the forty *logoi*. For this *logos* we possess some of Zeno's own words. Simplicius, who preserves them, quotes them in the course of a piece of commentatorial controversy; and it is necessary to reconstruct the original argument from two passages in Simplicius' text. Since scholars have not agreed on the reconstruction, I shall begin by displaying the two passages.[18]

In the first passage, Simplicius is concerned to refute the opinion of Alexander and Eudemus that Zeno 'rejected the One':

> In the treatise of his which contains many arguments, he proves in each one that anyone who asserts that there exist many things is committed to asserting opposites. One of these is an argument in which he proves that [i] if there exist many things, they are both large and small—large so as to be unlimited in magnitude, small so as to have no magnitude. Now in this he proves that [ii] what has neither magnitude, nor mass, nor bulk, would not even exist. '[iii] For', he says, 'if it were attached to something else that exists, it would not make it larger; [iv] for if it is of no magnitude but is attached, that thing cannot increase at all in magnitude. [v] And in this way what is attached will thereby be nothing. [vi] And if, when it is detached, the other thing is no smaller, and, when it is attached again, it will not grow, it is clear that what is attached is nothing, and likewise what is detached.' And Zeno says this not in order to reject the One, but [vii] to show that each of the many things has a magnitude—and an unlimited one at that (for there is always something in front of what is taken, because of the unlimited division). [viii] And he proves this having first proved that each of the many things has no magnitude from the fact that

each is the same as itself and one (174: *in Phys* 139.5–19; cf. **B 2** = 9 L).[19]

In the second passage, which is part of the same long note on *Physics* 187a1, Simplicius is arguing against Porphyry's view that the 'dichotomy' argument to which Aristotle refers belongs to Parmenides rather than to Zeno:

> And why should we waste words when [the argument] is actually produced in Zeno's own treatise? For in proving that if there exist many things the same things are unlimited and limited Zeno writes in these words: [ix] 'If there exist many things, it is necessary that they be as many as they are and neither more than themselves nor less. But if they are as many as they are, they will be limited. If there exist many things, the things that exist are unlimited. For there are always other things in the middle of the things that exist, and again others in the middle of those. And thus the things that exist are unlimited.' And in this way he proved their numerical unlimitedness from the dichotomy. Their quantitative unlimitedness [he proved] earlier by the same method of argument. [x] For having proved beforehand that if what exists had no magnitude it would not even exist, he continues: '[xi] and if there exist [many things], it is necessary for each to have a certain magnitude and mass, [xii] and for the one part of it to be separate from the other. [xiii] And the same argument holds of what protrudes; for that too will have a magnitude, and some part of it will protrude. [xiv] Now it is all one to say this of one case and to say it of every case; for no such part of it will be last, nor will there not be another part related to another.[20] [xv] Thus if there exist many things, it is necessary for them to be both small and large—so small that they have no magnitude, so large that they are unlimited' (175: *in Phys* 140.27–141.8: cf. **B 3** = 11 L; **B 1** = 10 L).

Sentence [ix] (= **B 3**) contains the *logos* of 'finite and infinite'; since it appeared in Zeno's treatise after the 'large and small', I shall postpone discussion of it. Sentence [x] shows that the argument in [xi]–[xiv] was preceded by the argument in [iii]–[vi]; and sentences [vii] and [viii] show that the argument in [xi]–[xiv] was preceded by the argument briefly retailed in [viii]. Simplicius does not state explicitly that the argument of [viii] preceded that of [iii]–[vi]; but the content of the two arguments, and the form of Zeno's antinomy, make that precedence clear.

[i] and [xv] give the conclusion of the *logos* of 'large and small'; it is striking:

(Z2) (a) If P, then everything has no magnitude, and (b) if P, then everything has infinite magnitude.

Given (Z2a), Zeno need only argue that everything has some positive magnitude; given (Z2b) he might rest content with a proof that everything has a finite magnitude: to urge both (Z2a) and (Z2b) is logically excessive; and Zeno's urging is a *tour de force*.

Zeno's argument for (Z2a) is given in sentence [viii]; the argument for (Z2b) is stated in [xi]–[xiv], and it is prepared for in [iii]–[vi]. These latter sentences argue for the lemma:

(L) If a exists, then a has a positive magnitude.

Thus from Simplicius' text we can reconstruct the following account of Zeno's *logos*:

(Z2a) = [viii];
lemma (L) = [iii]–[vi],
whence (Z2b) = [xi]–[xiv]:
hence (Z2) = [xv].

I shall accordingly discuss the *logos* in the order (Z2a); (L); (Z2b).[21]

(c) *Existence*

(Z2a) need not detain us long. Zeno appears to have moved from 'a is self-identical and one' to 'a is without magnitude'. Scholars mediate the move by 'a is partless', and refer to Melissus, **171**, and to Plato's *Parmenides*, 137CD.[22] I have already commented briefly on this argument (above p. 227). I am not sure that it was Zeno's (it makes no use of the premiss of self-identity); but I have no alternative to offer. It may be observed that the hypothesis, P, plays no part in the derivation of (Z2a); as we shall see, P is similarly inactive in the derivation of (Z2b): the antinomy works impartially against P and against monism.

What of the argument for (L)? Some scholars feel that it prevaricates upon the word 'nothing'[23] but I do not share the feeling, and I shall ignore Zeno's use of the word in [v] and [vi]. The logical articulation of [iii]–[vi] is not wholly clear: if we use '$a + b$' to mean 'the result of attaching a to b'; and 'mag: a' for 'the magnitude of a', then [iii], I think, expresses the following proposition:

(1) If mag: $a = 0$, then if b exists and a is attached to b then mag: $a + b$ = mag: b.

As far as I can see, [iv] merely repeats [iii]. As for [v], that states:

(2) If, if b exists and a is attached to b, then mag: $a + b$ = mag: b, then a does not exist.

[vi] repeats the matter of [v] and adds to it a parallel clause about 'detachment'. I assume that [vi], which Aristotle calls 'Zeno's axiom' (*Met* 1001b7 = **A 21**), is an improved or completed version of [v]; a similarly improved version of [iii] is needed, if any inference is to be made from [vi]. (1) and (2) immediately yield:
(3) If mag: $a = 0$, a does not exist.
If we make the harmless assumption that nothing can have a negative magnitude, then (3) yields (L).

Is (2), Zeno's unimproved axiom, true? The words '*prosgignesthai*' and '*apogignesthai*', which I translate 'be attached to' and 'be detached from', are standardly rendered by 'be added to' and 'be subtracted from'. That rendering gives encouragement to those who see a geometrical base to Zeno's paradox and construe (L) as a theorem about geometrical points;[24] but it is mistaken: Zeno is thinking of the collocation and dislocation of physical objects; and '$a + b$' denotes the complex object formed by juxtaposing, intermixing, fusing or otherwise uniting the two objects a and b. The term 'magnitude' in (2) is generally taken to mean 'size' or 'volume'. It is apparent, then, that (2) is not a logical truth; indeed, it turns out to be a contingent falsehood. It plainly presupposes that, in general, mag: $a + b$ = mag: a + mag: b; but that presupposition, as every schoolboy knows, is false: a pint of alcohol mixed with a pint of water does not yield a quart of liquor. Moreover, (2) itself, I am told, is false: one of the peculiarities of the stuff zeolite is that, when added to water, it does not increase the volume of the water: mag: $z + w$ = mag: w.

Zeno might attempt to escape from this objection in either of two ways. First, he might abandon the physical interpretation of 'attachment' and tell us that it is, after all, a mathematical operation that he has in mind. Alternatively, he might prefer to have 'magnitude' understood as 'mass'. (According to Simplicius, he uses *megethos, pachos,* and *onkos* indiscriminately.) On both readings, the presupposition that mag: $a + b$ = mag: a + mag: b turns out true: on the first reading, it is a tautology; on the second, a primitive version of the Law of Conservation of Matter.

Yet neither of those defences will save Zeno. (2) carries a second, more general, presupposition, namely that if a is attached to b then a must be the sort of thing to have a magnitude—a volume or a mass, Surely, though, I can 'attach' my shadow to a wall, or 'attach' a picture to a cinema screen: shadows and pictures occupy no volume and have no mass; the shadowy wall and the coloured screen have precisely the same magnitude as the sunlit wall and the vacant screen;

yet for all that cast shadows and projected pictures exist. And that appears to refute (2).

Aristotle anticipated and answered this objection: Zeno advances his axiom

> clearly assuming that what exists is a magnitude—and if a magnitude, corporeal (*sômatikon*); for that is what exists in all ways [i.e. is three-dimensional] (**176**: *Met* 1001b9 = **A 21**).

(2) holds only if *a* and *b* are three-dimensional, physical objects: I objected to (2) by citing cases in which *a* is a two-dimensional object; Aristotle suggests the simple retort: 'restrict *a* and *b* to three-dimensional objects'. It makes no odds whether we say that (2) is false but open to simple emendation; or rather that (2) is true when properly understood. The important fact is simply this: (2) is true if *a* and *b* are three-dimensional. And Zeno is surely entitled to that hypothesis: any pluralist will be proclaiming a world populated by fairly ordinary middle-sized objects; and it is such a pluralism that Zeno is out to attack. The commentators say as much in connexion with a later *logos*.

If (2) is true, so is (1); and thus Zeno has his conclusion. Moreover his conclusion need not decide between the two interpretations of 'magnitude'; for three-dimensional physical objects—bodies, for short—have both volume and mass. But victory is won at a price; and the price is triviality. The lemma (L), which reads like a strong ontological thesis, asserting that only things with magnitude can exist, turns out on examination to state no more than the analytic truth that all existent bodies occupy space and have a positive mass. From (L) nothing follows about the ontological status of shadows, of numbers, of points, of abstract entities—or of anything else.

The triviality of (L) may prove unimportant; what matters is whether it can function in the main argument for (Z2b). Yet it is, in a sense, distressing: the argumentative apparatus in [iii]–[vi] seems singularly pointless if (L) is as trifling as I claim; and some may still think that Zeno has stronger meat to cook. I can only say that no stronger conclusion will emerge from [iii]–[vi]; that there is no positive harm in impressing the truth of (L) by what is, after all, a sound argument; and that the interest of (L) lies in any case in its application to (Z2b), an application to which I now turn.

(d) *Infinite division*

The argument in [xi]–[xiv] is peculiarly difficult to grasp; and my presentation will, I fear, be both laborious and unconfident. First, let me offer a somewhat more precise version of its component sentences.

Sentence [xi] says that 'if there exist many things, it is necessary for each to have a certain magnitude and mass'; that, I assume, amounts to:
(1) If there exist objects $a_1, a_2, \ldots, a_n$, then for each i, mag: $a_i > 0$.
That is simply an application of the lemma (L). Sentence [xii] reads: '. . . and for the one part of it to be separate from (*apechein*) the other'; i.e.:
(2) If a_i exists, then there exist distinct parts of a_i, b_i and c_i.
I assume that the word *apechein* connotes nothing stronger than distinctness: that assumption is all that Zeno needs. Sentence [xiii]—'And the same argument holds of what protrudes'—applies (1) and (2) to one of the parts of a_i, say b_i. (I see no special significance in Zeno's label, 'what protrudes'.) And [xiv] asserts that (1) and (2) can be applied again to the parts of b_i, to the parts of the parts of b_i, and so on.

All that seems innocuous enough: how on earth are we to extract from it the lethal poison of (Z2b)? How can we generate, or seem to generate, infinitely large elephants from the little mice that play before us?

The rough answer to this question is not difficult to discover. By (2), every existent object contains infinitely many existent parts; and by (1) each of those parts has a positive magnitude. Now the magnitude of any object is equal to the sum of the magnitudes of its parts; and since any object has infinitely many parts, its magnitude is equal to the sum of the magnitudes of that infinity of parts. But the sum of infinitely many positive magnitudes is infinite; hence the magnitude of any object is infinite.

That, I think, is an uncontroversial expansion of Zeno's argument. The only premiss it requires which is not found in the Greek text is the thesis that the sum of an infinite set of magnitudes is infinite; and all scholars agree that some such thesis must be ascribed to Zeno. But the argument is still imprecise and impressionistic. I shall now attempt a more rigorous presentation. The ferociously technical aspect of what follows is, I believe, indispensable: if an argument is worth stating, it is worth stating precisely; and I cannot find a less unattractive route to precision than the one I follow here.

First, I need the notion of a *Zeno-set* or *Z-set*. Roughly speaking, a Z-set of an object a is any collection of all its parts: four legs and a top are a Z-set of the table I write upon; a few hundred pages, a spine, and two boards are a Z-set of the book you are reading; take a motor-mower engine to bits and beside you on the lawn you will have, if you are fortunate, a Z-set of the engine. Formally:

(D) $\{x_1, x_2, \ldots, x_n\}$ is a Z-set of y if and only if (a) every x_i is a proper part of y, (b) no x_i is a part of any other x_i, and (c) no part of y is not a part of the sum of all the x_is.

In place of Zeno's premiss (1) we can employ the simpler:

(3) If a exists, then mag: $a > 0$.

And in place of (2) we must use the more complex:

(4) If mag: $a > 0$, then there is a Z-set of a, $\{x_1, x_2, \ldots\}$, such that for every i mag: $x_i > 0$.

A further premiss is now required:

(5) If $\{x_{11}, x_{12}, \ldots\}$ is a Z-set of x_1, and $\{x_{21}, x_{22}, \ldots\}$ is a Z-set of x_2, and ... and $\{x_{n1}, x_{n2} \ldots\}$ is a Z-set of x_n, and $\{x_1, x_2, \ldots x_n\}$ is a Z-set of a, then $\{x_{11}, x_{12}, \ldots x_{21}, x_{22}, \ldots, \ldots x_{n1}, x_{n2} \ldots\}$ is a Z-set of a.

That is formidable in appearance; but it only expresses, in formal dress, the mundane truth that any object is made up of the parts of its parts.

From (3)–(5) I infer:

(6) If a exists, then for any n there is a Z-set of a, $\{x_1, x_2, \ldots, x_m\}$, such that $m > n$,

For suppose that the most numerous Z-set of a is k, or $\{x_1, x_2, \ldots, x_k\}$. Then mag: $x_k > 0$, and hence there is a Z-set of x_k, say $\{x_{k1}, x_{k2}, \ldots, x_{kj}\}$. But then there will be a Z-set of a $\{x_1, x_2, \ldots, x_{k-1}, x_{k1}, x_{k2}, \ldots, x_{kj}\}$; and that will be more numerous than k. Hence k is not the most numerous Z-set of a.

In effect, (6) says that a is infinitely divisible, or contains infinitely many parts. A further premiss, of self-evident truth, is now needed:

(7) If $\{x_1, x_2, \ldots x_n, \ldots\}$ is a Z-set of a, then mag: a = mag: x_1 + mag: x_2 + ... + mag: x_n + ...

I use the sign S_m^n to name the set $\{x_n, x_{n+1}, \ldots, x_m\}$; and '∞' for infinity. By (6), then, there is a Z-set of a S_∞^1; and hence, by (7):

(8) If a exists, then mag: a = mag: S_∞^1.

Finally, we need a premiss concerning the summing of infinite sets, viz:

(9) If for every x_i in S_∞^1 mag: $x_i > 0$, then mag: $S_\infty^1 = \infty$.

It is now a simple inference to:

(10) If a exists, mag: $a = \infty$.

And (10) is equivalent to (Z2b).

Evidently, the argument is unsound; and it has found no serious defenders. Yet its opponents are in disarray, and there is no agreement on just where the flaws—or the chief flaws—are to be found. In the next section I shall discuss five objections against Zeno.

(e) *The toils of infinity*

First, and most obviously, Zeno's opponents may deny (2) or (4): it is simply not true that every part of *a* has parts; it is simply not true that partition may continue *ad infinitum*. Physical bodies have minimal parts; and, being composed of a finite number of finite parts, they are felicitously finite in magnitude. In **174** and **175** Zeno is speaking of physical bodies: there is no reason to believe what he says in (2) and good reason to disbelieve it.[25]

That atomistic answer has left most Zenonians unmoved. No doubt Zeno is talking of the physical parts of physical bodies; but he need not be construed as talking of physical operations of division or splitting. Behind the physical façade of proposition (2) there lies a mathematical substance; and (2) rests not upon false or dubious physical theory but on a truth of stereometry: every geometrical solid s has a Z-set $\{s_1, s_2, \ldots\}$ all of whose members are geometrical solids; and since the magnitude of a physical body is determined by the volume of the geometrical solid which its spatial co-ordinates describe, if the volume is infinitely large, so too is the magnitude.

Some Greek thinkers were moved by that argument to posit indivisible geometrical magnitudes: just as physical division stops somewhere, so, they supposed, geometrical division has a terminus. Xenocrates, a pupil of Plato's, 'gave in to this argument about the dichotomy and accepted that everything divisible is many . . . for he said that there are atomic lines of which it is no longer true that they are many' (fr. 44 H = Simplicius, *in Phys* 138.10–6). Doubtless Xenocrates also postulated indivisible geometrical solids.[26] If a stereometrical atomism thus backs up physical atomism, premiss (2) may still be rejected.

Ancient critics observed, truly enough, that geometrical atomism emasculated their geometry (cf. Xenocrates, fr. 43 H); and they opined that Zeno's argument was bought off at suicidal expense. Modern critics need not at once concur; for they can propose a subtler version of the atomic objection: physical atomism, they allow, is irrelevant to Zeno's argument; and Euclidean solids are infinitely divisible. But between physical bodies and geometrical solids lies space. Zeno presupposes that space is infinitely divisible or continuous; i.e., he tacitly assumes that the geometry of space is, in that respect at least, Euclidean. But that assumption is unwarranted; indeed, the moral to be drawn from Zeno's paradoxes is precisely this: that space (and time) are not continuous.[27] Physical bodies have smallest physically separable parts; but that is no serious objection to Zeno. Euclidean geometry allows infinite division to its solids; but

245

that is no help to Zeno. Physical bodies occupy space; and in maintaining that bodies are infinitely divisible, Zeno is maintaining that space is infinitely divisible, that space has no minimal *quanta*. If we care to reject that assumption, we do not fall foul of geometry: we merely imply that the geometry of space is non-continuous. And we may reject premiss (2).

That sophisticated atomism is a tempting hare; but I shall not indulge in pursuit. For it seems to me that none of the arguments in favour of spatial atomism, and none of the arguments against spatial atomism, is cogent; and I incline to regard the question of the structure of space as an empirical one—to be settled, no doubt, by the abstract theorizings of the physicist rather than by microscopic inspection of pieces of space. If that is right, then we may say at least that Zeno's proposition (2) is not a truth of logic; but for all that, (2) may be true: it may be a truth of physical theory. And of course, almost all physicists hold that it *is* true. Further speculation on this topic would be idle: let us grant Zeno (2) and (4).

The second objection to Zeno's argument attacks proposition (9), his 'hidden premiss': '(9) proposes a principle for summing infinite series which is simply false; Zeno's arithmetic was naive, and a sophisticated mathematician will immediately refute his paradox. Z-sets of a are created by dichotomy: the first operation yields $\{b_1, b_2\}$, where mag: $b_1 = 1/2$ mag: a; the second operation yields $\{b_1, c_1, c_2\}$, where mag: $c_i = 1/2$ mag: b_i. And so on. Thus the magnitude of the infinite Z-set $\{b_1, c_1, d_1, \ldots\}$ is equal to $1/2$ mag: a + $1/4$ mag: a + $1/8$ mag: a + ... The infinite series to be summed is:

(S) $1/2 + 1/4 + 1/8 + \ldots$

Evidently, the sum of S does not exceed 1; and arithmeticians now make it 1 by definition. Zeno's infinite series is convergent; and the sum of a convergent series is finite. The principle enunciated in (9) is falsified by the very series Zeno means to apply it to: Zeno's hidden premiss was accepted by most ancient thinkers, with the honourable exception of Aristotle; but it is tediously false.'[28]

That objection is horribly confused; rather than anatomize its imperfections I shall show that it is undisturbing to any competent Zenonian. The text of **B 1** does, I think, lend plausibility to the claim that Zeno imagined his Z-sets as being generated in the way I have just described; but not all ancient commentators understood the generation in that light. Thus Porphyry restates the argument as follows:

If it is divisible, he[29] says, let it be divided in half, and then each of the parts in half. And if this happens in every case, it is clear, he says, that either there will remain some smallest, atomic magnitudes, infinite in number, and the whole will consist of smallest magnitudes infinite in number [sc. and so will be infinitely large], or else it will vanish and be dissolved into nothing and will consist of nothing. And both alternatives are absurd. . . .
(**175**: Simplicius, *in Phys* 139, 27–32).

Porphyry's argument was known to Aristotle (see *GC* 316a14–34; 325a8–12). Some scholars suppose it to be a Zenonian argument, related to but not identical with the argument of **B 1**; but Porphyry and Simplicius both treat it as a version of **B 1**, and I am inclined to take it as an ancient modification or interpretation of our argument.

The important point in Porphyry is this: the dichotomy does not yield Z-sets the magnitudes of whose members form a convergent series; the partitions are 'through and through'. Each part of a is divided, and every division produces a set whose members are equal in magnitude. Thus the second Z-set of a will not be $\{b_1, c_1, c_2\}$ but rather $\{c_1, c_1, c_3, c_4\}$, where each c_i has the same magnitude as each of its fellows. Let us define a Z*-set as a Z-set all of whose members are equal in magnitude; and let us replace premiss (4) by:
(4*) If mag: $a > 0$, then there is a Z*-set of a, $\{x_1, x_2, \ldots\}$ such that for every i mag: $x_i > 0$.
Premisses (5) and (7) must be correspondingly emended (the emendation of (7) is trifling, that of (5) more complicated); and the argument will proceed felicitously to (8). To reach (10), we need not (9) but:
(9*) If S^1_∞ is a Z*-set and for every i in S^1_∞ mag: $x_i > 0$, then mag: $S^1_\infty = \infty$
Unlike (9), (9*) is true; for the sum of an infinite series whose members each have the same finite magnitude is indeed, and evidently, infinite. I suppose that those later Greeks who adopted the 'hidden premiss' were in fact embracing (9*), on the tacit assumption that the elements to be summed were all of equal magnitude. I doubt if Zeno himself made that assumption; but it is enough that the assumption is readily superadded to his argument, and that the superaddition destroys the arithmetical objection.[30]

The third objection has Aristotelian roots. According to an Aristotelian *dictum*, the infinite exists only potentially: potentially, bodies may be divided infinitely often; actually, such a division is impossible. Infinite division cannot be actualized; the dichotomizing always comes to a finite stop; partition *ad infinitum* cannot be completed. Now Zeno's argument implies at (4) that infinite division is completable; and it is just there that Zeno goes astray.

Such an objection is worth pondering in connexion with the paradoxes of motion; but here it is readily dismissed. The premisses of the *logos* on 'large and small' contain no reference, explicit or implicit, to any process of dividing: Zeno is not enjoining us to cut, carve or chop up *a*; nor is he asking us to divide *a* 'in thought'. Like Leibniz, he holds that 'each portion of matter is not only infinitely divisible . . . but is also actually subdivided without end, each part into further parts' (*Monadology*, §65); but he does not say that every body *has been*, or *could be*, divided into parts—he asserts that it *has* parts. He is talking of a characteristic or state of bodies, not of an operation upon bodies. Since Zeno says nothing about dividing, he says nothing about dividing *ad infinitum*; and reflexions on the possibility of completed divisions are not germane to his argument.

Potentiality, too, is only a toy sword; it is not clear what application that notion has in the context of Zeno's argument. Aristotle applies his *dictum* to infinite processes and not to an infinity of parts; the *dictum* is, in Aristotle at least, a mere ukase; and in any event appropriate injections of the term 'potentially' into Zeno's argument would leave it with its force unimpaired.

The fourth objection comes from Thomas Hobbes. Hobbes had Zeno's Achilles in mind; but the considerations which led him to reject the Achilles as a 'sophistical caption' apply equally to our present argument. Hobbes accuses Zeno of mishandling the concept of infinity: 'The force of that famous argument of Zeno . . . consisted in this proposition, *whatsoever may be divided into parts, infinite in number, the same is infinite*: which he, without doubt, thought to be true, yet nevertheless is false. For to be divided into infinite parts is nothing but to be divided into as many parts as any man will. But it is not necessary that a line should have parts infinite in number, or be infinite, because I can divide and subdivide it as often as I please: for how many parts so ever I make, yet their number is finite' (*De Corpore* V.13).

Hobbes appears to vacillate between two objections. On the one hand, he seems to deny that *a* in fact has infinitely many parts; it has as many parts 'as you please', but your pleasure stops short of infinity. If that is his real intention, then he is, in effect, denying the validity of the move from (6) and (7) to (8): the introduction of the sign '∞' in (8) is illegitimate. But Hobbes does not explain *why* this is illegitimate, simply asserting that Zeno argues sophistically.

On the other hand, Hobbes appears to allow that *a* can be divided into infinitely many parts, but to draw the teeth of his admission by claiming that 'infinitely many' here simply means 'as many as you please'. If that is his real intention, then in effect he allows Zeno to proceed as far as (8) but no further; for on Hobbes's understanding of 'infinite', premiss (9*) is no more true than (9): the sum of as many finite parts as you like need not be infinite. Now Zeno must certainly allow that, given Hobbes's equation of infinity and the *ad lib*, premiss (9*) is false; but he is under no obligation to accept the Hobbesian equation. And indeed, that equation is false: there are infinitely many natural numbers; but that is not to say that there are as many numbers as you like; however many you like, there are more (indeed, infinitely many more).

Hobbes, I think, did not grasp the flaw in Zeno's argument; but his fingers came close to it, and he saw where the argument must be attacked, namely in its handling of the concept of *infinity*. My fifth and final objection to Zeno owes much to Hobbism; and I preface my remarks with a few elementary reflexions upon the notion of infinity.

It is peculiarly tempting to suppose that the phrase 'infinitely many' stands, so to speak, at the very end of the natural number series. If we start counting from 1, the numbers get bigger and bigger, until we pass from the large to the monstrously large, and from the monstrously to the incredibly large—and eventually, if only we went on for ever, we should reach the infinitely large. Thus 'There are infinitely many Fs' may seem to have the same logical structure as 'There are seventeen Fs'; and 'a can be divided infinitely many times' is, so to speak, the last member of a series which starts, modestly, with 'a can be divided once'.

That is all wrong: 'infinitely many' does not function like 'seventeen'; it does not specify a number of Fs or a fixed set of divisions. 'Infinitely many' is, on that score, more like 'as many . . . as you like' or 'more . . . than you could imagine'. Those latter phrases are not indefinite numerical adjectives like 'many' or 'a lot of'; but nor are they definite in the sense of specifying some particular number. 'Have as many chestnuts as you like' does not mean 'Have lots of chestnuts', nor 'Have n chestnuts' (for some determinate n); rather, it means something like: 'For any n, if you want n chestnuts, have n chestnuts'.

In a not wholly dissimilar fashion, 'infinitely many' is neither an indefinite modifier, like 'hundreds of', nor a specifying modifier, like 'seventeen'. To that extent Hobbes was right. But he erred when he went further and defined 'infinitely many' as 'as many as you please': the infinite contains as much as you please—and then more; it is inexhaustible, its contents are never used up. To say that a set contains infinitely many members is to say that, however many of its members you have picked out or enumerated, there are still more to count; more precisely, it is to say that for any positive integer n the set contains more than n members. Thus as a first definition of infinity I offer:

(Di) S contains infinitely many members if and only if for every n S contains more than n members.

Now the paradigm of an infinite set is the set of natural numbers or positive integers, $\{1, 2, 3, \ldots\}$. However many natural numbers you have taken, more remain; for if you have abstracted k numbers, at least $k+1$, the successor to k, remains to be abstracted. Pretty clearly, we might use that fact to give a second definition of infinity, viz:

(Dii) S contains infinitely many members if and only if S contains as many members as there are positive integers.

Definition (Di) is not technical; definition (Dii) leaves the infinity of the positive integers unaccounted for; a better definition is sought for. And one can be found (thanks mainly to the work of the German mathematician Dedekind) by way of the notion of a *one-to-one correlation*. Take any two sets of things, S and S': a relation, R, will set up a one-to-one correlation between S and S' if it pairs each member of S with exactly one member of S' and each member of S' with exactly one member of S. Consider a monogamous society, and let S be the set of husbands and S' the set of wives. Then the relation of *being married to* sets up a one-to-one correlation between husbands and wives; for each husband is married to exactly one wife, and every wife has exactly one husband married to her. Again, let S be the set of even positive integers, $\{2, 4, 6, \ldots\}$, and S' the set of positive integers, $\{1, 2, 3, \ldots\}$. Then the relation of *being double* sets up a one-to one correlation between S and S'; for every even positive integer is the double of exactly one positive integer, and every positive integer has exactly one even positive integer that is its double.

The new definition of infinity also requires the notion of a *proper subset*. That is readily explained: S is a proper subset of S' if and only if every member of S is a member of S' and not every member of S' is a member of S. Thus the set of husbands is a proper subset of the set of married people; for all husbands are married, but not all married people are husbands. And the set of even positive integers is a proper subset of the set of positive integers; for every even positive integer is a positive integer, but not every positive integer is even.

Now we can offer:

(Diii) S has infinitely many members if and only if there is a proper subset of S, S', and a relation R, such that R sets up a one-to-one correlation between S and S'.

Clearly, the set of natural numbers is infinite by (Diii); for the relation *double of* will set up a one-to-one correlation between the set of even integers and that set. Hence any set which is infinite by (Di) or (Dii) is infinite by (Diii).

Is any set that is infinite by (Diii) also infinite by (Di) and (Dii)? Suppose that S is infinite by (Diii) but not by (Dii). Then S contains fewer members than there are natural numbers. (I disregard, as irrelevant to Presocratic concerns, the higher infinities or the 'transfinite' numbers.) Hence for some k, S contains exactly k members; hence every subset of S contains less than k members; hence no subset of S can be correlated one-to-one with S; hence S is not, after all, infinite by (Diii). Any set infinite by (Diii) is infinite by (Dii), and by (Di); and since (Diii) is precise and explanatory, it is preferable to (Di) and (Dii) as a definition of infinity.

What is all that to Zeno? It helps us to show that Zeno's argument breaks down at the move from (6) and (7) to (8)—or rather, at the move from (6*) and (7*) to (8). I attempted to ease that move by suggesting that 'by (6) . . . there is a Z-set of a S_∞^1', i.e. a Z-set containing infinitely many members. Let us make that into an explicit inference from (6*), thus:

(11*) If a exists, then there is a Z*-set $\{x_1, x_2 . . .\}$ of a containing infinitely many x_is.

From (7*) and (11*), (8) is validly inferred; but without (11*) Zeno has no way of attaining (8); his argument turns on there being a Z*-set with infinite members.

Yet Zeno has no title to (11*). (11*) does not follow from (6*), nor from any other Zenonian premiss. (6*) does indeed show that a possesses infinitely many Z*-sets: the Z*-sets of a can be placed in one-one correspondence with the natural numbers; and Zeno's 'dichotomy' shows how that is so. But each Z*-set contains finitely many members. Thus let the Z*-sets be generated by successive dichotomies. Then the first Z*-set contains 2 members, the second 4, and so on: in general, the nth Z*-set contains 2^n members; and for every n, 2^n is finite. There are infinitely many Z*-sets of a. That is to say, for any integer n, there are more than n Z*-sets of a; the Z*-sets of a are as numerous as the integers; certain relations (e.g., *having twice as many members as*) set up a one-to-one correlation between proper subsets of the set of Z*-sets of a (e.g., the set of Z*-sets whose members are multiples of 4) and the set of Z*-sets itself. There are infinitely many Z*-sets of a. But the number of elements in any

Z*-set is finite: for any Z*-set S, there is a natural number k such that there are just k members of S.

It does not follow that no set of parts of a has infinitely many members; indeed, the fact that there are infinitely many Z*-sets of a suggests a way of constructing just such a set. A super-Z-set of $a \{x_1, x_2, \ldots\}$ takes x_1 from the first Z*-set of a; x_2 from the second Z*-set of a, where x_2 has no part in common with x_1; x_3 from the third Z*-set, having no part in common either with x_1 or with x_2; and so on. Clearly, super-Z-sets will have infinitely many members, since each super-Z-set of a has as many members as there are Z*-sets of a. Equally clearly, super-Z-sets are not Z*-sets; for the members of a super-Z-set are not all equal in magnitude. On the contrary, the magnitudes of members of any super-Z-set form a convergent series: $1/2, 1/4, 1/8 \ldots$ Thus if Zeno were to retreat from Z*-sets to super-Z-sets the traditional arithmetical objection would hold: the sum of the magnitudes of the elements of a super-Z-set is not infinite.

But if Zeno remains with ordinary Z*-sets, his paradox disappears. What follows from his argument about the magnitude of a? Nothing of any interest. By (7) and the principle that if m and n are finite, $m + n$ is finite, we can infer that mag: a is finite. If the Z*-sets are the products of dichotomy, then the magnitude of an element of the nth Z*-set of a will be equal to mag: $a/2^n$. Since the nth Z*-set of a has 2^n members, we may conclude, by (7*), that mag: $a = 2^n \frac{\text{mag: } a}{2^n}$ And that is an unexciting conclusion to Zeno's *logos*.

(f) *The totality of things*

I turn now to the *logos* of 'finite and infinite', which is contained in sentence [ix] of **175**. The *logos* concludes to the following antinomy:

(Z3) (a) If P, then there are finitely many existents, and (b) if P, then there are infinitely many existents.

The argument for (Z3a) is short: 'it is necessary that they be as many as they are . . . But if they are as many as they are, they will be limited'. I paraphrase: 'If there are many As, then there is some true proposition of the form: "There are as many As as Bs". Hence there is an answer to the question: "How many As are there?" Hence there is some true proposition of the form "There are n As", where n is a natural number.'

The argument has been called 'beautiful in its simplicity',[31] but it is merely *simpliste*. Zeno's final move supposes that a set S is finite if there is a set S' such that every member of S can be paired uniquely with a member of S' and vice versa; in other words, if we can set up a one-to-one correlation between S and S'. But as we have seen, that is not so: the set of even integers can be correlated one-to-one with the set of integers, though both sets are infinite. Zeno's argument is at once destroyed. Indeed, I find the 'proof' an uninstructive sophism.

The argument for (Z3b) is puzzling: 'There are always other things in the middle of the things that exist (*metaxu tôn ontôn*)'. Zeno is usually taken to mean that *between* any two existents there is always a third. And if Simplicius is reporting Zeno in unabbreviated form, that assertion stood bare of argument. Now between any two points on a line, there is indeed a third; and some scholars take Zeno to be speaking of geometrical points, and thus give his argument a happy gloss. Unfortunately, Zeno's text does not encourage that interpretation. Others suppose the following train of reasoning: 'If a and b were contiguous, they would be one object, not two. Hence they must be separated; and since, by Eleatic argument, there cannot be an empty space between them, they must be separated by a third object.' According to Aristotle, the Pythagoreans said that 'the void divides nature, the void being a sort of separation and dividing of contiguous things' (*Phys* 213b22–7 = **58 B 30**). Perhaps Zeno was implicitly rejecting their view? But that interpretation too requires us to read a great deal into a very plain text.

Perhaps '*metaxu tôn ontôn*' means not 'between the things that exist' but rather 'in the middle of any existent'. Then 'there are always other things *metaxu tôn ontôn*' means:

(1) For any x, if x exists there exists something distinct from and in the middle of x.

Now Zeno might surely have argued for (1) by appealing to an argument entirely analogous to that in **B 1**: if a exists, then a has some positive magnitude; and if a has a positive magnitude, then a is divisible into three parts, two 'outside' parts and a 'middle'. Simplicius, I think, took Zeno's argument in this way; at least, I can think of no other reason why he should have thought that the argument used the 'dichotomy'. The interpretation is linguistically permissible; and it gives Zeno the conclusion he requires without calling upon any extraneous Eleatic attitudes. Philosophically, of course, this reading of the *logos* of finite and infinite supplies no food for thought that has not already been digested in considering **B 1**.

(g) *One and many*

The fourth *logos* is the 'one and many'. Plato mentions it, and we have no reason to doubt that Zeno argued for:

(Z4) (a) If P, then everything is one, and (b) if P, then everything is many.

Zeno's own words have not survived; nor has any explicit doxographical account of the *logos*. But we can, I think, reconstruct at least part of Zeno's argument on the basis of some remarks of Simplicius and Philoponus.[32] The remarks go back to Eudemus, who gives the closest approximation to (Z4) that we possess:

> Zeno, the friend of Parmenides, tried to prove that it is not possible for what exists to be many because [i] nothing among the things that exist is one, and [ii] the many are a quantity of ones (*plêthos henadôn*)[33] (**178**: fr. 37aW = **A 21**).

Here [i], I take it, derives from (Z4b), [ii] from (Z4a).[34]

For (Z4b) we may again call upon Eudemus. Having retailed the anecdote of Zeno and the One (above, p. 235), he continues:

> He was puzzled, as it seems, by the fact that each of the perceptible things is called many both by way of predication (*katêgorikôs*)[35] and by partition, while the point cannot even be posited as one (for what neither increases when added nor diminishes when subtracted he thought not to be an existent).... But if points are of that character, and each of us is said to be many things (e.g., white, musical, etc.) and similarly with a stone (for each one can be infinitely split), how will there be any one? (**179**: fr. 37aW = Simplicius, *in Phys* 97.13–21; cf. **A 21**).

Eudemus' argument runs as follows: 'If there are many things, each is either [a] a perceptible object or [b] a point. If [b], then the object has no existence, and *a fortiori* is not "one" thing. If [a] then [i] the object is infinitely divisible and so is "many" not one; and [ii] the object, having many predicates true of it, is "many" not one.'

Eudemus' reconstruction is his own: he is not pretending to report an argument of Zeno's, but to discover why he should have been puzzled by 'the One'. But Eudemus bases himself firmly on Zenonian soil: [b] comes from **B 2**, and [a] [i] repeats the familiar move of **B 1**. [a] [ii] is a novelty to us; but I think we are entitled to trust Eudemus and to regard it too as Zenonian; and I suppose that it constituted Zeno's argument for (Z4b).[36]

The argument rests on the truism that everything has more than one property: Socrates is both pale and snub-nosed; Socrates possesses the property of pallor and also the distinct property of snub-nosedness. In general:

(1) $(\forall x)(\exists P)(\exists Q)(P$ is distinct from Q, and x has P, and x has $Q)$.

How did Zeno infer from (1) that 'everything is many'?

Most of the commentators suppose that he indulged in a naive and archaic confusion: muddling together predication and identity, Zeno managed to construe 'Socrates has pallor' as though it were 'Socrates is pallor'; and he thus read (1) as though it were:

(2) $(\forall x) (\exists P) (\exists Q) (P$ is distinct from Q, and $x = P$ and $x = Q)$.

Given (2) we can see how 'everything is many'; for everything is identical with at least two distinct things.

The confusion which encourages us to move from (1) to (2) was not unknown to the Greeks. According to Aristotle, in order to avoid the paradox of 'one and many' 'some did away with "is"' (e.g., Lycophron), and others emended the language, saying that the man (not is pale but) has paled, and (not is walking but) walks' (*Phys* 185b27–30 = **83 A 2**). Aristotle reports a diagnosis and a prophylactic. The diagnosis has it that our confusion between identity and predication is brought about by the word 'is': if we take 'Socrates is the Chairman' to assert an identity between Socrates and the Chairman, we may be seduced into taking 'Socrates is pale' to assert an identity between Socrates and pallor. The prophylactic is simple: abolish 'is'; instead of 'Socrates is pale' write 'Socrates pale' or 'Socrates has paled'.

The 'paradox' which worried Lycophron and the others seems trifling to us; but it clearly seemed serious to Zeno's contemporaries, and we may well imagine that (Z4b) trades upon it. (Note that Eudemus reported Zeno's argument in his *Physics*: Eudemus' *Physics* corresponds closely to Aristotle's, and the Eudemian fragment happens to answer to *Phys* 185b27–30.) For all that, I am not entirely happy in ascribing (2) to Zeno: (2) is contradictory in itself (for if $x = P$ and $x = Q$, then $P = Q$), and therefore not an ideal component in an antinomy. At all events, it is worth casting about for an alternative interpretation.

Let us return to Eudemus. According to him, 'Plato thought that "is" [sc. in "Socrates is pale"] does not signify what it does in the case of man, but that just as "is thoughtful" signifies to think and "is seated" to sit, so it is in the other cases too, even if there are no ready-made names for them' (fr. 37aW = Simplicius, *in Phys* 97.25–8). Plato's answer to a puzzle of predication distinguished, in effect, between the 'is' of essential and the 'is' of accidental predication. If that answer was appropriate, then it suggests a paradox about essence, rather than one about identity: '[a] Each thing is just one thing, i.e., has a unique essence. [b] If a has P, then having P is what a is; i.e., is the essence of a. Hence, by (1), each thing has more than one essence or is many.' If that Platonic puzzle seems anachronistic, let me double the offence by advertising to a peculiarly Aristotelian concern: the unity of definition. Thus: '[a] Each thing is a unity. [b] If a has P and Q, and having P does not involve having Q, nor vice versa, then a is a diversity; hence by (1), a is a diversity or "many".'[37]

These three diagnoses of Zeno's problem, the traditional one, the Platonic, the Aristotelian, are all unsatisfactory in one way or another; and it may be that no precise interpretation is possible. In his paradox of 'one and many', Zeno raised, in a vague and indeterminate fashion, several issues that were to excite and perplex his successors; he himself merely saw, or imagined, a conflict between 'being one' and 'being many', which properties all objects surely possess. It was left to Zeno's successors to distinguish particular knots in that tangled skein, and to pose plain puzzles to the adherents of pluralism. But note, again, that pluralism is not peculiarly vulnerable to this antinomy: Zeno's arguments, however they are elucidated, work whether a is a member of a numerous plurality or the sole inhabitant of the world: the 'one and many' is an antinomy of being, not a paradox of plurality.

(h) *The paradox of place*

I shall end the chapter by looking at two minor arguments which seem only loosely connected with the main theme of Zeno's *logoi*. These arguments are the paradox of place, and the paradox of the millet seed.

The paradox of place is twice adverted to by Aristotle (*Phys* 209a23; 210b22 = **A 24** = **13-14 L**), and it is discussed by Aristotle's commentators. Zeno's actual words do not survive; but an argument in Simplicius (*in Phys* 563.1–33) persuades me that the closest approximation to authenticity is achieved by Philoponus:

> For if everything that exists is somewhere, he used to say, and place too is something, then place too will be somewhere. Hence place will be in a place; and so *ad infinitum* (**180**: Philoponus, *in Phys* 510.4–6 = **16 L**; cf. Simplicius, *in Phys* 534.6–15).[38]

Zeno's immediate conclusion was, presumably, that there is no such thing as place. Conceivably, he then inferred that existent things are not in any place, and aimed to construct an antinomy:
(Z5) (a) If P, then everything is somewhere; and (b) if P, then everything is nowhere.
Here (Z5b) is the ultimate conclusion of the paradox of place; and

(Z5a) will have been inferred along the lines of **B 2**: if *a* exists, it has magnitude; if it has magnitude, it is spatially extended; hence it is 'somewhere'.[39] (Note again that in (Z5) the pluralist hypothesis is idle.)

The kernel of Zeno's argument is his assertion that everything that exists is 'somewhere' or occupies some place:

(1) If *a* exists, then for some *x* *a* occupies *x*.

The second premiss, that 'place too is something', may be construed as:

(2) If *a* occupies *b*, then *b* exists.

From (1) and (2) Zeno hopes to generate an infinite regress of places. Let us make the innocuous assumption that the relation of *occupation* is irreflexive, asymmetrical, and transitive; i.e., that:

(3) Nothing occupies itself.
(4) If *a* occupies *b*, *b* does not occupy *a*.
(5) If *a* occupies *b* and *b* occupies *c*, then *a* occupies *c*.

Now it is easy to prove from (1)—(5) that any existent body occupies infinitely many distinct places:

(6) If *a* exists, then for any *n* there are more than *n* distinct places occupied by *a*.

According to Zeno, (6) is absurd; hence (Z5b).

Is (6) absurd? Well, how can places be distinct other than by having distinct boundaries? And how can one and the same object, *a*, have more than one set of boundaries?

If (6) is unacceptable, does Zeno's argument for it fail? The ancient critics attack (1). According to Aristotle, the term 'occupy' is ambiguous: everything must indeed be 'in' something, but not all ways of being 'in' a thing are cases of occupying a *place*. Heat, say, is 'in' a body; but the body is a substrate, not a place, for heat (*Phys* 210b22–30). Thus (1) does not state any one truth because it does not state any one thing at all; and if it is made explicit that occupation in (1) is a matter of being in a place, then (1) is false, as Eudemus says: 'now if [Zeno] assumes that what exists is in a place, his assumption is incorrect; for neither health nor courage nor ten thousand other things would be said to be in a place' (fr. 78 W = **A 24**).[40]

I am, I confess, inclined to side with Zeno here, and to support some version of (1): if existents need not occupy places, then they exist in so far as they are related to some place holder, and they exist only in a derivative sense. But it is unnecessary to develop that line of thought here; for (1) is easily repaired against the Aristotelian attack. Zeno need only restrict *a* and *b* in (1) and (2) to things of a sort capable of being located in space; for surely anything that *can* occupy a place exists only so long as it actually *does* occupy a place. Premiss

(1) then asserts, uncontroversially, that any potential occupant of space does, if it exists, actually occupy a place.

Premiss (1) is true. Is (2) false? If (2) is true, then places are themselves capable of being located. It might be said that an object a occupies a place p if and only if the co-ordinates defining p determine the surfaces of a; and since places do not have surfaces, they are not locatable in space. But that is pedantry; why should we not say that a place p occupies a place p' if and only if the co-ordinates of p' determine the co-ordinates of p? In general, a occupies b if and only if the determining co-ordinates of a are the same as those of b. Necessarily, places have places: (2) is necessarily true. But the truth of (2) is bought at a price. For on that account of occupation, (3) and (4) are both false: occupation is neither irreflexive nor asymmetrical; for places are their own locations. As Newton put it: 'Times and spaces are, as it were, the places as well of themselves as of all other things'.

I do not insist on the Newtonian answer; for nothing, I think, hangs upon it. Some will accept Zeno's (1) and (2), rejecting (3) and (4). Others may prefer a weaker notion of existence, and deny (1); yet others will contrive reasonable grounds for rejecting (2). Zeno's argument certainly fails: it is interesting to observe that it fails even if we grant Zeno both of his explicit premisses.

(i) *The millet seed*

The paradox of the millet seed is reported by Simplicius:

> In this way [Aristotle] solves the problem which Zeno the Eleatic set for Protagoras the Sophist. 'Tell me, Protagoras,' he said, 'does a single millet seed make a sound when it falls? Or the ten thousandth part of a seed?' Protagoras said that it didn't. 'What about a bushel of millet seed', he said, 'does that make a sound when it falls, or not?' He said that the bushel did make a sound. 'Well', said Zeno, 'isn't there a ratio between the bushel and the single seed, or the ten-thousandth part of a single seed?' He agreed. 'Well then,' said Zeno, 'won't the sounds too stand in the same ratios to one another? For as the sounders are, so are the sounds. And if that's so, then if the bushel makes a sound, the single seed and the ten-thousandth part of a seed will make a sound too' (**181: A 29 = 38 L**).

Simplicius is reporting a later dramatization of the paradox; but Aristotle's testimony ensures that the argument itself is genuinely Zenonian (*Phys* 250a19 = **A 29 = 37 L**).

The argument is sometimes supposed to be an attack on

sense-perception: reason proves the millet seed to make a sound, even though our ears detect none. Archytas later asserted, conceivably with Zeno's millet seed in mind, that 'many sounds are not apprehensible by creatures of our nature, some because of the weakness of the blow [which produces them], others . . .' (47 **B** 1). The millet seed might, I suppose, illustrate a problem in the philosophy of perception; yet interest in such problems is not Eleatic. Nor will the millet seed argue for an Eleatic scepticism: at most it might persuade us of the uncontroversial fact that many things elude our perception even though they are intrinsically perceptible.

Imagine that one of Zeno's forty *logoi* aimed to prove:

(Z6) (a) If P, then each existent makes a sound, and (b) if P, then each existent is mute.

The millet seed argues for (Z6a); and we might easily concoct an inverted version of the same argument to support (Z6b). The suggestion is purely speculative and not worth developing; but the millet seed itself warrants another page.

The Megarian philosophers of the early fourth century, who are often spoken of as the successors to the Eleatic school, invented a series of logical puzzles. Two of them, the heap (*sôreitês*) and the bald man (*phalakros*) are near cousins to the millet seed. One grain of sand is not a heap, and the addition of one grain cannot turn what is not a heap into a heap; a man with a full head of hair is not bald, and the extraction of a single hair cannot make what is not bald bald: hence there are no heaps, and no bald men. The puzzles are jocular but the point they make is serious. They seem to provide counter-examples to the powerful logical tool of mathematical induction. The general formula for such an induction is this: Take an ordered sequence $\langle a_1, a_2, \ldots, a_n, \ldots \rangle$; if a_1, is F, and if, if a_n is F then a_{n+1} is F, then every a_i is F. The millet seed and the Megarian puzzles can be formulated as mathematical inductions: the as are bags of millet seed, each a_i containing exactly i seeds; and for 'F' read 'makes no audible sound on falling to the ground'. The conclusion, that every a_i is F, states the absurdity that no amount of millet seed makes a noise on falling.

It is often said that puzzles of this sort essentially use 'vague' concepts; and the moral is drawn that precise logical manoeuvres, such as mathematical induction, do not work for vague concepts. We might accept that and still worry about the Megarian puzzles: first, have they not shown a decisive logical flaw in such common notions as those of 'a heap' and of 'baldness'? And second, how are we to define the conditions a concept must satisfy if it is to be amenable to precise logical deployment?

Consideration of the millet seed thus opens some fairly large questions about the connexion between formal logic and ordinary language. Yet I am not sure that Zeno's paradox depends for its solution on an answer to those questions. After all, the predicate 'makes an audible sound' is not particularly vague: either I can hear the seed or I cannot; there is no halfway house between hearing and not hearing, in the way in which there seems to be between being bald and not being bald. Aristotle offers an answer to Zeno which in no way turns on the notion of vagueness: in effect, he challenges Zeno's implicit claim that if a_n makes no sound, then a_{n+1} makes no sound (cf. *Phys* 250a9–28). There is, for each of us, a threshold of audibility: the addition of a single seed to a parcel of millet may indeed make all the difference between audibility and inaudibility—even though that seed, falling alone, is not audible. Zeno, according to Aristotle, supposes that if n grains make a sound of volume V, that can only be because each grain makes a sound of volume V/n. And that assumption, which is not a logical but an empirical proposition, is false. Aristotle's diagnosis of Zeno's error, and his answer to Zeno's puzzle, seem to me to be correct.

XIII

Zeno: Paradox and Progression

(a) *Sprightly running*

Zeno's four arguments against motion are known to us from Aristotle's discussion of them in *Physics* Z. The Greek commentators on Aristotle for once fail us: they do not reproduce any of Zeno's own words, and with one trivial exception they provide us with no information we cannot glean from Aristotle's text. The paradoxes were famous in antiquity, and they influenced philosophers other than Aristotle: it is odd, as well as unfortunate, that our knowledge of them is virtually confined to the brief and polemical reports in the *Physics*.[1]

Z 9 contains Aristotle's main discussion: the section begins thus:

> There are four arguments of Zeno's about motion which provide difficulties for their solvers—first, the one about a thing's not moving because what is travelling must arrive at the half-way point before the end (we have discussed this earlier) . . . (**182**: *Phys* 239b9–14 = **A 25** = **19 L**).

I shall refer to this first paradox as the Dichotomy; it is also called the Stadium, but I reserve that title for the fourth paradox.[2]

Aristotle's earlier discussion of the Dichotomy appears in Z 2:

> That is why Zeno's argument assumes a falsehood—that one cannot pass through an unlimited number of things or touch an unlimited number of things individually in a limited time. For both length and time—and, in general, whatever is continuous—are called unlimited in two ways: either by division or as to their extremes. Now one cannot touch things unlimited in respect of quantity in a limited time, but one can so touch things

unlimited by division—for the time itself is unlimited in this way. Hence it is in an unlimited and not in a limited time that, as it turns out, one traverses the unlimited, and one touches the unlimited things in unlimited and not in limited times (**183**: *Phys* 233a21–31 = A 25 = 19 L).

From this critical appraisal, and the half-line of description in Z 9, we must reconstruct the Dichotomy.

Suppose that in a finite period of time T, a body b traverses a finite distance AB. Then at some instant within T b will 'touch' a_1, the mid-point of AB; and at some later instant, again with T, b will 'touch' a_2, the mid-point between a_1 and B; and so on: in general, for any a_i there is a point a_j, mid-way between a_i and B, which b will 'touch' at some instant within T. Thus within T b will 'touch' infinitely many points along AB; but that is impossible: hence b cannot traverse AB in T. And, in general, locomotion is impossible.

The exposition requires three preliminary comments. First, it interprets the Dichotomy in terms of a division which may be drawn thus:

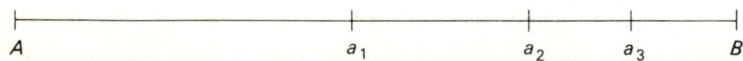

Aristotle's commentators prefer a different diagram:

Thus: 'Before reaching B, b must touch the midpoint a_1 of AB; and before reaching a_1, b must "touch" the midpoint a_2 of Aa_1 . . .'. Aristotle, I think, had the first diagram in mind;[3] and I rest on his authority. But it is to be observed that there is no interesting logical difference between the two ways of expounding the paradox. Many commentators suppose that, with the first diagram, Zeno attempts to show that no moving body can ever *complete* its journey: it can never take the last step to B, since there *is* no last step. With the second diagram, they say, Zeno shows, more strikingly, that no body can ever *start* its journey: it can never take its first step, since there *is* no first step to take. But that distinction is unimportant: with either diagram, Zeno means to show that no body can transverse a finite distance in a finite time—in other words, that no body can move. The first diagram does not allow travellers to begin but not end their journeys; for every journey begun is *eo ipso* a journey ended.

Second, we may wonder what is meant by 'touch' (*haptesthai*) in Aristotle's exposition, and why Zeno should think that moving bodies must 'touch' points in their travel. Some sources compare 'touching' to counting: b, they say, can no more 'touch' each a_i inside AB than he can count each a_i as he passes it; and some scholars have supposed that Zeno's original traveller went on a mental rather than a physical journey: b cannot run through AB in his mind, for he cannot, so to speak, give his mind in turn to each of the points in AB. 'Touching', on this view, is a sort of mental stopping: the physical runner 'touches' a_i in so far as, on passing a_i, he stops mentally and says to himself: 'This is a_i'.[4]

That interpretation is surely not Zenonian: Aristotle explicitly distinguishes between Zeno's paradox and the argument which requires the traveller to count the halfway points on his journey (*Phys* 263a6–11); and it is clear that the counting version was a vulgarization of Zeno's argument. 'Touching' in Zeno is what it sounds like: physical contact. Let us idealize the example: suppose b to be a perfect cube travelling along the straight path AB; and represent each a_i by a line across AB parallel to the front edge of b. Then b touches a_i if and only if a_i lies on the same plane as the front surface of b. Clearly, then, if b is to traverse AB, it must, in this sense, touch successively every a_i inside AB.

Third, we must be on our guard against the wiles of infinitude: in the paradox of 'large and small' Zeno falsely claimed an infinite regress; here does Zeno really show that b has infinitely many a_is to touch? It is easy to show that he does: the successive a_is are constructed by dichotomy; if $AB = 1$, then $Aa_1 = \frac{1}{2}$, $a_1a_2 = \frac{1}{4}$, $a_1a_3 = \frac{1}{8}$, and in general $a_n a_{n+1} = \frac{1}{2^n + 1}$. Thus the a_is can be put in one-one correspondence with the powers of 2; hence they can be put in one-one correspondence with the natural numbers, and they are infinitely numerous.

Were he to travel from A to B, b would perform infinitely many tasks: there are infinitely many a_is between A and B, each of which b must touch; there are infinitely many distinct propositions of the form 'b touches a_i', and if b reaches B every one of these propositions has been made true. Thus Zeno thinks to establish:
(1) If anything moves, it performs infinitely many tasks.
Since he holds it to be a truism that:
(2) Nothing can perform infinitely many tasks,
he concludes that nothing moves. Unless we are to follow Zeno into his immobile world, we must reject either (1) or (2). Philosophical controversy has settled about (2); but I shall begin my discussion with a few thoughts on (1).

Some philosophers reject (1): in running from A to B, they say, b

does not have to undertake, successively, infinitely many tasks; his run from A to B is not composed of an infinite sequence of progressively shorter runs. He performs one run, takes a hundred strides, feels fifty heart-beats, and so on; but he does not do or undergo an infinity of anything.

As an exercise in pure pedantry there is something to be said for that objection; for it is indeed mildly odd to call each of b's successive moves to the next a_i a 'run' or a 'task'. Yet the point is merely verbal: Zeno himself does not use the terminology; and if b need not perform infinitely many tasks, that does not show that he has not got infinitely many a_is to touch, infinitely many points to pass, infinitely many subsections of AB to traverse. The claim that b's operations are not 'tasks', or are only 'tasks' in a Pickwickian sense, is boring.[5]

Proponents of the boring claim sometimes mean to deny (1) outright; but sometimes they offer a slightly subtler suggestion: b's move from A to B, they suggest, is a *single* run, a *century* of paces, *half a century* of heart-beats, etc. To get from A to B requires the performance of many *finite* sets of tasks. Now, they continue, we can *describe* b's journey in terms of an infinite succession of tasks; but that does not show (1) to be true: the performances required of a locomotor can indeed be described in terms of infinity, but for all that they are finite performances.

I set down this view because I have frequently heard it; but I dismiss it shortly: if any piece of locomotion can be truly described as the successive performance of an infinity of operations, then (1) is true. There are no two ways about it: either the description does not apply, or else it does apply and (1) is true; you cannot allow the description and brush aside the infinity it imports.

A more interesting objection to (1) can be formulated: (1) is true only if space is continuous or infinitely divisible; for it rests upon the assumption that any stretch of space, AB, contains infinitely many spatial points, a_i. That assumption, which I adverted to in the previous chapter (above, pp. 245–6), is not examined in our ancient texts; and those philosophers who do examine it usually accept it on insufficient grounds, tacitly supposing that a continuous geometry is applicable to physical space (and to time). Any full-scale examination of Zeno's paradoxes would be obliged to discuss the geometry of space: for reasons I gave earlier, I shall not enter upon such a discussion here.

(b) *Infinity again*

There have been numerous and diverse attempts to deal with premiss (2); the most convenient approach begins by asking wherein the impossibility of infinite performances is judged to lie: what is it about infinite performance in general, or the infinite performance of b in particular, that involves an impossibility? I shall mention seven lines of argument.

First: 'b cannot run through infinitely many points; for that would mean that he traversed an infinite distance'. Many philosophers have faulted Zeno in the Dichotomy, as in the *logos* of 'large and small', for bad arithmetic.[6]. Let AB measure 1 mile; then in order to reach B, b must traverse $1/2 + 1/4 + 1/8 + 1/16 + \ldots$ miles. Now the sum of that series does not exceed 1 mile; but Zeno, it is alleged, supposed it to be infinitely great, and for that reason upheld (2).

If that was Zeno's reason for asserting (2), it was a tediously bad reason. And I am not confident that Zeno can be excused: if in the *logos* of 'large and small' he supposed the sum of $1/2 + 1/4 + 1/8 + \ldots$ to be infinitely great, then he may well have made the same supposition in the Dichotomy. But whatever Zeno may have argued, others have found (2) plausible despite a degree of mathematical expertise; and we cannot dismiss the Dichotomy on the grounds that Zeno misreasoned for (2).

Aristotle's criticism of the Dichotomy in *Physics* Z 2 suggests a second way of defending (2): 'Locomotion must take a finite period of time: b gets from A to B in T; but in order to touch infinitely many a_is, b requires an infinite span of time.' Thus (2) is true because we are all hemmed in by the finitude of our lives.

Aristotle's reply is apt: just as AB, though finite in extent, contains infinitely many points, a_i; so T, though finite in duration, contains infinitely many instants, t_i. Each a_i in AB can be uniquely paired with a t_i in T. Similarly, every spatial sub-interval $a_i a_j$ of AB can be uniquely paired with a temporal sub-interval $t_i t_j$ of T. If space is infinitely divisible, so too is time; and thus in his run from A to B, b will never be short of time; there are as many instants available for touchings as there are points to be touched.

Aristotle assumes that time, like space, is continuous. And Zeno might be defended by denying that assumption: space is continuous, but time is not; unlike space, time consists of a succession of discrete *minima*. Time is granular, space is smooth: the parallelism between the two dimensions is broken, and with it Aristotle's objection. One of Aristotle's successors, Strato of Lampsacus, apparently held this view; and it has its modern supporters. I content myself with asserting that it is based on a bad lot of arguments, and that its acceptance involves a host of difficulties.[7]

In any event, that strange view is not the only way of defending Zeno: the second defence of (2) fails; but (2) does not fall with it: (2)

has been upheld by men who are convinced of the continuous nature of time. Aristotle himself came to see that:

> But this solution [sc. that of Z 2] is adequate with regard to the questioner (for he asked whether one could traverse or count unlimited things in a limited time), but it is not adequate with regard to the facts and the truth; for if someone were to forget about the length and about asking whether one can traverse unlimited things in a limited time, and were to make this enquiry of the time itself (for the time has unlimited divisions), this solution is no longer adequate (**184**: *Phys* 263a15–22).

The observation that time as well as space is infinitely divisible only raises the further question of how we can endure through a finite stretch of time, if every such stretch contains limitless parts. Instead of one infinity to traverse, we have two: if AB is impenetrable, T is unendurable.

Aristotle is right: no Zenonian will be greatly moved by the solution of *Physics* Z 2. Aristotle himself suggests that we ignore AB and consider progress through T by itself; Zeno, I suspect, would have preferred to consider AB alone, without reference to T. Indeed, I am inclined to think that the reference to a finite time T did not occur in Zeno's original paradox: Zeno considered it impossible to touch infinitely many points; the impossibility is contained in the infinity of points, and factors of time are impertinent. Time is not, and need not be, mentioned in (2).[8]

After recanting his remarks in *Physics* Z 2, Aristotle essays a second solution to the Dichotomy; and his second solution suggests a third reason for upholding (2). Thus: 'If b is to touch infinitely many a_is, then an infinity of points must actually exist on AB; but there cannot *actually* be infinitely many existent points in a finite space.' That argument for (2) is of little intrinsic interest; but Aristotle's second solution to the Dichotomy warrants a moment's attention.

Here is the text:

> Hence we must say when asked if it is possible to traverse unlimited things—either in time or in distance—that in a way it is, and in a way it isn't: if they exist actually, it is not possible; if potentially, it is. For someone moving continuously traverses unlimited things incidentally, not absolutely; for it is incidental to the line to be unlimitedly many halves, but its essence and its being are different (**185**: *Phys* 263b3–9).

That is an obscure paragraph. I take Aristotle to mean that b may touch infinitely many a_is provided that the a_is do not all actually exist. Thus (2) would be true if touching a_i involved the actual existence of a_i; but in fact, the a_is need only exist potentially, and that they may do.

All that, I think, has little effect on any honest Zenonian: Aristotle simply asserts that b can touch the infinitely many a_is, provided that he touches them 'incidentally' and they exist 'potentially'. The Aristotelian jargon only partially disguises the fact that Aristotle is offering a denial of, and not an argument against, premiss (2).

But there is something of interest here: a sufficient condition for the 'actual' existence of a_i is b's stopping at a_i. According to Aristotle, b can touch the a_is as long as he does not stop at them, and hence actualize them. The keyword here is 'continuously (*sunechôs*)': b is safe, Aristotle opines, if he runs smoothly, leaving the infinite a_is in their state of innocent potentiality. Tolstoy agreed: referring to the Achilles, which raises the same puzzle as the Dichotomy, he wrote: 'The ancients regarded this as an unanswerable dilemma; its absurdity lies in the fact that the progress of Achilles is calculated on units with stoppage between, while it is in fact continuous' (*War and Peace*, bk 12, ch. XXII).

Consider a runner c who, like b, is set to traverse AB. c is allowed $2T$ for his performance; and he determines to produce a staccato run. Thus in $\frac{1}{2}T$ he runs from A to a_1; then he rests for $\frac{1}{2}T$ at a_1. In the next $\frac{1}{4}T$ he runs to a_2, and then rests for $\frac{1}{4}T$ at a_2. In general, he takes, like b, $T/2^n$ to traverse the interval $a_{n-1} a_n$; but, unlike b, he rests for $T/2^n$ at each a_n.

Aristotle will allow b to reach B, but will deny c his goal; for c's rest periods involve the impossible actualization of the infinitely numerous a_is. And, of course, though we meet b every day, we do not come across staccato runners like c. Much modern discussion of the Dichotomy has in fact focussed on staccato performances; and a central problem has been to determine the truth of (2) if the performances are discrete or staccato in the way in which c's is. We might, I think, intelligibly uphold (2) for c while rejecting it for b. Yet if that view seems reasonable, we have as yet no reason for accepting it. Aristotle's talk about actualized points is unconvincing; and no other argument yet allows us to distinguish between b and c in respect of (2). 'Intuition'—the kind name for untutored prejudice—favours b's chances above c's; but intuition is a fool's guide in this as in every other branch of philosophy.

Aristotle's double discussion of the Dichotomy is meritorious but not conclusive; and I turn now to the fourth of the seven reasons for maintaining premiss (2). It is comfortably simple: 'Infinite sequences of tasks have, by definition, no last member; and it is, trivially, impossible to complete a series of operations none of which is the last operation.'

Both premisses in this argument are false. The sequence actually employed in the Dichotomy does indeed lack a last member; but Zeno could easily have provided a sequence with both a last and a first member, as the following diagram shows:

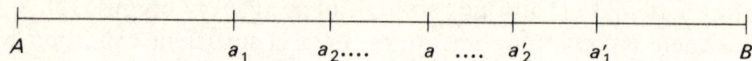

If b is to traverse AB, he must touch each of the infinitely many points $a_1, a_2, \ldots, a, \ldots a'_2, a'_1$. His first step is from A to a_1; his last is from a'_1 to B.

As for the second premiss, it owes the little plausibility it has to an equivocation: you might, I suppose, say that the 'completion' of a series of tasks is simply the performance of the last member of the series; I complete the crossword in entering the last light, I complete the book in writing the ultimate sentence. And in *that* sense of 'complete' (if it is really a sense at all), sequences with no last member cannot be completed. But the obvious sense of 'complete' does not yield that consequence: if S is the set of tasks $\{x_1, x_2, \ldots x_n, \ldots\}$, then b has completed S if and only if b has performed every x_i. To complete a set of tasks is to perform all the tasks, not to perform a *last* task. From 'b has performed every x_i' we cannot infer 'b performed one x_i after all the other x_is': even if S is finite, it need contain no last member; b may perform two, or three, or all of the x_is at the same time.

That simple reflexion may still some disquiet about the propriety of speaking of 'completing' an infinite sequence of operations; but it will leave some readers unsatisfied. Surely, they will feel, even if you do not need to perform a *last* task in S in order to complete your performance, yet you cannot *complete* S without coming to an end of your tasks; and your tasks, being infinite, have no end. Thus (2) is true; and its truth follows from the nature of completion: infinite tasks cannot, logically, be completed.

But that, too, is a bad argument; and it, too, trades on an equivocation. Someone who said 'b cannot come to an end of his tasks' might mean:

(3) $(\forall t)(\forall n)$ (if at t b has performed exactly n x_is, then there is an x_j that b has not performed by t).

He might, alternatively, mean:

(4) $(\forall t)(\exists j)$ (b has not by t performed x_j).

Now Zeno's premiss (2) is equivalent to (4); and if S is infinite it is

easy to demonstrate the truth of (3). But (3) and (4) are not equivalent; nor does (3) entail (4). By adding a further premiss:
(5) $(\forall t)\, (\exists n$ (by t b has performed exactly n x_is)
it is possible to deduce (4) from (3); but to assert (5) is precisely to deny that b can perform an infinite number of tasks—and that is the very proposition at issue. In short, to say that you can never get to the end of an infinite sequence either crudely reasserts that you cannot perform infinitely many tasks, or else observes (truly but irrelevantly) that whatever finite number of tasks you have performed more yet remain; neither assertion has any tendency to prove the truth of (2).

The next reason for supporting (2) turns on the notion of progress: 'If I perform a sequence of tasks, my performance is marked by a certain type of progress. I gradually tick off the tasks to be done, reducing their number until eventually all are finished and behind me. But if S is infinite, I can make no progress of that sort; for however many x_is I have performed, I still have exactly as many x_is left to perform: however many a_is b has touched, he still has exactly as many a_is left to touch. Performance depends on progress; infinitude mocks progress: (2), then, is true.'

The second premiss of this argument is true: if b has touched n a_is, he still has infinitely many a_is to go. In general, if S has infinitely many members, and S' is a finite subset of S, then $S-S'$ has as many members as S. (The series $\langle n, n+1, n+2, \ldots \rangle$, where n is any natural number, can be put in one-one correspondence with the natural numbers.)

What of the first premiss? I confess I see little force in it. It decrees that progress in the performance of a sequence of tasks must consist in the performance of a successively larger fraction of those tasks. If that decree is accepted, then many performances will exhibit no progress. If I design to break every window in the quadrangle, I need not throw successive stones and do my job piecemeal; a single bomb, suitably placed, will blow in all the windows at once. And in any case, it is unnecessary to accept the decree. I may surely make progress in my plan to defenestrate the quadrangle, even if the actual blowing in of the windows occurs all at an instant: my progress might well be measured by the length of time still to elapse before my object is attained. Similarly, we may say (if we wish) that b is progressing in his task of touching all the a_is, on the grounds that the time at which his task will be completed is getting nearer. In short, performance does not evidently require progress; and the notion of progress is in any case readily accommodated to apply to the performance of infinite tasks.

The sixth consideration advanced in support of (2) is more complex and more interesting. It invites us to consider the state of affairs that would hold were an infinite series of tasks to be successfully performed. Imagine a reading-lamp with a push-button switch for turning it on and off. The lamp is always either on or off; if it is on, a push of the switch turns it off; if it is off, a similar depression illuminates it. Take the lamp and depress its switch infinitely many times (first at noon, say; then at 12.30; then at 12.45 . . .). Now consider its state after the switchings are completed, at 1.00 p.m. Disregard any technological or physical obstacles which you may have met with and ask simply whether the lamp is on or off at 1.00 p.m. It cannot be on; for every time you switched it on you immediately switched it off again. It cannot be off; for every time you switched it off you immediately switched it on again. So it is neither on nor off. But by hypothesis it is always either on or off. The supposition of infinite switchings thus leads to an overt contradiction: premiss (2)—in a particular case at least—is established.[9]

That ingenious argument raises many questions; I shall not consider them in their generality, but instead construct a parallel argument for the Zenonian runner, and consider the credentials of that. 'Zeno's runner, b, has to complete the infinite set of tasks consisting of touching a_1, touching a_2, ... Suppose that b manages to complete his tasks: where is he at the moment of completion? Not, alas, at B; for B is not a member of the set of a_is, and each task which b performs brings him to an a_i. Nor beyond B; for no a_i is situated beyond B. Nor, thirdly, is he short of B, between A and B; for suppose he is at C, between A and B; then there are a_is (infinitely many of them) between C and B, and he has not after all completed his tasks. But clearly, after the completion of the tasks b must be either at B or beyond B or short of B. Hence he cannot complete his tasks.'

The argument sounds plausible; but its conclusion is invalidly drawn. More formally stated, the argument puts up for *reductio* the hypothesis that b completes his infinite tasks at some time t; and it does indeed reduce that hypothesis to absurdity, by showing that there is no consistent description of b's state at t. Hence we may conclude that there is no time at which b completes S. But from that we cannot infer that b does not complete S: he may complete S without there being any time which is the time of his completion, the last instant of his performance.

That contention may sound paradoxical; but in fact it only applies to the completion of S a general truth about the completion of any task or set of tasks. This general truth, which has nothing to do with the problems of infinity, was first grasped by Aristotle.[10] Take any change; i.e., suppose that at t a changes from being ϕ to being non-ϕ, thus:

Consider the point of change, t. If t is the last point in a's ϕness and also the first point in a's non-ϕness, then a is ϕ at t and a is non-ϕ at t. But that is impossible. Hence, in general, there can be no point that is both the first point of a's non-ϕness and the last point of a's ϕness. Suppose, then, that t is the first point of a's non-ϕness. Suppose there is a point t' prior to t which is the last point of a's ϕness. Since time is continuous, there are points t_1, t_2, . . . between t' and t (in fact there are infinitely many such points). At t_1 a is not ϕ, for t_1 is later than t'; and at t_1 a is not non-ϕ, for t_1 is prior to t. But that is impossible. Hence, in general, if there is a first point of a's non-ϕness there is no last point of a's ϕness. An exactly analogous argument shows that if there is a last point of a's ϕness there is no first point of a's non-ϕness.

The application to Zeno is plain. There is a first point of b's having completed the tasks in S—viz. the point at which he touches B. Hence there is no last point at which he completes the tasks in S; i.e., there is no last instant of his performance. That is no paradox: it simply brings out a general feature of all change: change can occur without there being a last moment of the unchanged state.

Thus the illustration of the lamp does show something about the logic of infinity; but it does not show that (2) is true. And I turn to the seventh and final argument for (2). The situation in which a performer of infinitely many tasks finds himself can be represented as a progress along an asymptotic curve:

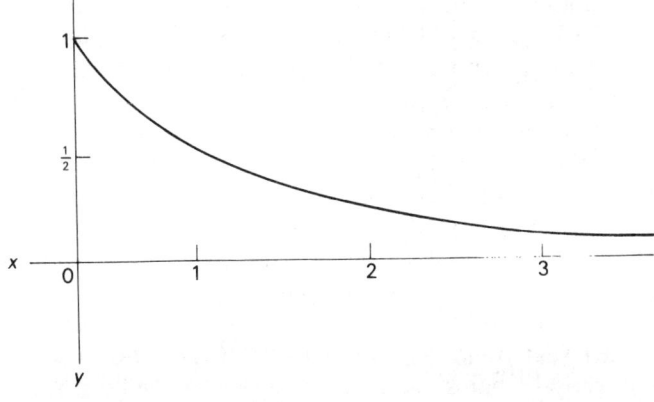

In the Zenonian case, the curve plots b's distance from B, the x-axis representing that distance, the y-axis marking off the a_is. The curve constantly approaches 0 but never reaches it. In general, progress *via* an infinite sequence of operations can be represented by an asymptotic line on a graph; and the discontinuity or gap between the line and the y-axis provides a puzzle; for it appears to mark a gap in the causal nexus of events. The runner's progress through the a_is is surely causally connected to his arrival at B; yet there is an unbridgeable gap between his arrival at the successive a_is and his arrival at B.

Thus, first, there is always a physical gap between b's position at the end of any run to an a_i and his goal. How can causation send its spark across that spatial chasm? Second, there is no event among the touchings of the a_is which may be linked to the arrival at B; for any causal chain would bind the arrival to the *last* touching, and there is no last touching. How can a causal chain hold firm when there is no link locked to its last link? Third, consider the period T during which b travels from A to B. There is no last instant of b's travelling, and hence no last instant in T. Let t be the first instant after T: given the details of b's progress we can say for any instant *within* T exactly where b will be: at t_i he will be at a_i. Yet we cannot in the same way predict where b will be at t. (Reconsider the lamp: the plan to switch it on at 12.30, off at 12.45, and so on enables us to predict the lamp's state at any time *between* 12.00 and 1.00; it does not license a prediction for 1.00.) How can a causal law cover that hole in the path of predictability?

Thus we have a seventh reason for upholding (2): 'If (2) were false, the great chains of causation would snap'.[11]

The argument deserves a longer presentation than I can give it here. I content myself with three summary observations. First, the argument does not show the truth of (2); at most it shows that (2) is true in a Laplacean world, where every event is causally determined by its predecessors; and no one has yet shown that our familiar world is Laplacean. Perhaps there are causal hiatuses; many philosophers and scientists hold that there are.

Second, the argument is stated too grossly. In the case of *some* infinite performances there seems no difficulty in formulating causal laws that 'bridge the gap'. The Zenonian runner provides such an example: given that he starts from A and proceeds at uniform speed through all the a_is, we can predict that he will be at B at a given time after his departure from A. The fact that the a_is are infinite and the distinct fact that no a_i is contiguous to B have no bearing on the question: causal 'chains'—a poor metaphor at the best of times—do not have to link events to their immediate neighbours; they can bind events together even if immediate neighbours are lacking.

Third, it is by no means clear that in *any* infinite performances there will or must be causal 'gaps'. Causal laws are empirical hypotheses; as far as I can see, nothing in the description of the infinite switchings of the lamp, or in any other infinite performance, rules out any causal hypothesis. Switch the lamp off at t_1, on at t_2; and so on. Is the state of the lamp at t predictable? Is it causally determined by its earlier states? Those questions cannot be answered *a priori*. Suppose that numerous experiments of such switchings were carried out, and that in all of them the lamp was found to be on at B; then we should have reason to favour the causal hypothesis that the lamp's state, after infinite switchings of the sort described, was *on*. Of course, a different result might be obtained: we might always find the lamp *off*; or there might be a random selection of *offs* and *ons*. Of course, we do not know, now, what the state at B would be. Of course, we shall never be able to conduct any such tests as those I have imagined. But those points are irrelevant: the seventh argument purports to show that only (2) will shield us from a world of random happenings. That is not so; and the notion of causation does not, I think, help us to ground our desire to believe (2).

I believe (2) to be false: of the many arguments designed to support (2), all are wanting in one or more particulars. But I cannot show that (2) is false; indeed, the reason why Zeno's Dichotomy is so fascinating an argument is to be sought in (2): men want to believe (2); they cannot believe that we possess infinite powers; and they keep producing ever more ingenious arguments in favour of Zeno. For all that, until a new batch of arguments comes forward I shall continue to reject Zeno's conclusion by rejecting (2).

(c) *Achilles and the tortoise*

The second paradox in Aristotle's list is the Achilles:

> Second is the one called Achilles. This says that the slow will never be caught in running by the fastest. For the pursuer must first get to where the pursued started from, so that it is necessary that the slower should always be some distance ahead (**186**: *Phys* 239b14–8 = A 26 = 26 L).

Take a racecourse, AB, of indefinitely great length. Let Achilles be placed at A; let the tortoise—as we have come to know his opponent—be placed at any point C between A and B; and at t let Achilles and the tortoise each begin to move towards B. (The paradox says—and need say—nothing about their relative speeds, about the absolute speed of either, or about the uniformity of either's progress.) Suppose that Achilles does catch up with the tortoise; i.e., that there is some point P on AB such that at some time t' after t both Achilles and the tortoise are at P. Since the tortoise has been moving towards B, P is between C and B, thus:

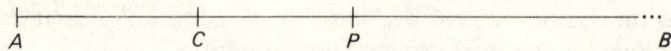

It follows that 'the pursuer must first get to where the pursued started from'; i.e., that at some time between t and t' Achilles is at C. Now when Achilles is at C, the tortoise is at some point, C_1, between C and B; but clearly Achilles must reach C_1 before t'; and when he is at C_1, the tortoise is already ahead, at C_2, between C_1 and B. And in general, if Achilles is at C_i, the tortoise is already at C_{i+1}, one step ahead of him. Thus 'it is necessary that the slower should always be some distance ahead', and Achilles can never catch the tortoise.

According to Aristotle, the Achilles paradox is merely a twopenny coloured version of the Dichotomy. Achilles is dramatized (*tetragôdoumenos*), but at bottom 'this argument is the same as the Dichotomy (only differing in that the added magnitude is not divided in half) . . . so that it necessarily has the same solution' (*Phys* 239b18–20; 25–6). Most modern scholars disagree with Aristotle; at all events, the Achilles is regularly discussed at length and in its own right, whereas the Dichotomy is regularly ignored. (Most of the arguments about infinite performances which I have examined under the rubric of the Dichotomy were originally advanced in connexion with the Achilles.) And at first sight, things do seem to go against Aristotle: according to the Dichotomy, Achilles can never reach the tortoise's starting position; according to the Achilles, even if he could do so, he could never catch the tortoise; in the Dichotomy, the race has a fixed finishing post, which can never be reached; in the Achilles, the finishing post itself is perpetually receding. Achilles, it seems, has double the toil and trouble of his undramatic counterpart in the Dichotomy. He cannot move; and if, *per impossibile*, he could, he would never reach his goal.

Nevertheless, a closer inspection of the Achilles vindicates Aristotle's judgment: the paradox, if not identical with the Dichotomy, is no more than the Dichotomy with an unharmonious coda.

The last step of the argument is invalid. From:
(1) For every i, if Achilles is at C_i, then the tortoise is at C_{i+1}, Zeno invites us, in effect, to infer:

(2) For every point p on AB, if Achilles is at p, the tortoise is at some point p' between p and B.

Now (1) is true; and Zeno's argument shows it to be true. And (2) does imply that Achilles never catches the tortoise. But (2) does not follow from (1). (2) could be inferred from the conjunction of (1) and:

(3) For every point p on AB, there is an i such that C_i is between p and B.

But clearly (3) is not available to Zeno. Every C_i is, by construction, between C and the hypothetical meeting point P; for C_i is simply the point on AB where the tortoise is at the time when Achilles is at C_{i-1}. Thus on the twin assumptions that the tortoise never ceases to move and that Achilles' speed is finite, for *no i* does $C_i = C_{i-1}$. But if $C_i = P$, then $C_i = C_{i-1}$; hence for no i does $C_i = P$. Evidently, no C_i is between P and B. Hence every C_i is between C and P. It follows that Achilles and the tortoise never meet at any C_i, as (1) says. But that conclusion is now seen to be the merest triviality: the two runners will never meet at any point before their first meeting point. From this, nothing like (2) follows; from the fact that they do not meet before they meet, we can scarcely infer that they never meet.

Aristotle saw all that very clearly: 'when [the tortoise] is ahead, he is not caught; but nevertheless he is caught if you grant that one can traverse a limited distance' (*Phys* 239b27–9). According to Aristotle, (1) is true but trivial. How, then, can we get any paradox out of the Achilles? Only, Aristotle implies, by denying that Achilles can traverse the finite distance AP. And how might Zeno propel us towards such a denial? Only, Aristotle implies, by adducing the considerations that he advanced in the Dichotomy. Thus (1) brings out, in a clear enough fashion, the fact that before Achilles reaches the tortoise he must touch infinitely many points; and it is easy to see from (1) that however close to the tortoise Achilles may be—however many C_is he may have successively touched—he still has infinitely many C_is still to touch before he reaches P. And such infinite performances are, Zeno invites us to suppose, impossible.

That manoeuvre reduces the Achilles to the Dichotomy; and any objections to the argumentation in the latter paradox will apply immediately to the former. I do not deny that the Achilles is both clever and elegant; but I agree with Aristotle that it raises no philosophical difficulties which its more prosaic predecessor has not already flushed out.

(d) *The arrow*

The third paradox of motion does break new ground. It is the Arrow. Aristotle's brief description and curt dismissal read thus:

> Third is the one we have just mentioned—that the travelling arrow is at rest. This comes about from assuming that time is composed of 'nows' (*ta nun*); for if that is not granted, there will be no deduction (**187**: *Phys* 239b30–3 = **A 27** = **28 L**).

Aristotle refers back to the opening of Z 9, where the transmitted text reads as follows:

> Zeno misargues; for if, he says, everything always rests or moves whenever it is against what is equal (*kata to ison*), and what is travelling is always in the now (*en tôi nun*), the travelling arrow is motionless (**188**: 239b5–7 = **A 27** = **29 L**).

After that brief report there is the same dismissal as at 239b30–3.

Two further, non-Aristotelian, texts may be adduced. Epiphanius gives the following report:

> He [sc. Zeno] also argues thus: what is moving moves either in the place in which it is or in the place in which it is not. And it moves neither in the place in which it is nor in that in which it is not. Therefore nothing moves (**189**: *adversus haereticos* III.11 = **18 L**).

The second text, from Diogenes, repeats the argument in an abbreviated form (IX.72 = **B 4** = **17 L**). Some scholars think that this dilemma is an independent Zenonian argument, the fifth paradox of motion; others, judging it feeble in itself, attach it to the Arrow: 'Either the arrow moves in the place where it is, or it moves in the place where it is not; evidently it cannot move in the place where it is not; by the Aristotelian argument it cannot move in the place where it is: hence it cannot move.' That reconstruction may possibly be right; but it has no ancient warrant. Moreover, the sources who ascribe the dilemma to Zeno are not unimpeachable; and elsewhere the dilemma is associated with the name of Diodorus Cronos.[12] I incline to the sceptical view that a later dilemma has been anachronistically fathered on Zeno. However that may be, I do not think that the dilemma is very exciting; and I shall confine my discussion to Aristotle's text.

That text is hard enough, in all conscience. It offers Zeno two premisses:

(1) If a is 'against what is equal' at t, then either a rests at t or a is moving at t.

(2) If *a* is moving at *t*, then *a* is 'in the now' at *t*.
From these propositions we are invited to conclude that:
(3) If *a* is moving at *t*, *a* is not moving at *t*.
And hence:
(4) *a* is not moving at *t*.
(I have replaced Aristotle's word 'travelling' (*pheromenon*) by 'moving' in (1) and (3); the terms are synonymous.)

The inference from (3) to (4) is valid; and it is worth noting that Zeno uses a subtle theorem of propositional logic later known as the *Lex Clavia*: if if P then not-P, then not-P. (The companion law, the *Consequentia Mirabilis*—if if not-P then P, then P—was used in a celebrated context by Aristotle.) The move from (3) to (4) is, however, the only uncontroversial element in the paradox: all scholars recognize the obscurity in (1) and (2) and the difficulty in moving from them to (3); and many philosophers deny that (4) is sufficient to establish Zeno's desired conclusion, that nothing moves. I shall first deal with (1) and (2).

(1) and (2) will not yield (3). Instead of (1) and (2) we might well expect:
(5) If *a* is 'against what is equal' at *t*, then *a* rests at *t*.
(6) If *a* is moving at *t*, then *a* is 'against what is equal' at *t*.
If we add the further premiss:
(7) If *a* rests at *t*, then *a* is not moving at *t*,
we can validly infer (3). Premiss (7), which may well seem a thoroughly trifling proposition, is easy enough to supply; but (5) and (6), neither of which follows from (1) and (2), surely need explicit statement. Scholars have accordingly emended the text of the *Physics* so as to produce (5) and (6).

The simplest means of producing (5) is the excision of the words 'or moves (*ê kineitai*) from 239b6; then (1) vanishes from the argument and is replaced by an explicit statement of (5). (6) might be derived from (2) in conjunction with:
(8) If *a* is 'in the now' at *t*, then *a* is 'against what is equal' at *t*.
It is possible to introduce (8) into Aristotle's text; but it is perhaps preferable to treat (8) as a suppressed premiss. Zeno states (2) and expects us to infer (6) by way of (8).[13]

Thus I suggest that Aristotle's text originally presented (5) and (2) explicitly, and expressly inferred (3) from those two premisses. And I suggest that Zeno's original argument started from (5), (2) and (8); that it first inferred (6) from (2) and (8); that it then inferred (3) from (5), (6) and (7); and that it finally inferred (4) from (3), concluding that nothing moves. The textual suggestions are, I think, of no great importance: what matters is that Zeno intended us to reach (3), and hence (4), from (5) and (6).

What, then, is the precise sense of Zeno's premisses? In particular, how are we to understand the two odd phrases 'in the now' and 'against what is equal'? 'The now (*to nun*)' is Aristotle's standard term for an instant of time; but it makes no sense to say, baldly, '*a* is at t', where t names some instant: I may be in a place, but I cannot simply be 'at a time'. We might construe 'is (*esti*)' strongly, as 'exists'; or, better, we might take it as a verb-variable, so that '*a* is in the now' means '*a* ϕs at t'—for some suitable verb ϕ and some definite instant t. (Aristotle says '*in* the now (*en tôi nun*)'; I say '*at t*': some philosophers find a significant difference here; but I think that 'at' is simply the appropriate English translation of '*en*'.)

The commentators all gloss 'is against what is equal' by 'occupies an equal space'; and the gloss is surely correct. Most of them add that 'an equal space' is elliptical for 'a space equal to its volume'; so that '*a* is against what is equal' becomes '*a* occupies a space equal to its own volume:

> No Creature loves an empty space;
> Their Bodies measure out their Place.

I accept that explanation: nothing else will give Zeno an argument of any plausibility.[14]

Thus interpreted, are Zeno's premisses true? Premiss (2) has become:

(2*) If a is moving at t, then there is some instant t' such that at t a is ϕing at t'.

And that is a tautology. The suppressed premiss (8) reads:

(8*) If there is some instant t' such that at t a is ϕing at t', then at t a occupies a space equal to its own volume.

That is a peculiar observation; and I cannot divine why Zeno should have propounded it. Indeed, the very notion of being 'in the now' seems only to add an unnecessary complication to Zeno's argument; for (6), which has now become:

(6*) If a is moving at t, then at t a occupies a space equal to its own volume,

can be justified on far less mysterious grounds: it is a necessary truth that everything always occupies a space exactly equal to its own volume; i.e., that for any object x and time t, the volume of space occupied by x at t is equal to the volume of x at t. For what is the volume of an object if not the amount of space it occupies? But then whether or not a is moving at t, a is 'against what is equal' at t; hence (6) is necessarily true.

What, then, of premiss (5)? If that is true, then Zeno has reached (4) and we are potentially in trouble. (5) now reads:

(5*) If a occupies at t a space equal to its own volume, then a rests at t.

Some philosophers hold that (5*) is not even coherent, let alone true. According to Aristotle, 'at an instant, it is not possible for anything to be either in motion or at rest' (*Phys* 239b1; cf. 234a32). Rest is a matter of endurance: things rest *for a period* of time; they cannot intelligibly be said to rest *at a point* in time. Aristotle has a multitude of followers. The question is usually discussed in connexion with Zeno's conclusion, (4); and I shall follow the custom. For at step (5) Zeno is easily and trivially defended; we need only replace (5*) by:

(5⁺) If a occupies at t a space equal to its own volume, then it is not the case that a is moving at t.

Indeed, (5⁺) not only evades the captious objection about rest; it also enables Zeno to dispense with the additional premiss (7): (5⁺) and (6*) together entail (3) with no more ado.

Those many thinkers who agree with Aristotle that 'at an instant, nothing moves' are obliged to accept (5⁺). And (6*) is certainly true. Since (5⁺) and (6*) entail (3), it seems that Zeno is vindicated: the moving arrow does not move.

(e) *Movement in a moment*

Russell, for one, happily assents to (4): Zeno, he says, did prove that 'we live in an unchanging world, and that the arrow, at every moment of its flight, is truly at rest. The only point where Zeno probably erred was in inferring (if he did infer) that, because there is no change, the world must be in the same state at one time as at another.' In short, (4), far from being a monstrous paradox, is 'a very plain statement of a very elementary fact'. But (4) does not entail the absence of motion. Rather, it enables us to see more clearly the real nature of motion: 'People used to think that when a thing changes, it must be in a state of change, and that when a thing moves, it is in a state of motion. This is now known to be a mistake. When a body moves, all that can be said is that it is in one place at one time and in another at another.'[15]

Russell's views are not entirely plain. I take it that he is saying three things about the inference from (4) to the denial of motion—strictly speaking, about the inference from:

(9) ($\forall t$) (if t is in T, then a is not moving at t),

to:

(10) a does not move during T.

Russell says *first* that the inference is invalid; *second*, that a correct understanding of the concept of motion will reveal its invalidity; and *third*, that Zeno may well not have made or intended the inference. I find Russell's view bizarre; on all three counts his reaction to the Arrow is mistaken. I take the points in reverse order.

First, then, all the ancient commentators treat the Arrow as part of Zeno's general attack upon motion. They plainly regard (4) as the penultimate step leading to a negation of motion: I see no reason to dispute their view; and I suppose that Zeno ended his argument by explicitly saying 'the arrow does not move'—indeed it is natural to construe Aristotle's words at 239b7 in precisely that way.

Second, let us consider Russell's account of motion. Russell naughtily describes it as a 'static' account; it can, I think, be formulated as follows:

(D1) a moves during T if and only if for every pair of distinct instants t_1 and t_2 in T there is an instant t_3 between t_1 and t_2 and a pair of distinct places p_1 and p_3 such as a is at p_1 at t_1 and a is at p_3 at t_3.

That looks needlessly complicated. In fact its complexities are necessary, and must be multiplied (as the ancients realized) if we are to say of spinning tops that they move. Zeno in (4) talks of motion at an instant; does (D1) show such talk to be odd? does it show the inference from (9) to (10) to be invalid? Motion at an instant is easily defined:

(D2) a is moving at t if and only if for some T t is within T and a moves during T.

Given (D2), (9) immediately implies (10): if (D1) and (D2) offer a correct account of motion, they do not thereby reveal the invalidity of the Zenonian inference. Quite the contrary. (I do not mean to imply that Zeno himself had in mind a Russellian account of motion. Nor do I think that there are just two ways of envisaging motion: the one given in (D1–2), and the one rightly rejected by Russell according to which motion is an intrinsic quality of the moving object, in much the way that triangularity is an intrinsic quality of a triangular object. My point is only that Zeno has nothing to fear from (D1).)

Finally, is the inference from (9) and (10), or from (4) to Zeno's immobile conclusion, valid? It seems to me gratuitously paradoxical to deny its validity: if the inference is invalid then we must, in Bergson's celebrated phrase, accept 'the absurd proposition that movement is made of immobilities'.[16] Every period of motion will consist of an infinite sequence of motionless states. Ordinary usage accustoms us to talk of 'motion at an instant': I can say that the car was travelling at 34 m.p.h. at the moment when the bus hit it; or that at 9.10 this morning I was cycling into College. And ordinary usage sanctions inferences of the relevant sort between statements of 'motion at an instant' and statements of enduring motion: if I claim to have been cycling between 9.05 and 9.15 I cannot consistently deny that I was cycling at 9.10; if the car moved steadily at 34 m.p.h. until it hit the bus, then it was moving at 34 m.p.h. when it hit the bus. Indeed, it is, I think, a general truth that if a ϕs during T, then a is ϕing at every instant t in T; and the acceptability of that proposition in no way depends on restricting the range of 'ϕ' to static verbs.

Why should any philosopher go against that natural mode of speech and argument? It cannot be said that the notion of 'motion at an instant' makes no sense; clearly it does make perfectly ordinary sense, and a sense that can be lucidly articulated in some such definition as (D2). Are there, then, hidden inconsistencies in the definition, or any that may replace it?

Some have argued as follows: 'All motion has duration, and it always makes sense to ask, of a moving object, how long it has moved for; consequently, the notion of instantaneous motion is logically contradictory; and thus motion at an instant is impossible.'[17] It is true that all motion involves duration: if a moves, then there is some period T such that a moves during T. And it does follow from this that instantaneous motion is a logical impossibility: 'a ϕs instantaneously' means, I take it, that for some t a ϕs at t and for no T does a during T. In that sense some things, e.g., dying or learning—may or may not be instantaneous; and some things, of which change and all its species are the most conspicuous examples, are necessarily not instantaneous. But that does not show that the argument I have just considered is sound; for its final step involves a gross confusion: it is one thing to reject instantaneous motion, another to reject motion 'at an instant'. To believe that motion at an instant is possible is to believe that 'a moves at t' is consistent; to believe that instantaneous motion is impossible is to believe that 'a moves at t' and for no T does a move during T' is inconsistent. Plainly, those two beliefs are compatible: I uphold motion 'at an instant'; but I also believe that if a moves then for some T a moves during T, and thus I reject instantaneous motion.

Aristotle provides a different argument against motion at an instant: 'That nothing moves at an instant is evident thus: if it did, a thing could move both quicker and slower. Let N be an instant, and let the faster thing have moved the distance AB at N (*en autôi*). Now at the same instant (*en tôi autôi*) the slower thing will have moved a shorter distance, say AC. But since the slower has moved through AC in the whole instant, the faster will have moved [through AC] in a

281

shorter time than this—so that the instant will have been divided. But that is impossible—hence it is not possible to move at an instant' (*Phys* 234a23–31).

There are two related errors in this argument. The first is more evident in the translation than in the Greek: it consists in treating the term 'instant (*nun*)' as though it connoted a period of time, as though it were the last member of the set of terms that includes 'year', 'day', 'hour', 'minute', 'second'. In English we do sometimes talk of things happening 'in an instant', and the same idiom is, I suppose, possible in Greek. But when we say 'in an instant' we are using the term 'instant' loosely, as a synonym for 'split second'. Aristotle misses this point; and his argument depends on his construing '*en tôi nun*' as though it were logically on a par with '*en miai hôrai*' ('in an hour').

The second, allied, error, is harder to exhibit clearly. It lies in Aristotle's supposition that 'the faster thing has moved the distance AB *en autôi*'. Behind that supposition lies the truism that if a has moved at all, then there is some distance through which a has moved. But from that truth Aristotle falsely infers that if a moved at t, then there is some distance through which a moved at t, say the distance AB. Now he might properly have inferred that there is some distance through which a was moving at t: at t a was moving from A to B if t falls within a period of constant motion T and if during T a moved from A to B. But from 'a was moving from A to B at t' we cannot infer 'a moved from A to B at t'. Indeed, we cannot, in general, infer 'a ϕed at t' from 'a was ϕing at t' (as, in another context, Aristotle in effect recognizes). I was eating breakfast at 8.45, but I did not eat breakfast at 8.45; I was reading a book at 10.30, but I did not read a book at 10.30. In general, if '$a\phi$s' entails 'for some T, $a\phi$s during T', then 'a is ϕing at t' does not entail 'a ϕs at t'.

Thus Aristotle's argument against motion 'at an instant' fails. And I know of no other, more compelling, argument.

I end this section by considering Aristotle's objection to the Arrow: he says simply that 'time is not composed of indivisible nows' (239b8). I take it that he means to ascribe the following argument to Zeno:

(11) ($\forall t$) (if t is in T, a is not moving at t).
(12) T is composed of the set of instants it contains.
Hence:
(13) a does not move during T.

Here (11) represents (4), and (13) is a version of Zeno's wholesale rejection of locomotion. And Aristotle objects that (12) is false.

I have two comments. First, we might disagree with Aristotle about

(12) and yet agree with him that the argument from (11) to (13) is unsound. For the pattern of inference represented by (11)–(13) is invalid: it is a case of the 'fallacy of composition', the fallacy of arguing from 'All the parts of X are F' to 'X is F'. (All the molecules that make up this glass of beer are tasteless, so the beer is tasteless.) Second, I see no reason to ascribe Aristotle's argument to Zeno: Zeno infers (13) directly from (11). There is no need to invoke (12); and hence no occasion to charge Zeno with a fallacy of composition.

(f) *The arrow blunted*

If I am right, we cannot allow Zeno to reach proposition (4) without giving him his conclusion that motion is impossible. Since (6*) is true, we must reject (5*); and indeed (5*) seems to me to be clearly false: objects do, at every instant in their temporal careers, occupy a space exactly equal to their volume at that instant. And they do even if they are in motion throughout their temporal careers. Why should anyone find that puzzling?

Some might argue as follows: 'If we think of the arrow as occupying a given position for a time of zero duration, it will be obvious enough that it cannot be moving *then*: it will have no time in which to move.'[18] That is a bad argument: a needs time to move from A to B; but a needs no time *to be moving* from A to B. The arrow is moving at t; it does not follow, as I have already said, that the arrow *moves* through some distance at t. If that argument lies behind (5*), then (5*) is not established.

But the argument makes no essential reference to the space which a occupies at t; and I suspect that a different consideration operated on Zeno's mind. I suspect that he argued as follows: 'If at t a occupies a space no greater than itself, then a has no room in which to move. Moving involves the transition from one place to another, and hence occupancy of more than one place. But at t a occupies just one place, viz. the place marked out by its own boundary.' That argument too is bad; and the grounds of its badness have already been presented: if a moves, then there are two points, A and B, such that a moves from A to B; and if a is moving at t, there are points A and B such that at t a is moving from A to B. But it does not follow that if a is moving at t, then there are points A and B such that at t a moves from A to B. Similarly if I smoke my pipe, there is a plug of tobacco which I consume in the process; and if I am smoking a pipe at t, then there is a plug of tobacco which I am consuming at t. But it does not follow—and it is not true—that if I am smoking a pipe at t, then there is a plug of tobacco which I consume at t.

It is perhaps worth setting out in one paragraph the various facts about motion which I have tried to express and to advocate. First, motion requires duration: 'a moves' entails 'For some period T, a moves during T'. Second, motion requires extension: 'a moves' entails 'For some distance AB, a moves from A to B.' Third, motion 'at an instant' requires durational motion: 'a is moving at t' entails 'For some period T, a moves during T'. Fourth, motion 'at an instant' requires motion through a space: 'a is moving at t' entails 'For some distance AB, a moves from A to B'. Fifth, motion 'at an instant' does *not* require instantaneous motion: 'a is moving at t' does not entail 'for no period T, a moves during T'. Sixth, motion 'at an instant' does *not* require instantaneous transition: 'a is moving at t' does not entail 'For some distance AB, a moves from A to B at t'. There is evidently much more to be said about the logic of motion than that. But I believe that the six facts I have just listed are sufficient to show that the customary answers to Zeno's Arrow are mistaken. Zeno's argument is valid; but it relies on a false premiss.

There remains the possibility of an eleventh hour reprieve: so far I have taken Aristotle's phrase 'the now' to denote an instant; and one of my complaints has been against the misconstrual of instants as small periods of time. Now some scholars suppose that Zeno's argument should in fact be conducted entirely in terms of periods of time, and not at all in terms of instants. I do not think that Aristotle's text encourages such a supposition; and I do not believe that we can seriously hope to recover a genuinely Zenonian argument behind a distorted Aristotelian presentation. Nonetheless, it is clearly desirable to see what difference might be made to the penetrative powers of the Arrow if it is freed from the notion of movement 'at an instant'.

In the new version proposition (5) is replaced by:

(14) If a occupies during T a space equal to its own volume, then a is at rest during T.

As it stands, (14) seems plausible, or at least more plausible than (5). But in fact it is ambiguous. Its plausible sense is more explicitly given by:

(14a) If there is a place p equal to the volume of a such that at every instant t in T a occupies p, then a is at rest during T.

Indeed, (14a) is not only plausible: it is evidently true. Clearly, however, (14a) and (6) do not together entail (4). To secure the entailment, (6) too must be replaced by a proposition talking about periods of time. The proposition required is:

(15) If a is moving during T, then there is a place p equal to the volume of a such that at every instant t in T a occupies p.

And just as (14a) is evidently true, so (15) is evidently false.

If (14) is read as (14a), the Arrow has no penetration. The alternative reading of (14) is:

(14b) If at every instant t in T there is a place p such that a occupies p at t, then a is at rest during T.

A suitable replacement can be found for (6) which, together with (14b) entails (4). And that replacement will be true. But now (14b) turns out to be false; for the antecedent of (14b) is compatible with there being distinct places $p_1, p_2 \ldots$ which a occupies at distinct instants $t_1, t_2 \ldots$ in T; and occupancy of distinct places during T is incompatible with rest during T. Thus if (14) is interpreted as (14b) the Arrow gets no further. And I conclude that the proposal to read Zeno's paradox in terms of periods of time rather than in terms of instants has no philosophical merit. Not only does it fail to give Zeno a better argument; it also fails to raise any interesting philosophical puzzles.

Let me end my discussion of the Arrow with two negatively polemical remarks. It is usually supposed that Zeno's paradox carries with it some philosophical theory about the nature of time; and Zeno's commentators regularly adduce rival theories in the course of their reflexions upon it. My discussion has shown the falsity of that common supposition; for in expounding and criticizing the Arrow I have neither explicitly nor implicitly invoked any theory of time. In particular, I have not accused Zeno of treating time as being 'composed of instants'; nor have I ascribed to him the view that time is made up of 'atomic minimal parts'; nor have I made him assume that motion proceeds cinematographically. The paradox, as we should expect and desire, is innocent of any such theories: it presupposes only the two harmless and common notions that there are instants, as well as periods, of time; and that things move, if at all, at instants.

Many scholars find an architectonic structure uniting Zeno's four surviving paradoxes of motion: the paradoxes form a dilemmatic attack upon movement, the Dichotomy and the Achilles supposing that time and space are infinitely divisible, the Arrow and the Stadium supposing that there are indivisible spatial and temporal *quanta*. My account of the Arrow seems to me to have revealed the falsity of that neat fantasy.

(g) *The stadium*

The fourth and final paradox is the Stadium:

[i] The fourth is the one about equal bodies which move alongside equal bodies in the stadium from opposite directions—the ones from the end of the stadium, the others from the middle—at equal speeds, in which he thinks it follows that half the time is equal to its double. [ii] The misargument consists in requiring that [a body travelling] at an equal speed travels for an equal time past a moving body and a body of the same magnitude at rest. That is false. [iii] E.g., let the stationary equal bodies be *AA*; let *BB* be those starting from the middle of the *A*s (equal in number and in magnitude to them); and let *CC* be those starting from the end (equal in number and in magnitude to them, and equal in speed to the *B*s). [iv] Now it follows that the first *B* and the first *C* are at the end at the same time, as they are moving past one another. [v] And it follows that the *C* has passed all the *A*s, and the *B* half; [vi] so that the time is half, [vii] for each of the two is alongside each for an equal time. [viii] And at the same time it follows that the first *B* has passed all the *C*s. [ix] For at the same time the first *B* and the first *C* will be at opposite ends, [x] being an equal time alongside each of the *B*s as alongside each of the *A*s, as he says, [xi] because both are an equal time alongside the *A*s. [xii] This is the argument, and it rests on the stated falsity (**190**: *Phys.* 239b33–240a18 = A 28 = 35 L).

The outline of that argument is clear enough. We have three equinumerous groups of bodies in a stadium, and the bodies are all equal in size. How many bodies each group possesses is not stated: the number is immaterial to the argument; and I shall take the simplest case, that in which each group contains just two bodies.[19] Aristotle does not say that the members of each group are contiguous and arranged in a row (like the carriages of a railway train); but the argument plainly requires that assumption. One row of bodies, the *A*s, is stationary. The *B*s and the *C*s move; and I shall refer to the leading *B* and the leading *C* as B_1 and C_1.

Aristotle gives, in [i] and [iii], a description of the stadium before the *B*s and *C*s begin their movements. I shall call this the *starting position*. Then [iv]–[x] list three things that 'follow' once the moving bodies have left the starting position. Let us call the starting time t_1; then at some later point, t_2, the bodies will be in what I shall call the *crucial position*. And if we consider what has happened during *T*, the interval between t_1 and t_2, we shall (according to Zeno), be faced with paradoxical or contradictory results. The problems of interpretation are thus three: first, to determine the starting position, at t_1; second, to determine the crucial position, at t_2; third, to discover what paradox is supposed to arise from our consideration of T, and how it is supposed to arise. The problems cannot be tackled separately; but it helps, I think, to begin by looking at the second of the three things that allegedly 'follow'.

That second result is stated in [v]–[vii], which describe, or partially describe, the state of the stadium at the crucial time, t_2. The description contains a vagueness; but I shall simply assume that the phrases 'the B' and 'the C' in sentence [v] denote the *first B* and the *first C*. Thus sentence [v] asserts that at t_2 the first C has passed all the As and the first B has passed half the As; C_1 has passed two As, B_1 has passed one A. Given that the Cs and the Bs are proceeding at the same speed, we can infer that at some time prior to t_2—call it, for the moment, t_x—the stadium looked like this:

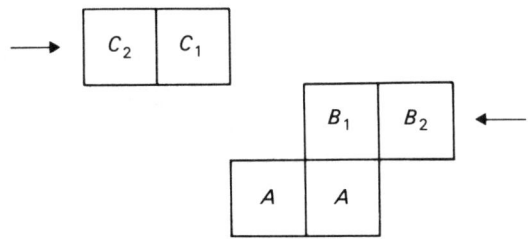

fig. 1

As far as t_2 goes, each of the following two diagrams seems to be consistent with the words of Aristotle's description:

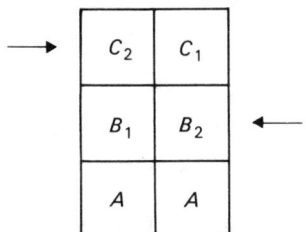

fig 2.1

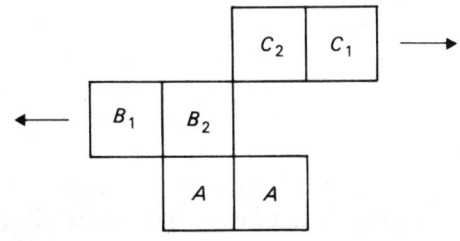

fig 2.2

Now Zeno infers in [vi] that 'the time is half'. The obvious expansion of this reads: 'the time taken by B_1 to get from its *fig. 1* position to its new position is half that taken by C_1 to get from its *fig. 1* position to its new position'. And Zeno's argument for that, in [vii], glosses as follows: 'In the interval between *fig. 1* and the new position, B_1 has passed half as many As as C_1 has; and both B_1 and C_1 are travelling at the same speed.' That reasoning allows us to fix on *fig. 2.1* as the correct diagram for t_2.

Let us now glance briefly at the *first* result, stated in [iv]. I assume that the time of this result is the same as the time of the second result, i.e. t_2. The run of the text favours the assumption; and if we introduce a further time I see no way of reconstructing any argument. At t_2, then, B_1 and C_1 are 'at the end'. That phrase is wholly opaque. Four glosses at least are possible; and three of those glosses produce a plurality of diagrams. But given that *fig. 2.1* represents the stadium at t_2, we can limit the choice to two diagrams. (a) If 'at the end' means 'at the [opposite] end[s of the As]', then the diagram must be *fig. 2.1* itself. (b) If 'at the end' means '[each] at the end [of the other's row]', the diagram must be:

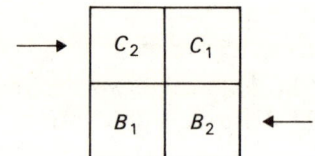

fig. 3

One manuscript has a reading which shows that *fig. 3* represents an ancient interpretation; and since we do not want the second result merely to repeat the first, we should clearly plump for (b) and *fig. 3*.

We have thus identified the 'crucial position' as the position diagrammed in *fig. 2.1*, and it is an obvious conjecture that *fig. 1* represents the starting position at t_1. Can that conjecture be supported from the text?

Aristotle describes the starting position twice, in [i] and in [iii]. The latter sentence adds something to the former: it specifies that the Bs start 'from the middle of the As'. In *fig. 1* they do; and the Cs similarly start 'from the end [of the As]'. That confirms that *fig. 1* represents the starting position of the three rows at t_1.

There is an objection to my reconstruction. If the bodies start in the position depicted in *fig. 1* they will never reach the position of *fig. 2.1*; it is logically impossible, given the conditions Zeno stipulates, that both *fig. 1* and *fig. 2.1* should depict points in the careers of the Bs and Cs. But that objection is not fatal: Zeno, after all, is trying to find contradictions in the concept of motion; and we should not necessarily be dismayed to find that his paradoxes represent as achieved what in reality and logic is impossible. The question, then, is not: Can *fig. 1* yield *fig. 2.1*? It is: Can Zeno have thought, or have made it seem plausible to think, that *fig. 1* yields *fig. 2.1*? And we might attempt to answer that question by looking at the *third* result, sentences [viii]–[xi].

Textually, that too is uncertain. In [viii], at 240a13, where I translate 'the first B', most manuscripts read '*ta B*', 'the Bs'. Given that reading, we should have 'at the same time'—i.e. at t_2—the following position:

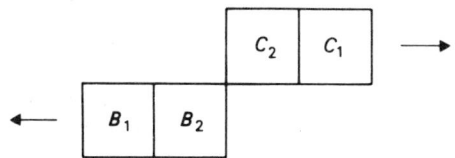

fig. 4

Now *fig. 4*, though a part of *fig. 2.2.*, is not reconcilable with *fig. 2.1*. Nor can I find any plausible argument which makes use of *fig. 4*. Consequently, the majority reading must be rejected; and we must read either '*to B* (the B)' or '*to prôton B* (the first B)'.[20]

We now have an argument designed to show that the third result actually occurs: i.e., that:
(1) At t_2 B_1 has passed both C_1 and C_2.
The text presents three sentences: sentence [ix] gives:
(2) At t_2 B_1 is against C_2 and C_1 is against B_2.
Sentence [x] gives:
(3) C_1 is alongside each B for the same length of time that it is alongside each A.
Sentence [xi] gives:
(4) The Bs and the Cs spend an equal time alongside each A.
Each of these three sentences allegedly supports its predecessor. Can anything be made of the argument?

Proposition (2) re-expresses the first result; and (1) follows easily enough from it and the initial description of the stadium. Proposition (4) is true, given the equal speed of the Cs and the Bs. Zeno, I suppose, argued thus: 'If, as (4) says, B_1 spends n time units against an A, and C_1 spends n time units against an A, then plainly B_1 spends n time units against C_1. Thus (3) is established.[21] And since by t_2 C_1 has been alongside *two* As, it must—by (3)—have been alongside two Bs as well. Hence (2). Finally, given the starting conditions, we may deduce (1).'

Let me now try to restate Zeno's whole argument in briefer and more perspicuous fashion. Suppose that at t_1 the As, Bs and Cs are arranged as in *fig. 1*; and let the Bs and Cs move as specified. Let t_2 be the time at which C_1 has passed every A. Now C_1 has passed two As and hence two Bs; therefore *fig. 2.1* represents the position at t_2. C_1 and B_1 each take n units of time to pass a body. Hence T, the period from t_1 to t_2, is $2n$ units long. But in T B_1 has passed only one A. Hence $T = n$. Hence $T = \frac{1}{2}T$.[22]

The argument is not sound; but no version of the Stadium will yield a sound argument. It is not elegant; but Aristotle's text does not suggest an argument with the elegance of the Achilles. I am inclined to think that this reconstruction is as close to Zeno as anything we can now produce; and I have expounded it at some length because it goes against the prevailing orthodoxy.

Different interpretations fall into two classes. First, there are those which agree that *fig. 1* represents the starting position.[23] Such interpretations are only minor variants on mine; and they do not require special discussion. Second, there are those which abandon *fig. 1* and adopt as a starting position:

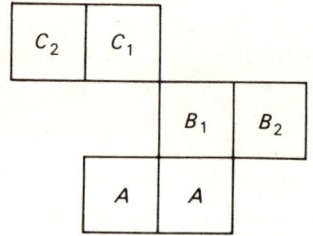

fig. 5

From *fig. 5* the position of *fig. 2.1* is easily reached; and in that lies the advantage of *fig. 5* over *fig. 1*. For my part, as I have already intimated, I do not think that the advantage is very great. And on the other side, adoption of *fig. 5* requires two changes in the text of **190**, one of which is most implausible.[24] But I shall not pursue the question further: philosophically speaking, it matters little whether we choose *fig. 1* or *fig. 5*.

(h) *A most ingenious paradox?*

Thus far I have concentrated on textual *minutiae* and little problems of interpretation; and it may well be wondered whether such attention is worth the paper it consumes. Aristotle dismisses Zeno's argument curtly enough: Zeno, he says, wrongly assumes that the Cs will take as long to pass a moving B as they will to pass a stationary A. To most scholars the criticism seems both apt and conclusive: the paradox of the Stadium is philologically the most complicated of Zeno's four arguments; philosophically it is the simplest and the least interesting—correct a childish mistake and all is in motion again. As Eudemus long ago saw, the puzzle is 'very silly, because the misargument is obvious' (fr. 106W = **A 28**).

Moved by those considerations, yet convinced of Zeno's logical acumen, some scholars have inferred that Aristotle has misrepresented Zeno. Zeno's argument, they say, in fact assumed that the As, Bs and Cs were *minimal* bodies, indivisible atoms of stuff. And it further assumed that the time taken for a B or a C to pass a stationary A was a *minimal* period of time, an indivisible temporal *quantum*. Given those two assumptions, the Stadium becomes a sound and a significant argument; for in effect it shows that absurd results follow from such an atomic attitude to matter and time. The Stadium, in short, is an early essay in the logic of the continuum.[25]

I do not deny the philosophical interest of that sophisticated version of the Stadium paradox; but it was not Zeno's. There is no evidence that anyone prior to Zeno had entertained the atomistic theory he is imagined to be attacking; and there is no reason why he should himself have invented such a theory simply to knock it down. The sophisticated Stadium has no historical support. Nor is the train of reasoning which introduced it very compelling. It is simply false that Zeno was a brilliant logician who would never have committed an elementary error—I have already discussed more than one argument indubitably Zenonian and of less subtlety than the Aristotelian Stadium. Indeed, a stronger case can be put: the Aristotelian Stadium, as it stands, is not immensely impressive; but it points to a crucial feature in the concept of locomotion. In short, the Aristotelian Stadium is philosophically important, and not 'very silly'.

I offer the following argument as a refurbished account of the Stadium. 'Our concept of motion is intimately connected with the two continua of space and time. The concept is linked logically to those two notions in a variety of ways; two of the most important are mirrored in these two implications:

(1) If a moves past a sequence of n Fs and each F is k units long, then a moves nk units.

(2) If a moves for a period of T units at a constant speed of j u.p.u., and covers m units in that time, then $T = m/j$ units.

Now consider *fig. 5* and *fig. 2.1*. Substitute B_1 for a in (1) and (2): it is easy to show, by two applications of (1) and (2), that T, the period from t_1 to t_2, is equal to $\frac{1}{2}T$. For the passage of B_1 past the single A gives $T = 1k/j$. And the passage of B_1 past the two Cs gives $T = 2k/j$.

Thus the concept of motion implies (1) and (2); and (1) and (2) lead to contradiction. Hence the concept of motion is incoherent. Hence nothing can move.'

Such a reconstruction has two points in its favour. First, it relates the Stadium to Zeno's general attack on motion; most accounts do not explain the connexion between the fourth paradox of motion and Zeno's overall aim. Second, it provides an interesting argument against motion. For I am inclined to think that both (1) and (2) would have commended themselves to Zeno's contemporaries, and do commend themselves to us in our unthinking moments. Our conception of locomotion is such that (1) and (2) seem to be implicit in it; yet (1) and (2) lead to unacceptable results. Zeno infers, I suggest, that the concept of motion is inconsistent; we may prefer to say that men who subscribe to (1) and (2) confusedly grasp the consistent concept of motion. The mode of expression is immaterial: if we are to move in the Stadium we must articulate a concept of motion which does not give rise to (1) and (2).

Aristotle's answer to Zeno may now seem as unsatisfactory as in reality it is: according to Aristotle, Zeno ignores the fact that the *As* are stationary and the *Bs* moving. The criticism is not profound: where, we may ask, does Aristotle's objection fit into the argument based on (1) and (2)? How would he reject those twin principles? What notion of movement would he supply which avoids (1) and (2)? I do not say that those questions are unanswerable; I do say that they are unanswered, and that that fact makes Aristotle's reply to Zeno inadequate.

An adequate reply to Zeno, and an adequate account of motion, would focus on the truth that motion is a relational thing: '. . . it doth not appear to me that there can be any motion other than *relative*: so that to conceive motion, there must be conceived two bodies, whereof the distance or position in regard to each other is varied. Hence if there was only one body in being, it could not possibly be moved. This seems evident, in that the idea I have of motion doth necessarily include relation' (Berkeley, *Principles of Human Knowledge*, §CXII).

Motion, in brief, is relative not absolute. That slogan may mislead; and it is worth stating clearly two things that it does not imply. First, it does not imply the incoherence of 'absolute' motion in Newton's sense: Newtonian 'absolute' motion is merely a privileged form of relative motion; for according to Newton a body is in 'absolute' motion if it is changing position relative to absolute space. (It is a further question whether anything can be made of absolute space.) Second, the rejection of 'absolute' motion does not require a wholesale change in our everyday language of movement. For though we do regularly speak as though motion were absolute, it is fairly simple to translate such talk into talk of motion relative to our human inertial frame, the earth: 'he's moving' can regularly be taken as elliptical for 'he's changing position relative to (some point on) the earth's surface'. (Regularly, but not, of course, always: in the enclosed world of an aeroplane or a ship we naturally take the enclosing vehicle as our reference frame; and Christmas cracker puzzles, such as the conundrum of the man running round the monkey, remind us that all is not plain sailing here.)

To say that motion is relative is to say no more than this: 'a moves' only makes sense if it is taken as elliptical for some two-place predication of the form 'a changes position relative to b'. 'a moves' is comparable to 'a leads' or 'a follows'; leading and following are relational notions, even though we often and intelligibly use the verbs without explicitly mentioning a *relatum*: and just as 'a leads' is elliptical for 'a leads b', so is 'a moves' elliptical for 'a moves vis-à-vis b'. There is, of course, nothing unusual in having such elliptical, absolute-seeming, uses for essentially relational verbs; in the case of 'move', however, there is a peculiar danger of taking the absolute-seeming use at face value, and inventing an absolute quality of motion to serve as *denotatum* for the absolute verb. (I suspect that this connects with the old Aristotelian view that motion is immediately perceptible, a 'simple idea': if we can simply *see* that a thing is in motion, surely motion is an intrinsic quality and not a relation?)

What bearing has the relativity of motion on the Stadium? It allows us to retain the essence of implications (1) and (2) while rejecting their cruel accidents. Thus, to take the case of (1), we shall have:

(1*) If a moves past a sequence of n Fs and each F is k units long, then relative to those Fs a moves nk units.

The plausibility of (1) carries over to (1*) and (1*) contains the truth which (1) strove in vain to express. Moreover (1*) has no hard consequences, once we realize that there is no contradiction between 'a moves n units relative to b' and 'a moves m units relative to c' (where $b \neq C$ and $n \neq m$). For I may move relative to one thing while resting relative to another—there are a thousand everyday examples of that.

I do not claim that only a relative concept of motion will answer Zeno's argument; but that such a concept is both correct in itself and sufficient to answer Zeno seems clear enough. If Zeno's Stadium encourages us to clarify our conception of motion in that way, then that, I submit, is enough to make an honest argument of it. Zeno, of course, did not intend his Stadium to refute 'absolute' motion and elicit a relativized concept; and indeed he does not seem to have stirred any of his successors to develop such a sanitary notion. For all that, the Stadium does show, in a pointed and pregnant way, the need for a subtler concept of locomotion than we are apt at first sight to formulate. And that turns the paradox of the Stadium, in its plain Aristotelian form, into an argument of some significance.

(i) *Two last remarks*

I end my long consideration of Zeno's paradoxes with two general comments.

First, what, we may wonder, is the connexion between the four paradoxes on motion and the Platonic schema into which I attempted to fit the paradoxes of plurality? We may always suppose that the arguments about motion, which Aristotle treats as a unitary group and which according to Elias constituted an independent Zenonian volume, were in their original form a separate publication. We might indeed conjecture that they were worked out later in Zeno's life, the fruits of his intellectual maturity.

On the other hand, Plato names 'at rest and moving' as one of the set of opposites which Zeno proved to hold of 'the many' (*Phaedrus* 261D = **A 13**). Thus one case of the Platonic schema will be:

(Z7) (a) If P, then everything moves, and (b) if P, then nothing moves.

Here (Z7a) will have required no special argument: evidently, the 'many things' which the pluralists admit do, all of them, move. And it is not vastly implausible to see the four paradoxes of motion as intended to support (Z7b). In that case, the paradoxes will, originally, have appeared in Zeno's juvenile book, alongside the other arguments I have dissected; and some later editor will have assembled them in a little treatise of their own, preserving their philosophical content while divesting them of their original polemical form.

Second, what general portrait of Zeno emerges from these two chapters? My discussion has, I think, confirmed the view I sketched on an earlier page (above, p. 236). Zeno 'put forward no view of his own but puzzled further about' Eleatic issues (pseudo-Plutarch, **A 23**). Zeno was no original philosopher; he is not a member of the long line of thinkers stretching from Thales to Melissus, men of vast learning, wide pretensions, profound insights. Rather, he puzzled: negative, destructive, polemical, Zeno was the first of the 'Sophists'. His aims were critical, not constructive; his methods subtle not solid.

Yet from his Sophist's quiver he drew a few darts of brilliance and acuity; and those darts have made him a prince of philosophers *malgré lui*.

XIV

The Ports of Knowledge Closed

(a) *Parmenides on sense and reason*

'Antisthenes the Cynic, unable to answer [Zeno's arguments against motion], got up and walked, deeming a proof by action more potent than any logical confutation' (Elias, **29 A 15**). Zeno's paradoxical conclusions disagree outrageously with what we like to call 'common sense'; and if common sense has no part to play in the serious dramas of science, in philosophy it often assumes a leading role. Moreover, in its antagonism to Elea, common sense has a powerful ally: perception. We perceive, everyday, the falsity of Eleatic metaphysics and Zenonian immobility; and our common sense is trustworthy just because it is securely backed by those quotidian perceptions.

The Eleatics, naturally enough, became enrolled in the sceptical army: in the crude words of Aëtius, 'Parmenides says that the senses are false' (**28 A 49**). Sextus, our chief quarry for ancient scepticism, numbers Parmenides among his tribe (*adv Math* VII. 114); and Timon, the sceptical satirist, praised Parmenides, 'who turned his thoughts from the delusion of fantasy' (fr. 44 = **A 1**). Aristotle sums it up: the Eleatics 'pass over perception and disregard it, thinking that one should follow reason. . . . In the light of their arguments this seems to follow; in the light of the facts it is near to madness to hold such opinions' (*GC* 325a13–18 = **A 25**).

No Eleatic could be unaware of the way in which his conclusions disregard the data of perception; and we might expect some little argument from Elea to excuse or justify its high-handed treatment of the chief instrument of Ionian science. Epistemology, after all, was in existence, a young discipline but not an infant; and if Parmenides had a sceptical predecessor in Xenophanes, he had an opponent in

Heraclitus. A philosopher of the fifth century could not simply shrug off his epistemological commitments.

In fact we find little in the Eleatic fragments; and the little we find is probably all there ever was. Nothing suggests that Zeno wrote in an epistemological vein; for Melissus we possess one substantial fragment, but no hint that his work contained anything further of that sort; and for Parmenides we have a few brief lines.

In support of his claim that Parmenides 'makes it clear that one should not attend to the senses but to reason', Sextus quotes text **153**; and Diogenes quotes the same lines in the same connexion (IX. 22 = **A 1**). Plainly, the later tradition knew no other sceptical utterances from Parmenides. (The quatrain on thought, **B 16**, is irrelevant here: it will be considered in volume 2.) I transcribe **153** again (see above, p. 170):

> Do not let much-experienced habit force you along this road,
> to let run an aimless eye and an echoing ear
> and a tongue; but judge by argument (*logôi*) the much-
> contending refutation uttered by me.

The lines do not argue for scepticism: they enjoin, they do not reason. But many scholars find in them a wholesale rejection of sense-perception. I think that the lines say both more and less than that.

First, the lines mention the tongue; and the tongue is the organ of speech as well as of taste. I agree with those scholars who attend to the former function and suppose that Parmenides has in mind not gustatory illusions (never a very rich source of sceptical argument) but rather the perils inherent in ordinary language. The empty words of mortals, which Parmenides lists at **156**. 40–1, habitually trip off our tongue; and if we let them do so, they will lure us, like a fatal *ignis fatuus*, along the marshy path of Opinion.[1] It seems probable that the 'echoing ear' is to be understood in the same fashion. Parmenides is not thinking of auditory illusions; he is warning us against listening to the foolish words of other mortals which perennially seduce us from the narrow path of Truth. Compare Heraclitus' advice to disregard other men's flowers and 'seek for ourselves' (above, p. 145). If I am right, then two of the three organs mentioned in **153** feature not as instruments of disreputable sense-experience but as channels for the subtle and semi-conscious insinuation of mortal opinion. The lines in **153** do more than warn against the errors of the senses.

Second, **153** does less than utter a general warning against perception. The lines occur in a specific context and their moral has a specific point: it is not that the senses are in general to be distrusted;

it is that the senses are not to be used against Parmenides' 'much-contending refutation'. Parmenides' request, as I have already remarked, is entirely just: when we turn to the backgammon board, we may find it impossible to believe that the Way of Truth is the way to metaphysical bliss; but that is no disproof of Parmenides' contentions. If we are to reject Parmenides' conclusion, then we must match reason with reason: we must show where his argument goes wrong.

In sum, 153 has very little to do with scepticism. Parmenides is saying no more than this: 'If you think my argument wrong, then *prove* it wrong; don't fall back into the lazy habits of common sense.' I do not deny that Parmenides was an enemy of the senses and that he 'hurled the senses out of truth' (pseudo-Plutarch, **A 22**). But that enmity is left implicit in Parmenides' poem: we have no formal argument for scepticism in the text, and no explicit statement of scepticism. Parmenides made no contribution to the history of Pyrrhonism.

(b) *Melissus on perception*

The case is otherwise with Melissus. Fragment **30 B 8** is long, but it merits a complete translation:

[i] Now this argument is the greatest sign that there is only one thing; but there are the following signs too.

[ii] If there were many things, they would have to be such as I say the one thing is. For if there is earth and water and air and fire and iron and gold and living and dead and black and white and the other things which men say are real—if there are these things, and we see and hear correctly, then each of them must be such as it first seemed to us, and must not change or become different (*heteroion*), but each thing must always be just as it is.

[iii] But now we are saying that we see and hear and grasp (*sunienai*) correctly; but what is hot seems to us to become cold, and what is cold hot, and what is hard soft, and what is soft hard, and living creatures seem to die and to come into being from what is not alive, and all these seem to alter (*heteroiousthai*), and what was and is now seem to be in no way homogeneous; but the iron which is hard seems to be rubbed away by the finger . . . ,[2] and so do gold and stone and everything else that seems to be strong, {Hence it follows that we neither see nor know what is the case[3]} and earth and stone seem to come into being from water.

[iv] Now these things are not in agreement with one another. For although we say that the many things both are eternal and

have forms and strength, they all seem to us to alter and to change from the state in which they are at any time seen.

[v] It is clear, then, that we do not see correctly, and that those many things do not correctly seem to be. For they would not change if they were real, but they would be just as each seemed to be; for nothing is greater than what is real. But if they change, what is has perished and what is not has come into being. Now in this way if there were many things they would have to be such as the one thing is (**191**).

As paragraph [i] explicitly states, the burden of **191** is to provide additional support for monism: the 'argument' to which [i] refers is presumably that of **164**; whether **191** contains all the additional 'signs' that Melissus promises is unknown. Aristocles, who quotes part of [ii] and [iii], says that Melissus 'wants to show that none of the phenomena and things we see exists in reality' (**A 14**); and Simplicius introduces **191** to illustrate Melissus' attitude to sense-perception. And those ancient critics were at least half correct; for one of the things Melissus attempts to do in **191** is to argue that 'we do not see correctly'.

The argument is in *reductio* form. Paragraph [ii] sets out the hypothesis to be reduced; it is in fact the conjunction of:
(1a) There exists several things, $a_1, a_2, \ldots a_n$,
and
(1b) Our senses are veridical.
Melissus' illustrations for (1a) sound strange to modern ears; but they doubtless reflect the various pluralisms, lay and professional, that Melissus met with in his philosophical conversations.[4] The conjunct (1b) is usually stated for the cases of sight and hearing; but I assume that Melissus has the general case in mind, and I believe that by '*sunienai* (grasp)' in [iii] he means 'perceive'.

Paragraph [ii] also begins the *reductio*: asserting, reasonably, that each member of the plurality in (1a) would have to have the properties which the Eleatic deduction has shown to be essential to all existents, Melissus infers in particular that:
(2) No a ever changes.
He also argues, with needless ingenuity, that:
(3) If a_i seems ϕ at t, then a_i is always ϕ.

Paragraph [iii] looks more seriously at (1b): any number of changes seem to take place; the hardest things are rubbed away, and the most different things emerge from one another. Our senses tell us that everything changes; hence, by (1b), we get to:
(4) Every a_i constantly changes.

(The word 'constantly' is not in Melissus' text; but it is, I think, implicit in the last phrase of paragraph [iv].)

The argument is now over; for, as [iv] points out, (2) and (4) 'are not in agreement with one another'. Thus [v] concludes to the negations of (1a) and (1b): 'we do not see correctly, and . . . those many things do not correctly seem to be'.[5] The remainder of [v] merely repeats the assertion made in [ii], that from (1a) an Eleatic can properly derive (2) and (3): if the many things are *real*, then the predicates of Eleatic metaphysics must hold of them.

What are the merits of this ingenious piece of reasoning? First, it is worth noting that, despite [i], it does not purport to be entirely independent of Eleatic metaphysics; on the contrary, the move from (1a) to (2) explicitly applies familiar Eleatic properties to a putatively plural world. Such an application might seem wholly trivial: apply monism itself, and (1a) leads at once to a contradiction. But that would be unbearably jejune; and Melissus does not intend it. In his move to (2) he applies (T 7), the thesis that what exists does not alter. Now (T 7) was indeed inferred from (T 5), the thesis of monism; but it also inferred directly from (T 1), the thesis that what exists cannot be generated (above, p. 215), and paragraph [v] serves the important function of indicating that it is that second inference that Melissus means to call upon. In short, Melissus argues that any pluralist must accept at least (T 1), and hence (T 7); and that then pluralism collapses. The 'neo-Ionians', to whom the first chapters of volume 2 are devoted, did, some of them, attempt to hold both (T 1) and pluralism.

Aristocles introduces his quotation of [ii]–[iii] with a scathing criticism:

> Now this is most absurd: showing by argument that [the senses] are useless, in fact they continually rely heavily upon them—Melissus, who wants to show that none of the phenomena and the things we see exists in reality, proves it by means of the phenomena themselves.

Having quoted Melissus' own words he proceeds:

> When he says this, and much more in the same vein, one might well ask him: 'Is it not by perception that you know that what is now hot later becomes cold?'—and similarly in the other cases. For as I said, he will be found to be doing away with and refuting the senses by means of a peculiar trust in them (**192: A 14**).

Aristocles here initiates a longstanding objection to scepticism of the senses: in order to construct their arguments, the sceptics have to start from the data of perception; so based, their arguments are bound to be self-refuting. Melissus relies heavily on the senses; for he sets down (1b) as a premiss, and construes it in the strongest way possible, as saying that every sense report is true. Having said that, he proceeds to infer the falsity of all sense reports. What could be more absurd?

The charge of self-refutation may stand against some sceptics, but it has no hold on Melissus. Aristocles has misread Melissus' argument: Melissus does not assert that (1b) is true—he presents it as a hypothesis which he will show to be false. Nor does he assert that (2) is true; for (2) depends upon (1b). The only fact about the senses to which Melissus does commit himself is this: that, according to our senses, things change. To believe that is not to show 'a peculiar trust' in the senses.

Aristocles' charge of self-refutation fails, but there is a sound point in his criticism. Melissus construes (1b) in a strong fashion; and no self-respecting partisan of the senses would maintain that every sense report is true. In fact, Melissus does not need the strong construe of (1b); without it he will get neither (3) nor (4)—but he does not really use (3), and he does not require (4). To discover a contradiction he need only establish the contradictory of (2), which is not (4) but:
(5) Some a_i sometimes changes.
However weak we care to make (1b), it will surely remain powerful enough to give (5): the man who pretends to place some trust in his senses and yet believes that the world is an unchanging place can hardly be taken seriously. Partisans of the senses must not believe everything their favourites tell them; but their partisanship is empty if they deny such propositions as (5).

A more tolerable objection remains: 'Melissus' handling of the *reductio* is poor: the conjunction of (2) and (5) is certainly a contradiction; but Melissus cannot infer that both (1a) and (1b) are false: at most he can infer the negation of their conjunction, "Not both (1a) and (1b)".' That objection is sound; and it makes a fatal breach in Melissus' argument as he states it. But it is possible to repair the wall and restore the argument.

Since he cannot retain both (1a) and (1b), Melissus' opponent has two positions open to him: he may abandon (1a) and hold to (1b); or he may maintain (1a) and give up (1b). The first of those positions is quickly demolished by an argument closely parallel to that of **191**: if our senses are veridical, then we live in a plural world. Just as any serious advocate of (1b), however weakly he construes it, must admit the truth of (5), so any serious advocate of (1b) must allow that the world exhibits diversity and is not a monolithic whole. It is absurd to support the senses and be a monist. Melissus' opponent must therefore retreat to the second position; and that too must be abandoned if Melissus can prove:

(6) If there exist several things, $a_1, a_2, \ldots a_n$, then our senses are veridical.

Now Melissus will certainly have reflected that it is only sense perception which suggests a plural world: reason, as the Eleatic deduction shows, leads inexorably to monism. That reflexion will not yield (6) but it will yield:

(7) If there is reason to believe that there exist several objects, $a_1, a_2, \ldots a_n$, then our senses are veridical.

I imagine that even pluralists who deny Melissus' rational path to monism will be prepared to accept (7). In itself (7) does not suffice to demolish the second position; but it does show that any occupant of that position is committed to:

(8) There exist several things and there is no reason to believe that there exist several things.

Propositions of the same form as (8)—'*P* and there is no reason to believe that *P*'—are not self-contradictory; but anyone who holds to (8) is thereby acting irrationally, in one clear sense of that term. Many philosophers will maintain that some irrationalities of that sort are acceptable: there are some things we may or even must believe in the absence of reasons; but even if that is true, it seems unlikely that (8) can be numbered among such favoured propositions. I conclude that in (8) Melissus has a final answer to his opponent: the argument of 191 cannot be rationally defeated. Of course, Melissus has not proved scepticism; he has argued that, given the fundamental thesis of Eleatic metaphysics, (T 1), scepticism can be securely established by way of (T 7). The argument is not general: it is tied to Eleatic theory; but it is, for all that, ingenious and powerful.

Appendix A Sources

Our knowledge of the Presocratic philosophers is almost entirely indirect; for even where we possess their actual words, those words are preserved, fragmentarily, as quotations in the works of later authors. The sources we rely upon for *testimonia* and fragments span two millennia: they differ widely, one from another, in their literary aims, their historical competence, and their philosophical interests.

This appendix lists *in chronological order* the ancient authors I have quoted from or alluded to in the text and the notes. Some of the authors are (from a Presocratic point of view) of minor or minimal importance. A single asterisk is prefixed to the names of the more freely flowing sources; and those few gushing streams are marked by a pair of stars. Each name is followed by a date, often roundly given, and the briefest of biographical sentences. When a 'principal work' is named, that is not necessarily the author's major *opus*, but rather the book which holds most interest for students of the Presocratics.

Where no edition of the ancient text is mentioned, the reader may assume that I have used only the excerpts printed in Diels-Kranz. In citing editions I use these abbreviations:
CIAG *Commentaria in Aristotelem Graeca* (Berlin, 1881–1909)
OCT Oxford Classical Texts
SdA *Die Schule des Aristoteles*, ed. F. Wehrli (Basel, 1967–9²)

HERODOTUS: $c.485-c.430$; the father of history. Edition: OCT, Hude.
HIPPOCRATES: $c.480-c.400$. The Hippocratic *corpus* is a compilation of works of various dates and of a medical character; perhaps none of them was written by the great Hippocrates himself. Abbreviations:
cord de corde
morb de morbo

morb sacr   *de morbo sacro*
nat puer   *de natura puerorum*
vet med   *de vetere medicina* (ed. Festugière [218])
vict   *de victu*
Edition: Littré, Paris, 1839–61.
ISOCRATES: 436–338; orator, statesman, and opponent of the Academy. Edition: Teubner, Benseler and Blass.
XENOPHON: *c*.430–*c*.355; general, historian, and pupil of Socrates. Principal work: *Memorabilia*. Edition: OCT, Marchant.
*PLATO: 427–347; his dialogues contain numerous references to his Presocratic predecessors. Edition: OCT, Burnet.
SPEUSIPPUS: d.340; Plato's nephew and successor as head of the Academy; only fragments of his writings survive. Edition: Lang, Bonn, 1911.
XENOCRATES: fl. second half of fourth century; pupil of Plato who succeeded Speusippus as head of the Academy. Only fragments remain. Edition: Heinze [311].
**ARISTOTLE: 384–322; son of a doctor, pupil of Plato, and master of those who know. Abbreviations and editions:
An   *de Anima* (OCT, Ross)
APst   *Posterior Analytics* (OCT, Ross)
Cael   *de Caelo* (OCT, Allan)
EE   *Eudemian Ethics* (Teubner, Susemihl)
EN   *Nicomachean Ethics* (OCT, Bywater)
fr.   *Fragmenta* (Teubner, Rose)
GA   *de Generatione Animalium* (OCT, Drossaart Lulofs)
GC   *de Generatione et Corruptione* (Joachim, Oxford, 1922)
HA   *Historia Animalium* (Louis, Paris, 1964–9)
Met   *Metaphysics* (OCT, Jaeger)
Meteor   *Meteorologica* (Fobes, Cambridge Mass, 1919)
PA   *de Partibus Animalium* (Loeb, Peck)
Phys   *Physics* (OCT, Ross)
Poet   *Poetics* (OCT, Kassel)
Pol   *Politics* (OCT, Ross)
Resp   *de Respiratione* (in *Parva Naturalia*, Ross, Oxford, 1955)
Rhet   *Rhetoric* (OCT, Ross)
Sens   *de Sensu* (in *Parva Naturalia*, Ross, Oxford, 1955)
Top   *Topics*, including *Sophistici Elenchi* (OCT, Ross)
Pseudo-Aristotelian works:
lin insec *de lineis insecabilibus* (Timpanaro Cardini, Milan, 1970)
MM   *Magna Moralia* (Teubner, Susemihl)
MXG   *de Melisso, Xenophane, Gorgia* (Teubner, Apelt)

Prob   Problems (Teubner, Ruelle)
HERACLIDES PONTICUS: *c*.390–*c*.310; Platonist and Pythagorean, renowned as a dandy. Only fragments survive. Edition: SdA VII.
*THEOPHRASTUS: 371–287; Aristotle's greatest pupil and his successor. Only fragments survive. Abbreviation:
Sens   de Sensu
Edition: Diels [4].
ARISTOXENUS: b. *c*.370; musical theorist with Pythagorean interests. Edition: SdA II.
DICAEARCHUS: b. *c*.340; Aristotelian philosopher, only fragments of whose writings are preserved. Edition: SdA I.
*EUDEMUS: fourth century; pupil of Aristotle, philosopher, and historian of mathematics. Edition: SdA VIII.
MENO: fourth century; pupil of Aristotle, and author of history of medicine.
EPICURUS: 342–270; founder and eponym of Epicureanism, a philosophy strongly influenced by Democritus. Principal work: *Letter to Herodotus*. Abbreviations:
ad Hdt   Letter to Herodotus
ad Men   Letter to Menoeceus
Edition: Arrighetti, Turin, 1960.
HERMIPPUS: third century BC, follower of Callimachus; sensational biographer.
SATYRUS: third century BC, peripatetic biographer.
TIMON: 320–230; sceptic philosopher and poet. Edition: Diels [3].
ERATOSTHENES: *c*.280–200; geographer, scholar, and librarian at Alexandria.
CRATES OF MALLOS: mid-second century; scholar and librarian at Pergamum.
SOTION: second century BC, peripatetic historian of philosophy.
ARIUS DIDYMUS: first century BC; Stoic philosopher, teacher of Augustus.
ALEXANDER POLYHISTOR: *c*.105–*c*.25 BC; a Greek who became a Roman prisoner of war and then a polymath. Principal work: *Hypomnemata Pythagorica*.
DEMETRIUS OF MAGNESIA: flourished *c*.50 BC; a source for Diogenes Laertius.
CICERO: 106–43 BC: statesman, orator, master of prose, poet *manqué*, and amateur philosopher.
LUCRETIUS: 97–55 BC; Roman interpreter of Epicureanism in rough hexameters. Work: *de Rerum Natura*. Edition: OCT, Bailey.
PHILODEMUS: *c*.80–*c*.35 BC; Epicurean philosopher, fragments of

whose works were discovered in the lava of Vesuvius.

NICOLAUS OF DAMASCUS: fl. second half of first century BC; historian and polymath, who wrote commentaries on Aristotle.

DIODORUS SICULUS: fl. $c.35$ BC; author of a *Universal History*. Edition: Teubner, Vogel and Fischer.

DIONYSIUS OF HALICARNASSUS: fl. end of first century BC; historian, and leading literary critic.

STRABO: 64 BC–AD 20; Romanophile Greek geographer.

AGATHEMERUS: first century AD; geographer.

OVID: 43 BC–AD 18; amatory poet. Principal work: *Metamorphoses*. Abbreviation and edition:

Metam   *Metamorphoses* (Ehwald and Albrecht, Zürich, 1966)

PHILO: $c.10$ BC–$c.$AD 40; Jewish theologian and philosopher.

VITRUVIUS: fl. $c.$AD 30; leading Roman authority on architecture.

SENECA THE YOUNGER: AD 4–65: politician, Stoic philosopher, playwright. Principal works: *Quaestiones Naturales; Letters*.

PLINY THE ELDER: 23–79: minor politician and omnivorous observer, killed while scrutinizing the eruption of Vesuvius. Work: *Naturalis Historia*.

*PLUTARCH: 45–$c.120$. Biographer and philosopher, whose numerous philosophical essays are known collectively as the *Moralia*. Abbreviations and editions:

adv Col   *adversus Colotem* (Teubner, Pohlenz and Westman)
aud poet   *de audiendis poetis* (Teubner, Bernardakis)
comm not   *de communibus notitiis* (Teubner, Pohlenz)
exil   *de exilio* (Teubner, Bernardakis)
Plat quaest   *Platonicae quaestiones* (Teubner, Hubert)
soll anim   *de sollertia animalium* (Teubner, Hubert)
tranq   *de tranquillitate animae* (Teubner, Bernardakis)

*AËTIUS: fl. $c.100$. Eclectic philosopher, whose doxography (the *Placita* or *Opinions*) was reconstructed by Diels from Stobaeus and pseudo-Plutarch (2). Edition: Diels [4].

NICOMACHUS OF GERASA: $c.100$; Neoplatonist mathematician.

FAVORINUS: $c.80$–$c.150$, hermaphrodite, favourite of Hadrian, friend of Plutarch, polymath.

JULIUS SORANUS: fl. 100–140; leading physician and author of history of medicine.

PTOLEMY: fl. $c.140$. Geographer, mathematician and astronomer. Principal work: *Syntaxis mathematica*—the '*Almagest*'. Edition: Teubner, Heiberg.

THEON OF SMYRNA: first half of second century; Platonist mathematician.

ARISTOCLES: second century, teacher of Alexander of Aphrodisias and historian of philosophy.

GALEN: 129–199; the most celebrated doctor of the age, and a copious author.

HERMOGENES: b. c.150; orator and rhetorician.

TERTULLIAN: 160–220; Christian theologian with rhetorical and legal interests.

AULUS GELLIUS: second century, antiquarian and grammarian; his *Noctes Atticae* is a philosophico-legal miscellany.

JULIUS POLLUX: second century; successful teacher of rhetoric. Work: *Onomasticon*.

DIOGENES OF OENOANDA: second century; Epicurean, who had his philosophy inscribed on stone. Edition: Teubner, Chilton (several new fragments not yet collectively published).

HARPOCRATION: ? second-century lexicographer.

PSEUDO-PLUTARCH (1): mid-second century, author of *Stromateis*, a doxographical compilation. Edition: Diels [4].

*PSEUDO-PLUTARCH (2): mid-second century, author of an *Epitome* of the *Placita* (see Aëtius). Edition: Diels [4].

TATIAN: second half of second century, Christian apologist and rhetorician.

*CLEMENT OF ALEXANDRIA: c.150–215, the first major Christian philosopher. Principal work: *Stromateis*.

AELIAN: fl. second half of second century, author of miscellaneous natural histories.

ATHENAGORAS: fl. c.180, Athenian philosopher and Christian apologist.

**DIOGENES LAERTIUS: ? third century; scissors and paste historian of philosophy. Work: *Lives of the Philosophers*. Edition: OCT, Long.

PHILOSTRATUS: third-century sophist and author of *Lives of the Sophists*.

CENSORINUS: third-century Roman grammarian. Principal work: *de die natali*.

HERMIAS: ? third to sixth century, author of *Gentilium Philosophorum Irrisio*. Edition: Diels [4].

*SEXTUS EMPIRICUS: fl. 180–200, massive compiler of sceptical *topoi* and our main source for ancient scepticism. Abbreviations and Editions:

adv Math   Against the Mathematicians (Teubner, Mau)
Pyrr Hyp   Outlines of Pyrrhonism (Teubner, Mau).

ALEXANDER OF APHRODISIAS: fl. c.200, seminal commentator on the works of Aristotle. Abbreviation:

quaest nat   quaestiones naturales
Edition: CIAG.

APPENDIX A SOURCES

ATHENAEUS: fl. *c*.200, author of the anecdotal miscellany, *Deipnosophistae*.

*HIPPOLYTUS: d. 235: presbyter of Rome, opposed to the Establishment. Principal work: *Refutatio Omnium Haeresium* (*Ref. Haer*). Edition: Diels [4].

PLOTINUS: 205–70, the principal philosopher of the period between Aristotle and Aquinas. Work: *Enneads*.

DIONYSIUS OF ALEXANDRIA: flourished *c*. 250, episcopal opponent of atomism.

PORPHYRY: 234–303, Neoplatonist pupil of Plotinus. Abbreviations and editions:
de Abst   *de Abstinentia* (Teubner, Nauck)
VP   *Vita Pythagorae* (Teubner, Nauck)

ACHILLES: third-century astronomer and mathematician.

EUSEBIUS: *c*.260–340, bishop of Caesarea and leading churchman; principal work: *Praeparatio Evangelica* (*PE*).

ANATOLIUS: fl. 270. Bishop of Laodicea, saint, Aristotelian, and mathematician.

CHALCIDIUS: 256–357, Christian philosopher; his Latin commentary on Plato's *Timaeus* had enormous influence on later ages.

IAMBLICHUS: fourth-century pupil of Porphyry. Abbreviations and editions:
comm math sc   *de communi mathematica scientia* (Teubner, Festa)
VP   *de Vita Pythagorica* (Teubner, Deubner)

LACTANTIUS: fl. *c*.320, prolific Christian author, influenced by the Platonic and hermetic traditions. Principal work: *de Ira*.

THEMISTIUS: 317–388, Constantinopolitan orator and philosopher, who paraphrased Aristotle's works.

EPIPHANIUS: *c*.315–403, bishop of Salamis. Edition: Diels [4].

AUGUSTINE: 354–428, saint and church father, author of *Confessions* and *City of God*.

SERVIUS: fl. *c*.400, grammarian and author of celebrated commentary on Vergil.

MACROBIUS: early fifth century, author of the literary symposium, *Saturnalia*.

*STOBAEUS: early fifth-century excerptor with particular interest in philosophy. Work: *Florilegium*. Edition: Diels [4].

HESYCHIUS: fifth-century lexicographer.

THEODORETUS: 393–466, Bishop of Cyrrhus, Christian apologist.

BOETHIUS: d. 480, the last of the Romans; author of the *Consolatio Philosophiae* and numerous more professional works.

CLAUDIANUS MAMERTINUS: d. 474, Neoplatonist. Principal work: *de statu animae*.

APPENDIX A   SOURCES

PROCLUS: c.410–485, leading Neoplatonist philosopher and author of valuable commentaries on Plato's dialogues. Abbreviations and editions:
in Parm   Commentary on the *Parmenides* (Cousin, Paris, 1864)
in Tim   Commentary on the *Timaeus* (Teubner, Diehl)
PSEUDO-GALEN: c.500, author of *Historia Philosopha*. Edition: Diels [4].
EUTOCIUS: c.500, Byzantine mathematician who wrote commentaries on Apollonius and Archimedes.
AMMONIUS: c.440–520. A pupil of Proclus and leading Platonist of the Alexandrian school; commentator on Aristotle and influential teacher. Edition: CIAG.
PHILOPONUS: c.490–570, Christian pupil of Ammonius; author of commentaries on Aristotle. Edition: CIAG.
**SIMPLICIUS: fl. c.550, Ammonius' greatest pupil, and a major source for early Greek philosophy. Edition: CIAG.
OLYMPIODORUS: second half of sixth century, pupil of Ammonius and commentator on Plato.
ELIAS: end of sixth century, pupil of Olympiodorus and commentator on Aristotle. Edition: CIAG.
SUDA: tenth-century, a large Byzantine lexicon, formerly known as Suidas.
HISDOSUS: fl. c.1100, wrote on Plato's psychology.
TZETZES: c.1110–85, leading Byzantine scholar.
ALBERTUS MAGNUS: c.1200–80; St Albert the Great, teacher of Aquinas and Parisian exponent of Aristotle.
SCHOLIASTS on various authors: the margins of many ancient manuscripts contain notes or 'scholia'; the dates and identities of most scholiasts are unknown.

Appendix B Chronology

Our evidence for Presocratic chronology is scrappy, confused and unreliable: few thinkers can be dated with any precision; and monumental dispute governs all. My chronological table, then, has no high aspirations: its sole aim is to provide the reader with a rough and approximate idea of the temporal relationships that hold among the Presocratic philosophers. The table is tentative (broken lines indicate uncertainty); and it represents orthodoxy (in so far as any view here is orthodox). The reader who is hungry for more information should begin by consulting the relevant pages of Guthrie [25] or of Zeller-Mondolfo [26].

Timeline of Ancient Greek Philosophers (BC 620–350)

Philosopher	Approximate Date Range (BC)
Thales	~624–546
Anaximander	~610–546
Pherecydes	~585–520
Anaximenes	~585–525
Pythagoras	~570–495
Heraclitus	~535–475
Epicharmus	~530–450
Parmenides	~515–450
Hippasus	~530–450
Xenophanes	~570–475
Alcmeon	~500–450
Anaxagoras	~500–428
Empedocles	~490–430
Zeno	~490–430
Protagoras	~490–420
Gorgias	~485–380
Archelaus	~480–430
Melissus	~470–430
Antiphon the Orator	~480–411
Hippon	~470–430
Socrates	~470–399
Antiphon the Sophist	~470–410
Thrasymachus	~459–400
Lycophron	~450–400
Hippias	~460–400
Ion of Chios	~480–420
Philolaus	~470–385
Diogenes of Apollonia	~460–390
Leucippus	~460–390
Democritus	~460–370
Prodicus	~465–395
Critias	~460–403
Diagoras	~460–400
Eurytus	~450–390
Cratylus	~440–390
Archytas	~435–347
Plato	~428–348

Notes

The text of the book is intended to be self-sufficient; and the reader who ignores these notes should not find the main narrative broken or its arguments enthymematic. The notes are designed to serve four subsidiary functions.

First, they supply additional references to the ancient texts. (For the abbreviations used see the Note on Citations, and Appendix A.)

Second, the notes broach issues too technical or too narrow to justify inclusion in the body of the book.

Third, they explain (and sometimes attempt to justify) disputed readings, translations, or interpretations which the main narrative adopts without comment.

Fourth, there are some selected references to the secondary literature. (References consist of the author's name; a numeral, in square brackets, keying the work to the Bibliography; and, usually, a page or chapter number.) It is customary in scholarly works to compile references, pious and polemical, to authors who agree and disagree with a given interpretation. That practice is a pedantic pleasantry, of little value to the reader; and, apart from acknowledgments of direct quotations, I only provide references where they are likely to yield a useful supplement to my own remarks. The reader who seeks bibliographical assistance will find it, I hope, in the Bibliography.

I *The Springs of Reason*

1 On Hippias as a source for Aristotle see esp. Snell [13]; also Stokes [56], 50–60. Democritus also wrote about Thales: Diogenes Laertius, I.11 = **68 B 115a**.
2 Cf. e.g., Epicharmus, **23 B 4.5**; Anonymous Iamblichi, **89 A 4.3**.
3 See Alexander, *quaest nat* II.23, a text which includes Empedocles, **31 A 89**; Anaxagoras, **59 A 98a**; Diogenes, **64 A 33**; Democritus, **68 A 165**.

4 Propositions (4) and (5) are also found in Diogenes Laertius, I.27 = **A 1**; Scholiast to Plato, **A 3**; Simplicius, Servius, **A 13**; etc. (see Classen [88], 939). The two theses may conceivably have formed parts of a full cosmogony and cosmology (thesis (5) was used in the explanation of earthquakes: Seneca, **A 15**) see West [87], 172–6; [59], 208–13.
5 Stokes [56], 283, n. 113, suggests that the analogy with wood was intended to show only the *possibility* of the earth's floating on water; Kirk-Raven [33], 88, think that the analogy may have been supplied by Aristotle and doubt that Thales ever considered the problem of the earth's stability. Neither view is plausible.
6 Some scholars are content with the explanation that Thales was adopting an Egyptian myth: see especially Hölscher [91], 40–8 (the explanation is already in Plutarch, **A 11**, and Simplicius, **A 14**). Thales' tour of Egypt (Proclus, **A 11**, etc.) is of dubious historicity.
7 On Alcman see West [87] and [108]; on poetico-mythological cosmogony see Stokes [109]; Kirk-Raven [33], 24–72; Hölscher [91], 49–82; Schwabl [107], 1437–74.
8 West [59], 75. On Pherecydes see especially West [59], chh. 1–2; Kirk-Raven [33], 48–72. Some scholars have thought that Pherecydes' aim was to interpret the old mythological cosmogonies in the new Milesian spirit (see Jaeger [48], 67–72; *contra:*; Vlastos [161], 106–10).
9 So, e.g., Guthrie [25], I.46–9; the scepticism of Dicks [42], 298, etc., is excessive.
10 References in Classen [88], 941–3 (mathematics), 943–5 (astronomy). Extreme scepticism in Dicks [86]; extreme credulity in van der Waerden [58], 86–90; a balanced view in Burkert [173], 415–17. (Note that Herodotus did not credit the stories of Thales' engineering feats: they are 'the common tale of the Greeks'. For late Thaletan romance see Classen [88], 931–5.) Thales is the archetypical geometer for Aristophanes: *Birds*, 995, 1009; *Clouds*, 215. Three of the books ascribed to Thales concern astronomy (**B 1, B 2, B 4**); but all the ascriptions are almost certainly wrong.
11 On this report see especially Gladigow [89].
12 According to Proclus, Thales 'is said to have called equal angles "similar" in the archaic fashion' (**A 20**): this may come from Eudemus, and Eudemus' source may have been Hippias (cf. **86 B 12** = Eudemus, fr. 133 W). But we cannot infer that either Eudemus or Hippias possessed, or claimed to possess, a written work by Thales.
13 But (a) the central portion of Parmenides' poem has survived entire (see above, p. 155); (b) Gorgias' *Helen* is complete, and I shall treat it as a piece of philosophy (see vol. 2, pp. 221–8); and (c) some of the fifth-century works in the Hippocratic canon have a strong philosophical bias (see above, p. 139).
14 Fragments in Diels [4], 473–527. The long fragment on perception is edited by Stratton [14] who gives (51–64) a useful appreciation of Theophrastus' faults and merits. Most scholars, following Diels, hold that the *Phusikôn Doxai* was a comprehensive history of early Greek thought; and they infer that the Presocratic material extracted from that work has a better evidential standing than the stuff we quarry from Aristotle's treatises. Steinmetz [5] argues that the title '*Phusikôn Doxai*' was given to the collection of studies on individual Presocratics listed in Diogenes Laertius, V.42–7; that those studies were used by Theophrastus in his *Physics*; and that it is that latter work which formed Simplicius' main source. If Steinmetz is right, then the Theophrastan material is exactly comparable to the doxographical notices which we read in the Aristotelian treatises.

II Anaximander on Nature

15 For the case against Aristotle see Cherniss [6]; McDiarmid [7] completes his companion study of Theophrastus by asserting that he 'is a thoroughly biased witness and is even less trustworthy than Aristotle' (133). The best defence of Aristotle is still that in Guthrie [8] (but see Stevenson [9]); the best defence of Theophrastus is in Mondolfo-Tarán [131], CXCIII–CXCVIII.

16 The classic study is Diels' magisterial *Doxographi Graeci*. There is a useful summary of Diels in Burnet [31], and a detailed illustration in Stokes [56], ch. 3.

1 An epitome (or perhaps the work itself) survived to the time of Apollodorus; Anaximander may have gone to press at the age of 64 (see Diogenes Laertius, II.2 = **12 A 1**; cf. West [59], 76, n. 1). On Theopompus' report (Diogenes Laertius, I.116 = *FGrH* 115 F 71 = **7 A 1**) that Pherecydes 'was the first to write about nature and the birth of the gods', see Kahn [90], 6, n. 2; 240.

2 For a fine sketch of Anaximander's intellectual range see Kahn [90], 82–4; a main thesis of Kahn's book is the domination of later Presocratic speculation by Anaximander's conception of science.

3 See especially Kahn [90], 58–63; cf. Tannery [29]; Rescher [97] ('an intellect ... audacity': Rescher, 731).

4 On *metabiônai* see Kahn [90], 67; Kahn shows (70–1) that Plutarch's story in **A 30** is mere romance.

5 See, e.g., Anaxagoras, **59 A 42**; Democritus, **68 A 139**; Diodorus Siculus, I.7.

6 On Xenophanes' theory see Guthrie [25], I.387–90. The observations were repeated in the fifth century by Xanthus of Lydia, *FGrH* 765 F 12.

7 First quotation from Kahn [90], 97; second from Popper [35], 140. There is a splenetic attack on Kahn's 'monstrous edifice of exaggeration' in Dicks [65], which Kahn [66] answers. Both authors are unconvincingly extreme: see Burkert [173], 308–10.

8 Cf. Diogenes Laertius, II.1 = **A 1**; Suda, **A 2**; Simplicius, *in Cael* 532.14.

9 A version of the Principle may have been used by Parmenides (see below, p. 187); it is employed at *Phys* 203b25–8, a passage which may have Milesian origins (cf. Hussey [34], 18).

10 Kahn [90], 77.

11 Aristotle, *Cael* 295a16–b9 = **31 A 67**; see Bollack [349], III.242–4.

12 See *Phaedo* 108E; *Timaeus* 62D. The ascription to Empedocles is probably a loose reference to **31 A 67**; that to Parmenides, an inference from the spherical symmetry of his world (**28 B 8**.42–4); that to Democritus a plain error (cf. *Cael* 294b13). *Pace* Robinson [98], there is nothing in the argument which exceeds Anaximander's capacities or conflicts with the rest of his astronomy.

13 Some scholars think that Xenophanes' earth was not literally of infinite depth and that he was not seriously tackling Anaximander's problem (e.g., Kirk-Raven [33], 175–6); but see Stokes [56], 75; 286, nn. 18–19. Empedocles **31 B 39** is generally taken as a criticism of Xenophanes (see *Cael* 294a25); *contra*: Bollack [349] III.242.

14 Anaximenes, Anaxagoras, Democritus (*Cael* 294b13 = **13 A 20**); Xenophanes (Simplicius, **21 A 47**); Empedocles (*Cael* 295a15 = **31 A 67**). Eudemus, fr. 145 W = **12 A 26**, has Anaximander's earth move: either Theon has garbled Eudemus (Kahn [90], 54), or the text is corrupt (Burkert [173], 345, n. 38).

15 Sweeney [57], ch. 1, gives a full account of the voluminous publications on this topic from 1947 to 1970. The most distinguished contribution is Kahn [90].

16 Cf. Simplicius, *in Phys* 465.5-10, who probably alludes to Anaximander, though he names no name. (In *Cael* 615.15 names Anaximander; but that is in connexion with quite another argument.)
17 Kahn [101].
18 See Hölscher [91], 10-12; and especially Schwabl [99], 60-4; *contra*: Kahn [90], 37-8.
19 The precise extent of the fragment is uncertain: see especially Kahn [90], 168-78; and, more sceptically, Dirlmeier [100].
20 For controversy see McDiarmid [7], 138-40, n. 46; Kahn [90], 30-2; Kirk [92], 324-7. I follow Stokes [56], 28-9; 274-6.
21 The role of the 'opposites' in Anaximander's thought is obscure: see especially Lloyd [64], 260-70; Kahn [90], 40-1; Hölscher [91], 31-2. For a detailed account of the 'opposites' in early Greek thought see Lloyd [50], ch. 1.
22 Conflationists have been worried by the plurals in [iv] (*ex hôn . . . tauta . . .*), covertly making them singular or else asserting that 'the unlimited' is a mixture and hence a plurality. The grammatical difficulty vanishes once it is seen that [iii] and [iv] need not belong together. Kahn [90], 181-3, argues that 'the things that exist' in [iv] cannot be the ordinary furniture of the world but must be the elements 'from which' and 'into which' those things come and go. That makes for a tortuous construe.
23 This interpretation is strongly advocated by Schwabl [99]. He sets out from [vi], where he alleges that 'them (*auta*)' must refer to 'generation' and 'destruction' in [iv]. That gives a good sense to '*legôn auta*' ('calling them thus by . . .'), but it is otherwise implausible. Most interpreters take '*auta*' in [vi] to have the same reference as '*auta*' in [v], i.e. the elements. That gives a good sense to [vi], but it puts a great strain on the Greek. I suspect that '*auta*' in [vi] should be changed to '*autos*' ('himself speaking thus . . .') or else excised.
24 Kirk-Raven [33], 116-17, suggest that Anaximander actually used the Homeric formula 'immortal and ageless (*athanatos kai agêrôs*)', and that Aristotle and Hippolytus have each preserved a half of it.
25 A lucid account in Kirk-Raven [33], 110-12; cf. Gottschalk [104], 40-7. On the *metaxu* passages see Kahn [90], 44-6; Hölscher [91], 34-7. On *migma* see Vlastos [111], 76-80; Seligman [102], 40-9; Hölscher [91], 16-17.
26 See **59 B 12**; cf. Dicks [42], 57; Guthrie [25], II.296.
27 B 3 is generally rejected as spurious, and the language shows that it cannot be a *verbatim* report; but it may well be a fair paraphrase of Anaximenes (see West [59], 100, n. 3). The first 'and' in the quotation may belong to Olympiodorus, so that he preserves two fragments rather than one; certainly, the two parts of B 3 hang only loosely together.
28 If argument (B) does not belong to Anaximander, I guess that in **A 14** Aëtius has written 'Anaximander' by mistake for 'Anaximenes'.
29 The etymology is entertained and rejected by Kahn [90], 231-3; see further Solmsen [103], 123-4; Classen [94], 44-5 (cf. Aristotle, *Phys* 204a2,13). On '*apeiros*' in general see Guthrie [25], I.85-7.
30 'Like a fog-bank': Rescher [97], 719.

III Science and Speculation

1 See Hippolytus, **A 7**; Aristotle, *Meteor* 354a28 = **A 14**; Aëtius, **A 12**, **A 14**, **A 15**; Pliny, **A 14A**. The report of Eudemus, fr. 145 W = **A 16**, that Anaximenes first saw that the moon shines with borrowed light, is unreliable (see Guthrie

[25], I.94, n. 2). On Anaximenes' meteorology see Aristotle, *Meteor* 365b6 = **A 21**; Aëtius, **A 17, A 18**; Galen, **A 19**.

2 See Simplicius, **59 A 41**; Diogenes Laertius, IX.57 = **64 A 1**. 'In the eyes of his contemporaries, and for long after, Anaximenes was a much more important figure than Anaximander' (Burnet [31], 78).

3 See especially Stokes [56], 30–65. McDiarmid [7], 92, asserts that 'it is an obvious historical impossibility that any Presocratic should have held this concept [sc. of *hulê*], for the concept implies a grasp of the notion of identity and of the distinction between subject and attribute'. That argument barely deserves refutation.

4 Jaeger [48], 24.

5 A passage from Simplicius has puzzled commentators:

> Anaximenes says that when thinned the air becomes fire, when condensed, wind.... For in his case alone Theophrastus in his *History* [i.e. in the *Phusikôn Doxai*] speaks of rarefaction and condensation. But it is clear that the others too used rareness and denseness (*in Phys* 149.30–150.1; cf. **A 5**).

Elsewhere, in passages presumably derived from Theophrastus, Simplicius and the other doxographers use '*manôsis*' and '*puknôsis*' of many Presocratic cosmogonies. (See, e.g., *in Phys* 202.32–203.5; 1266.33–8; 1319.17–27; cf., e.g., Aristotle, *Phys* 187a15; *GC* 330b10.) Simplicius does not report (*pace* Cherniss [6], 13, n. 55) that according to Theophrastus only Anaximenes used rarefaction and condensation; nor (*pace* Stokes [56], 273, n. 22) can he mean that Theophrastus used the words '*manôsis*' and '*puknôsis*' only in connexion with Anaximenes. Perhaps he means that in his *History*, as opposed to his *Physics*, Theophrastus speaks of rarefaction and condensation only in the case of Anaximenes. If so, then we shall infer that Simplicius' principal Theophrasten source was not the *History* (see above, p. 313, n. 14); and we may wonder how Theophrastus described non-Anaximenean cosmogonies in the *History*. Klowski [106] argues that the operation of condensation and rarefaction was an invention of Theophrastus, falsely fathered by him on the Presocratics; Stokes [56], 43–8, argues that condensation and rarefaction do not imply an Aristotelian interpretation of Anaximenes' air. Neither argument appeals.

6 Sambursky [53], 10–11; cf. Guthrie [25], I.126–7. It should in fairness be added that, in Sambursky's opinion, 'it is a far cry from the speculative teaching of Anaximenes to the extremely abstract calculations of the physicist and mathematician of today' (11).

7 The term 'felting' for condensation ('*pilêsis*', '*pilousthai*': Hippolytus, **A 7**; pseudo-Plutarch, **A 6**) has been thought Anaximenean; but it is common in the doxographers (see Diels-Kranz [1], III.352b).

8 But the point is controversial: Guthrie [25], I.131, n. 1.

9 Burnet [31], v; cf. 24–8. Popper [35] gives a strong statement of Burnet's thesis, on grounds diametrically opposed to those of Burnet.

10 See especially Cornford [114]. According to Raven [178], 175, Presocratic thought tends to rely 'on dogmatic reasoning alone' and shows 'a cheerful ignorance of the conditions of scientific knowledge'.

11 Vlastos [115], 53.

12 See Sambursky [53], 283–41. On the vagueness endemic in Presocratic science see especially Vlastos [115], 51–3; Dicks [42], 60–1.

13 Lloyd [113] gives an excellent account of the place of experiment in early Greek thought; the best examples are in Hippocrates, *morb* IV.39; *nat puer* 17.
14 Jones [49], 44.
15 Sambursky [53], 89, is mistaken when he says that experiment is 'now the final arbiter of every theory' and contrasts this modern notion with that of the Greeks. At 231-8 he argues in detail that lack of experimentation gravely impeded the advance of Greek science; but at 235 he observes that 'the heavenly phenomena display all the ideal qualities of a laboratory experiment'.
16 Kahn [66], 112. 'The apparently bizarre speculations of the early thinkers are rarely entirely divorced from observation, but sometimes depend on rather extravagant extrapolation from it' (Guthrie [25], II.188). But note first, that the word 'extrapolation' implies an hypothesis about Milesian procedure which we cannot test; and second, that the 'extravagance' is not shown by reliance on a paucity of data, but rather by a carefree connexion between data and theory. Dicks [65], 36, affirms that the Presocratics *'were not scientists*—and actual observation seems to have played a very minor part in their astronomical theories'. Of course, it does not matter a hang whether the Presocratics made their own observations (like Kepler), or simply worked from reports of others (like Newton).
17 Examples collected in Kranz [121]; Lloyd [50], part II. See also Baldry [122], and the celebrated paper by Diller [120], who judges that Anaximenes marks 'the birth of the analogical method' (35).
18 Text and interpretation are disputed: Guthrie [123], Longrigg [124], and especially Schwabl [125].
19 A full examination of **26** in Alt [127], who concludes (unconvincingly) that it is a fragment of Diogenes of Apollonia. Although **26** contains anachronistic vocabulary (Alt [127], 129-30) and has been judged a fabrication (especially Reinhardt [30], 175), I side with those who find it Anaximenean in content (see Guthrie [25], I.131-2). Most scholars take *'hoion . . . kai . . .'* for an inferential construction: 'just as . . . so . . .'. (For different ways of construing the inference see Kirk-Raven [33], 158.) It is better to read *'hoion'* as 'e.g.', the doxographer's introduction to the quotation which follows; and I guess that the *'kai'* is doxographical, conjoining two quotations. See especially Longrigg [126].

IV The Natural Philosophy of Heraclitus

1 Popper [137], I.17; Hegel [27], 279. On Heraclitus' early followers see Diogenes Laertius, IX.6 = **A** 1; for early exegetes, *id.*, IX.15 = **A** 1; Antiphanes, fr. 113 K. An exhaustive discussion of the traditions and controversies surrounding Heraclitus' life in Marcovich [140], 246-56.
2 On Hippolytus see Reinhardt [30], 158-63; Hershbell [17]; on Clement see Reinhardt [135]; on the Stoics see Hölscher [79], 150-3; Marcovich [140], 315-17.
3 Note that Pythagoras was incarnated as a Delian diver: above, p. 108.
4 Numerals succeeded by '**M**' refer to the fragments in the edition of Marcovich [129]; whether or not that arrangement is correct, it is vastly superior to that of Diels-Kranz.
5 On Heraclitus' 'Orakelstil' see especially Hölscher [79], 136-41.
6 Some scholars deny that Heraclitus wrote a book and suppose instead a disjointed set of aphorisms (e.g., Kirk [136], 7). That view explains the ordering of the fragments in Diels-Kranz: the nature of Heraclitus' effusions prohibits systematic

arrangement, and Diels took the alphabetical order of the quoting authorities as a suitably arbitrary schema within which to print the fragments. There are ancient references to Heraclitus' book (Aristotle, *Rhet* 1407b16 = **A 4**; Diogenes Laertius, IX.1,5, 6, 7, 12 = **A 1**); but that book might have been an anthology of saws. But fragment **33** = **B 1** = **1 M** both by its form and by its content promises a continuous and systematic treatise (see, e.g., Guthrie [25], I.406–8; Kahn [139], 189–91).

7 See, e.g., Guthrie [25], I. 420–4; Hölscher [79], 130–43; Marcovich [129], 2–11; and, for a clear exposition of the right view, West [59], 124–9.

8 See, e.g., Snell [144], 139; West [59], 113–14. That will explain the initial 'and (*de*)' in **33**, if explanation is needed.

9 See the useful table in Kirk [136], 47.

10 Cf. **B 64** = **79 M**:

The thunderbolt steers all things (cf. **B 41** = **85 M**).

But the connexion between the *logos* and the thunderbolt is uncertain: see Kirk [136], 356–7; West [59], 142–4. On **B 114** see p. 132.

11 For the text of **34** see Marcovich [129], 125. I take 'conjunctions' to mean 'composite things', i.e. to denote the ordinary furniture of the world; and I suppose that the first three clauses of the fragment say that 'all composite things are both unities and diversities' (see, e.g., Snell [146]; Kirk [136], 173–7).

12 For the text see Ramnoux [142], 461–3. Kirk [136], 70, thinks that **35** presents an inference from the *logos*; Stokes [56], 102, says that 'it is apparent from **B 50** that the unity of all things is the principal content of the Logos'. Neither view is in the text.

13 '*Palintonos harmoniê*' or '*palintropos harmoniê*'? 'Back-stretched connexion' or 'back-turning connexion'? For the controversy see Marcovich [129], 215–16. On *harmoniê* see also Stokes [56], 94–7; on *-tonos* and *-tropos*, Hussey [34], 43–5. I doubt if anything turns on the textual dispute: even if we could decide between *-tonos* and *-tropos*, it is not clear that they need bear significantly different senses; even if they do, it is not clear how far we may press the analogy with bow and lyre; even if we squeeze the analogy dry, we have no reason to take **36** as the key statement of the *logos* and to force the other fragments into its mould.

14 On text and interpretation of **40** see Jones [149]. I agree that the fragment must be read in two parts (Clement does not quote it as a continuous piece), and that the final '*ê genesthai gên*' should be excised.

15 Against *ekpurôsis* see especially Reinhardt [135] and [30], 163–201. For *ekpurôsis* see especially Mondolfo-Tarán [131], CLXXVII–CXCIII, 109–18. Mondolfo convinces me that at *Phys* 205a1–4 and *Cael* 279b12–17 = **A 10** Aristotle ascribes *ekpurôsis* to Heraclitus; he fails to show that the ascription was correct.

16 **B 76** = **66**(e) **M** carries the implication more clearly; but that fragment is probably a Stoic perversion of **B 36**. See Marcovich [140], 264.

17 I quote Guthrie [25], I.438–9; Kahn [139], 190. See also Hölscher [79], 139–40, 148–9 (but Hölscher's view is unclear to me: at 139–40 he says that in Heraclitus analogies take the place of proofs; at 145 he implies that analogies are a form of proof); von Fritz [62], 230–4, who says that in Heraclitus *nous* is pure insight; Cleve [37], 108 ('he is no proving and arguing philosopher.... Presenting no proof whatsoever, he appeals to faith and hope, pronouncing his Logos dogma like a prophet').

18 See especially Fränkel [145]; cf. Reinhardt [134], 72–5.

19 See especially Reinhardt [30], 206–7; Snell [144], 130–1; Kirk [136], 244, 366. Reinhardt denies that Heraclitus held a 'Flusslehre'; but he says that 'Heraclitus' fundamental idea . . . is the most perfect conceivable opposite of the Theory of Flux: stability in change; constancy in alteration; . . . unity in duality; eternity in ephemerality' (207). But that describes, in high-flown language, something very like the Theory of Flux.

20 References in Marcovich [129], 194–205.

21 On the *de victu* see especially Joly [153] (date, c.500: 203–9; influence from Heraclitus: 19–91); see also Wasserstein [152]; Mondolfo-Tarán [131], 231–4. Epicharmus 23 B 2 (above, p. 106) has been held to show acquaintance with the Theory of Flux: see especially Bernays [133]; Mondolfo-Tarán [131], XLII–LXIV; *contra*: Reinhardt [30], 120–1. Melissus 30 B 8 may hint at the Theory.

22 On Plato's doxographical talents see especially Mondolfo-Tarán [131], LXXXIV–CXVIII; on Plato and Heraclitus, ibid., CXVIII–CLVIII.

23 See Marcovich [129], 206–14, with references. Bollack-Wismann [143] accept all three quotations as genuine and independent fragments (87–8, 173–4, 268–9); most scholars pick upon one as the original.

24 Plutarch quotes **45**; his text continues as follows:

> It is not possible to step into the same river twice, according to Heraclitus, nor to touch twice a mortal substance the same in its character; but with a sharpness and celerity of change *it disperses and gathers together* again (or rather, not again or later, but at the same time it comes together and disintegrates), and *it approaches and departs*.

Some scholars claim the italicized words for Heraclitus (but see Marcovich [129], 207–14); if they are right, the Flux interpretation of the river fragment is assured.

25 Popper [137], I.11; [151], 159 (italics Popper's); Hegel [27], 287. For a different comparison between Heraclitus and Wittgenstein's *Tractatus* see Hussey [34], 59.

26 Reinhardt [30], 220; cf. Popper [35].

27 Another possibility is:

(3*) $(\forall \phi)(\forall x)(\phi x$ if and only if $\phi' x)$:

'opposites' are one in that they are mutually implicative. That, I suspect, is as suitable an interpretation as (2); but it raises all and only the problems raised by (2).

28 Kirk [136], 70.

29 See Stokes [56], 90–100, who distinguishes five relations involved in the Unity Thesis: opposites may be (i) logically indistinguishable, (ii) ascribed to the same object, (iii) mutually successive, (iv) mutually validating, and (v) 'the kind exemplified by B 61'. Now (iv), exemplified in **B 23 = 45 M** and **B 111 = 44 M**, has nothing to do with the Unity Thesis; and the cases Stokes lists under (i), (iii) and (v) can all be accommodated under (ii).

30 See Kirk [136], 139–48; Reinhardt [134], 91, n. 31 (whose reading, *tauto de ge zôn* . . ., I accept); cf. Plato, *Cratylus* 440A.

31 See Stokes [56], 93, who concludes with the romantic hypothesis that Heraclitus 'was only a step from knowing that there was something wrong somewhere in the argument; only he could not lay his finger on the flaw and continued to proclaim the paradoxes with his unique vigour'.

32 Plato, *Euthydemus* 293B 'may be the first extant text in which it is implicitly recognized that the factors of *respect* and *time* must be taken into account in deciding whether two assertions in which contrary attributes are predicated of a single subject contradict one another' (Lloyd [50], 138).

33 **B 48 = 39 M**:

A name of the bow is life (*bios*), its function death.

(*Bios* means both 'bow' and 'life'.) See, e.g., Snell [144], 141–5. But there is no call to take that quip as philosophy. On **B 23 = 45 M**, sometimes taken to illustrate the Unity Thesis, see especially Mouraviev [130], 114–17.

34 Sextus, *Pyrr Hyp* I.210–1, II.63, explicitly ascribes this type of argument to Heraclitus.

35 See Stokes [56], 97–8; completely different interpretations in, e.g., Hölscher [79], 153–6, and Mouraviev [130], 122–5.

36 I side with those scholars who see no cosmological significance in **55** (see, e.g., Kirk-Raven [33], 190–1; *contra*: e.g., West [59], 121–3). On the sense of *anô katô* see Reinhardt [135], 62. The puzzle still troubled Aristotle: *Phys* 202b12–6.

37 According to Philo, **A 6a**, Heraclitus offered 'immensa atque laboriosa argumenta' for his *logos*: the surviving *argumenta* are usefully catalogued in Marcovich [140], 286–91.

38 Guthrie [25], I.461; contrast ibid. II.246: 'we can only study these philosophers in the light of our own conceptions, nor would the study be of much value if we did not'. Stannard [119], 198, n. 19, suggests that it is silly to accuse Heraclitus of violating the Law of Contradiction since 'there was no "Law of Contradiction" prior to Aristotle's formulation of logical rules'. Perhaps that is a joke.

39 *Ta enantia* and *ta antia* do not appear in the fragments (Kranz' change of *tauta* into *tantia* in **B 23 = 45 M** is implausible; *antion* appears as a preposition in **B 120 = 62 M**). Text **35** and **B 67 = 77 M**, taken in conjunction with Hippolytus' glosses, suggest that Heraclitus never spoke of 'the opposites'.

V The Divine Philosophy of Xenophanes

1 There are two exceptions to this generalization: Democritus (Diogenes Laertius, IX.41 = **68 B 5**; vol. 2, p. 5); and Gorgias (Olympiodorus, **82 A 10**). On Aristotle, *Met* 984a11 = **31 A 6**, see vol. 2, p. 4.

2 For the Milesian aspect of Xenophanes' work see especially Heidel [160], 268–72 (*contra*: Fränkel [215], 339–40). According to Theophrastus, Xenophanes had 'heard' Anaximander: Diogenes Laertius IX.21 = **A 2**.

3 Sextus, Galen, and Simplicius could not find copies of Xenophanes' works (**A 35**, **A 36**, **A 47**): Aristotle's cutting appraisal (*Met* 986b21–5 = **A 30**) may have dulled interest in Xenophanes' thought.

4 A poem *Concerning Nature*: Crates of Mallos, *ad* **B 30**; Pollux, *ad* **B 39**; Stobaeus, **A 36**. For the majority view see especially Burnet [31], 121–6 (I quote 116); Steinmetz [159], 54–68; *contra*: see especially Untersteiner [156], CCXLII–CCL.

5 Cherniss [32], 18; similar judgments are legion.

6 On the sentence from the *Sophist* see especially Stokes [56], 50–2; for the issue in general, ibid., ch. 3. Mondolfo-Taran [131], C–CXIV, offer a spirited defence of the doxography. According to Simplicius:

> Theophrastus says that Xenophanes . . . supposes that the principle is one, or that what exists is one . . ., but he [i.e. Theophrastus] agrees that the account of his [i.e. Xenophanes'] opinion belongs to an inquiry other than that into nature (**A 31**).

Theophrastus did not say (*pace* Jaeger [48], 40) that Xenophanes was not a *phusiologos*; rather, he said that Xenophanes' alleged monism was not a 'physical' opinion (he probably gave Xenophanes a physical theory of elements: Diogenes Laertius, IX.19 = **A** 1). The inquiry to which Xenophanes' monism belongs is theology (see Diels [4], 480 n, recanting the view he expressed at 101-10): Xenophanes' theological monotheism was lightheartedly construed by Plato as an ontological monism; Theophrastus solemnly indicates that Plato is romancing. It is another question whether Parmenides was in any sense a 'pupil' of Xenophanes (Aristotle, *Met* 986b22 = **A 30**; Simplicius, **A 31**; etc.): one man

7 Vlastos [161], 92; contrast Burnet [31], 13-15; on 'the secular character of the earliest Ionian philosophy'. Where religiosity is concerned I am tone-deaf: it is certain that many of the Presocratics had something to say about the gods; whether or not they were religious men I cannot tell.

8 Nietzsche [28], 385; Jaeger [48], 49, 92. Cf. Kirk-Raven [33], 171; Cleve [37], 27-8; *contra*: Reinhardt [30], 100: 'the tradition compels us to replace Xenophanes the mystic by Xenophanes the dialectician'.

9 That the major gods were ungenerated was clear to Pherecydes, **7 B 1**; and note the apophthegm ascribed to Thales: 'What is divine?—That which has neither beginning nor end' (Diogenes Laertius, I.36 = **11 A 1**).

10 Note the strange phrase *'theoi aeigenetai'* (e.g., *Iliad* II.400; III. 296); Callimachus, *Hymn to Zeus* 1-10, says that Zeus was born, 'but you have not died; for you exist forever'.

11 The section of the *MXG* on Xenophanes is usually dismissed as worthless (e.g., Jaeger [48], 51-4; Guthrie [25], I.367-8); but the old arguments in Reinhardt [30], 89-96, still convince me that the *MXG* relies on Theophrastus and hence has some historical value (cf. Steinmetz [159], 49-51; von Fritz [158], 1548-52). (On the other hand, the attempt in Untersteiner [156], XVII-CXVIII, to date the *MXG* to *c*.300 BC is feeble and confused.)

12 On Epicharmus see especially Berk [172]. For his philosophical interests see Diogenes Laertius, VIII.78 = **23 A 3** (cf. Berk [172], 80-5). Some make him a Pythagorean (Diogenes Laertius, VIII.78 = **A 3**; Iamblichus, **A 4**); but see Burkert [173], 289, n. 58; Thesleff [175], 84. That he criticized Xenophanes is attested by Aristotle (*Met* 1010a5 = **21 A 15**; cf. Alexander, *in Met* 308.12; and see especially Reinhardt [30], 122-5). Of the many fragments collected in Diels-Kranz, most are forgeries (see Athenaeus, **A 10**; Diels-Kranz I.193-4). **B 1-B 6** are quoted by Alcimus, a fourth-century historian of Sicily: he argued against Plato's pupil Amyntas that Platonism was in all essentials anticipated by Epicharmus. **B 1** and **B 2** seem to be genuine (Berk [172], 88-93); and **B 5** probably is too (ibid., 98-9).

13 See e.g. Kirk-Raven [33], 170. On 'polar expressions' see Wilamowitz [18], III.230-1; Lloyd [50], 90-4. Aristophanes, *Clouds* 573-4, may be a reminiscence of **B 23**.1; but his expression is not 'polar'.

14 See especially Stokes [56], 76-9, who thinks that this view gives the 'plain, ordinary meaning' of the Greek (83). A survey of interpretations in Untersteiner [156], XLIII-XLIX.

15 Euripides imitates Xenophanes in fr. 282 = **C 2** (cf. **B 2**, and see Athenaeus, *ad* **C 2**); see Nestle [459], 560-3; Dodds [43], 197, n. 20.

16 *orthôs*: for the logical sense of the word see Wilamowitz [18], III.18-19 (the MSS. read *ontôs*—an accurate gloss). Cf. *MXG* 977a31-3 = **A 28**: 'the divine is by its nature (*pephukenai*) not mastered'.

17 Diogenes Laertius, IX.19 = **A 1**, adds 'and does not breathe'; and the addition may be genuine (see Kahn [90], 98, n. 2).

18 Cf. Anaxagoras, **59 B 12**; Diogenes, **64 C 3** (pseudo-Hippocrates) and **C 4** (Philemon); and Critias, **88 B 25**. 17.
19 Cf. *MXG* 977b27 = **A 28**: 'Again, he assumes that god is most masterful (*kratistos*), meaning by this most powerful and best'. For the essential goodness of gods see especially Aristotle, *Cael* 279a30-5, and Euripides, fr. 292.7 ('if gods do anything evil, they are not gods').
20 See Antiphon, **87 B 10**:

> For this reason it lacks nothing and takes nothing from anything, but is unlimited and unlacking.

(Antiphon is almost certainly talking about god.) Socrates thought that 'to lack nothing is a divine characteristic . . . and what is divine is most powerful' (Xenophon, *Memorabilia*, I.vi.10). So too Diogenes the Cynic: 'It is proper to gods to lack nothing' (Diogenes Laertius, VI.105). *MXG* 977b27-30 = **A 28** objects that Xenophanes' almighty god is not conventional (*kata nomon*) (cf. Adkins [207], 26, n. 4). But Xenophanes 'everywhere starts from the definitions of the nature of the gods given by popular religion' (Drachmann [164], 19); rather, he forms his concept of the divine from the core of characteristics essential to the gods of popular thought.

21 'He remains in the same state' translates *en tautôi mimnei* (cf. Epicharmus, **23 B 2**.9; Euripides, *Ion* 969); thus line 1 of **62** asserts immutability, and line 2 adds immobility. But *en tautôi mimnei* may rather mean 'he stays in the same place'; in which case *oude* in line 2 may have the force of 'for . . . not . . .', so that **62** asserts immobility in line 1 and justifies the assertion in line 2.
22 Cf. 886D; 889A–890A; [Hippocrates], *morb sacr* 1-5; Plutarch, *Nicias* 23; see Guthrie [25], III.227-8. There is a long-standing controversy over the identity of the atheist philosophers attacked in *Laws* X: see especially Tate [167]; Guthrie [25], III.115-16; De Mahieu [168].
23 For the ascription, see especially Jaeger [48], 31-2, 203-6, n. 44 (comparing Diogenes, **64 B 5**); *contra*: e.g., Vlastos [161], 114, n. 75.
24 See especially Guthrie [25], I.376-80; Untersteiner [156], LXX–LXXVI, CXC–CCIV.

VI Pythagoras and the Soul

1 On Pythagoras' life see especially Guthrie [25], I.173-81; Burkert [173], ch II.2 ('There is not a single detail in the life of Pythagoras that stands uncontradicted': ibid., 109). On the extreme difficulty of getting to grips with Pythagoreanism see the wise words of Guthrie [25], I.146-56; Burkert [173], 1-14.
2 See Diogenes Laertius, VIII.6-8 = **14 A 19**; Iamblichus, **A 17**; Galen, **A 18**; see especially Burkert [173], 218-20 (who deals adequately with Ion, **36 B 4**, and Heraclitus, **22 B 129**, texts which appear to ascribe writings to Pythagoras).
3 See the list in van der Waerden [408] (cf. Aristoxenus, **58 D 6**, § 198); a full account of the pseudepigrapha in Thesleff [174] and [175].
4 Mathematics: e.g., Proclus, **58 B 1**; Aristoxenus, **B 2**; Diogenes Laertius, VIII.11. (Pythagoras' theorem: Proclus, **58 B 19**; Diogenes Laertius, VIII.12. See especially Burkert [173], 409-12, 428-9.) Astronomy: e.g., Aëtius, **41 A 7**; Diogenes Laertius, VIII.48 = **28 A 44**. Harmonics: e.g., Xenocrates, fr. 9 H; Iamblichus, *VP* 115. (Harmonics and astronomy as sister sciences: Archytas, **47 B 1**; Plato, *Republic* 530D. Music of the spheres: Aristotle, *Cael* 290b12–

291a28 = **58 B 35**. See especially Burkert [173], 350-7; West [108], 11-14.) Metaphysics: Aristoxenus, **58 B 2**.
5 In what follows I rely heavily on Burkert [173] (see also Reinhardt [30], 131-6; Heidel [406], 350-4); for critical comment on Burkert's scepticism see Van der Waerden [408], 277-300; De Vogel [181], ch. 3; Kahn [177].
6 Our sources for Pythagoreanism fall into five classes (see especially Burkert [173], ch. II.1; Philip [180], 8-23): (a) the genuine fragments of Philolaus and Archytas (see vol. 2, Ch. IV); (b) a handful of pre-Aristotelian reports, most of which are mentioned in the present chapter (see Burkert [173], 109, n. 64; Morrison [182], 136-41); (c) fourth-century accounts, mostly fragmentary (in general see von Fritz [183], 173-9), including Aristotle (see especially Guthrie [25], I.214-16; Philip [413], and [180]), Dicaearchus, Eudemus, Heraclides, Timaeus, Speusippus; (d) neo-Pythagorean writers such as Porphyry, Iamblichus and Nicomachus; (e) the usual compilers, such as Diogenes Laertius.
7 Iamblichus, *comm math sc* 76.16-78.8 (cf. *VP* 81, 87-9); see Burkert [173], 193-7, 206-7 (*contra*; Philip [180], 28-9).
8 For the *acousmata* see **58 C**, with Burkert [173], ch. II.4. Aristoxenus, **58 D**, contains a lot of sensible stuff about ethics, political theory and education; but it is probably a fourth century version of the *acousmata* (Burkert [173], 107-9).
9 Pythagoras is sometimes called a shaman (e.g., Burkert [173], 162-5; cf. Dodds [43], ch. 5); but I doubt if the phenomenon of shamanism sheds any light on early Greek philosophy (see Philip [180], 158-62; Kahn [177], 30-5).
10 The passage is from Porphyry, *VP* 19; for the attribution to Dicaearchus see Burkert [173], 122-3.
11 'Metempsychosis' is the orthodox name for the view later and more accurately referred to as '*palingenesis*' or '*metensômatôsis*' (Servius, *ad Aen* III.68).
12 See *Meno* 81AD; *Phaedo* 70A; etc. (see especially Long [188], 65-86).
13 References in Burkert [173], 126, n. 38; cf. Herodotus, II.18; Hellanicus, *FGrH* 4 F 73. Reinhardt tried to find cyclical transmigrations in Heraclitus (Reinhardt [30], 191-9); some scholars find them in Parmenides' Way of Opinion (cf. Simplicius, *ad* **28 B 13**). For Egyptian origins of Pythagoreanism see also Isocrates, *Busiris* 28 = **14 A 4**; Suda, **7 A 2**; and see Philip [180], 189-91; Burkert [173], 126.
14 Numerals followed by 'Z' refer to the order of the fragments in Zuntz [193]. The fish in **86** is a dolphin: Wilamowitz [194], 635-6.
15 **B 129** is often mistranslated; for the correct version see, e.g., Zuntz [193], 208-9. Most scholars see a reference to Pythagoras (see Burkert [173], 137-8); but that is far from certain. Ion, **36 B 4**, ascribes some doctrine of survival to Pythagoras, but does not explicitly refer to metempsychosis; so too Herodotus, IV.95-6 = **14 A 2**.
16 There is no reason to doubt Diogenes' reference to Pythagoras (see Burkert [173], 120, n. 1), though Diogenes is of course wrong to refer to Pythagoras' *own* incarnations. Reference to later Pythagorean texts on metempsychosis in Thesleff [175], Subject Index IV; but some later Pythagoreans played the doctrine down (see Burkert [173], 124). I have nothing whatever to say about Orphism (see, e.g., Burkert [173], 125-33).
17 I note the probable answers of Empedocles to my peripheral questions. Hippolytus, **31 A 31**, implies that all *psuchai* transmigrate, but **B 112**.4 and **B 113**.2 suggest that transmigration is limited to an *élite* (but see Burkert [173], 136-7). As far as we can tell, all animals and at least some plants receive *psuchai*. There is a cycle of transmigration with a fixed time-table (**B 115**) (on a

Pythagorean time-table see Diogenes Laertius, VIII.14; Thesleff [175], 171, n. 21); and transmigrations are hierarchically arranged (see Zuntz [193], 232–4). There is no evidence for gaps between incarnation or for *post mortem* Judgment. A moral theory is erected on the doctrine (above, pp. 122–6).
18 E.g., *Iliad* XIX.350–4; *Odyssey* X.229–40; see especially Bacigalupo [189], 267–76.
19 Metempsychosis is ascribed to Pherecydes (Suda, **7 A 2**; see, e.g., Vlastos [161], 110, n. 60); for Epimenides see Dodds [43], 143. Note that Heraclitus **22 B 129** accuses Pythagoras of plagiarism.
20 See, e.g., Long [188], 2; Jaeger [48], 84–5. Burnet [185], 257, claimed that the personal *psuchê* was an invention of Socrates, and many scholars have believed him. But see, e.g., Zuntz [193], 270; Lloyd-Jones [51], 8–10. There is no standard Greek terminology for personhood (see especially Dodds [43], 138–9); but we can hardly say that 'strictly speaking, a doctrine of personal immortality could scarcely be developed without a word for "person"' (Kahn [493], 13, n. 24). The notion of an occult, non-personal self seems to figure in the doctrine of Pindar, fr. 116 B (see Burnet [185], 249–51; Kahn [493], 12–13), but that has nothing to do with the orthodox Pythagorean doctrine.
21 This argument, the *auxanomenos logos*, has had a long history. For the ancient part of the story see Plutarch, *Moralia* 1083AD and Bernays [198]; for the modern part see R. Hall 'Hume's Use of Locke on Identity', *Locke Newsletter* 5, 1974, 56–75. **88** has often been connected with Pythagoreanism for the absurd reason that the debtor's opening remarks refer to a Pythagorean 'Lehre vom Geraden und Ungeraden'.
22 Burkert [173], 136.
23 Burkert [173], 136.
24 According to Plutarch, Empedocles denied that we can remember our earlier incarnations (*ad* **31 B 116**); but Empedocles certainly claimed some such memories. In Plato the connexion between pre-existence and recollection is familiar. Further texts on Pythagorean mnemonics: Cicero, *Cato* 11.38; Proclus, *in Tim* 124.4–13; Porphyry, *VP* 40; Diodorus, X.viii (see Burkert [173], 213, n. 19; Gladigow [187], 412–14). But memory was cultivated in Greece, and a good memory is an advantage even to the non-Pythagorean sage (see, e.g., Aristophanes, *Clouds* 129, 414; Plato, *Republic* 486D).
25 I think that this argument lies behind the remarks in Diogenes of Oenoanda, fr. 34 Ch (cf. new fr. 2: M. F. Smith, 'New Readings in the Text of Diogenes of Oenoanda', *CQ* n.s. 22, 1972, 162); see Chilton [22], 85–8; 128–30.
26 Kahn [177], 167.
27 Cf. Herodotus, II.123 = **14 A 1**; Alexander Polyhistor, *apud* Diogenes Laertius, VIII.28 = **58 B 1a**; Cicero, **7 A 5**.
28 See especially Guthrie [25], I.351–7; Mugler [201], who argues ingeniously that men die and their *psuchai* survive because their physiological cycles break down and their psychic cycles are eternal. With **93** compare Heraclitus, **22 B 103**; [Hippocrates], *de victu* 19 = **22 C 1** (see Reinhardt [134], 76–80).
29 On *aeikinêton* ('ever-moving') and the variant *autokinêton* ('self-moving') see especially Robinson [202], 111–12, with references; on the sense of *pasa psuchê*, ibid., 111 (see also Hackforth [203], 64–6; Robinson [205]). This argument for immortality was one of the most quoted passages of Plato: see references in Moreschini's edition of the *Phaedrus*.
30 See, e.g., Skemp [204], 5–6; Burkert [173], 296, n. 97. The argument was

connected with Alcmeon by Simplicius: *in An* 32.1-13. See further Stella [200], 276-7, for other Platonic references.
31 So too Philoponus, *in An* 71.6; Sophonias, *in An* 11.25.

VII The Moral Law

1 Pythagorean abstention was a standard butt of comedy (see **58 E**); but the nature and extent of the practice was hotly debated from the time of Aristoxenus (see especially Burkert [173], 180-3).
2 Zuntz [193], 183.
3 Omitting line 4 with Wilamowitz [194], 634, and Zuntz [193], 194-6.
4 In line 2 I translate Zuntz' *oiktra toreunta*: that emendation makes sense, the MSS. text does not.
5 Burkert [173], 180; a more careful assessment in von Fritz [183], 195-7. For Theophrastus, see Porphyry, *de Abst* III.26 (Burkert [173], 122, n. 6); for Xenocrates, fr. 98 H (cf. Hippolytus *ad* **31 B 115**; Diodorus, X.vi.1). Note also the Empedoclean sentiments in the speech of Ovid's Pythagoras (*Metam* XV.75-175, 457-78; on Ovid's sources here see van der Waerden [184], 854-5).
6 P. D. Singer, 'Animal Liberation', *New York Review of Books*, XX.5, 1973, 18.
7 Cf. Diogenes Laertius, IX.12 = **22 A 1**:

> Some entitle Heraclitus' book *Muses* [cf. Plato, *Sophist* 242D = **A 10**], others *Concerning Nature*; Diodotus calls it
> A certain Steering to a Balanced Life,
> others *Judgment* [*gnômê*: cf. **B 41**), *Manners* [*êthê*: cf. **B 78**], *Turnings* [*tropai*: cf. **B 31**], *One Universe for All* [cf. **B 89**].

The MSS. text is corrupt, and I have tacitly emended it in places; at any event, it is plain that more than one ancient scholar found moral philosophy at the core of Heraclitus' book.

8 I quote only the second half of **B 5**: the first half, though on the related topic of ritual observances, seems to be a separate fragment. See also **B 14** = **87 M**; **B 15** = **50 M**.
9 Heraclitus' views on psychology and death are controversial (see especially Marcovich [140], 303-5; Nussbaum [477]). I offer a brief sketch of one possible reconstruction: 'Souls are fiery (Aëtius, **18 A 9**), and the drier they are the better (**B 118** = **68 M**; cf. **B 119** = **69 M**); "for souls it is death to become water" (**B 36** = **66 M**: cf. **B 76** = **66 (e) M**; **B 77** = **66 (d) M**; and perhaps **B 12** = **40 M**). But **B 36** does not imply that all souls do in fact become wet and die; and there may well be survival for some. Thus something unexpected awaits us after we die (**B 27** = **74 M**; cf. **B 98** = **72 M**); and the fate we meet with then depends upon the life we lead now (**B 25** = **97 M**; **B 136** = **96 (b) M** (see Kirk [213]; West [214]); cf. **B 63** = **73 M**; **B 24** = **96 M**). Souls are immortal (Aëtius, **A 17**); and perhaps they undergo a cyclical series of incarnations (**B 88** = **41 M**)'. See further, vol. 2, pp. 171-2.
10 See also: **B 29** = **95 M**; **B 66** = **82 M** (but see below, n. 20). Other moralizing fragments: **B 43** = **102 M**; **B 95** = **110 M** (perhaps to be connected with **B 117** = **69 M**); **B 110** = **71 M**.
11 'What must be', *chreôn*, is in fact an emendation. See also **B 137** = **28 (d) M**; Aëtius, I.28.1; pseudo-Galen, 42.
12 See Aëtius, Censorinus, **A 13** = **65 M**; Aëtius, **A 18**; Plutarch, Philo, Censorinus, **A 19** = **108 M**; cf. **B 100** = **64 M**. See especially Reinhardt [134], 75-83; Kirk [136], 295-305.

13 This interpretation of **109** is taken from Cleve [37], 83–7; see further Marcovich [140], 309–10.
14 On early uses of *nomos* see especially Ostwald [211], 20–54; he ends by distinguishing no less than thirteen senses of the word.
15 Clearly descriptive *nomoi*: Aeschylus, *Choephori* 400; Sophocles, *Antigone* 613; Euripides, fr. 346. Clearly prescriptive *nomoi*: Aeschylus, *Supplices* 670; Sophocles, *Antigone* 450; Euripides, *Hippolytus* 1328. See also Dover [206], 256–7.
16 Vlastos [111], 56; cf. Jaeger [48], 115–16; Lloyd [50], 210–32. Cornford [40], 21, says that 'the word "law" is missing from the vocabulary of Greek science. "Law" suggests a rule of behaviour, an enactment associated with the notions of cause and effect, of action and its consequences.' Cornford here seems to confuse prescriptive and descriptive laws; and he is quite mistaken in saying that legislative vocabulary was foreign to Greek science.
17 *Kata to chreôn*: some scholars see a normative notion in the phrase—'what should be' rather than 'what must be' (see especially Fränkel [230], 187–8). Even if that is right, Anaximander exhibits the confusion between descriptive and prescriptive laws which I am labouring here.
18 Justice figures in other Heraclitean fragments: on **B 23** = **45 M** see Mouraviev [130]; on **B 28** = **20 + 19 M** see above, p. 145; on **B 66** = **82 M** see below, n.20.
19 For the conjunction of **B 114** and **B 2** see Marcovich [129], 91–2. **B 114** may have followed close upon 33 (so West [59], 117; cf. Sextus, **A 16**), thereby giving prominence to the ethical content of Heraclitus' book. The text of **B 2** is uncertain. Sextus' MSS. read:

> Going on a little, he adds: For that reason one should follow what is *koinos*, for what is *koinos* is *xunos*; yet . . .

Diels-Kranz print:

> Going on a little, he adds: For that reason one should follow what is *xunos* (that is, what is *koinos*—for the *koinos* is *xunos*); yet . . .

I adhere to the orthodox opinion, which accepts this text and treats the parenthesis as an un-Heraclitean gloss on the rare word *xunos*. West [59], 118, begins the quotation at the word 'yet', ascribing the preceding clause to Sextus (cf. Bollack-Wismann [143], 65); that is implausible.
20 **B 66** = **82 M** reads:

> Fire, coming upon them, will judge and convict all things.

Its authenticity is defended by, e.g., Marcovich [129], 435; but Reinhardt [135], 64–7, argues—to my mind cogently—that it is Hippolytan, not Heraclitean. **B 33** = **104 M** reads:

> It is a *nomos* too to obey the will of one.

Some take 'one' to refer to God; but the presence of 'too' (*kai*) is against this. The fragment should rather be connected with **B 49** = **98 M** and **B 121** = **105 M**.

VIII *The Principles of Human Knowledge*

1 I follow the text suggested by Wachtler [199], 34–8 (cf. Stella [200], 237, n. 1).
2 *Iliad* II.484–6 (trans. Chapman); cf. Theognis, 141–2; Pindar, *Nemean* VI.1–6;

Herodotus, VI.50; Heraclitus, **22 B 78** = **90 M**, B 79 = **92 M**; Philolaus, **44 B 6**. See especially Snell [55], ch. 7.
3 Lloyd-Jones [51], 35.
4 But Xenophanes was not a pure sceptic in Sextus' opinion: see *Pyrr Hyp* I.223-5 = **A 35**; II.18; III.219; *adv Math* VII.48-52. See also Aristocles, **A 49**, and Diels [3], 45. I am not sure how Xenophanes' rejection of diviniation (Cicero, Aëtius, **A 52**; pseudo-Galen, 105) connects with his scepticism.
5 In line 1 I read *iden* rather than *genet'* (see Fränkel [215], 342-3). An alternative translation of line 2 runs: '. . . and concerning what I say about everything'. In line 3, *tuchoi* may mean '. . . if he should happen . . .' rather than '. . . if he should actually manage . . .'. In line 4 I take *pasi* to be masculine; if it is neuter, the line reads: 'but in the case of all things, there is only belief'. The fragment is frequently cited or alluded to: see references in Diels [3], 45.
6 See especially Heitsch [217] 208-16.
7 See also Varro, *apud* Augustine, *Civitas Dei*, VII.17:

> sed ut Xenophanes Colophonius scribit, quid putem, non quid contendam, ponam. Hominis est enim haec opinari, dei scire.

8 For the phrase, used to refer to Ionian science, see, e.g., Plato, *Apology*, 18B; cf. Aristophanes, *Clouds* 187-95 (see Mejer [529]).
9 So Sextus, *adv Math* VII.48-52; Epiphanius, III.9. Timon reproaches Xenophanes for 'dogmatizing' about God (frr. 59-60 = **A 35**); and some scholars hold that Xenophanes' positive theology rules out a sceptical interpretation of **121** (e.g., von Fritz [158], 1557-8; Rivier [216], 55-7). But I do not see that Xenophanes' theology is 'dogmatic'; and I suppose that **124** is Xenophanes' anticipatory response to Timon's charge.
10 *adv Math* VII.48-52; 326. Plato, *Meno* 80D, perhaps suggests the same interpretation (see Fränkel [215], 344).
11 Clement paraphrases Xenophanes; Diels' tentative restoration of the original verses has become canonical, but it is speculative.
12 See B 40 = **16 M**; B 57 = **43 M**; B 106 = **59 M**; B 129 = **17 M**; B 81 = **18 M** (see Reinhardt [219]); B 42 = **30 M**.
13 See the table in Kirk [136], 47. With **128** compare *Odyssey* XVIII.130-7; Archilochus, fr. 68 D. I read *hokoiois* (Bergk) for *hokosoi*.
14 Cf. Archytas, **47 B 3**:

> . . . to discover without inquiring is difficult and rare, with inquiry it is plain sailing and easy—but impossible if you do not know how to inquire.

15 I follow, doubtingly, Mouraviev [130], 118-22.
16 Plutarch, *adv Col* 1118C, interprets **136** differently: 'I probed myself' (cf. B 116 = **23 (e) M**); see Westman [15], 295-7. Cf. Epicurus, fr. 117 Us.; *contra*: Dio Chrysostom, 54.2.
17 **137** is imitated by Democritus, **68 B 64** (cf. **B 65**); with **138** contrast Ion, **36 B 4**. For a related distinction between polymathy and wisdom see Anaxarchus, **72 B 1**; Plato, *Laws* 819A; see Pfeiffer [24], 138.
18 See especially Archytas, **47 B 3**; Plato, *Phaedo* 99C; cf. Xenophanes, **21 B 3.1**; Pindar, *Olympian* II.86-8 (see Ramnoux [142], 324-5); Parmenides, **28 B 1.32**; Empedocles, **31 B 14**. For Heraclitus see B 17 = **3 M**; B 55 = **5 M**; and note *didaskein* in B 40 = **16 M**.
19 Some translate: 'The things of which there is sight, hearing, perception

(*mathêsis*)—these I prefer' (see Marcovich [129], 21); but that does not agree with Heraclitus' use of *manthanein*.
20 So Fränkel [145], 271–2; Cherniss [32], 15. For the obvious interpretation see Diogenes Laertius, IX.7 = **A 1**. Note that the heavenly bodies are carried about in *skaphai* or basins (Diogenes Laertius, IX.9 = **A 1**; Aëtius, **A 12**).
21 **B 46** = **114 M** reads thus:

> He used to say that thinking was a sacred disease (*hieros nosos*: epilepsy), and that sight deceives.

(cf. **B 131** = **114 (d) M**). The second clause of **B 46** is surely derived from **B 107** = **13 M**. The first clause is presented as an apophthegm, not as a quotation. Its meaning is anyone's guess. **B 46** does not require a sceptical interpretation.

22 Many scholars feel that there is an incompatibility between **141** and **137**. On my interpretation of **137** there is evidently no incompatibility; but neither is there on the orthodox interpretation. For on that interpretation, **137** denies that polymathy is a sufficient condition for wisdom, while **141** asserts that it is a necessary condition. On the pre-philosophical background to **141** see Stokes [56], 88–9.
23 Nussbaum [477], 10.
24 Alcman, fr. 125 P reads:

> Experience (*peira*) is the beginning of learning.

Lanza [223], argues cogently that 'Alcman' here is a mistake for 'Alcmeon'. (The same mistake is certainly made at Theodoretus, *curatio* V.17). Note that the fragment fits well with the *Phaedo* theory. Cornford [114], 34, says that 'in the practical art of medicine we find the root of empirical epistemology'; but he is right only *per accidens*: Alcmeon's epistemology has no logical connexion with his medical practice. Vlastos [115], 47–8, finds no empiricist epistemology before *Phaedo* 96B (in which, by implication, he sees no Presocratic traces).

IX Parmenides and the Objects of Enquiry

1 See the condemnatory judgments of Plutarch, **A 16**, Proclus, **A 17**, **A 18**, and Simplicius, *in Phys* 7.3, 21.19. On Parmenides' style see Diels [224], 4–11; Mourelatos [237], ch. 1.
2 In line 29 I read *eukukleos*; for the variant, *eupeitheos* ('persuasive'), see, e.g., Diels [224], 54–7. In line 31, 'these' (*tauta*) are the mortal opinions (*contra*; Schwabl [243]; Reale [269], 226–34). I omit lines 31b–32, which are among the most disputed in Parmenides' poem. I incline to take *perônta* (read *perôntas*?) as masculine, and to accept Diels' *dokimôs* for *dokimôs*; thus I translate:

> ... you will learn ... the way in which men were bound to judge the things that seem to be, since they always journey through them all.

i.e., 'You will learn how men who always have appearances thrust upon them could not help believing them to be real.' But the sentence does not have the importance some would ascribe to it: the central problem of the relationship between the Way of Truth and the Way of Opinion can be securely established without reference to lines 31b–32. The arrangement of the verses at the end of **B 1**, and their connexion with **150** and **156**, are disputed (see Bicknell [228]); I follow the orthodoxy of Diels-Kranz. But Bicknell [229] plausibly puts **B 10** after **B 1**.

3 It contained some interesting astronomy (see **A 37-44**; **B 10-15**): Parmenides is said to have identified the Morning Star with the Evening Star (Diogenes Laertius, IX.23 = **A 1**; Aëtius, **A 40a**), and to have been the first upholder of a spherical earth (Diogenes Laertius, IX.21 = **A 1**; VIII.48 = **A 44**). On the contents of the Way of Opinion see especially Hölscher [227], 106-23, who suggests connexions with the later theories of Empedocles and Philolaus.

4 For this translation see, e.g., Tarán [226], 41-4, with references. The traditional translation is: 'Thinking and being are the same' (e.g., Kahn [253], 721-4); but I can make no sense of that unless it is glossed in such a way as to make it equivalent to the translation I prefer. Full details of interpretations of **149** in Untersteiner [225], CII-CVI.

5 The grammar is horrid: should we read *legei te noei t'*, taking *to* as a relative pronoun? Then translate: 'It is necessary for what one says and thinks to be being'. Other interpretations documented in Untersteiner [225], CIX, n. 29.

6 See especially Verdenius [233], 65-6; Mourelatos [237], 68-70. Kahn [253], 713, n. 18, and Mourelatos [251], render *phrazein* in **148**.8 by 'point out' and gloss *legein* and *phasthai* by 'say truly'; but that gloss is unacceptable. In this context reference is often made to von Fritz [62]. But I do not know what von Fritz thinks he has shown. Originally, perhaps, *nous* referred to insight or intuitive knowledge. But even in Homer and Hesiod, *nous* is not always veridical; i.e., you can *noein* that P though P is false. Hence *nous* is nearer to thought than to knowledge. By the fifth century, *nous* covers reflective thought and intellect in general (see also Furley [186], 8-10).

7 Kahn [253], 703, n. 4, offers a different account of **148**. 2: *noêsai* is 'loosely epexegetical . . . with *hodoi*'; i.e. 'what ways of enquiring there are that lead to thought'.

8 The reference of *tautês* in **150**.3 has caused some difficulty (see especially Stokes [56], 112-15); but as far as I can see that word refers simply enough to the Road discussed in **148** and **150**.1-2 (see Cornford [242], 99-100).

9 The second half of **148**.3 is syntactically ambiguous: the *esti* in *ouk esti mê einai* may be either 'personal' or 'impersonal' ('It is not for not being' or 'It is not possible for it not to be'). Line 5 proves that the *sense* is: 'It cannot not be'; and I take it that either syntax will yield that sense.

10 See especially Kahn [255]; there is a useful table on p. 82 presenting a summary classification of the roles played by *einai*.

11 Eudemus, fr. 43 W = **A 28**, says that the Eleatics ignore different uses of *einai*; but the Peripatetic and the modern accusations are quite distinct. Furth [257] maintains that the notions of existence and of the copula are 'impacted or *fused* in the early Greek concept of being' (243). He cites no evidence; and he does not explain the difference between fusion and confusion. Kahn [255], 320-3, argues that existential *einai*—his Type VI—was invented in the fifth century; but I cannot distinguish Type VI from the early Type I.

12 '. . . negative judgments (*hoi apophatikoi logoi*), as Parmenides says, fit principles and limits' (Scholiast to Euclid, **A 22a** in Untersteiner's edition); but the sense and reliability of the report are uncertain.

13 The veridical use of *einai* is discussed in Kahn [252], and applied to Parmenides in Kahn [253]. Kahn's view is complicated by the fact that he maintains first that the veridical use of *einai* involves both the existential and the predicative uses ([253], 712), and second, that Parmenides' *esti* means both 'it is the case' and 'it

exists' (ibid., 336). Mourelatos [237], ch. 2 and Appendix 2, claims to follow Kahn; but he says that *esti* is the 'is' of 'speculative predication' (predication which gives insight into the identity of something or says what it is). That is not a special sense of *esti*; nor can I give any account of the three Roads in terms of it. Hölscher [227], 79 and 98, holds that *esti* is neither existential nor predicative: it means 'seiend sein', 'Bestand haben', 'wahr sein'. Jones [258], 290–1, thinks that Parmenides is proposing a new sense of *einai*, which he explains in **149**. None of these modern suggestions has any linguistic or interpretative plausibility; and none is worth considering unless there are grave objections to the existential construe of *esti*.

14 Some scholars talk vaguely of an 'indefinite' subject. Loenen [238], 12–14, emends line 3 to read: . . . *hopôs esti ti kai hôs* . . . ('that something (*ti*) is . . .'). Untersteiner [225], LXXV–XC, takes the subject of *esti* to be *hê* [*hodos*], 'the one [road]'; and **156**.17–18 supports the suggestion. But that gives Parmenides grammar at the cost of sense.

15 Reinhardt [30], 60, supposes a lost line before **148** in which Parmenides refers to *to eon*; Cornford [231], 30, n. 2, emends line 3 to read: *Hê men hopôs eon esti* . . .

16 Tugendhat [256], 137, says that 'what Parmenides is dealing with is that (i.e. "the Whole") which previous philosophers had always dealt with'; so that the philosophically educated reader will grasp the subject of the poem at once (cf. Verdenius [233], 32: Verdenius, 73–5, argues that the poem was explicitly entitled *Concerning Nature*). The Milesians had indeed described the universe as a whole; but they had not, in any very obvious sense, made statements about 'the Whole'.

17 See especially Owen [244]; I quote from Stokes [56], 119–22.

18 As well as (4), (3) yields:
(4a) If O can exist, then O can be thought of —
there are no unthinkable mysteries. Parmenides does not need (4a) for his argument; for some reflexions on it see Anscombe [250], 128–32.

19 Parmenides had an ancient reputation for criticizing his predecessors (Simplicius, **A 19**; Plutarch, *adv Col* 1124C); but no details survive. For references to the modern controversy over the mortals of **150** see Untersteiner [225], CXII–CXVII; Mondolfo-Tarán [131], XLVI–LXIV.

20 *Pantôn* is usually taken as neuter; then 'the path of all things is backward turning' is part of mortal opinion. For the translation adopted in the text see Stokes [56], 116–17; Ballew [267], 194–5.

21 Parallelism with **156**.40 supports it; comparison with **B 8**.57–8 suggests that 'the same and not the same' means 'the same as itself and not the same as other things'.

22 See further J. Barnes, *The Ontological Argument* (London, 1972), 39–45.

23 Basson [265], 83.

24 Gorgias worked by 'putting together what others had said' (*MXG* 979a14); the *MXG* specifically mentions Melissus and Zeno (979a22; b22–5).

25 So Diels-Kranz, who do not even print the *MXG*.

X Being and Becoming

1 Diels [224], 25–6, guessed that we possess nine-tenths of the Way of Truth and one tenth of the Way of Opinion. On the status of **B 4** see above, p. 213.

Loenen [238], 75-7, discovers three new fragments of the Way of Truth, of which he thinks we have only a small portion. He has convinced no one.
2 Discussion of **155** in Jameson [266] (sceptical) and Ballew [267] (over-elaborate). Hölscher [227], 77, locates **155** between **B 1** and **148**, and supposes that the goddess means only that the order of the two Ways is indifferent.
3 Owen [244], 322.
4 For 'signs' (*sêmata*) see **B 8**.55, which indicates that the 'signs' are the characterizing properties of what exists and not proofs that what exists has those properties.
5 Diels-Kranz, and many others, print *esti gar oulomeles* . . . (cf. Untersteiner [225], XXIX). Their source is Plutarch, *adv Col* 1114C. But Plutarch is quoting from memory; and the words *esti gar* are plainly Plutarch's and not a part of his quotation (see Westman [15], 236-9). *Oulon mounogenes*, which I translate, has the support of Simplicius, Clement and Philoponus; it was the standard text in late antiquity; and most modern scholars now accept it.
6 *Ateleston* is defended by Untersteiner [225], XXX-XXXI; most scholars emend to *êde teleion* or the like ('and complete'). (References in Tarán [226], 88-93). For *atalanton* see Empedocles, **31 B** 7.19 (cf. T. J. Reilly, 'Parmenides, Fragment 8.4: a correction', *AGP* 58, 1976, 57).
7 Numerals followed by '**R**' refer to the edition of Melissus by Reale [269].
8 See Reale [269], 31-2; Jouanna [270], 314-23.
9 Melissus is talking about 'whatever is' (**B 1**); equivalently, he is supposing that 'something is' and asking what follows from that supposition (Simplicius *ad* **B 1**; *MXG* 974a2 = **A 5**). His subject is not 'the Whole' or 'Nature' or 'Being' or any of those odd things.
10 After (T 12), the *MXG* adds:
    (12a) O is not mixed
    (974a24-b2 = **A 5**). See especially Reale [269], 305-8.
11 'Not existing, it exists': *esti mê on*. Most scholars translate 'it is non-existent', gratuitously importing into the text a confusion between existential and predicative *einai*.
12 In his paraphrase Simplicius says:

> Melissus begins his treatise on generation and destruction thus: 'If it is nothing, what could be said about this as if it were something existent?' (*ad* **B 1**).

Reale [269], 34-6, 368-9, prints this as a genuine fragment (cf. Burnet [31], 321, n. 5). But *MXG* 975a34-5 implies that Melissus produced no such argument. If he did, he was of course only epitomizing Parmenides.
13 The MSS. read *ho ti ên* ('whatever was'): I accept the conjecture of Loenen [238], 144-7, *ho ti esti* (but see Reale [269], 59, n. 60; 370).
14 Note that Parmenides deals with generation and destruction together: Melissus probably does not deal with destruction until **B 7**.
15 See Wiesner [273]: Diels took lines 7-9a to be directed against generation, 9b-10 against growth. Calogero took 7-11 to be against generation, 12-13 against growth. For the colourless use of 'grow' (*auxanesthai*) see, e.g., Empedocles **31 B** 17.1.
16 The dilemmatic interpretation pairs 'Neither . . .' (*oute* . . . in line 7) with 'Nor . . .' (*oud'* . . . in line 12). It is tempting to emend *oud'* to *out'*. My interpretation pairs *oud'* with the *de* of line 9.
17 Aristotle's commentators find the dilemma in Melissus (**A 10aR**); but the text of

Melissus nowhere hints at a dilemma, and the *MXG* implies that there was none (see especially 975a22–32 = **A 5**). There is a dilemma in Gorgias, **157** § 71; but it is a bastard: in the disjunction, *ek mê ontos* or *ex ontos*, the first *ek* introduces a generator, the second does not. Aristotle also refers to the dilemma (*Phys* 191a23); but in his dilemma, *ek* does not introduce a generator at all.

18 See especially Stokes [56] 253–5: Anaxagoras and Empedocles attempted to answer Parmenides' argument, and they saw in it no more than the claim that every generation requires an instigating cause (against their answers Aristotle later applied the Principle of Sufficient Reason: *Phys* 252a4).

19 Lloyd [50], 103–6, observes that the disjuncts in line 11 are not exhaustive, and he faults Parmenides for relying on a false 'principle of Unqualified Exclusion'; but the 'principle' of line 11 is the conclusion of an argument, not an assumption.

20 See especially Reinhardt [30], 39–42; further references in Tarán [226], 95–102. Stokes [56], 310, n. 78, notes a number of places where scribes have erred over negation signs.

21 I translate the MS. text; many emend (references in Tarán [226], 104–5).

22 Thus I doubt if line 5 rests on two premisses: *homou pan*, proved in 6b–21, and *suneches*, proved in 22–5 (Schofield [275], 118–19); nor am I sure that the *suneches* of line 6a should be linked to that of line 25. Certainly, *hen, suneches* does not repeat *oulon, mounogenes* (Stokes [56], 308, n. 68). On *hen* in the sense of *suneches* see Stokes [56], 13–15.

23 Adherents of (a) must gloss line 5 thus: 'it is the case neither that O used once to exist [but does so no longer], nor that O will exist [but does not yet]'. Against that gloss see especially Owen [274], 320–2; but see Schofield [275], 122–4.

24 See Owen [274], 318–19; criticized by Schofield [275], 128–9.

25 I prefer *esti de* to Diels-Kranz' *esti te kai* ('Since it did not come into being, it both is and always was...'); and I take 'unlimited' in a temporal sense (*contra*: Reale [269], 82–6, but the point has no substantial significance). Raven [178], 82–4, refers to Aristotle, *Cael* 268a10 = **58 B 17**, and to Ion, **36 B 1**; he conjectures that Ion and the Pythagoreans objected against Parmenides that his 'One', like everything else, would be a plurality of beginning, middle and end, and he supposes that Melissus in **159** was out to scotch that objection.

26 For the temporal use of *pan* see B 7.3. Most scholars take *pan* spatially. Reale [269], 86–98, argues that his interpretation saves Melissus from Aristotle's objection; similarly Cherniss [6], 67–71, and Verdenius [278]. But at best those interpretations displace the fallacy, and do not avoid it; and the spatial reading of *pan* introduces a foreign element, and a wholly disputable premiss, into Melissus' argument.

27 *Top* 167b13–20; 168b35–40 = **A 10**. The details of Aristotle's accusation are not clear: see Reale [269], 73–7.

XI *Stability and Change*

1 References in Reale [269], 77–9; cf. *MXG* 975b38–976a13. Gorgias certainly made the inference (**157** §§ 68–9); cf. *MXG* 979b21–3: 'if it is ungenerated, he [sc. Gorgias] assumes, by the axioms of Melissus, that it is unlimited': but see Nestle [260], 555); so too did Metrodorus, **70 A 4** (pseudo-Plutarch).

2 See especially Reale [269], 98–104; he treats the last sentence of **162** as a fragment of Melissus, and infers that the fallacious deduction of spatial infinity

'should be considered a closed chapter in the history of the interpretation of Melissus'.

3   At line 49 I read *toigar* (Wilamowitz); the MS. reading, *hoi gar* gives the wrong logical connective.
4   For the use of *mallon hêtton* see [Plato], *Minos* 313B.
5   For the doxography see, e.g., Hippolytus, **A 33**; Aëtius, **A 31**.
6   References in Untersteiner [225], CLXIII, n. 174; cf. Simplicius, **A 20**:

> If he says that the one existent is 'like the bulk of a well-rounded ball', do not be surprised; for because of his poetry he also indulges in a sort of mythical fiction.

7   'But a plurality of spheres could not be close-packed.' (a) In the *Timaeus* Plato invents a vacuumless world of close-packed figures, which geometry will not allow to pack close enough: Parmenides may have made the same mistake. (b) Did Parmenides ever reject vacuums? (above, p. 222) (c) A very clever person might toy with the idea of packing the interstices between the spheres with infinitely many ever smaller spheres.
8   For the insertion of 'unlimited' see Reale [269], 121, n. 51. **B 5** reads:

> If it was not one, it would be limited against something else.

I guess that this is a paraphrase of **164** rather than a separate fragment.
9   Kirk-Raven [33], 300.
10 The dots mark the omission of '*en hôi pephatismenon esti*'. I adopt the translation suggested by Hölscher [227], 99–100, paraphrasing thus: 'If you think, your thought bears on that existing thing, whatever it may be, which makes the utterance conveying your thought something more than a mere "name".' But that is difficult; and the phrase has suggested numerous different interpretations.
11 Woodbury [283], argued for the reading *onomastai* instead of *onom' estai*, translating: 'with reference to it (sc. *to on*) are all the names given that mortals ...' (cf., e.g., Mourelatos [237], 180–5). But that gives a remarkably feeble sense. For the orthodoxy, to which I adhere, see, e.g., Tarán [226], 129–36.
12 On homogeneity see especially Reale [269], ch. V. I accept the interpretation of *homoios* given by the *MXG* (976a14–8 = **A 5**); and I suppose that the argument in the *MXG* is Melissan (*contra*: e.g., Stokes [56], 151; Solmsen [282], 9, nn. 18–19).
13 Owen [244], 92, takes *homoion* adverbially: 'it all exists to a similar extent'; but that does not seem to me to affect the argument. Owen, ibid., finds the premiss of lines 22–5 in line 11; Stokes [56], 136, finds it in line 16.
14 *Leusse d' homôs apeonta noôi pareonta bebaiôs*. Diels-Kranz read *homôs* as 'nevertheless'; I prefer to take it for *homoiôs* (see Bollack [284], 56, n. 3). The point of the adverb is this: 'Don't make any distinction between the absent and the present'. *Noôi* is often connected with *apeonta ... pareonta* ('things absent and things present to your mind': cf., e.g., *Iliad* XV.80); it might go both with *leusse* and with *apeonta ... pareonta*; it might go just with *leusse ... apeonta*. And a little ingenuity will conjure up a dozen different construes of the line. On *kata kosmon* in line 4 see Tarán [226], 47–8.
15 The suggestion is from Hölscher [227], 117–18. Bicknell [228], 47–8, puts **167** between **151** and **156**; for attempts to insert **167** into **156** see Untersteiner [225], CXLVI, n. 107.
16 Covotti proposed *apolluoi ti* ('nor would it lose anything') for *apoloito* (see Reale

[269], 388). That gives a neater contrast between (T8) and (T9); if it is accepted, we may suppose Melissus to have taken destruction as the limiting case of loss.

17 Accepting Heidel's emendation (*metakosmêtheiê ti tôn eontôn* for *metakosmêthentôn eontôn ti ê*); see Reale [269], 389–90.
18 Omitting *to hugies kai*, with Gomperz. The MS. text reads: 'for what is healthy and what is would perish'.
19 Sentences [i]–[xviii] and [xix]–[xxvii] may be independent fragments (see Solmsen [282], 10). For various attempts to elucidate **168** see Reale [269], 386–8.
20 Cf., perhaps, Empedocles, **31 B 17**.31: 'If they were destroyed continually, they would not exist': 'if there is any destruction, destruction will continue; and so, in the course of infinite time, all will be destroyed'. I translate *toinun* as 'again'; the normal translation, 'therefore', does not help; and *toinun* is not inferential in Melissus (cf. **158**, **159**; and see J. D. Denniston, *The Greek Particles* (Oxford, 1954²), 574–7).
21 A *kosmos* is an arrangement or structure; *metakosmêthênai* must mean here 'change structure', 'be rearranged' (see Diller [540], 363; cf. Reale [269], 164–70).
22 I follow Loenen [238], 162–4. The rival translations of the first sentence are equivalent, given (T4). For the import of *ouk oun . . . ge . . .* in the third sentence see Denniston, *opus cit.*, n. 20 (above), 422–5.
23 We may smell the old Melissan fallacy in sentence [xxiii]; but if it is there, it does not infect the main argument of the passage.
24 The second clause of **169** admits of different translations: 'If it moves, it does not exist'; 'It cannot be a moving thing'; 'If it moves, it is not [full]'. Fortunately, those variants make no difference to the argument.
25 For *houneken* meaning 'because' see especially Fränkel [230], 191–2; further references in Untersteiner [225], CLV, n. 140.
26 I read *epidees s·m mê eon de*, which was certainly Simplicius' text (see Coxon [287], 72–3); and I follow Hölscher [227], 53, in translating *mê eon* by 'otherwise'. Other suggestions listed in Untersteiner [225], CLVI, n. 145.
27 Lines 22–5 do not reject vacuums as such (*pace* Guthrie [25], II.33), but at best only internal vacuums. According to Raven [178], 29, 'there is . . . no need to argue that these lines [sc. **156**.7–9] are simply a rejection of the Void'; but the lines say nothing at all about the void. **167** rejects intra-mundane void, but leaves open the possibility of extra-mundane void. In any case, none of this helps the argument of lines 30–2.
28 *Principles of Philosophy* II.40 (*Oeuvres*, ed. Adam and Tannery, VIII.65); cf. II.4 (*Oeuvres*, VIII.42); letter to More of 1649 (*Oeuvres*, V.267 = *Philosophical Letters*, ed. Kenny, 237–45). See also Capek [390], 54–8.
29 In these paragraphs I draw heavily on D. H. Sandford, 'Locke, Leibniz and Wiggins on Being in the Same Place at the Same Time', *PR* 79, 1970, 75–82.
30 I append a pleasant curio:

> There are some who think it evident from the rare and dense that there is void. For if nothing is rare and dense, nothing can come together and felt up. And if that cannot happen, either motion will simply not occur or the universe will swell like the sea, as Xuthus said (Aristotle, *Phys* 216b22–6 = **33 A 1**).

Did Xuthus, whom Simplicius calls a Pythagorean and who may have lived in the second quarter of the fifth century, imagine a full and finite universe in which motion nevertheless took place? (The internal convolutions would produce ripples or waves on the outer surface of the world.) If so, was he objecting to a finite and motionless Parmenidean sphere? And did Melissus invent an infinite universe partly to combat that suggestion? Speculation is seductive (see Kirk-Raven [33], 301-2).

31 According to Aristotle, Parmenides and Melissus do not admit the existence of non-perceptible things (*Cael* 298b21 = **28 A 25**; cf. Alexander, *apud* Simplicius, *in Cael* 560.5-10).

32 The text of **B 9** in Diels-Kranz runs together **170** and **171**. For the argument see above, p. 240, on Zeno; Plato, *Sophist* 244E-245A.

33 Simplicius, *ad* **160**, refers to 'limitlessness in respect of sublimity'; see also Loenen [238], 157-8; Vlastos [289], 34-5. *Contra*: e.g., Guthrie [25], II.110, n. 2.

34 Gomperz [288] argued that *asômatos* means the same as *leptos*: not 'incorporeal' but 'fine, not dense'; Guthrie [25], II.110-13, holds that it means 'non-finite and imperceptible' (cf. Reale [269], 211-20). Gomperz and Guthrie suggest that *pachos* is not solidity but 'palpable density'.

35 Incorporeality is not ascribed to O by the *MXG*; and *MXG* 976a10-13 and 28-31 = **A 5** imply that Melissus made no explicit statement about the corporeality of O.

36 According to Cherniss [32], 21, Parmenides thinks that his argument 'precludes the possibility of any characteristic [sc. of what is] except just *being*' (cf. Furth [257], 264-7). That view—which is a *communis opinio*—is surely absurd.

37 So Popper [35], 79; Mourelatos [237], xi.

XII Zeno: Paradox and Plurality

1 Russell [316], 347; cf. Russell [318], 175: 'They are not . . . mere foolish quibbles: they are serious arguments, raising difficulties which it has taken two thousand years to answer, and which even now are fatal to the teachings of most philosophies.' It is Russell's advocacy which has spurred modern philosophers to take Zeno seriously; but it should be said that Russell himself acknowledges that the decisive turn in Zeno's fortunes was due to the work of the Frenchmen, Tannery, Noël, and Brochard. For the history of Zeno's reputation see Cajori [295].

2 The reports, most worthless, about Zeno's life are discussed by von Fritz [298], 53-5. The curious will read the Arabic life of Zeno by Mubaššir, printed in Jacoby [457].

3 Aristotle discusses four paradoxes of motion; Elias says there were five (**A 15**: see Untersteiner [293], 68), and Simplicius thinks there may have been more than four (*in Phys* 1012.27-9). Bicknell [342], 103-5, suggests that the argument in Diogenes Laertius, IX.72 (above, p. 276), may have been the fifth paradox.

4 'He wrote *Disputes, Account of Empedocles, Against the Philosophers, Concerning Nature*' (Suda, **A 2**). *Disputes* and *Against the Philosophers* may be the forty *logoi*; for the Empedoclean title, see below, n. 6. Some natural science is ascribed to Zeno in Diogenes Laertius, IX.29 = **A 1** (cf. Aëtius, I.7.27-8); but the value of the report is uncertain (see Untersteiner [293], 14-17; Longrigg [300]). The report that Zeno wrote dialogues (Diogenes Laertius, III.48 = **A 14**) is merely confused (Untersteiner [293], 62-3).

5 A complex architecture was first suggested by Tannery [29], ch. 10, and developed by Noël and Brochard (see Cajori [295]); it was revived by Owen [307], whose view is tellingly criticized by Stokes [56], 188-93.

335

6 The literature is immense: for the view that Zeno is reacting against Pythagoreans see especially Tannery [29], ch. 10; Raven [178], ch. 5; *contra*; e.g., Burkert [173], 285–8, with references. The ancient assertions that Zeno was a Pythagorean (Proclus, **28 A 4**; Strabo, **28 A 12**) are worthless. Gaye [340], 106–16, argues that the Stadium was aimed against Empedocles (see Suda, **A 2**, above, n. 4); but he does not convince.

7 But Protagoras is said to have written against the monists (Porphyry, **80 B 2**); and some scholars (e.g., Nestle [260]) think that Gorgias, **82 B 3**, is a skit on Eleaticism.

8 In a passage designed to show that 'excessive subtlety produces great evil and is hostile to truth', Seneca asserts that 'Zeno . . . says that nothing exists'; and 'if I believe Parmenides, there exists but one thing—if Zeno, not even one' (*Epistle* 88.44–5: cf. **A 21**). Dillon [294] draws attention to Proclus, *in Parm* 862.25ff: Proclus says that Zeno used the argument of *Parmenides* 131B3–6, to prove that 'the many share in some one thing, and are not deprived of one even if they stand very far apart from one another'. Dillon wonders if that comes from a positive Zenonian argument for monism; but I am sceptical.

9 Alexander's view is uncertain: at 138.3–30 Simplicius says that Alexander shared Eudemus' opinion and borrowed it from him; at 99.12–16 he says that Alexander wrongly argued that Eudemus did not ascribe an attack on monism to Zeno.

10 Numerals followed by 'L' refer to the arrangement in Lee [292].

11 According to Owen [307], 140–1, 'Zeno's major question is: if you say there are many things in existence, how do you distinguish your individuals?' But that view rests on one among several readings of the Eudemus fragment; and no reading will show that this little anecdote enshrines Zeno's 'major question'.

12 Aristotle, fr. 65 R³ = **A 10** (see especially Fränkel [308], 199 n. 1); cf. Diogenes Laertius, IX.25 = **A 1**; Suda, **A 2**; Philostratus, **A 9**. For different interpretations of Aristotle's remark see Lee [292], 7–8, 113–19; von Fritz [298], 78.

13 According to Alcidamas, Zeno later in life 'philosophized on his own account' (Diogenes Laertius, VIII.56 = **31 A 1**; *contra*: pseudo-Plutarch, **29 A 23**).

14 *Antilogikos*: Plato, *Phaedrus* 261D; Plutarch, **A 4**; *eristikos*: Epiphanius, III.11; pseudo-Galen, 3. Modern advocates of an antilogical Zeno include Bayle [299], note B; Fränkel [308]; Solmsen [301]. Against them, see especially Vlastos [303].

15 I guess that the two conjuncts of (Z) are what Plato calls the 'hypotheses' of Zeno's *logoi*; so that the 'first hypothesis of the first *logos*' (*Parm* 127D) will be (Z1a).

16 Proclus, *in Parm* 619.34–620.3 adds 'equal and unequal'; Isocrates X.3 adds 'possible and impossible'. See also the suggestions in Cornford [231], 58.

17 Proclus, *in Parm* 721.25–726.27, has a long and tedious discussion; clearly, he had no textual evidence. For some guesses at Zeno's reasoning see, e.g., Untersteiner [293], 47–51.

18 It is disputed how much of Zeno's work Simplicius had access to: see Guthrie [25], II.81, n. 3; Vlastos [309], 137, n. 7. The course of Simplicius' argument in 138.3–141.10 is controversial (see especially Solmsen [301], 128–31); but this is not the place for an analysis.

19 In [vi] I retain the MSS. reading *esti* for Diels' *estai*. In [vii] I accept Fränkel's palmary emendations: *apeiron* for *apeirôn*; *ek tou* placed after *pollôn*. The general sense of Simplicius' report is uncontroversial.

20 Gomperz emends *oute* to *hôste* in [xiii]; his text translates: '. . . for no part of

it will be last in such a way that there will not be another part related to another'. That expresses the same sentiment as the MSS. text, but more elegantly.

21 The argument for (Z2b) in no way depends on that for (Z2a) (*pace* Fränkel [308], 211-12, 216, n. 2); nor can **B 1** be read as a self-standing argument for (Z2) (*pace* Solmsen [301], 131-7).

22 So, e.g., Fränkel [308], 212; Vlastos [309], 119-20. See also Xenocrates, fr. 44 H = Simplicius, *in Phys* 138.10-13.

23 Fränkel [308], 217-20, finds 'a very great difference' between 'what is added is nothing' and 'what is added does not exist', and he suggests that Zeno passed from the former to the latter by way of the Polypheman fallacy. I cannot see that the fallacy infects Zeno's argument.

24 For the geometrical interpretation see especially Grünbaum [313], ch. III, who holds that Zeno's arguments 'were designed to show that the science of geometry is beset by paradox' (3). Salmon [296] opines that 'the force of this argument is geometrical' (13); but he recognizes that Zeno's paradoxes 'are—so to speak—paradoxes of applied mathematics. No theory of pure mathematics can fully resolve them' (34).

25 'That no physical cut or fission is intended here is quite obvious' (Vlastos [309], 125): Zeno is certainly not thinking of cuts which an engineer can make 'with his present tools'; but he is certainly thinking of physical bodies, and claiming that they have physical parts.

26 See further Xenocrates, frr. 43-9 H. Plato too believed in atomic lines (Aristotle, *Met* 992a22; Alexander, *in Met* 120.6); but we are not told why (and Vlastos [401], 125, n. 28, doubts the report). The ancient evidence is confusing. (a) The argument of Zeno's which precipitated atomic lines is usually identified as the Dichotomy (see especially [Aristotle], *lin insec* 986a17-28 = Xenocrates, fr. 42 H = **A 22**), but sometimes as the present argument against pluralism (see Alexander, **A 22**: cf. Furley [387], 81-3). (b) Aristotle, *Phys* 187a1-3, says that 'some' gave in to the 'dichotomy' and posited atomic magnitudes: he probably refers to the Abderite atomists (see Ross [12], 479-80; Furley [387], 81-3), but all his ancient commentators refer to Xenocrates.

27 See especially Grünbaum [313], 40-64. On Epicurus' spatial atomism see Luria [398], 148-72; Mau [402]; Vlastos [401].

28 This, the classical solution, is plainly stated by Descartes in a letter to Clerselier of 1646 (*Oeuvres*, ed. Adam and Tannery, IV.445-7 = *philosophical Letters*, ed. Kenny, 196-9); see further Cajori [295], 79-80. Fränkel [308], 226-7, attempts to pre-empt it by denying that (Z2b) states that the many things will be infinite in magnitude; but see Furley [387], 68-9. Zeno's 'hidden premiss' was set down as a luminous truth by Epicurus (*ad Hdt* 57: cf. Furley [387], 14-16), and generally adopted by the later tradition (e.g., Sextus, *Pyrr Hyp* III.44; Simplicius, *in Phys* 141.15-16; 459.25-6; *in Cael* 608.12-15; 635.11-26: cf. Vlastos [297], 370b-371a). See below, n. 30.

29 'He' in Porphyry's text, which Simplicius quotes *verbatim*, refers to Parmenides; but Simplicius is right in maintaining that the dichotomy argument belongs rather to Zeno.

30 Aristotle, *Phys* 206b7-9, knows that (9) is not unrestrictedly true. I incline to speculate that Zeno imagined that (9) held without restriction; that Aristotle scotched that supposition; and that Epicurus saw that a restricted version of (9) was defensible. Later subscribers to Zeno's 'hidden premiss' tacitly suppose the Epicurean version of it. Vlastos [309], 131-3, thinks Zeno assumed that any infinite sequence must have a smallest member. If that assumption were true,

then (9) would hold unrestrictedly. But the assumption is false; and there is no evidence that Zeno made it.
31 Vlastos [297], 371b. Vlastos says that only a Cantorian sophistication can pinpoint Zeno's error; but we do not need the 'diagonal method' to show how Zeno errs. The concept of one-one correspondence is expounded most famously by Gottlob Frege (*Foundations of Arithmetic*, §63); but, as Frege points out, it is already present in that most unsophisticated of mathematicians, David Hume.
32 See especially Simplicius, *in Phys* 96.15-99.31, quoting Alexander and Eudemus; Philoponus, *in Phys* 42.9-45.15 (cf. **A 21** and **3-8 L**).
33 For *plêthos henadôn* see, e.g., Philoponus, *in Phys* 42.21; 24 (cf. *sunthesis tôn kath' hen* in Gorgias, **157** § 74). For the sense of *henas* see, e.g., Plato, *Philebus* 15A: *henas* does not mean 'arithmetical unit', and it is a mistake (*pace* Raven [178], 71-2) to invoke any 'Pythagorean' theory about arithmetical units.
34 Simplicius is quoting Alexander's quotation of Eudemus; and Simplicius says that the argument Alexander retails is not in Zeno's book (*in Phys* 99.18). Eudemus is hardly inventing: either the argument fell out of Zeno's book in the millennium separating Eudemus from Simplicius; or else Simplicius means only that the argument does not occur *verbatim* in Zeno.
35 Solmsen [301], 128, n. 38, connects *katêgorikôs* with the Aristotelian categories. But the rest of the quotation shows that '*a* is many *katêgorikôs*' simply means '*a* is many in virtue of the predicates (*katêgoriai*) true of it'.
36 The ascription to Zeno is also made by Alexander (*apud* Simplicius, *in Phys* 96.22-30) and by Philoponus (see especially *in Phys* 42.24-8 = **8 L**, with an anachronistic illustration). For doubts about the ascription see, e.g., Lee [292], 27-9; Burkert [173], 286-8.
37 Lycophron tackled this, or a very similar, puzzle: pseudo-Alexander, **83 A 1**.
38 The main text is Simplicius, *in Phys* 562.1-564.13; further references in Lee [292], 36. Diels-Kranz, I.498, accept Calogero's suggestion that *in Phys* 562.3-6 is an actual fragment of Zeno; but Simplicius himself makes it clear first that he does not possess Zeno's own words here, and second that he does not believe that the form of the argument given at 562.3-6 is authentic.
39 Philoponus, *in Phys* 513.8-12, did not know what point Zeno was trying to make; Cornford [231], 148-9, constructs a slightly different dilemma.
40 So too Plato, *Timaeus* 52 B. Zeno's premiss is used by Gorgias, **157** §§ 69-70 (*MXG* 979b25 explicitly ascribes to Gorgias this use of 'Zeno's argument about place'); it appears at *Parmenides* 145E, 151A; according to Aristotle, *Phys* 208a30, it was a commonplace (cf. Kahn [255], 237: it was 'firmly grounded in the idiomatic expression of existence').

XIII Zeno: Paradox and Progression

1 Texts collected in Lee [292] (**19 L-36 L**, with supplementary references). The Greek commentators say that Achilles' rival was a tortoise (the tortoise is not in Aristotle; Plutarch races a tortoise against a horse); apart from that, they add nothing (see Ross [12], 71). Aristotle probably found the arguments already numbered; he refers to previous attempts at a solution (*Phys* 239b11); and he remarks upon a non-Zenonian version of the Dichotomy (above, p. 263). (Aristotle may have composed a monograph on Zeno (Diogenes Laertius, V.25; cf. Untersteiner [293], 74); Heraclides Ponticus did (Diogenes Laertius, V.17).) Favorinus said that 'Parmenides and many others' raised the Achilles paradox (Diogenes Laertius, IX.29 = **A 1**).

2 'The Dichotomy' derives from *Phys* 239b22 = **L 26** (on 187a3 = **A 22**, see above, p. 337, n. 26); 'the Stadium' derives from *Top* 160b8 = **A 25**. Aristotle himself probably knew no title for the paradox (see Vlastos [321], 95, n. 2).
3 Cf. *Phys* 239b18–20 = **A 26** = **26 L**; and note that the 'counting' version requires this diagram. See, e.g., Fränkel [308], 204, n. 3; Vlastos [321], 95–6.
4 Cf. *Phys* 263a6–11; *lin insec* 968a18–b4; see Furley [387] 70–1; Grünbaum [313], 70 (Zeno is 'enticing us to attempt a one-by-one contemplation in thought' of all the temporal parts of the runner's task). On the counting paradox itself see Grünbaum [313], 90–2; Black [326], 100–8.
5 Cf. Black [326], 108, who distinguishes between 'the finite number of real things that the runner has to accomplish and the infinite series of numbers by which we describe what he actually does' (cf. Grünbaum [313], 73–8; and especially Wisdom [328]). Some scholars discuss the Dichotomy in terms of 'making infinitely many runs'; they declare that the term 'run' has two senses; and they find an equivocation in Zeno (see especially Grünbaum [313], 73–8; Vlastos [321]). I cannot find two relevant senses of 'run'; nor does Zeno himself say anything about 'making infinitely many runs'.
6 E.g., C. S. Peirce: 'This ridiculous little catch presents no difficulty at all to a mind adequately trained in mathematics and in logic' (*Collected Papers*, VI.122). Peirce is talking of the Achilles; but his remarks apply equally to the Dichotomy.
7 For Strato see fr. 82 W = Sextus, *adv Math* X.155; on the thesis he adopts see Grünbaum [313], 50–2.
8 But Ross [12], 73–4, argues strongly that Aristotle's objection in Z 9 is cogent *ad hominem*, and hence that Zeno himself did mention the finitude of *T*; and Grünbaum [313], 52, thinks it is the temporal aspect of the Dichotomy which 'constitutes the heart of the conviction' which it often carries (cf. Ushenko [314], 157).
9 The lamp was introduced into the literature, with far more finesse than in my sketch, by Thomson [331].
10 For Aristotle's discussion see *Phys* 234a24–b9; 235b6–32; 236a7–27; 236b32–237b22; 238b36–239b4; 263b15–264a6. My argument in the text abstracts from those remarks and is not an interpretation of them.
11 This argument is adapted from some subtler remarks in Bostock [322].
12 Diodorus' dilemma is designed to show that *atoms* do not move (fr. 123 D = Sextus, *adv Math* X.86–90; cf. frr. 116–24 D); he also offered, apparently as a distinct argument, something answering to Aristotle's non-dilemmatic text (Sextus, *adv Math* X.112).
13 On the text of *Phys* 239b5–7, see especially Ross [12], 657–8, whom I follow.
14 See especially Vlastos [335], 3, n. 2 (Fränkel [308], 209, n. 5, and Untersteiner [293], 149–51, offer different explanations). The 'space equal to itself' is the *place* of an object, in the strict Aristotelian sense (*Phys* 209a33; 211a2); it is that notion of place which is employed in the Paradox of Place. The Arrow is presented in characteristically Aristotelian terminology; but it is fruitless to attempt to recover Zeno's phraseology.
15 Russell [316], 347, 350; [317], 65. Epicurus, fr. 278 Us, and Diodorus Cronus, frr. 121–9 D, advance theories of motion interestingly similar to Russell's (see Furley [387], 131–5).
16 Bergson [320], 63.
17 Adapted from Black [338], 138–9; Black's own conclusion is that there are two senses of 'move'.

18 Vlastos [335], 11.
19 At 240a5-7 the MSS. offer a choice of readings: '*A*', '*AA*', '*AAA*', '*AAAA*', etc.; Ross rightly plumps for '*AA*', but that does not mean that Aristotle had precisely two *A*s in mind: '*ta AA*' means simply 'the *A*s'.
20 Palaeographically there is nothing to choose between '*to B*' and '*to prôton B*' (abbreviated to '*to a B*'); and one MS. reads '*to a B*' (see Ross [12], 665). Bicknell [341], 43, defends '*ta B*'.
21 Thus I retain sentence [x], which many editors excise (see especially, Ross [12], 665).
22 The Greek at 240a1 ('half the time is equal to its double') may mean either '$\frac{1}{2}T = T$' or '$\frac{1}{2}T = 2T$'; see, e.g., Lee [292], 88; Gaye [340], 100-1; Stokes [56], 329, n. 31.
23 A classical example in Bayle [299], n.F; a modern example in Bicknell [341] (but Bicknell [342], 81, recants).
24 (i) Defenders of *fig. 5* must change the text at 240a6: they must either (a) omit 'of the *A*s (*tôn A*)' after 'starting from the middle'; or else (b) add 'of the *B*s (*tôn B*)' after 'starting from the end'. One MS. offers '*tôn B*', several omit '*tôn A*' (see Ross [12], 663). (ii) At 240a11 most MSS. and the Greek commentators read '*ta A*', which I translate; two MSS. read '*ta B*'. Adherents of *fig. 5* have a choice: either (a) they accept '*ta B*' instead of '*ta A*' and interpolate '*ta A*' later in the sentence ('the *C* had passed all the *B*s and the *B* half the *A*s')—so Diels-Kranz; or else (b) they omit '*ta A*' ('the *C* has passed all, and the *B* half'), and gloss the resulting sentence as 'the first *C* has passed all the *A*s and the first *B* has passed half the *A*s' (so Ross [12], 662). (ib) is tolerable, and (ia) may well be right; but both (iia) and (iib) are counsels of desperation, defensible only if *fig. 5* must at all costs be established.
25 The inventor of the sophisticated Stadium was Tannery [29], ch. 10 (further references in Guthrie [25], II.95-6); *contra*: e.g., Furley [387], 73-4; Stokes [56], 185-7. Sextus, *adv Math* X.144-7, preserves an argument similar to the Stadium which explicitly uses *minima*; see also Bayle [299], n. G.

XIV *The Ports of Knowledge Closed*

1 So Cornford [231], 32, referring to [Hippocrates], *de victu* I.23; Verdenius [233], 55, referring to 156.38-41; cf. Antiphon, 87 B 44 (Diels-Kranz, II.348.6).
2 I do not translate *homoureôn* (*homou rheôn*?), the sense of which is obscure.
3 The bracketed sentence makes no sense here, where it stands in Simplicius' text. Karsten transposed it to follow '. . . from water' at the end of [iii], and most scholars accept his transposition. But the sentence is inapposite at the end of [iii]. Moreover, it is linguistically objectionable: *hôste* and *sumbainein* are used in a sense that is not Presocratic; we have *ta onta* for *ta eonta*; and *gignôskein* misinterprets *sunienai*. The sentence is a marginal gloss written in a later jargon.
4 Melissus refers simply to 'men' (*hoi anthrôpoi*): he is attacking the *communis opinio*, not any particular philosophical school (see Reale [269], 242-52). Mourelatos [237], 362-3, says that Melissus 'does not, of course, intend the paradoxical and self-contradictory thesis that *this* to which I point (the earth, the sea) does not exist. The verb "to be" here has a special sense'. The thesis is not self-contradictory, and Melissus surely did intend it: it is paradoxical—but what is Eleaticism if not paradoxical?
5 I.e. '$a_1, a_2, \ldots, a_n$ seem to be real, but in fact are not so' (see Loenen [238], 133-4). The usual translation reads: '. . . those things do not correctly seem to be many'.

Bibliography

The bibliography has two functions: it gives detailed references to the various books and articles cited in the Notes; and it attempts to provide an intelligible and articulated guide to the vast modern literature on the Presocratics. The second aim accounts for the arrangement of the bibliography; the first explains the inclusion of some fairly minor items.

I use the following abbreviations:

ABG   *Archiv für Begriffsgeschichte*
AC   *Acta Classica*
AGP   *Archiv für Geschichte der Philosophie*
AJP   *American Journal of Philology*
An   *Analysis*
APQ   *American Philosophical Quarterly*
BICS *Bulletin of the Institute of Classical Studies*
BJPS *British Journal for the Philosophy of Science*
CP   *Classical Philology*
CQ   *Classical Quarterly*
CR   *Classical Review*
H   *Hermes*
HSCP *Harvard Studies in Classical Philology*
JHI   *Journal of the History of Ideas*
JHP   *Journal of the History of Philosophy*
JHS   *Journal of Hellenic Studies*
JP   *Journal of Philosophy*
M   *Mind*
MH   *Museum Helveticum*
Mnem *Mnemosyne*
NGG   *Nachrichten von der Gesellschaft der Wissenschaft zu Göttingen*
PAS   *Proceedings of the Aristotelian Society*
PCPS *Proceedings of the Cambridge Philological Society*
Phlg *Philologus*
Phron *Phronesis*
PQ   *Philosophical Quarterly*
PR   *Philosophical Review*

BIBLIOGRAPHY

QSGM   *Quellen und Studien zur Geschichte der Mathematik*
RE   Pauly-Wissowa's *Realenkyklopädie der klassischen Altertumswissenschaft*
REA   *Revue des Études Anciennes*
REG   *Revue des Études Grècques*
RhM   *Rheinisches Museum*
RM   *Review of Metaphysics*
SO   *Symbolae Osloenses*
TAPA   *Transactions of the American Philological Association*
WS   *Wiener Studien*

A: GENERAL

I: Texts

The standard work on the Presocratics, a monument to scholarship and an indispensable aid, is:
[1] H. Diels and W. Kranz: *Die Fragmente der Vorsokratiker* (Berlin, 1960^{10})
The fragments, but not the *testimonia*, are Englished in:
[2] K. Freeman: *The Pre-Socratic Philosophers* (Oxford, 1946)
For the poetical Presocratics it is worth consulting:
[3] H. Diels: *Poetarum Philosophorum Fragmenta* (Berlin, 1901)

The doxography is finely discussed, and the main texts printed, in another magisterial work by Diels:
[4] H. Diels: *Doxographi Graeci* (Berlin, 1879)

Editions of texts of individual Presocratics are listed under the appropriate heading in part B of the bibliography; editions of certain other ancient authors are mentioned in the next section, and in Appendix A.

II: Source Criticism

Most scholars accept the reconstruction of the doxographical tradition which Diels established in [4]; but there are some important qualifications in:
[5] P. Steinmetz: *Die Physik des Theophrasts*, Palingenesia I, Bad Homburg, 1964)
and some intemperate disagreements in Gershenson-Greenberg [361].

The historical value of the doxography is a matter of grave dispute. A lengthy denunciation of Aristotle was made in:
[6] H. F. Cherniss: *Aristotle's Criticism of Presocratic Philosophy* (Baltimore, 1935)
and Theophrastus was attacked in similar vein by:
[7] J. B. McDiarmid: 'Theophrastus on the Presocratic Causes', *HSCP* 61, 1953, 85-156 = Furley-Allen [70]
Most books on the Presocratics contain appreciations of the doxography. Against Cherniss see especially:
[8] W. K. C. Guthrie: 'Aristotle as an Historian of Philosophy', *JHS* 77, 1957, 35-41 = Furley-Allen [70]
Guthrie's paper has been examined in turn by:
[9] J. G. Stevenson: 'Aristotle as Historian of Philosophy', *JHS* 94, 1974, 138-43
A wealth of relevant material can be found in the classic commentaries of:
[10] R. D. Hicks: *Aristotle: de Anima* (Cambridge, 1907)
[11] W. D. Ross: *Aristotle's Metaphysics* (Oxford, 1924)
[12] W. D. Ross: *Aristotle's Physics* (Oxford, 1936)

And there is a brilliant paper on a nice detail by:
[13] B. Snell: 'Die Nachrichten über die Lehre des Thales und die Anfänge der griechischen Philosophie- und Literaturgeschichte', *Phlg* 96, 1944, 170–82 = Snell [82]

On Theophrastus see Steinmetz [5], and the Introduction to:
[14] G. M. Stratton: *Theophrastus and the Greek Physiological Psychology before Aristotle* (London, 1917)
Plutarch's testimony is analysed by:
[15] R. Westman: *Plutarch gegen Colotes*, Acta Philosophica Fennica VII (Helsinki, 1955)
[16] J. P. Hershbell: 'Plutarch as a Source for Empedocles Re-examined', *AJP* 92, 1971, 156–84
And on Hippolytus consult:
[17] J. P. Hershbell: 'Hippolytus' *Elenchos* as a Source for Empedocles Re-examined', *Phron* 18, 1973, 97–114

The major commentaries on the classical authors frequently shed incidental light on the Presocratics; I have found myself most often helped by:
[18] U. von Wilamowitz-Moellendorf: *Euripides: Herakles* (Berlin, 1895)
[19] T. L. Heath: *The Thirteen Books of Euclid's Elements* (Cambridge, 1926^2)
[20] C. Bailey: *Epicurus* (Oxford, 1926)
[21] C. Bailey: *Lucretius: de Rerum Natura* (Oxford, 1947)
[22] C. W. Chilton: *Diogenes of Oenoanda* (London, 1971)
[23] M. L. West: *Hesiod: Theogony* (Oxford, 1966)
Finally, no one should fail to peruse the opening chapters of:
[24] R. Pfeiffer: *A History of Classical Scholarship*, I (Oxford, 1968)

III: General Histories

English readers will find a treasury of humane scholarship in the first three volumes of:
[25] W. K. C. Guthrie: *A History of Greek Philosophy* (Cambridge, 1962, 1965, 1969)
Zeller's handbook, *Die Philosophie der Griechen*, has undergone several revisions since its first appearance in 1892; the fullest and most recent edition—still incomplete—is:
[26] E. Zeller and R. Mondolfo: *La Filosofia dei Greci nel suo sviluppo storico* (Florence, 1932–)
Philosophers will enjoy the relevant chapters of:
[27] G. W. F. Hegel: *Lectures on the History of Philosophy*, trans. E. S. Haldane and F. H. Simson (London, 1892; first publishing of German text, 1840)
and also:
[28] F. Nietzsche: *Die Philosophie im tragischen Zeitalter der Griechen*, in vol. III of Nietzsche's *Werke*, ed. K. Schlechta (Munich, 1956; first published in 1872)
Of other general accounts of Presocratic thought, the most influential have been:
[29] P. Tannery: *Pour l' histoire de la science Hellène* (Paris, 1887)
[30] K. Reinhardt: *Parmenides und die Geschichte der griechischen Philosophie* (Bonn, 1916)
([30] is, for my money, the most sparkling book in the whole field)
[31] J. Burnet: *Early Greek Philosophy* (London, 1930^4)
[32] H. F. Cherniss: 'Characteristics and Effects of Presocratic Philosophy', *JHI* 12, 1951, 319–45 = Furley-Allen [70]

There are sober introductions in:
[33] G. S. Kirk and J. E. Raven: *The Presocratic Philosophers* (Cambridge, 1962⁴)
[34] E. Hussey: *The Presocratics* (London, 1972)
And a spirited introduction in:
[35] K. R. Popper: 'Back to the Presocratics', *PAS* 59, 1958/9, 1-24 = K. R. Popper: *Conjectures and Refutations* (London, 1969³) = Furley-Allen [70]
See also:
[36] T. Gomperz: *Greek Thinkers* (London, 1901-12)
[37] F. M. Cleve: *The Giants of Pre-Sophistic Greek Philosophy* (The Hague, 1965)
[38] G. Calogero: *Storia della logica antica* (Bari, 1967)

IV: Monographs

I list here a number of books which bear upon particular aspects of early Greek thought: their titles on the whole are adequate guides to their contents.
[39] J. I. Beare: *Greek Theories of Elementary Cognition* (Oxford, 1906)
[40] F. M. Cornford: *The Laws of Motion in Ancient Thought* (Cambridge, 1931)
[41] F. M. Cornford: *Principium Sapientiae* (Cambridge, 1952)
[42] D. R. Dicks: *Early Greek Astronomy to Aristotle* (London, 1970)
[43] E. R. Dodds: *The Greeks and the Irrational* (Berkeley, Cal., 1951)
[44] H. Fränkel: *Early Greek Poetry and Philosophy*, trans. M. Hadas and J. Willis (Oxford, 1975)
[45] T. L. Heath: *Aristarchus of Samos* (Oxford, 1913)
[46] T. L. Heath: *A History of Greek Mathematics* (Oxford, 1921)
[47] W. W. Jaeger: *Paideia* (Oxford, 1939-45)
[48] W. W. Jaeger: *The Theology of the Early Greek Philosophers* (Oxford, 1947)
[49] W. H. S. Jones: *Philosophy and Medicine in Ancient Greece* (Baltimore, 1946)
[50] G. E. R. Lloyd: *Polarity and Analogy* (Cambridge, 1966)
[51] H. Lloyd-Jones: *The Justice of Zeus* (Berkeley, Cal., 1971)
[52] C. W. Müller: *Gleiches zu Gleichen—ein Prinzip frühgriechischen Denkens* (Wiesbaden, 1965)
[53] S. Sambursky: *The Physical World of the Greeks* (London, 1956)
[54] B. Snell: *Die Ausdrücke für den Begriff des Wissens in der vorplatonischen Philosophie*, Philologische Untersuchungen 29 (Berlin, 1924)
[55] B. Snell: *The Discovery of Mind* (Oxford, 1953)
[56] M. C. Stokes: *One and Many in Presocratic Philosophy* (Washington, DC, 1971)
[57] L. Sweeney: *Infinity in the Presocratics* (The Hague, 1972)
[58] B. L. van der Waerden: *Science Awakening*, trans. A. Dresden (New York, 1961)
[59] M. L. West: *Early Greek Philosophy and the Orient* (Oxford, 1971)

I append to this section a number of articles of a general scope. The first two are seminal pieces:
[60] W. A. Heidel: 'Qualitative Change in Pre-Socratic Philosophy', *AGP* 19, 1906, 333-79 = Mourelatos [72]
[61] W. A. Heidel: '῾Περὶ Φυσέως: A Study of the Conception of Nature among the Pre-Socratics', *Proceedings of the American Academy of Arts and Sciences* 45, 1910, 77-133
The next article is of wider scope than its title suggests, being a comprehensive account of early notions of cognition:

[62] K. von Fritz: 'Νοῦς, νοεῖν and their Derivatives in Presocratic Philosophy', *CP* 40, 1945, 223-42 and 41, 1946, 12-34 = Mourelatos [72] = Gadamer [71]
With Jones [49], compare:
[63] J. Longrigg: 'Philosophy and Medicine: some early Interactions', *HSCP* 67, 1963, 147-76
With Lloyd [50], compare:
[64] G. E. R. Lloyd: 'Hot and Cold, Dry and Wet, in early Greek Thought', *JHS* 84, 1964, 92-106 = Furley-Allen [70]
With Dicks [42], compare:
[65] D. R. Dicks: 'Solstices, Equinoxes and the Presocratics', *JHS* 86, 1966, 26-40
and the reply by:
[66] C. H. Kahn: 'On Early Greek Astronomy', *JHS* 90, 1970, 99-116
Finally, note the interesting piece on the Derveni papyrus by:
[67] W. Burkert: 'Orpheus und der Vorsokratiker', *Antike und Abendland* 14, 1968, 93-114

V: Anthologies

[68] V. E. Alfieri and M. Untersteiner (eds): *Studi di Filosofia Greca* (Bari, 1950)
[69] J. P. Anton and G. L. Kustas (eds): *Essays in Ancient Greek Philosophy* (Albany, New York, 1971)
[70] D. J. Furley and R. E. Allen (eds): *Studies in Presocratic Philosophy* (London, 1970, 1975)
[71] H. G. Gadamer (ed.): *Um die Begriffswelt der Vorsokratiker* (Darmstadt, 1968)
[72] A. P. D. Mourelatos (ed.): *The Presocratics* (Garden City, New York, 1974)

VI: Collected Papers

[73] J. Bernays: *Gesammelte Abhandlungen* (Berlin, 1885)
[74] F. M. Cornford: *The Unwritten Philosophy* (Cambridge, 1950)
[75] H. Diller: *Kleine Schriften zur antiken Literatur* (Munich, 1971)
[76] H. Fränkel: *Wege und Formen frühgriechischen Denkens* (Munich, 1960^2)
[77] K. von Fritz: *Grundprobleme der Geschichte der antiken Wissenschaft* (Berlin, 1971)
[78] O. Gigon: *Studien zur antiken Philosophie* (Berlin, 1972)
[79] U. Hölscher: *Anfängliches Fragen* (Göttingen, 1968)
[80] W. Nestle: *Griechische Studien* (Stuttgart, 1948)
[81] K. Reinhardt: *Vermächtnis der Antike* (Göttingen, 1966^2)
[82] B. Snell: *Gesammelte Schriften* (Göttingen, 1966)
[83] F. Solmsen: *Kleine Schriften* (Hildesheim, 1968)
[84] M. Untersteiner: *Scritti Minori* (Brescia, 1971)

VII: Bibliography

There are excellent bibliographies in Guthrie [25], Sweeney [57], and Mourelatos [72]; see also:
[85] G. B. Kerferd: 'Recent Work on Presocratic Philosophy', *APQ* 2, 1965, 130-40
And of course most of the books and papers I list here contain a multitude of further references.
   Bibliographies date quickly. The reader may keep abreast of the tide by consulting

BIBLIOGRAPHY

L' Année Philologique, Repertoire bibliographique de la Philosophie de Louvain, and *The Philosophers Index*, periodicals which, taken together, catch all the new literature on the subject.

B: PARTICULAR

The second half of this bibliography is divided into sections that correspond to the chapters of the book. Items referred to in one section will often contain material relevant to other sections; and many of the works listed in part A—notably Guthrie [25]—will profitably be consulted in connexion with every chapter.

Chapter I

On Thales in general see:
[86] D. R. Dicks: 'Thales', *CQ* n.s. 9, 1959, 294–309
[87] M. L. West: 'Three Presocratic Cosmologies', *CQ* n.s. 13, 1963, 154–76
[88] J. C. Classen: 'Thales', *RE* suppt. 10, 1965, 930–47

Literature on the notion of *psuchê*, on the stability of the earth, and on early cosmogony, is given on later pages (below, pp. 351, 346, 347). On Thales' mathematical achievements see chapter 4 of Heath [46]; and:
[89] B. Gladigow: 'Thales und der διαβήτης', *H* 96, 1968, 264–75
For the sources see the items in part A, section II, especially Guthrie [8] and Snell [13].

Chapter II

The classic study of Anaximander's thought is:
[90] C. H. Kahn: *Anaximander and the Origins of Greek Cosmology* (New York, 1960)
(I might observe that Kahn's book is crammed with wise and stimulating thoughts on every aspect of early Greek philosophy.) Out of numerous general studies of Anaximander I pick:
[91] U. Hölscher: 'Anaximander und die Anfänge der Philosophie', *H* 81, 1953, 255–77 and 385–417 = Hölscher [79] = Furley-Allen [70]
[92] G. S. Kirk: 'Some Problems in Anaximander', *CQ* n.s. 5, 1955, 21–38 = Furley-Allen [70]
[93] J. C. Classen: 'Anaximander', *H* 90, 1962, 159–72
[94] J. C. Classen: 'Anaximandros', *RE* suppt. 12, 1970, 30–69

Anaximander's 'Darwinism' is discussed ably by:
[95] J. H. Loenen: 'Was Anaximander an Evolutionist?', *Mnem* s. 4, 7, 1954, 215–32
and it is worth reading:
[96] G. Rudberg: 'Empedokles und Evolution', *Eranos* 49, 1951, 23–30

Anaximander's mathematical astronomy has often been described: see in particular chapter 4 of Tannery [29], and chapter 4 of Heath [45]; and the dispute between Dicks ([65] and [42]) and Kahn ([90] and [66]). See also:
[97] N. Rescher: 'Cosmic Evolution in Anaximander', *Studium Generale* 11, 1958, 718–31 = N. Rescher, *Essays in Philosophical Analysis* (Pittsburgh, Pa., 1969)
And on the stability of the earth:
[98] J. Robinson: 'Anaximander and the Problem of the Earth's Immobility', in Anton-Kustas [69]

The best discussions of the Anaximandrian fragment are in Kahn [90] and in:
[99] H. Schwabl: 'Anaximander—zu den Quellen und seiner Einordnung um vorsokratischen Philosophie', *ABG* 9, 1964, 59-72
See also:
[100] F. Dirlmeier: 'Der Satz des Anaximandros', *RhM* 87, 1938, 376-82 = F. Dirlmeier, *Ausgewählte Schriften* (Heidelberg, 1970) = Gadamer [71]
[101] C. H. Kahn: 'Anaximander and the Arguments concerning the ἄπειρον at *Physics* 203b4-15', *Festschrift Ernst Kapp* (Hamburg, 1958)
(Kahn thinks he has discovered a second fragment of Anaximander in the text of the *Physics*.)
There is a full-length study of Anaximander's 'unlimited' principle by:
[102] P. Seligman: *The Apeiron of Anaximander* (London, 1962)
and several useful papers, including:
[103] F. Solmsen: 'Anaximander's infinite: traces and influences', *AGP* 44, 1962, 109-31 = Solmsen [83]
[104] H. B. Gottschalk: 'Anaximander's Apeiron', *Phron* 10, 1965, 37-53
[105] P. J. Bicknell: τὸ ἄπειρον, ἄπειροs ἀήρ and τὸ περιέχον', *AC* 9, 1966, 27-48

Chapter III

Less attention has been paid to Anaximenes than to Anaximander. In addition to the general histories, chapter 2 of Stokes [56], and a few studies of detail, I know only:
[106] J. Klowski: 'Ist der Aër des Anaximenes als eine Substanz Konzipiert?', *H* 100, 1972, 131-42
The topic of ancient cosmogonical thought has been far more intensely discussed; the most comprehensive piece is:
[107] H. Schwabl: 'Weltschöpfung', *RE* suppt. 9, 1962, 1433-1589
On Pherecydes see especially West [59], chapters 1-2; and on the tantalizing fragment of Alcman:
[108] M. L. West: 'Alcman and Pythagoras', *CQ* n.s. 17, 1967, 1-15
For Hesiod see West [23], and:
[109] M. C. Stokes: 'Hesiodic and Milesian Cosmogonies', *Phron* 7, 1963, 1-35, and 8, 1963, 1-34
[110] J. Klowski: 'Zum Entstehen der Begriffe Sein und Nichts und der Weltentstehungs- und Weltschöpfungstheorien im strengen Sinne', *AGP* 49, 1967, 121-48 and 225-54
Milesian cosmogony is also discussed in Kahn [90] and in Hölscher [91]; and in a classic paper by:
[111] G. Vlastos: 'Equality and Justice in early Greek cosmologies', *CP* 42, 1947, 156-78 = Furley-Allen [70]
Finally, read:
[112] F. Solmsen: 'Aristotle and Presocratic Cosmogony', *HSCP* 63, 1958, 265-82 = Solmsen [83]
The question of the scientific standing of Presocratic thought has produced a large literature. The best general survey is in Sambursky [53]; and there is an invaluable article by:
[113] G. E. R. Lloyd: 'Experiment in Early Greek Philosophy and Medicine', *PCPS* n.s. 10, 1964, 50-72
F. M. Cornford more than once advanced the extreme view that the Presocratics were not, and did not mean to be, scientists: see Cornford [41], [74], and:

[114] F. M. Cornford: 'Was the Ionian Philosophy Scientific?', *JHS* 62, 1942, 1-7 = Furley-Allen [70]
Against Cornford see especially:
[115] G. Vlastos: review of Cornford [41], *Gnomon* 27, 1955, 65-76 = Furley-Allen [70]
(And compare the dispute between Dicks and Kahn, above, p. 346).

At the other extreme, Sir Karl Popper has lavishly praised Presocratic science: see Popper [35]. Against Popper:
[116] G. S. Kirk: 'Popper on Science and the Presocratics', *M* 69, 1960, 318-39 = Furley-Allen [70]
[117] G. S. Kirk: 'Sense and Common Sense in the Development of Greek Philosophy', *JHS* 81, 1961, 105-17
See also Popper [151]; and:
[118] G. E. R. Lloyd: 'Popper versus Kirk: a Controversy in the Interpretation of Greek Science', *BJPS* 18, 1967, 21-39
I mention too:
[119] J. Stannard: 'The Presocratic Origin of Explanatory Method', *PQ* 15, 1965, 193-206

Analogy has long been recognized as a characteristic of early Greek thought. See especially Part II of Lloyd [50];
[120] H. Diller: '$\mathring{o}\psi\iota\varsigma\ \mathring{\alpha}\delta\acute{\eta}\lambda\omega\nu\ \tau\grave{\alpha}\ \varphi\alpha\iota\nu\acute{o}\mu\epsilon\nu\alpha$', *H* 67, 1932, 14-42 = Diller [75]
and:
[121] W. Kranz: 'Gleichnis und Vergleich in der frühgriechischen Philosophie', *H* 73, 1938, 99-122
See also:
[122] H. C. Baldry: 'Embryological Analogies in Presocratic Cosmogony', *CQ* 26, 1932, 27-34
and compare Fränkel [145], and Regenbogen [520].

On Anaximenean details see:
[123] W. K. C. Guthrie: 'Anaximenes and $\tau\grave{o}\ \kappa\rho\upsilon\sigma\tau\alpha\lambda\lambda o\epsilon\iota\delta\acute{\epsilon}\varsigma$', *CQ* n.s. 6, 1956, 40-4
[124] J. Longrigg: '$\kappa\rho\upsilon\sigma\tau\alpha\lambda\lambda o\epsilon\iota\delta\tilde{\omega}\varsigma$', *CQ* n.s. 15, 1965, 249-52
[125] H. Schwabl: 'Anaximenes und die Gestirne', *WS* 79, 1966, 33-8
[126] J. Longrigg: 'A Note on Anaximenes fragment 2', *Phron* 9, 1964, 1-5
[127] K. Alt: 'Zum Satz des Anaximenes über die Seele—Untersuchung von Aëtius $\pi\epsilon\rho\grave{\iota}\ \mathring{\alpha}\rho\chi\tilde{\omega}\nu$', *H* 101, 1973, 129-64
[128] G. B. Kerferd: 'The Date of Anaximenes', *MH* 11, 1954, 117-21

Chapter IV

The fragments of Heraclitus are best studied in the edition of:
[129] M. Marcovich: *Heraclitus* (Merida, 1967)
That edition can be supplemented by:
[130] S. Mouraviev: 'New Readings of Three Heraclitean Fragments (B 23, B 28, B 26)', *H* 101, 1973, 114-27
All other texts pertaining to Heraclitus are collected and annotated in:
[131] R. Mondolfo and L. Tarán: *Eraclito—testimonianze e imitazione* (Florence, 1972)
For bibliography see:
[132] E. N. Roussos: *Heraklit-Bibliographie* (Darmstadt, 1971)
There are three landmarks in modern Heraclitean studies. First:

[133] J. Bernays: *Heraclitea* (Bonn, 1848) = Bernays [73]
(see also papers II–IV in [73]); second, the work of Karl Reinhardt:
[134] K. Reinhardt: 'Heraclitea', *H* 77, 1942, 225–48 = Reinhardt [81] = Gadamer [71]
[135] K. Reinhardt: 'Heraklits Lehre vom Feuer', *H* 77, 1942, 1–27 = Reinhardt [81]
as well as chapter 3 of Reinhardt [30]; and, third:
[136] G. S. Kirk: *Heraclitus: the Cosmic Fragments* (Cambridge, 1962²)

The best general account of Heraclitus' thought is perhaps that in Guthrie [25], I, ch. VII. There is a stimulating piece which appears as chapter 3 of volume I of:
[137] K. R. Popper: *The Open Society and its Enemies* (London, 1966⁵)
See also:
[138] G. Vlastos: 'On Heraclitus', *AJP* 76, 1955, 337–66 = Furley-Allen [70]
[139] C. H. Kahn: 'A New Look at Heraclitus', *APQ* 1, 1964, 189–203
[140] M. Marcovich: 'Herakleitos', *RE* suppt. 10, 1965, 246–320
[141] W. J. Verdenius: 'Der Logosbegriff bei Heraklit und Parmenides', *Phron* 11, 1966, 81–99
Idiosyncratically French accounts may be read in:
[142] C. Ramnoux: *Héraclite, ou l' homme entre les choses et les mots* (Paris, 1959)
[143] J. Bollack and H. Wismann: *Héraclite ou la Séparation* (Paris, 1972)

The peculiarities of Heraclitus' style have been analysed by:
[144] B. Snell: 'Die Sprache Heraklits', *H* 61, 1926, 353–81 = Snell [82]
[145] H. Fränkel: 'A Thought Pattern in Heraclitus', *AJP* 59, 1938, 309–37 = Fränkel [76] = Mourelatos [72]
[146] B. Snell: 'Heraklits Fragment 10', *H* 76, 1941, 84–7 = Snell [82]
and in Hölscher [79].

On Heraclitean fire see Reinhardt [135] and:
[147] G. S. Kirk: 'Natural Change in Heraclitus', *M* 60, 1951, 35–42 = Mourelatos [72]
[148] W. J. Verdenius: 'Heraclitus' Conception of Fire', in J. Mansfeld and L. M. de Rijk (eds), *Kephalaion: studies in Greek philosophy and its continuation offered to Professor C. J. de Vogel* (Assen, 1975)
[149] H. Jones: 'Heraclitus: Fragment 31', *Phron* 17, 1972, 193–7
[150] R. Mondolfo: 'The evidence of Plato and Aristotle relating to the ekpyrosis in Heraclitus', *Phron* 3, 1958, 75–82

The Theory of Flux is denied to Heraclitus by Reinhardt and by Kirk; it is vindicated for him by Mondolfo-Tarán [131];
[151] K. R. Popper: 'Kirk on Heraclitus, and on Fire as the Cause of Balance', *M* 72, 1963, 386–92 = K. R. Popper, *Conjectures and Refutations* (London, 1969³)
[152] A. Wasserstein: 'Pre-Platonic Literary Evidence for the Flux Theory of Heraclitus', *Atti di XII Congresso Internazionale di Filosofia* (Florence, 1960), 11, 185–91
Wasserstein's brief discussion of the *de victu* can be supplemented by:
[153] R. Joly: *Recherches sur le traité pseudo-hippocratique du Régime* (Paris, 1960)
The Cratylan texts are examined by:
[154] G. S. Kirk: 'The Problem of Cratylus', *AJP* 72, 1951, 225–53
[155] D. J. Allan: 'The Problem of Cratylus', *AJP* 75, 1954, 271–87

Finally, on the Unity of Opposites, see the various works by Reinhardt and Kirk.

Items bearing on Heraclitus' moral theories and on his psychology can be found below, p. 352 and vol. 2, p. 328.

Chapter V

There is an edition of Xenophanes by:
[156] M. Untersteiner: *Senofane—testimonianze e frammenti* (Florence, 1956)
For general accounts of Xenophanes' thought see chapter 2 of Reinhardt [30], chapter 3 of Stokes [56], and:
[157] K. Deichgräber: 'Xenophanes περὶ φυσέως *RhM* 87, 1938, 1-31
[158] K. von Fritz: 'Xenophanes', *RE* 9A, 1967, 1541-62
[159] P. Steinmetz: 'Xenophanesstudien', *RhM* 109, 1966, 13-73
And on his Ionian interests see especially:
[160] W. A. Heidel: 'Hecataeus and Xenophanes', *AJP* 64, 1943, 257-77
  There is a fine paper on Presocratic theology by:
[161] G. Vlastos: 'Theology and Philosophy in Early Greek Thought', *PQ* 2, 1952, 97-123 = Furley-Allen [70]
and useful material can be found in:
[162] O. Gigon: 'Die Theologie der Vorsokratiker', *Entretiens Hardt* 1, 1954, 127-55 = Gigon [78]
[163] W. Fahr: Θεοὺς νομίζειν', Spudasmata 26 (Hildesheim, 1969)
It is still worth reading:
[164] A. B. Drachmann: *Atheism in Pagan Antiquity* (London, 1922)
  For Milesian theology see chapter 2 of Jaeger [48], and:
[165] D. Babut: 'Le Divin et le Dieu dans la pensée d' Anaximandre', *REG* 84, 1972, 1-32
and for Heraclitus see:
[166] H. Fränkel: 'Heraclitus on God and the Phenomenal World', *TAPA* 69, 1938, 230-44 = Fränkel [76]
The atheists of *Laws* X are rooted out by:
[167] J. Tate: 'On Plato: *Laws* X, 889CD', *CQ* 30, 1936, 48-54
[168] W. de Mahieu: 'La doctrine des Athées au Xe livre des Lois de Platon', *Revue belge de philologie et d'histoire* 41, 1963, 5-24; and 42, 1964, 16-47
  On Xenophanes' theology see especially chapter 3 of Jaeger [48]; and also:
[169] W. Pötscher: 'Zu Xenophanes frag. 23', *Emerita* 32, 1964, 1-13
[170] G. Calogero: 'Senofane, Eschilo e la prima definizione dell' onnipotenza di dio', in Alfieri-Untersteiner [68]
[171] H. A. T. Reiche: 'Empirical Aspects of Xenophanes' Theology', in Anton-Kustas [69]
Finally, the Epicharman material is all judiciously examined by:
[172] L. Berk: *Epicharmus*, diss. Utrecht (Groningen, 1964)

Chapter VI

The study of Pythagoreanism has been advanced to a new level of sanity and scholarship by:
[173] W. Burkert: *Lore and Science in Ancient Pythagoreanism* (Cambridge, Mass., 1972; first German edition, 1962)
The main problem of interpretation, that of distinguishing early from late doctrine, should be approached with the help of:
[174] H. Thesleff: *An Introduction to the Pythagorean Writings of the Hellenistic Age*, Acta Academiae Aboensis Humaniora XXIV.3 (Åbo, 1961)
[175] H. Thesleff: *The Pythagorean Texts of the Hellenistic Period*, Acta Academiae Aboensis Humaniora XXX.1 (Åbo, 1965)

and see also:
[176] H. Dörrie: 'Der nachklassische Pythagoreismus', *RE* 24, 1963, 268-77
There is an excellent introduction to early Pythagoreanism in:
[177] C. H. Kahn: 'Pythagorean Philosophy before Plato', in Mourelatos [72]
Of other general studies I mention:
[178] J. E. Raven: *Pythagoreans and Eleatics* (Cambridge, 1948)
[179] K. H. Ilting: 'Zur Philosophie der Pythagoreer', *ABG* 9, 1964, 103-31
[180] J. A. Philip: *Pythagoras and Early Pythagoreanism* (Toronto, 1966)
[181] C. J. de Vogel: *Pythagoras and Early Pythagoreanism* (Assen, 1966)
For Pythagoras himself consult:
[182] J. S. Morrison: 'Pythagoras of Samos', *CQ* n.s. 8, 1958, 198-218
[183] K. von Fritz: 'Pythagoras', *RE* 24, 1963, 171-268
[184] B. L. van der Waerden: 'Pythagoras', *RE* suppt 10, 1965, 843-64
And see also West [108].
Literature on Pythagorean science is given in vol. 2, p. 325.
On early Greek notions of the *psuchê* or soul see the celebrated study by Dodds [43]; and also:
[185] J. Burnet: 'The Socratic Doctrine of the Soul', *Proceedings of the British Academy* 7, 1915/16, 235-59
[186] D. J. Furley: 'The Early History of the Greek Concept of Soul', *BICS* 3, 1956, 1-18
[187] B. Gladigow: 'Zum Makarismos des Weisen', *H* 95, 1967, 404-33
There is a thorough survey of Greek texts on metempsychosis in:
[188] H. S. Long: *A Study of the Doctrine of Metempsychosis in Greece from Pythagoras to Plato* (Princeton, N.J., 1948)
and a wealth of material in:
[189] M. V. Bacigalupo: 'Teriomorfismo e trasmigrazione', *Filosofia* 16, 1965, 267-90
For Plato see:
[190] R. S. Bluck: 'Plato, Pindar and Metempsychosis', *AJP* 79, 1958, 405-14
and for Pindar:
[191] K. von Fritz: ' Ἐστρὶς ἑκατέρωθι in Pindar's Second *Olympian* and Pythagoras' Theory of Metempsychosis', *Phron* 2, 1957, 85-9
[192] D. McGibbon: 'Metempsychosis in Pindar', *Phron* 9, 1964, 5-12
The Empedoclean material is edited and discussed in:
[193] G. Zuntz: *Persephone* (Oxford, 1971)
who draws on the study by:
[194] U. von Wilamowitz-Moellendorf: 'Die Καθαρμοί des Empedokles', *Sitzungsberichte der preussischen Akademie*, 1929, 626-61 = Wilamowitz-Moellendorf, *Kleine Schriften* I (Berlin, 1935)
See also:
[195] O. Skutsch: 'Notes on Metempsychosis', in his *Strudia Enniana* (London, 1968)
[196] M. L. West: 'Notes on newly-discovered fragments of Greek authors', *Maia* 20, 1968, 195-205
On the phenomenon of shamanism see Dodds [43], chapter 5; and:
[197] J. D. P. Bolton: *Aristeas of Proconnesus* (Oxford, 1962)
And for the *auxanomenos logos*:
[198] J. Bernays: 'Epicharmos und der αὐξανόμενος λόγος', *RhM* 8, 1853, 280-8 = Bernays [73]

Further material is listed in vol. 2, p. 329; and for Empedocles' natural philosophy see vol. 2, p. 322.

There are two long studies of Alcmeon:
[199] J. Wachtler: *De Alcmaeone Crotoniata* (Leipzig, 1896)
[200] L. A. Stella: 'Importanza di Alcmeone nella storia del pensiero greco', *Memorie della Reale Accademia Nazionale dei Lincei*, s.6, VIII.4, 1939, 233-87
On the argument for immortality see:
[201] C. Mugler: 'Alcméon et les cycles physiologiques de Platon', *REG* 71, 1958, 42-50
Plato's version is analysed in:
[202] T. M. Robinson: 'The Argument for Immortality in Plato's *Phaedrus*', in Anton-Kustas [69]
and there are helpful comments in:
[203] R. Hackforth: *Plato's Phaedrus* (Cambridge, 1952)
[204] J. B. Skemp: *The Theory of Motion in Plato's Later Dialogues* (Amsterdam, 1967^2)
[205] T. M. Robinson: *Plato's Psychology* (Toronto, 1970)
Further literature on Alcmeon is given on p. 353 and vol. 2, p. 329.

Chapter VII

The best introduction to early Greek thought on moral matters is:
[206] K. J. Dover: *Greek Popular Morality in the Time of Plato and Aristotle* (Oxford, 1974)
There is much of value in Dodds [43], Lloyd-Jones [51], and:
[207] A. W. H. Adkins: *Merit and Responsibility* (Oxford, 1960)
And it is still worth reading Essay 2 in:
[208] A. Grant: *The Ethics of Aristotle* (Oxford, 1885^4)
For Empedocles, see the works cited under Chapter VI, especially Zuntz [193].

Heraclitus is exhibited as a moralist in chapters 4-6 of West [59]; and the main fragment on his ethics is discussed by:
[209] H. Blass: *Gott und die Gesetze*, Schriften zur Rechtslehre und Politik 12 (Bonn, 1958)
[210] A. P. D. Mourelatos: 'Heraclitus, fr. 114', *AJP* 86, 1965, 258-66
The intricacies of the concept of *nomos* are unravelled by:
[211] M. Ostwald: *Nomos and the Beginnings of the Athenian Democracy* (Oxford, 1969)
and there is further material in Vlastos [111] and Popper [137].

On some matters of detail see:
[212] H. Fränkel: 'Heraclitus on the Notion of a Generation', *AJP* 59, 1938, 89-91 = Fränkel [76]
[213] G. S..Kirk: 'Heraclitus and Death in Battle (fr. 24 D)', *AJP* 70, 1949, 384-93
[214] M. L. West: 'A pseudo-fragment of Heraclitus', *CR* n.s. 18, 1968, 257-9

Chapter VIII

On the popular origins of scepticism see chapter 7 of Snell [55]. Xenophanes' epistemology is discussed in the studies listed under Chapter V, and in a fine piece by:
[215] H. Fränkel: 'Xenophanesstudien', *H* 60, 1925, 174-92 = Fränkel [76] = Mourelatos [72]

Fränkel is supported by:
[216] A. Rivier: 'Remarques sur les fragments 34 et 35 de Xénophane', *Revue de Philologie* 30, 1956, 37-61
and ably criticized by:
[217] E. Heitsch: 'Das Wissen des Xenophanes', *RhM* 109, 1966, 193-235
The Hippocratic treatise *On Ancient Medicine* is edited by:
[218] A. J. Festugière: *Hippocrate: L' Ancienne Médicine* (Paris, 1948)
and it is discussed in Jones [49].

To the literature on Heraclitus given under Chapter IV I add two pieces on minor topics:
[219] K. Reinhardt: 'Κοπίδων ʼΑρχηγός', *H* 63, 1928, 107-10 = Reinhardt [81]
[220] G. S. Kirk: 'The Michigan Alcidamas Papyrus; Heraclitus Fr. 56 D; The Riddle of the Lice', *CQ* 44, 1950, 149-67
The theory of the *Phaedo* was attributed to Alcmeon by:
[221] R. Hirzel: 'Zur Philosophie des Alkmäon', *H* 11, 1876, 240-6
See also:
[222] D. Lanza: 'L' ἐγκέφαλος e la dottrina anassagorea della conoscenza', *Maia* 16, 1964, 71-8
[223] D. Lanza: 'Un nuovo frammento di Alcmeone', *Maia* 17, 1965, 278-80

Chapter IX

The best edition of the fragments of Parmenides is still:
[224] H. Diels: *Parmenides' Lehrgedicht* (Berlin, 1897)
More recent editions include:
[225] M. Untersteiner: *Parmenide—testimonianze e frammenti* (Florence, 1958)
[226] L. Tarán: *Parmenides* (Princeton, N.J., 1965)
[227] U. Hölscher: *Parmenides: Vom Wesen des Seiendes* (Frankfurt am Main, 1969)
Further suggestions of an editorial nature can be found in:
[228] P. J. Bicknell: 'A New Arrangement of Some Parmenidean Verses', *SO* 42, 1968, 44-50
[229] P. J. Bicknell: 'Parmenides, fragment 10', *H* 98, 1968, 629-31
There are three classic studies of Parmenides: that in Reinhardt [30]; and:
[230] H. Fränkel: 'Parmenidesstudien', *NGG* 1930, 153-92 = Fränkel [76] = Furley-Allen [70]
[231] F. M. Cornford: *Plato and Parmenides* (London, 1939)
Comprehensive accounts of Parmenides' thought can also be found in:
[232] G. Calogero: *Studi sull' Eleatismo* (Rome, 1932)
[233] W. J. Verdenius: *Parmenides* (Groningen, 1942)
[234] A. H. Coxon: 'The Philosophy of Parmenides', *CQ* 28, 1934, 134-44
[235] W. Bröcker: 'Parmenides', *ABG* 9, 1964, 79-86
[236] U. Hölscher: 'Parmenides', in Hölscher [79]
[237] A. P. D. Mourelatos: *The Route of Parmenides* (New Haven, Conn., 1970)
See also chapter 5 of Stokes [56], and the heterodox views of:
[238] J. H. M. M. Loenen: *Parmenides, Melissus, Gorgias* (Assen, 1959)
On the prologue to Parmenides' poem see:
[239] C. M. Bowra: 'The Proem of Parmenides', *CP* 32, 1937, 97-112
[240] W. Burkert: 'Das Proömium des Parmenides und die Katabasis des Pythagoras', *Phron* 14, 1969, 1-30
[241] D. J. Furley: 'Notes on Parmenides', in E. N. Lee, A. P. D. Mourelatos and R.

Rorty (eds), *Exegesis and Argument: Studies in Greek Philosophy presented to Gregory Vlastos*, Phron suppt. 1, 1973

The best discussion of the relation between the Way of Truth and the Way of Opinion is that in chapter 1 of Reinhardt [30]; see also:

[242] F. M. Cornford: 'Parmenides' Two Ways', *CQ* 27, 1933, 97–111
[243] H. Schwabl: 'Sein und Doxa bei Parmenides', *WS* 66, 1953, 50–75 = Gadamer [71]
[244] G. E. L. Owen: 'Eleatic Questions', *CQ* n.s. 10, 1960, 84–102 = Furley-Allen [70]

And compare:

[245] A. P. D. Mourelatos: 'The Real, Appearances and Human Error in Early Greek Philosophy', *RM* 19, 1965, 346–65

On the content of the Way of Opinion consult, e.g., Popper [35]; and

[246] J. S. Morrison: 'Parmenides and Er', *JHS* 75, 1955, 59–69
[247] A. A. Long: 'The Principles of Parmenides' Cosmogony', *Phron* 8, 1963, 90–107 = Furley-Allen [70]

The argument about the Three Roads is brilliantly analysed by Owen [244], who is criticized by:

[248] S. Tugwell: 'The Way of Truth', *CQ* n.s. 14, 1964, 36–41

See also:

[249] E. Heitsch: *Gegenwart und Evidenz bei Parmenides*, Abhandlungen der Akademie der Wissenschaft und Literatur (Mainz, 1970)

and the interesting paper by:

[250] G. E. M. Anscombe: 'Parmenides, Mystery and Contradiction', *PAS* 69, 1968/9, 125–32

On Parmenides' conception of *nous* or thought see Snell [54], von Fritz [62], and:
[251] A. P. D. Mourelatos: 'φράζω and its derivatives in Parmenides', *CP* 60, 1965, 261–2

The 'veridical' interpretation of *einai* is advanced in several papers by Charles Kahn:

[252] C. H. Kahn: 'The Greek Verb "to be" and the Concept of Being', *Foundations of Language* 2, 1966, 245–65
[253] C. H. Kahn: 'The Thesis of Parmenides', *RM* 22, 1968/9, 700–24
[254] C. H. Kahn: 'More on Parmenides', *RM* 23, 1969/70, 333–40
[255] C. H. Kahn: *The Verb Be in Ancient Greek* (Dordrecht, 1973)

And see Mourelatos [237]. Kahn is criticized by:

[256] E. Tugendhat: 'Das Sein und das Nichts', in *Durchblicke: Festschrift für Martin Heidegger zum 80. Geburtstag* (Frankfurt am Main, 1970)

A 'fused' account of *einai* is propounded in:

[257] M. Furth: 'Elements of Eleatic Ontology', *JHP* 6, 1968, 111–32 = Mourelatos [72]

and criticized by:

[258] B. Jones: 'Parmenides' "The Way of Truth"', *JHP* 11, 1973, 287–98

See also:

[259] W. J. Verdenius: 'Parmenides B 2.3', *Mnem* s.4, 15, 1962, 237

For Gorgias' treatise *Concerning What is Not* see, besides Calogero [232] and Loenen [238]:

[260] W. Nestle: 'Die Schrift des Gorgias "Ueber die Natur oder über das Nichtseiende"', *H* 57, 1922, 551–62 = Nestle [80]

BIBLIOGRAPHY

[261] O. Gigon: 'Gorgias' "Ueber das Nichtsein"', *H* 71, 1936, 186–213 = Gigon [78]
[262] W. Bröcker: 'Gorgias contra Parmenides', *H* 86, 1958, 425–40
[263] G. B. Kerferd: 'Gorgias on Nature or that which is not', *Phron* 1, 1955, 3–25
[264] J. M. Robinson: 'On Gorgias', in E. N. Lee, A. P. D. Mourelatos and R. Rorty (eds), *Exegesis and Argument: Studies in Greek Philosophy presented to Gregory Vlastos*, *Phron* suppt 1, 1973

Chapter X

There are general accounts of Parmenides' metaphysical deduction in most of the major studies cited under Chapter IX; see also:
[265] A. H. Basson: '"The Way of Truth"', *PAS* 61, 1960/1, 73–86
And on Parmenides' 'circular' logic consult:
[266] G. J. Jameson: '"Well-rounded Truth" and Circular Thought in Parmenides', *Phron* 3, 1958, 15–30
[267] L. Ballew: 'Straight and Circular in Parmenides and the *Timaeus*', *Phron* 19, 1974, 189–209
   The problems raised by Parmenides' prospectus in B 8.3–5 are discussed by, e.g., Owen [244], Schofield [275], and:
[268] J. R. Wilson: 'Parmenides, B 8.4', *CQ* 2 n.s. 20, 1970, 32–5
   Melissus has been less well served than his master; but there is a first-rate edition:
[269] G. Reale: *Melisso—testimonianze e frammenti* (Florence, 1970)
and useful chapters in Calogero [232] and Loenen [238]. On Melissus' importance see:
[270] J. Jouanna: 'Rapports entre Mélissos de Samos et Diogène d'Apollonie, à la lumière du traité hippocratique de natura hominis', *REA* 67, 1965, 306–23
[271] J. Klowski: 'Antwortete Leukipp Melissos oder Melissos Leukipp?', *MH* 28, 1971, 65–71
   Studies devoted to Parmenides' arguments against generation and destruction include:
[272] C. M. Stough: 'Parmenides' Way of Truth, B 8.12–3', *Phron* 13, 1968, 91–108
[273] J. Wiesner: 'Die Negation der Entstehung des Seienden', *AGP* 52, 1970, 1–35
And Eleatic views on time are discussed by:
[274] G. E. L. Owen: 'Plato and Parmenides on the Timeless Present', *Monist* 50, 1966, 317–40 = Mourelatos [72]
[275] M. Schofield: 'Did Parmenides discover Eternity?', *AGP* 52, 1970, 113–35
[276] J. Whittaker: *God, Time and Being*, *SO* suppt. 23, 1971
See also:
[277] W. C. Kneale: 'Time and Eternity in Theology', *PAS* 61, 1960/1, 87–109
And on Melissus B 2:
[278] W. J. Verdenius: 'Notes on the Presocratics VII', *Mnem* s.4, 1, 1948, 8–10

Chapter XI

The interpretation of Parmenides' ball or 'sphere' has much engaged scholars; for a selection of views see Coxon [234], Owen [244]; and
[279] G. Rudberg: 'Zur vorsokratischen Abstraktion', *Eranos* 52, 1954, 131–8

[280] J. Mansfeld: 'Σφαιρῆς ἐναλίγκιον ὄγκῳ', *Akten des XIV Internationales Kongress für Philosophie* (Vienna, 1970), 5, 414–9
[281] J. Bollack and H. Wismann: 'Le moment théorique (Parménide fr. 8.42–9)', *Revue des sciences humaines* 39, 1974, 203–12

Eleatic monism has, surprisingly, been less discussed; in addition to the commentaries I note only:
[282] F. Solmsen: *The 'Eleatic One' in Melissus*, Mededelingen der koninklijke nederlandse akademie van wetenschappen 32.8 (The Hague, 1969)
(But on Parmenides B 8.34–41 see also:
[283] L. Woodbury: 'Parmenides on Names', *HSCP* 63, 1958, 145–60 = Anton-Kustas [69])

Fragment B 4 of Parmenides is scrutinized by:
[284] J. Bollack: 'Sur deux fragments de Parménide (4 et 16)', *REG* 70, 1957, 56–71
And the Parmenidean attack on motion is discussed in:
[285] M. C. Stokes and G. S. Kirk: 'Parmenides' Refutation of Motion', *Phron* 5, 1960, 1–22
[286] P. J. Bicknell: 'Parmenides' Refutation of Motion and an Implication', *Phron* 12, 1967, 1–6
See also:
[287] A. H. Coxon: 'The Manuscript Tradition of Simplicius' Commentary on Aristotle's *Physics* i–iv', *CQ* n.s. 18, 1968, 70–5

Finally, on the solidity or corporeality of Melissus' being see:
[288] H. Gomperz: 'ἀσώματος', *H* 67, 1932, 155–67
[289] G. Vlastos: review of Raven [178], *Gnomon* 25, 1953, 29–35 = Furley-Allen [70]
[290] N. B. Booth: 'Did Melissus believe in incorporeal being?', *AJP* 79, 1958, 61–5
[291] M. Untersteiner: 'Un aspetto dell' Essere melissiano', *Rivista critica di storia della filosofia* 8, 1953, 597–606 = Untersteiner [84]

Chapter XII

The texts bearing upon Zeno have been edited by:
[292] H. D. P. Lee: *Zeno of Elea* (Cambridge, 1936)
[293] M. Untersteiner: *Zenone—testimonianze e frammenti* (Florence, 1963)
See also:
[294] J. Dillon: 'New Evidence on Zeno of Elea?', *AGP* 56, 1974, 127–31
The history of Zenonian scholarship is recounted in:
[295] F. Cajori: 'The History of Zeno's Arguments on Motion', *American Mathematical Monthly* 22, 1915, 1–6, 38–47, 77–82, 109–15, 143–9, 179–86, 215–20, 253–8, 292–7
And there is an anthology (with an excellent bibliography) by:
[296] W. C. Salmon (ed.): *Zeno's Paradoxes* (Indianapolis, Ind., 1970)
For a lucid introduction to Zeno and his problems see:
[297] G. Vlastos: 'Zeno of Elea', in P. Edwards (ed.), *Encyclopaedia of Philosophy* (New York, 1967)
Compare:
[298] K. von Fritz: 'Zenon von Elea', *RE* 10 A, 1972, 53–83
It is a pleasure to read:
[299] P. Bayle: 'Zeno of Elea', *Historical and Critical Dictionary*, trans. R. H. Popkin (Indianapolis, Ind., 1965)
See also, on a minor matter:
[300] J. Longrigg: 'Zeno's Cosmology?', *CR* n.s. 22, 1972, 170–1

BIBLIOGRAPHY

The crucial passage from the *Parmenides* has recently been thrice examined:
[301] F. Solmsen: 'The Tradition about Zeno of Elea Re-examined', *Phron* 16, 1971, 116–41 = Mourelatos [72]
[302] K. von Fritz: 'Zeno of Elea in Plato's *Parmenides*', in J. L. Heller and J. K. Newman (eds), *Studia Turyniana* (Urbana, Ill., 1974)
[303] G. Vlastos: 'Plato's Testimony concerning Zeno of Elea', *JHS* 95, 1975, 136–63

On the aim of Zeno's paradoxes see:
[304] N. B. Booth: 'Were Zeno's Arguments a reply to attacks upon Parmenides?', *Phron* 3, 1957, 1–9
[305] N. B. Booth: 'Were Zeno's arguments directed against the Pythagoreans?', *Phron* 3, 1957, 90–103
[306] N. B. Booth: 'Zeno's Paradoxes', *JHS* 78, 1957, 189–201

On the architecture of the paradoxes see especially:
[307] G. E. L. Owen: 'Zeno and the Mathematician', *PAS* 58, 1957/8, 199–222 = Salmon [296] = Furley-Allen [70]
Owen's thesis is rejected by Stokes [56], chapter 7, and by Furley [387], chapter 5

Discussion of the paradox of 'large and small' was put on a sound scholarly footing by:
[308] H. Fränkel: 'Zeno of Elea's Attacks on Plurality', *AJP* 63, 1938, 1–25 and 193–206 = Fränkel [76] = Gadamer [71] = Furley-Allen [70]
For further discussion see Owen [307], Furley [387], chapter 5; and
[309] G. Vlastos: 'A Zenonian Argument against Plurality', in Anton-Kustas [69]
[310] W. E. Abraham: 'The Nature of Zeno's Argument against Plurality', *Phron* 17, 1972, 40–53

On the issue of geometrically indivisible magnitudes see:
[311] R. Heinze: *Xenokrates* (Leipig, 1892)
[312] A. T. Nicol: 'Indivisible Lines', *CQ* 30, 1936, 120–6
and the papers listed in vol. 2, p. 324.

Since Russell's persuasive advertisements modern philosophers have taken Zeno seriously. The most sophisticated and exhaustive modern treatment is:
[313] A. Grünbaum: *Modern Science and Zeno's Paradoxes* (London, 1968) = (in part) Salmon [296]
See also the Introduction to Salmon [296] and:
[314] A. P. Ushenko: 'Zeno's Paradoxes', *M* 55, 1946, 151–65
[315] H. N. Lee: 'Are Zeno's Paradoxes Based on a Mistake?', *M* 74, 1965, 563–70

Chapter XIII

Bertrand Russell more than once gave crisp accounts of Zeno's four paradoxes of motion; see:
[316] B. Russell: *The Principles of Mathematics* (London, 1903), chapters 42–3
[317] B. Russell: *Mysticism and Logic* (London, 1917), chapter 5
[318] B. Russell: *Our Knowledge of the External World* (London, 1956^2) chapter 6 = Salmon [296]
Russell was influenced by the brilliant assessment in chapter 10 of Tannery [29], on which see also:
[319] F. Cajori: 'The Purpose of Zeno's Arguments on Motion', *Isis* 3, 1920/1, 7–20
Philosophers will enjoy chapter 4 of:
[320] H. Bergson: *Creative Evolution* (London, 1964) = Salmon [296]
And Grünbaum [313] again has much of value to say.

BIBLIOGRAPHY

The best scholarly study of the first two paradoxes, the Dichotomy and the Achilles, is:
[321] G. Vlastos: 'Zeno's Race Course', *JHP* 4, 1966, 96-108 = Furley-Allen [70]
And on all four paradoxes the notes in Ross [12] are invaluable; on Aristotle's interpretation of Zeno see also:
[322] D. Bostock: 'Aristotle, Zeno and the Potential Infinite', *PAS* 73, 1972/3, 37-53
There are numerous modern attempts to grapple with the complex issues that Zeno raises:
[323] C. D. Broad: 'Note on Achilles and the Tortoise', *M* 22, 1913, 318-19
[324] W. V. Metcalf: 'Achilles and the Tortoise', *M* 51, 1942, 89-90
[325] G. Ryle: *Dilemmas* (Cambridge, 1954), chapter 3
[326] M. Black: 'Achilles and the Tortoise', *An* 11, 1950/1, 91-101 = M. Black, *Problems of Analysis* (London, 1954)
[327] M. Black: 'Is Achilles still Running?', in M. Black, *Problems of Analysis* (London, 1954)
[328] J. O. Wisdom: 'Achilles on a Physical Racecourse', *An* 12, 1951/2, 67-73 = Salmon [296]
[329] R. Taylor: 'Mr. Black on Temporal Paradoxes', *An* 12, 1951/2, 38-44
[330] J. Watling: 'The Sum of an Infinite Series', *An* 13, 1952/3, 39-46
[331] J. Thomson: 'Tasks and Supertasks', *An* 15, 1954/5, 1-13 = Salmon [296]
[332] P. Benacerraf: 'Tasks, Supertasks, and the Modern Eleatics', *JP* 59, 1962, 765-84 = Salmon [296]
[333] J. Thomson: 'Comments on Professor Benacerraf's Paper', in Salmon [296]
[334] C. S. Chihara: 'On the Possibility of Completing an Infinite Process', *PR* 74, 1965, 74-87
On the third paradox, the Arrow, see especially:
[335] G. Vlastos: 'A Note on Zeno's Arrow', *Phron* 11, 1966, 3-18 = Furley-Allen [70]
Among modern studies I mention:
[336] P. E. B. Jourdain: 'The Flying Arrow—an Anachronism', *M* 25, 1916, 42-55
[337] L. Greenberg: 'A Note on the Arrow in Flight', *PR* 59, 1950, 541-2
[338] M. Black: 'The Paradox of the Flying Arrow', in M. Black, *Problems of Analysis* (London, 1954)
[339] V. C. Chappell: 'Time and Zeno's Arrow', *JP* 49, 1962, 197-213
Finally, for detailed analysis of the Stadium see:
[340] R. K. Gaye: 'On Aristotle *Physics* Z ix, 239b33-240a18', *Journal of Philology* 31, 1910, 95-116
[341] P. J. Bicknell: 'The Fourth Paradox of Zeno', *AC* 4, 1961, 39-46
[342] P. J. Bicknell: 'Zeno's Arguments on Motion', *AC* 6, 1963, 81-105

Chapter XIV

For literature relevant to this chapter see the general studies listed under Chapter IX, and the items on post-Eleatic epistemology in vol. 2 under Chapter X.

C: APPENDIX

The following works which bear primarily on the subject matter of volume 2 are also referred to in the present volume:
[349] J. Bollack: *Empédocle* (Paris, 1965-9)

[361] D. E. Gershenson and D. A. Greenberg: *Anaxagoras and the Birth of Physics* (New York, 1964)
[387] D. J. Furley: *Two Studies in the Greek Atomists* (Princeton, N.J., 1967) = (in part) Mourelatos [72]
[390] M. Capek: *The Philosophical Impact of Contemporary Physics* (Princeton, N.J., 1961)
[398] S. Luria: 'Die Infinitesimaltheorie der antiken Atomisten', *QSGM* B 2, 1932, 106-85
[401] G. Vlastos: 'Minimal Parts in Epicurean Atomism', *Isis* 56, 1965, 121-47
[402] J. Mau: 'Was there a Special Epicurean Mathematics?', in E. N. Lee, A. P. D. Mourelatos and R. Rorty (eds) *Exegesis and Argument: Studies in Greek Philosophy presented to Gregory Vlastos*, *Phron* suppt 1, 1973
[406] W. A. Heidel: 'The Pythagoreans and Greek Mathematics', *AJP* 61, 1940, 1-33 = Furley-Allen [70]
[408] B. L. van der Waerden: 'Pythagoreische Wissenschaft', *RE* 24, 1963, 277-300
[413] J. A. Philip: 'Aristotle's Source for Pythagorean Doctrine', *Phoenix* 17, 1963, 251-65
[457] F. Jacoby: *Diagoras δ Ἄθεος*, Abhandlungen der Akademie der Wissenschaften, Berlin, 3, 1959
[459] W. Nestle: *Euripides der Dichter der griechischen Erklärung* (Stuttgart, 1901)
[477] M. C. Nussbaum: 'ψυχή in Heraclitus', *Phron* 17, 1972, 1-16 and 153-70
[493] C. H. Kahn: 'Religion and Natural Philosophy in Empedocles' Doctrine of the Soul', *AGP* 42, 1960, 3-35 = Anton-Kustas [69] = Mourelatos [72]
[520] O. Regenbogen: 'Eine Forschungsmethode antiker Naturwissenschaft', *QSGM* B 2, 1930, 131-82
[529] J. Mejer: 'The Alleged New Fragment of Protagoras', *H* 100, 1972, 175-8
[540] H. Diller: 'Die philosophiegeschichtliche Stellung des Diogenes von Apollonia', *H* 76, 1941, 359-81 = Diller [75]

D: ADDENDA (1978)

Several valuable studies in Presocratic philosophy have appeared since my typescript was submitted to the publishers in August 1976. I mention here a small selection.

To section *A V* add:
[72A] C. J. Classen (ed.): *Sophistik* (Darmstadt, 1976)
[72B] R. A. Shiner and J. King-Farlow (eds): *New Essays on Plato and the Presocratics*, *Canadian Journal of Philosophy* suppt 2 (Guelph, 1976)
Classen's volume contains an excellent bibliography.

To section *B, Chapter II* add:
[101A] M. C. Stokes: 'Anaximander's Argument', in Shiner-King-Farlow [72B]
and to *Chapter III*:
[112A] C. J. Classen: 'Anaximander and Anaximenes: the Earliest Greek Theories of Change?', *Phron* 22, 1977, 89-102

For *Chapter IV* there is a study of Heraclitus' influence on the Stoics by:
[131A] A. A. Long: 'Heraclitus and Stoicism', Φιλοσοφία 5, 1975/6, 133-56
and a thorough examination of the Unity of Opposites by:
[155A] C. J. Emlyn-Jones: 'Heraclitus and the Identity of Opposites', *Phron* 21, 1976, 89-114

For *Chapter IV* see:
[206A] A. C. Lloyd: 'The Principle that the Cause is greater than its Effect', *Phron* 21, 1976, 146-55

BIBLIOGRAPHY

which examines the history of what I call the Synonymy Principle (above, p. 119).

Parmenides continues to attract scholarly attention. There are at least two full-length studies:

[238A] K. Bormann: *Parmenides* (Hamburg, 1971)

[238B] J. Jantzen: *Parmenides zum Verhältnis von Sprache und Wirklichkeit*, Zetemata 63 (Munich, 1976)

and it is worth reading three long review articles:

[238C] C. H. Kahn: review of Tarán [222], *Gnomon* 40, 1968, 123–33

[238D] L. Tarán: review of Mourelatos [237], *Gnomon* 48, 1977, 651–66

[238E] A. Graeser: 'Vier Bücher zur Eleatik' (reviews of Mourelatos [237], Heitsch [249], Bormann [238A], Newiger [264A]), *Göttingische Gelehrter Anzeigen* 230, 1978, 37–69

(I must apologize for omitting [238A] and [238C] from the body of the Bibliography.)

On Parmenides' rejection of the Roads of Ignorance, see:

[250A] T. M. Robinson: 'Parmenides on the Ascertainment of the Real', *Canadian Journal of Philosophy* 4, 1975, 623–33

[250B] R. Bosley: 'Monistic Argumentation', in Shiner-King-Farlow [72B]

[250C] A. Graeser: 'Parmenides über Sagen und Denken', *MH* 34, 1977, 145–55

Kahn's views on *einai* have been further discussed in:

[255A] C. H. Kahn: 'Why Existence does not emerge as a Distinct Concept in Greek Philosophy', *AGP* 58, 1976, 323–34

[255B] E. Tugendhat: review of Kahn [255], *Philosophische Rundschau* 24, 1977, 161–76

See also:

[255C] U. Hölscher: *Der Sinn von Sein in der älteren Griechischen Philosophie*, Sitzber.Heidelberg.Ak.Wiss., phil.-hist.Kl. 1976.3 (Heidelberg, 1976)

Mourelatos has refined his account of Parmenidean *einai*:

[259A] A. P. D. Mourelatos: 'Determinacy and Indeterminacy, Being and Non-Being, in the Fragments of Parmenides', in Shiner-King-Farlow [72B]

On Gorgias' treatise I ought to have referred to:

[264A] H. J. Newiger: *Untersuchungen zu Gorgias' Schrift Über das Nichtseiende* (Berlin, 1973)

On the matter of monism, *Chapter XI*, see:

[282A] J. Barnes: 'Parmenides and the Eleatic One', *AGP* 60, 1978

To *Chapter XII* and Dillon [294] add:

[294A] J. Dillon: 'More Evidence on Zeno of Elea?', *AGP* 58, 1976, 221–2

On the logic of change (above, p. 271) see:

[334A] R. Sorabji: 'Aristotle on the Instant of Change', *PAS* suppt 50, 1976, 69–89

And on Diodorus' Zenonian arguments:

[342A] D. Sedley: 'Diodorus Cronus and Hellenistic Philosophy', *PCPS* 23, 1977, 74–120

Indexes

Compiled by Antony Feeny

(i) *Passages*

Alcman,	fr. 125	328n.24		A 10	97
Alcmeon,	24 A 1	115, 116		A 12	41, 53–4
	A 4	117		A 14	53–4, 315n.1
	A 5	149			
	A 11	149		A 15	53–4
	A 12	116		A 17	53–4
	B 1	137		A 21	54, 316n.1
	B 2	115		B 1	46
Alexander,	*quaest nat* II.23 312n.3			B 2	53, 55, 317n.19
Anaxagoras,	59 A 41	316n.2			
	A 42	314n.5		B 3	35, 315n.27
	A 98a	312n.3	Antiphon,	87 B 10	322n.20
	B 12	315n.26, 322n.18	Archytas,	47 A 24	204, 332n.2
				B 3	259, 327n.18
Anaxarchus,	72 B 1	327n.17	Aristotle, *An*	403b25–7	7
Anaximander,	12 A 1	32, 314n.8		403b28–31	118
	A 9	29, 43		405a19–21	6
	A 10	20, 43		405a29–b1	116
	A 11	24		407b20	103
	A 14	30, 315n.28		411a7	9, 97
	A 15	30, 31		413a22–5	7
	A 16	30		414a12	7
	A 17	30, 97	*Cael*	279a30–5	322n.19
	A 26	24, 314n.14		279b12–7	318n.15
	A 27	21		294a12–20	10
	A 30	21–3		294a25	314n.13
	B 1	29		294a28–31	9
Anaximenes,	13 A 5	43, 44		294a32–3	10
	A 7	39, 46, 53–4, 97, 315n.1		295a16–b9	314n.13
				295b10–16	24

INDEXES

Aristotle, *Cael* (cont.)
295b30–3	26
298b21	335n.31
fr.65	336n.12
191	107
GC 314a8	41
325a13–8	296
325a15–6	201
Met 983b6–27	41
983b20–2	5, 9
984a7	63
985b26	180
986b21	84, 320n.3
986b24	98
986b29	206
1000a9–20	95
1001b7	241–2
1010a5	32n.12
1010a7–15	68
1012a24	69
1023a26	39
Meteor 353b6–11	21
354a28	315n.1
365b6	316n.1
Phys 185b27–30	255
186a9	180
190a23	185
202b12–16	320n.36
203b4–15	31
203b13–15	97
203b18–20	30
203b25–9	314n.9
204b22–9	30
205a1–4	318n.15
206b7–9	337n.30
207a15–7	202
208a7–10	35
209a23	256
210b22	256–7
213b22–7	253
216b22–6	334n.30
233a21–31	261–73
234a23–31	281–2
239b1	279
239b5–7	276–85
239b9–13	261–73, 338n.1
239b14–18	273–5
239b18–20	274, 339n.3
239b25–6	274
239b27–9	275
239b30–3	276–85
239b33–240a18	286–90
250a19	258
252a4	332n.18
253b9–11	77
263a6–11	263
263a15–22	266
263b3–9	266–7
Rhet 1373b6	123
1399b6–9	86
1407b16	58, 318n.6
Top 166b37–167a20	73
167b13–20	332n.27
MXG 974a12–4	208, 331n.10
975a3	184
975a22–32	332n.17
975a34–5	331n.12
976a10–13	335n.35
977a10–980b22	173
977a14–22	86–7
977a24–9	90–1
977b1	98
977b27–30	322n.20
979a14	330n.24
979b25	338n.40

Augustine, *civitas Dei*
VII.17	327n.7

Cratylus, **65 A 4** 68
Critias, **88 B 25** 322n.18

Democritus,
68 A 139	314n.5
A 165	312n.3
B 5	320n.1
B 64	327n.17
B 115a	312n.1

Diodorus,
I.7	314n.5
X.6.2	110

Diogenes of Apollonia,
64 A 1	316n.2
A 33	312n.3
B 5	322n.23

Diogenes Laertius,
I.11	312n.1
16	155
23	12–13
24	6
27	97
36	321n.9

INDEXES

	116	314n.1	
II.2		314n.1	
22		58	
V.42–7		313n.14	
VI.105		322n.20	
VII.87		133	
VIII.4–5		108	
6–8		322n.2	
36		104	
78		321	
83		115–16	
IX.6		58, 317n.1, 318n.6	
15		127, 317n.1	
16		57	
19		98, 321n.17	
21		320n.2, 329n.3	
22		297	
23		329n.3	
24		217	
41		320n.1	
57		316n.2	
72		276	
111		138	

Diogenes of Oenoanda, fr.34 324n.25
Dissoi Logoi, 90 A 5 51, 169

Empedocles, 31 A 31 323n.17
A 67 314n.12
A 72 22
A 89 312n.3
B 11 185
B 12 185
B 17.31 334n.20
B 39 314n.13
B 57–62 22
B 84 53
B 100 53
B 112–13 323n.17
B 115 104, 124, 323n.17
B 117 103, 323n.14
B 129 104, 323n.15
B 135 123
B 136 125
B 137 124
B 146 104
Epicharmus, 23 A 3 321n.12

A 15 321n.12
B 1 87, 321n.12
B 2 106–7, 319n.21, 321n.12, 324n.21
B 4 312n.2
B 5 74, 321n.12

Epiphanius,
adv haer III.9 327n.9
III.11 276, 336n.14
Euclid, *Elements* I.26 13
Eudemus, fr.37a 235, 254–5
41 205
43 176, 329n.1
65 204
78 257
106 291
145 314n.14, 315n.1

Euripides,
Hercules 1341–6 90–1
fr.292.7 322n.19
Eusebius, PE XI.28.9 116

Gorgias, 82 A 10 320n.1
B 3 171, 173–4, 182–3, 332n.1, 336n.7

Heraclitus, 22 A 1 57, 58, 127, 145–6, 317n.1, 328n.20
A 4 58, 318n.6
A 5 63
A 6 65
A 6a 320n.37
A 8 127
A 10 61, 318n.15
A 16 147
A 17 325n.9
B 1 58–9, 77, 128, 135, 318n.6, 326n.19
B 2 59, 132, 326n.19
B 3 147

363

Heraclitus (cont.)
B 4	74	B 66	326n.20
B 5	127, 325n.8	B 67	320n.39
B 7	147	B 74	145
B 9	74	B 76	318n.16
B 10	60, 64, 318n.13	B 78	144–5
B 12	66	B 79	144
B 13	74	B 80	60, 65, 127, 130–1, 135
B 15	75	B 81	327n.12
B 16	133	B 88	67, 72–3, 325n.9
B 17	144, 147	B 89	59
B 22	144	B 90	61, 63, 128
B 23	319n.29, 320n.39	B 91	66, 319n.24
B 25	127, 325n.9	B 93	58
B 26	74	B 94	128, 130–1
B 27	133, 325n.9	B 96	127
B 28	133, 145	B 101	145
B 30	61–3, 67, 128	B 101a	145
B 31	61, 63, 67, 318n.14	B 102	131
B 34	59	B 103	75, 324n.28
B 35	147	B 104	144
B 36	325n.9	B 106	327n.12
B 40	146, 327n.12	B 107	147–8, 328n.21
B 41	128, 318n.10	B 111	144, 319n.29
B 42	327n.12	B 112	133
B 44	132	B 114	59, 128–32, 326n.19
B 45	144–5	B 118	325n.9
B 46	328n.21	B 121	326n.20
B 48	319n.33	B 123	76, 77, 144
B 49	66, 326n.20	B 125	66
B 50	60, 63, 70, 145, 318n.12	B 126	67
B 51	60	B 129	146, 322n.2, 324n.19, 327n.12, 328n.22
B 52	128		
B 53	127		
B 54	76	Herodotus, II.123	103
B 55	147, 327n.1	IV.95	102, 323n.15
B 56	76, 147		
B 57	72, 327n.12	Hesiod,	
B 58	72	Works and Days 276–85	129
B 59	75	Hicetas, **50 A 1**	28
B 60	75	Hippasus, **18 A 7**	63
B 61	73, 74, 319n.21	Hippo, **38 B 2**	96
B 64	128, 318n.10	Hippocrates, vet med 1	139
		9	143

364

INDEXES

Hippolytus,		
ref haer	I.2	42
Homer, *Iliad*	I.290	86
	II.484–6	93, 137
	XIX.418	131
Odyssey IV.379		93
	468	93
Iamblichus, *comm math sc* 76–8 323n.7		
	VP 165	108
Ion,	36 B 4	323n.15
Lycophron,	83 A 2	255
Melissus,	30 A 1	217
	A 4	180
	A 5	181, 184, 205, 208, 331n.9, 332n.17, 333n.12, 335n.35
	A 7	180
	A 7a	180
	A 8	201
	A 10a	180–1, 331n.17
	A 13	217
	A 14	299–301
	B 1	181, 184–5, 331n.9, n.12
	B 2	181, 194–6, 200
	B 3	181, 200, 332n.25
	B 4	181, 200–1
	B 5	181, 333n.8
	B 6	181, 205
	B 7	181, 207, 214–19, 224–6
	B 8	181–2, 227, 229–30, 298–302, 319n.21
	B 9	182, 210, 227–8, 240
	B 10	181, 219–20, 228

Ovid, *Metam* XV.158–64 111		
Parmenides,	28 A 1	296, 297, 329n.3
	A 12	122
	A 13	155
	A 19	330n.19
	A 20	333n.6
	A 22	298
	A 24	206, 299
	A 25	296, 335n.31
	A 27	202
	A 28	176, 329n.11
	A 34	156
	A 37–44	329n.3
	A 49	296
	B 1	156–7, 328n.2
	B 2	157–65
	B 3	157, 165, 329n.4
	B 4	213
	B 5	177
	B 6	158–60, 165–9, 329n.9
	B 7.1–2	158, 168
	3–6	170, 297–8
	B 8.1–4	179–80, 331n.5
	5–21	169, 184–94, 331n.15
	22–5	210–12, 334n.27
	26–33	220–2
	34–41	206–7, 229
	42–9	201–4
	50–2	156
	55	331n.4
	60–1	156
	B 10–15	329n.3
	B 16	297
Pherecydes,	7 A 1	314n.1
	A 2	323n.13, 324n.19
	B 1	321n.9
Philo, *quis rerum divinarum heres sit* 43.214		72
Plato, *Apology* 23D		95
Cratylus 402A		65

INDEXES

Plato (*cont.*)
   Euthydemus 293B   65
   Laws 819A   327n.17
      967A   95
   Meno 81AD   323n.12
   Parmenides 127A–128E   231–6, 336n.15
      137CD   240
   Phaedo 70A   323n.12
      96B   149–50
   Phaedrus 245C–246A   117, 119, 324n.29
      261D   237, 294, 336n.14
   Sophist 242DE   84
   Theaetetus 179D–183D   68
      183E   180
   Timaeus 44D   118
      37D–38A   192
Plutarch, *adv Col* 1124C   330n.19
      1126A   122
   de E apud Delphos 393AB   193
   Pericles 32   95
Proclus, *in Parm* 619.34   336n.16
      721.25   336n.17
      862.25   336n.8
Ptolemy, *Syntaxis* I.7   28
Pythagoras,   **14 A 1**   103, 324n.27
      A 2   102, 323n.19
      A 4   323n.13
      A 7   107
      A 8   108
      A 8a   103, 114
      A 19   322n.2

Seneca, *nat quaest* 6.10   54
   epistle 88.44–5   336n.8
Sextus, *adv Math* VII.
      48–52   327nn.4, 9, 10
      65   173
      66–76   182–3
      77–82   173–4
      114   296–7
      127   125
   Pyrr Hyp I.210   70, 326n.19
      223–5   327n.4
Simplicius, *in An* 32.1–13   324n.30
   in Phys 97.9–99.31   235
      97.13–21   254
      97.25–8   255

      138.3–139.23   235, 336n.9
      138.10–6   245
      139.5–19   238–52
      140.27–141.8   239–53
      534.6–15   256
      563.1–33   256
Sophocles, *Electra* 62–4   110

Thales,   **11 A 1**   6, 12, 13, 96, 114, 313n.4, 321n.9
      A 3   313n.4
      A 12   5, 9, 11
      A 14   9, 10
      A 20   13, 313n.12
      A 22   6, 9, 97
      A 23   9, 97
      B 1–4   313n.10
Theophrastus, *Sens* 25   149
      26   149
Timon,   fr.44   296
      59   99, 327n.9
      60   98, 327n.9

Xenocrates, fr.44   245
Xenophanes,   **21 A 1**   98, 321n.17
      A 2   320n.2
      A 12   86
      A 28   86–7, 90–1, 98, 321n.16, 322n.19
      A 29   84
      A 30   99, 320n.3, n.6
      A 31   90–1, 98, 320n.6
      A 32   90–2
      A 33   21, 93
      A 34   84
      A 35   98, 99, 320n.3, 327n.4
      A 36   320n.3
      A 47   314n.14, 320n.3
      B 2   122
      B 3   122
      B 7   104

INDEXES

	B 11	93–4, 122	Zeno,	29 A 1	335n.4, 338n.1
	B 12	122		A 2	335n.4
	B 14	86, 142		A 10	336n.12
	B 15	92–3, 142		A 13	237, 294
	B 16	93, 142, 327n.11		A 14	335n.4
	B 18	139		A 15	233, 296
	B 23	89–92		A 16	235
	B 24	93		A 21	241–2, 254
	B 25	93		A 23	294
	B 26	85, 94, 322n.21		A 24	256–8
	B 29	41		A 25	261–73, 291
	B 32	96		A 26	273–5
	B 33	42		A 27	276–85
	B 34	83–4, 138–41		A 28	286–90
	B 35	140		A 29	258
	B 36	139–40		B 1 + 2	234, 237–52, 254
	B 38	142		B 3	234, 237, 239, 252–3
	C 1	90–1		B 4	276
Xuthus,	33 A 1	334n.30			

(ii) *Persons*

Aetius, on Alcmeon 116–17
Alcman 12, 328n.24
Alcmeon, life and works 115; an empiricist 149–50; on immortality of the soul 115–20; on scepticism 137–9
Alexander, on Zeno and the One 238, 338n.34
Anaxagoras, on the expanding universe (?) 35; *see also* 20, 51, 52, 83, 95, 332n.34
Anaximander, Chapter II *passim*; influence 19–20, 314n.2; astronomy 48; on the 'unlimited' 28–37 (the fragment 29; the doxography 29–31; cosmogony 32–7); on natural law 130, 326n.17; stability of earth 23–8, 314n.12; theology 97; zoogony 20–3
Anaximenes, Chapter III *passim*; relation to Anaximander 38; on air 35, 44–7, 316n.5; astronomy 38, 315n.1; material monism 39–44; scientific pretensions 48–52, 317n.16; stability of earth 27; theology 97
Antiphon, on God 322n.20

Aquinas, St Thomas, on generation and destruction 197–8
Archytas, on space 204; on Zeno's deafness 258–9
Aristocles, on Melissus 299–301
Aristophanes 26, 95–6, 313n.10
Aristotle, as source for Presocratics 314n.15;
on Alcmeon: immortality of the soul 116–17;
on Anaximander: astronomy 23–6; cosmogony 30–6; the 'unlimited' 97;
on Cratylus 68;
on the Eleatics: perception 296, 335n.31; infinity 201–2;
on Empedocles: ethics 123; generation and change 197;
on Heraclitus: cosmogony 61–3; *logos* 58; Unity of Opposites 69–71, 73, 79–80;
on Melissus: and change 216; monism 208–9; *see also* 180, 194, 196;
on Parmenides: monism 206;
on Pythagoras: metempsychosis

367

INDEXES

Aristotle (*cont.*)
  103, 107; void 253;
  on Thales: 5–14, 42;
  on Xenophanes: divine generation 87, 89; god 98–9;
  on Zeno: Achilles 273–5; arrow 276–84, 339n.8; Dichotomy 261–3; 265–8, 270, 337n.26; infinity 337n.30; magnitude 242; method 236; millet seed 258–60; One and Many 255–60; place 256–7; Stadium 285–94;
  on infinite divisibility 247–8; on generation and change 197; on science and theology 98; on knowledge 149–50; on material monism 39–44; on scientific enquiry 172; on soul and life 7, 118–19; on the verb 'to be' 160–1
Arius Didymus, on Xenophanes' god 139

Bentham, Jeremy, on animals 126
Bergson, Henri, on motion 280
Berkeley, George, on causation 119; on thought and existence 170–1; on motion 192; on the Book of Nature 148

Cleanthes 57
Clement, on Heraclitus 57; on Xenophanes 93
Coleridge, Samuel Taylor, on Zeno 231
Cratylus, on change 68–9

Dedekind, R., on infinity 250
Democritus, against cosmogony 62; on solidity 224–5; *see also* 26, 51, 320n.1
Descartes, René, on causation 119; on matter and space 223; and the Synonymy Principle 88; on Zeno 337n.28
Dicaearchus, on Pythagoras 102–3, 114
Diodorus Cronus, on motion 276
Diodotus, on Heraclitus 127
Diogenes of Apollonia 26, 51, 149
Diopeithes 95

Empedocles, and analogy 53; astronomy 26; ethics 123–6; on generation 185; metempsychosis 103–4, 323n.17; on blood and thought 149; zoogony 22; *see also* 20, 51, 52, 83, 332n.18
Epicharmus, on personal identity 106–7; on relativism 74; parody of Xenophanes' theology 87–9; *see also* 321n.12
Epicurus 87, 337n.28
Epiphanius, on Zeno's arrow 276
Eudemus, on Melissus 205; on Parmenides 206; on Thales 12, 13, 313n.12; on Zeno: the One 235, 238; place 257; One and Many 254–5
Euripides, theology of 90–1, 94, 95; *see also* 26, 321n.15

Frege, Gottlob, on number 208–9, 338n.31

Gorgias, on non-entity 171, 173–4, 182–3, 235; *see also* 320n.1, 330n.24, 332n.1, 338n.40

Hecataeus, criticized by Heraclitus 144, 146
Hegel, G. W. F. 51, 57
Heraclides Ponticus, on Pythagoras 108; on Zeno 338n.1
Heraclitus, Chapter IV *passim*; writings and style 57–8, 317n.6, 325n.7; use of argument by 63–4, 318n.17;
  epistemology: apparent scepticism 144–50; empiricism 144–51, 297; personal discovery 145–9
  ethics: 127–35, 325n.7; law and justice 98, 125–35; immortality 114
  philosophy of science: outline 60; *logos* 59;
    monism 60–4
    flux: sources 65; the river fragments 66, 319n.24; and observation 66–7; rival interpretations of 67–9;
    unity of opposites: Aristotle's interpretation of 69–71,

368

73; versions of 70–3, 319n.29; and flux 72–3; and observation 73–5 criticisms 75–81
Herodotus, on metempsychosis 103; on Thales 12
Hesiod, and natural law 129; *see also* 36, 87, 94, 122, 144, 146
Hicetas, on heavenly motion 28
Hippasus 101
Hippias, on Thales 6, 8, 9, 13, 313n.12
Hippo, and atheism 96; on water 11; *see also* 51
Hippocrates, and scientific experiment 317n.13; on Heraclitus and flux 65, 319n.21; *vet med* and empiricism 143–4, and scepticism 139–40; *see also* 26, 51
Hippolytus, on Anaximander 24; on Anaximenes 97; on Heraclitus 57, 63, 70
Hobbes, Thomas, on infinity 248–9
Homer, and theriomorphism 105, 116; and theology 86, 89, 94
Hume, David 114, 338n.31

Iamblichus, on Pythagoreanism 101

Keats, John, on knowledge 146
Kepler, J. 128

Leibniz, G. W., on divisibility of matter 248; on Identity of Indiscernibles 193, 208; on Presocratics xii; and Principle of Sufficient Reason 24; and solidity 224–5
Locke, John, on essence 77; on knowledge and scepticism 137, 146, 172; on personal identity 107–10, 114; on solidity 223–4; on the soul 105–6; *see also* 3, 10
Lycophron, on One and Many 255, 338n.37

Marx, Karl 134
Melissus, Chapters X–XI *passim*; life and works 180; metaphysical system: summary of 181, 228–30; and impossibility of change 214–7, 299; and eternity 194–7; and generation 184–5, 197–9, 331n.17; and homogeneity 207–10; and indivisibility 219–20, 227–8; and infinity 200–1; and monism 205, 299–302; and impossibility of motion 217–19, 221–2, 226; and sense-perception 298–302, 335n.31; on solidity 223–8, 335n.34
Mill, J. S. 133–4

Newton, Sir Isaac, on motion 292; on place 258; *see also* 101, 102
Nietzsche, F., on Heraclitus 58; on Xenophanes 85

Parmenides, Chapters IX–XI *passim*; work and influence 155; summary of system 228–30
  Prologue 156–7
  The three Roads 158–65; meaning of *noein* 158; meaning of *esti* 160–1, 329n.13; subject of *esti* 161–3, 330n.16
  Paths of Ignorance 165–72: Road (B) 165–7; Road (C) 167–70; assessment of argument 171–2; formalization of argument 174–5
  Way of Truth, sketch of 176–80: on change and motion 214, 220–2; on finitude 201–4, 333n.7; on generation and destruction 184–92, 197–9; on continuity 210–13; on timelessness 190–4, 197
  and Milesian monism 41, 51–2; not a monist 205–7; and politics 121–2; on reason and perception 296–8; and Xenophanes 320n.6; and Zeno 231–6
Pherecydes 12, 313n.8, 314n.1, 321n.9, 324n.19
Philo, on Unity of Opposites in Heraclitus 71
Philoponus, on Zeno 254, 256
Pindar 104
Plato: on Alcmeon, and knowledge 149; and immortality of soul 116–20;

Plato (*cont.*)
  on Heraclitus, and flux 65–6, 68–9; and temporal qualifiers 319n.23
  on Melissus 180, 205
  on Pythagoreanism 101, 103
  on Xenophanes 84, 320n.6; and knowledge 140–1; and god 95
  on Zeno 231–6, 294; and finite/infinite 253; and One/Many 255–6
Pliny 196
Plutarch, on Anaximenes 46; pseudo-Plutarch on Xenophanes' monotheism 90–2
Porphyry, on Pythagoras 101; on Zeno and dichotomy 239, 246–7
Proclus, on Thales 313n.12; on Zeno 233, 336n.8
Ptolemy, on stability of earth 28
Pyrrho 137
Pythagoras, Chapter VI *passim*; life and influence 100–3; denounced by Heraclitus 144, 146; and immortality 114, 116; on metempsychosis 103–14 (and the soul 103–6; rational foundations 106–11; and disembodiment 111–14)
Pythagoreanism: ethics 122–3; form and number 45; and Parmenides 234; and position of earth 27–8; sources 323n.6; and Zeno 253

Russell, Bertrand, on Zeno 231, 279–80, 335n.1

Sextus Empiricus, on Gorgias 173–4; on Heraclitus 147; on Parmenides 296–7; on Xenophanes 138, 327n.4
Simplicius, on Anaximander 29–34; on Anaximenes 45, 316n.5; on Heraclitus 63; on Melissus 180, 208, 227, 299, 331n.12; on Parmenides 155, 176, 213; on Xenophanes 90–2; on Zeno 235, 238–9, 241, 247, 253–4, 256, 258, 336n.18, 337n.29, 338n.34
Socrates, on Heraclitus 58; on theology 95–6, 322n.20; on knowledge 149; on Zeno 232–3;
  see also 3, 51
Solon 122
Sophocles 123
Speusippus 101
Spinoza, B. 145
Strato 265

Thales, Chapter I *passim*; on immortality of soul 114; on magnets 5–9; and mathematics 12–13, 313n.10; originality of 11–12, 313n.6; tradition and interpretation 13–16; on stability of earth 9–10, 313n.5; theology 97; on water as material principle 9–11, 42
Theognis 122
Theophrastus, as source for Presocratics 14, 313n.14; on Alcmeon 149; on Anaximander 21; on Anaximenes 316n.5; on Empedocles 124; on Heraclitus 58; on Parmenides 206; on Thales 11–12; on Xenophanes 84, 320n.6
Timon, on Parmenides 296; on Xenophanes 98–9, 327n.9
Tolstoy, Leo, on Zeno 267

Xenocrates, on divisibility 245; on metempsychosis 124
Xenophanes, Chapter V *passim*; life and works 82–4; astronomy 26–7; on metempsychosis 104; and material monism 41–2, 320n.6; scepticism 137–43, 327n.9
  theology 84–94: immobility of god 85, 322n.21; divine generation 86–9; monotheism 89–92; and anthropomorphism 92–3; divine perfection 93–4, 322n.20; and science 95–9
Xuthus 334n.30

Zeno, Chapters XII–XIII *passim*; life and works 231–6, 294–5, 335n.4; influence 231; in Plato 232; writings 233–4; method 235–6; and Parmenides 177, 205, 231–6; on monism 235, 336n.8

INDEXES

attack on plurality 237–60, 294;
  mode of argument 237–8
    Large/Small paradox 237–52
    Finite/Infinite paradox 237,
      238, 239, 252–3
    One/Many paradox 253–6
    Millet seed 258–60
    Place 256–8
  attack on motion 261–95

Achilles 274–5
Arrow 276–85: motion at an
  instant 279–83
Dichotomy 261–73:
  exposition 261–3;
  objections 263–73
Stadium 285–94: exposition
  285–90; relativity of
  motion 290–4

(iii) *Topics*

Acousmata 102, 323n.8
Air, in Anaximenes, as god 97; as
  material principle 44–7, 316n.5;
  unlimited nature 35, 38
Analogy, use of 52–6; types of 54–5;
  objections to 54–6; in Anaximenes
  53–5, 317n.19; in Empedocles 53;
  in Heraclitus 63–4, 318n.13; in
  Thales 10, 313n.5
Animals, in Empedoclean ethics
  123–6; *see also* Zoogony
Astronomy, in Anaximander 20,
  23–8, 48; in Anaximenes 38, 54;
  in Thales 12; and theology 95–6
Atheism 95–7; 322n.20

Being (*einai*), in Parmenides 159–61,
  329n.13

Causation, in Alcmeon 119–20;
  Synonymy Principle 88, 119; in
  Xenophanes' epistemology 142–3
Change (*kinêsis* 220), rejected by
  Melissus 214–17, by Parmenides
  169, 193–4, 220–2; and generation
  197–9; and perception 299–302;
  see also Flux, Motion
Condensation, and rarefaction
  (*puknôsis, manôsis* 44, 316n.5), in
  Anaximenes 44–7, 48, 52; in
  Heraclitus 63; in Thales 42
Conflagration (*ekpurosis*), in Heraclitus
  (?) 61–2, 318n.15
Continuity, in Parmenides, spatial
  202–4; temporal 210–11; in Zeno
  265–7
Contradiction, in Heraclitus 79–81,
  320n.38
Corporeality, of Anaximander's

principle 34; in Empedocles 103–4;
  and Heraclitus' monism 60–4; of
  Melissus' One 224–8, 335n.34; of
  Parmenidean beings 201–4; of
  Pythagoras' soul 111–14; of
  Xenophanes' god 98–9; of items
  in unZenonian pluralities 241–2,
  245–6
Cosmogony, in Anaximander 28–37;
  in Anximenes 42–3, 44–7; not in
  Heraclitus 61–2; Milesian 38–44, 62;
  in Thales 9–11, 42
Critical method 50–2, 170

Density, of air in Anaximenes 44–7,
  52; of Melissus' One 226; of water
  in Thales 42
Divisibility, in Zeno 243–52, 261–75
Doxography 13–15, 303–9, 313n.4

Earth, stability of, in Anaximander
  23–8, 314n.16; in Anaximenes 27,
  38; in Thales 9–10, 313n.5
Elements, the four 29–34
Empiricism, in Heraclitus and
  Alcmeon 144–51
Epistemology *see* Empiricism,
  Perception, Scepticism
Essence, in Heraclitus 77; in Zeno
  255
Ethics, of Empedocles 122–6; of
  Heraclitus 59, 127–35
Evolution 22
Existence, impossibility of, in Gorgias
  173–4, 182–3; and void, in Melissus
  218–19; in Parmenides: and
  generation 185–92; and thought
  157–72, 206–7; and time 190–4; in
  Zeno: potential and actual 266–7;

371

INDEXES

Existence (*cont.*)
and spatial location 257–8; *see also* Being
Experiment, in early Greek thought 317nn.13–16; in Milesians 48–9; *see also* Science

Fate, in Heraclitus 127
Fire, in Heraclitus: and flux 67; as god 98; as material principle 60–4
Flux *see* Heraclitus (Index ii)

Generation and Destruction, logic and language of 39–42, 72–3, 197–9; in Anaximander 29–36; in Milesian cosmogony 41; rejected by Melissus 184–5, 195–6, 200–1, 214, 216, 302, 331n.7; rejected by Parmenides 169, 185–92, 221; of gods in Xenophanes 85–6, 321n.9; *see also* Cosmogony
Geometry, in Thales 12; and Zeno's paradoxes 245–6, 337n.26
God *see* Theology

Homogeneity, of Parmenidean beings 201–4, 210–12; of Melissus' One 207–10, 214–15
Identity, personal, in Locke and Pythagoras 107–11; of temporal instants in Parmenides 193–4, 197; and predication, in Zeno 255
Immortality, personal, in Alcmeon 115–20
Indivisibility, in Melissus 219–20, 227–8; in Parmenides 211–13; in Zeno 234, 245, 276–85
Inductive method, and the Milesians 49–50, 55; *see also* 150, 259
Infinity, of *Urstoff*, in Anaximander 28–36, 43, 97; meaning of *apeiros* 36; of space, in Melissus 200–1; not in Parmenides 201–4; in Zeno's paradoxes, analysis of 249–52

Justice (*dikê* 129–30), cosmic, in Anaximander 130; in Heraclitus 130–5; *see also* Law

Knowledge, *eidenai*, meaning of 138

Law (*nomos* 128–9, 326n.16), in Heraclitus 129–35
Logic, in Parmenides 176–7; in Zeno 235–6, 259, 277; *see also* Reasoning

Magnets, in Thales 5–9
Mathematics, and Pythagoreanism 101–2; and Thales 12, 13, 213n.10
Measurement, in Milesian science, lack of 48
Memory, in Alcmeon's epistemology 149–50; cultivated by Pythagoras 108–11
Metempsychosis, terminology of 323n.11; in Empedocles 103–4, 124–6, 323n.17; in Pythagoras 103–15; *see also* Soul
Methodology 47–52, 52–6; of Zeno 235–6
Monism, material, in Anaximander 29, 43; in Anaximenes 43–4; in Heraclitus 60–4; in Thales 11, 42–3 real, in Eleatics 204–7, 208–10, 214–16, 299–302
Monotheism, in Heraclitus 98, 127; in Xenophanes 89–92
Moral philosophy *see* Ethics
Motion, of the soul 116–20; rejected by Melissus 217–19; by Parmenides 206, 213, 220–2; by Zeno Chapter XIII *passim*

Nature (*phusis*) 19–20, 77; *see also* Essence
Necessity (*anankê*), in Heraclitean ethics 128–35

Observation, scientific use of, by Anaximander 21; by Anaximenes 46–50, 54; by Heraclitus: and flux 65–9; and Unity of Opposites 71–5; by Thales 7, 11; and stability of earth 27–8; *see also* Empiricism, Science
One, the, subject of Parmenides' poem (?) 162; foreshadowed by Xenophanes (?) 98; attacked by Zeno (?) 235, 238, 254; *see also* Monism

INDEXES

Opposites, in Anaximander 43; in Anaximenes 46–7; *see also* Heraclitus (Index ii)

Pantheism, in Heraclitus 98; in Thales 97; in Xenophanes 99
Perception, in Heraclitus 144–50; attacked by Melissus 298–302, 335n.31; by Parmenides (?) 170, 296–8; by Zeno (?) 258–9
Person, concept of 107, 115, 324n.20; *see also* Soul
Predication, and Parmenides' use of *esti* 160–1, 330n.13; in Zeno's One/Many paradox 254–5
Principle (*archê* 29, 39), 'unlimited', in Anaximander 29–36, 38, 42–3; air in Anaximenes 43–7, 55; fire in Heraclitus (?) 60–4, 76; water in Thales 9–11, 15, 42; *see also* Cosmogony, Monism
Principle of Sufficient Reason, in Anaximander 24–6, 38; in Leibniz 24; in Parmenides 187, 222, 322n.18
Psychology, of Heraclitus 325n.9; of Thales 6–9, 12

Reasoning, use of, by Presocratics 3–5; by Heraclitus 63–4, 70–3, 75, 79–80; by Melissus Chapters X–XI *passim*; by Parmenides Chapters IX–XI *passim*; by Pythagoras 107–11; by Xenophanes 85, 92, 94, 140–1; by Zeno Chapters XII–XIII *passim*; *see also* Logic

Scepticism, and Heraclitus 144–5; in Melissus 298–302; in Parmenides (?) 296–8; in Xenophanes 138–43
Science 47–56; and analogy 53–6; in Anaximander 23, 25; in Anaximenes 46–7; and Elea 229–30; in Heraclitus 61, 71, 78, 81; in Pythagoreanism 101–2; and theology 95–9; *see also* Experiment, Measurement
Senses *see* Perception
Shamanism 323n.9
Solidity 223–8
Soul (*psuchê* 6–7, 105–6), immortality of, in Alcmeon 115–20; *see also* Metempsychosis, Person, Psychology
Style, literary, of Anaximander 38; of Heraclitus 57–8; of Melissus 180; of Parmenides 155; of Xenophanes 83; of Zeno 231
Theodicy, in Heraclitus 131
Theology, in Heraclitus 98, 128–35; in Milesians 96–7; in Xenophanes 84–94
Thought (*noein* 158–9, 329n.6), and existence, in Gorgias 173–4; in Parmenides 157–9, 162–72, 186–8, 206–7
Time, in Melissus 194–7; in Parmenides: and generation 186–94, 221; continuity in 210–12; in Zeno, divisibility of 261–73, 276–85
Transmigration of souls *see* Metempsychosis

Unity of Opposites *see* Heraclitus (Index ii)
Unlimited (*apeiros*) *see* Infinity

Vegetarianism, in Empedocles 123–6
Void, rejected by Melissus 218–19; by Parmenides (?) 222, 334n.27; in Pythagoreanism 253; and solidity 223–8; in Xuthus 334n.30

War and Strife, in Heraclitus 60, 65, 79, 127–8, 130
Water, in Thales: as god 97; as material principle 9–11, 42; as support of earth 9–10, 313n.5; in Xenophanes 21

Zoogony, of Anaximander 20–3; of Empedocles 22

Concordance

Barnes	Diels-Kranz	Barnes	Diels-Kranz
1	11 A 1	32	(see Diels-Kranz,
2	11 A 22		I.488.30–5)
3	11 A 12	33	22 B 1
4	11 A 14	34	22 B 10
5	11 A 20	35	22 B 50
6	12 A 10	36	22 B 51
7	12 A 30	37	22 B 80
8	12 A 27	38	22 B 30
9	21 A 33	39	22 B 90
10	12 A 26	40	22 B 31
11	12 A 11	41	22 A 5
12	50 A 1	42	22 A 6
13	12 A 9 + B 1	43	22 B 12
14	12 A 15	44	22 B 49a
15	12 A 16	45	22 B 91
16	12 A 15	46	22 B 125
17	12 A 1	47	22 B 126
18	13 B 3	48	65 A 4
19	13 A 7	49	(see Diels-Kranz,
20	21 B 29		I.491.39–42)
21	21 B 33	50	22 B 88
22	(Hippolytus, *ref haer* I.2)	51	22 B 57
23	12 A 10	52	22 B 61
24	13 A 5	53	23 B 5
25	13 B 1	54	22 B 26
26	13 B 2	55	22 B 60
27	13 A 7	56	22 B 103
28	13 A 12	57	22 B 59
29	13 A 14	58	22 B 15
30	13 A 15	59	22 B 123
31	13 A 17	60	22 B 54

CONCORDANCE

Barnes	Diels-Kranz
61	22 B 56
62	21 B 26
63	21 B 14
64	21 A 12
65	21 A 28
66	23 B 1
67	21 B 23.1
68	21 A 28
69	21 A 31
70	21 A 32
71	21 C 1
72	21 B 23.2
73	21 B 15
74	21 B 24
75	21 B 25
76	21 B 11
77	(Plato, *Laws* 967A)
78	21 B 32
79	11 A 1
80	11 A 22
81	13 A 10
82	21 A 30
83	21 A 35
84	14 A 8a
85	14 A 1
86	31 B 117
87	21 B 7
88	23 B 2
89	14 A 8
90	(Diodorus, X.6.2)
91	(Ovid, *Metam* XV.158–64)
92	11 A 1
93	24 B 2
94	24 A 12
95	(Eusebius, *PE* XI.28.9)
96	24 A 1
97	24 A 12
98	(Plato, *Phaedrus* 245C–246A)
99	31 B 135
100	31 B 115.3–6
101	31 B 137
102	31 B 136
103	22 B 5b
104	22 B 53
105	22 B 25
106	22 B 96
107	22 B 64
108	22 B 41
109	22 B 52
110	(Hesiod, *Works and Days* 276–85)
111	22 B 94
112	22 B 102
113	22 B 114 + B 2
114	22 B 44
115	22 B 16
116	22 B 28
117	22 B 17
118	22 B 112
119	24 B 1
120	21 B 34
121	(Hippocrates, *vet med* § 1)
122	21 B 18
123	21 B 36
124	21 B 35
125	21 B 16
126	21 B 38
127	(Hippocrates, *vet med* § 9)
128	22 B 17
129	22 B 104
130	22 B 111
131	22 B 79
132	22 B 78
133	22 B 45
134	22 B 28
135	22 B 101a
136	22 B 101
137	22 B 40
138	22 B 129
139	22 B 55
140	22 B 7
141	22 B 35
142	22 B 107
143	24 A 11
144	24 A 5
145	28 B 1.28–31
146	28 B 8.50–2
147	28 B 8.60–1
148	28 B 2
149	28 B 3
150	28 B 6
151	28 B 7.1–2
152	90 A 5
153	28 B 7.3–6

CONCORDANCE

Barnes	Diels-Kranz
154	82 B 3.77–82
155	28 B 5
156	28 B 8.1–51
157	82 B 3.66–76
158	30 B 1
159	30 B 2
160	30 B 3
161	30 B 4
162	30 A 8
163	47 A 24
164	30 B 6
165	28 A 24
166	30 A 5
167	28 B 4
168	30 B 7
169	30 B 10
170	30 B 9
171	30 B 9
172	(Plato, *Parmenides* 127A–128E)
173	29 A 16
174	29 B 2
175	29 B 3 + B 1
176	29 A 21
177	(Simplicius, *in Phys* 139.27–32)
178	29 A 21
179	29 A 21
180	(Philoponus, *in Phys* 510.4–6)
181	29 A 29
182	29 A 25
183	29 A 25
184	(Aristotle, *Phys* 263a15–22)
185	(Aristotle, *Phys* 263b3–9)
186	29 A 26
187	29 A 27
188	29 A 27
189	(Epiphanius, *adversus haereticos* III.11)
190	29 A 28
191	30 B 8
192	30 A 14

Diels-Kranz	Barnes
11 A 1	1, 79, 92
11 A 12	3
11 A 14	4
11 A 20	5
11 A 22	2, 80
12 A 1	17
12 A 9	13
12 A 10	6, 23
12 A 11	11
12 A 15	14, 16
12 A 16	15
12 A 26	10
12 A 27	8
12 A 30	7
12 A 33	9
12 B 1	13
13 A 5	24
13 A 7	19, 27
13 A 10	81
13 A 12	28
13 A 14	29
13 A 15	30
13 A 17	31
13 B 1	25
13 B 2	26
13 B 3	18
14 A 1	85
14 A 8	89
14 A 8a	84
21 A 12	64
21 A 28	65, 68
21 A 30	82
21 A 31	69
21 A 32	70
21 A 33	9
21 A 35	83
21 A 7	87
21 B 11	76
21 B 14	63
21 B 15	73
21 B 16	125
21 B 18	122
21 B 23	67, 72
21 B 24	74
21 B 25	75
21 B 26	62
21 B 29	20

CONCORDANCE

Diels-Kranz	Barnes	Diels-Kranz	Barnes
21 B 32	78	22 B 91	45
21 B 33	21	22 B 94	111
21 B 34	120	22 B 96	106
21 B 35	124	22 B 101	136
21 B 36	123	22 B 101a	135
21 B 38	126	22 B 102	112
21 C 1	71	22 B 103	56
22 A 5	41	22 B 104	129
22 A 6	42	22 B 107	142
22 B 1	33	22 B 111	130
22 B 2	113	22 B 112	118
22 B 5b	103	22 B 114	113
22 B 7	140	22 B 123	59
22 B 10	34	22 B 125	46
22 B 12	43	22 B 126	47
22 B 15	58	22 B 129	138
22 B 16	115	23 B 1	66
22 B 17	128	23 B 2	88
22 B 22	33	23 B 5	53
22 B 25	103	24 A 1	96
22 B 26	54	24 A 5	144
22 B 27	117	24 A 11	143
22 B 28	116, 134	24 A 12	94, 97
22 B 30	38	24 B 1	119
22 B 31	40	24 B 2	93
22 B 35	141	28 A 24	155
22 B 40	137	28 B 1	105
22 B 41	108	28 B 2	148
22 B 44	114	28 B 3	149
22 B 45	133	28 B 4	167
22 B 49a	44	28 B 5	155
22 B 50	35	28 B 6	150
22 B 51	36	28 B 7	151, 153
22 B 52	109	28 B 8	146, 147, 156
22 B 53	104	29 A 16	173
22 B 54	60	29 A 21	176, 178, 179
22 B 55	139	29 A 25	182, 183
22 B 56	61	29 A 26	186
22 B 57	51	29 A 27	187, 188
22 B 59	57	29 A 28	190
22 B 60	55	29 A 29	181
22 B 61	52	29 B 1	175
22 B 64	107	29 B 2	174
22 B 78	132	29 B 3	175
22 B 79	131	30 A 5	166
22 B 80	37	30 A 8	162
22 B 88	50	30 A 14	192
22 B 90	39	30 B 1	158

CONCORDANCE

Diels-Kranz	Barnes		Diels-Kranz	Barnes
30 B 2	159		31 B 117	86
30 B 3	160		31 B 135	99
30 B 4	161		31 B 136	102
30 B 6	164		31 B 137	101
30 B 7	167		47 A 24	163
30 B 8	190		50 A 1	12
30 B 9	170		65 A 4	48
30 B 10	169		82 B 3	154, 157
31 B 115	100		90 A 5	152